Property Investing

ALL-IN-ONE

FOR DUMMIES®

by Roy Barnhart, Colin Barrow, James Carey, Morris Carey,
Robert Griswold, Gene Hamilton, Katie Hamilton,
Jeff Howell, Tony Levene, Don R Prestly, and Jeff Strong

Edited by Melanie Bien

BICENTENNIAL
1807
WILEY
2007
BICENTENNIAL

John Wiley & Sons, Ltd

Property Investing All-in-One For Dummies®

Published by
John Wiley & Sons, Ltd
The Atrium
Southern Gate
Chichester
West Sussex
PO19 8SQ
England

E-mail (for orders and customer service enquires): cs-books@wiley.co.uk

Visit our Home Page on www.wiley.com

For general information on our other products and services, please contact our Customer Care Department within the U.S. at 800-762-2974, outside the U.S. at 317-572-3993, or fax 317-572-4002.

For technical support, please visit www.wiley.com/techsupport.

Wiley also publishes its books in a variety of electronic formats. Some content that appears in print may not be available in electronic books.

British Library Cataloguing in Publication Data: A catalogue record for this book is available from the British Library

ISBN: 978-0-470-51502-0

Printed and bound in Great Britain by Bell & Bain Ltd, Glasgow

10 9 8 7 6 5 4 3 2 1

WILEY

About the Authors

Melanie Bien is associate director at independent mortgage broker Savills Private Finance. Before joining SPF at the end of 2004, she was personal finance editor and property writer on the *Independent on Sunday*. She has written about buy-to-let for a variety of national newspapers, magazines, and Web sites, and written several books and pamphlets to accompany television programmes on property makeovers and design, buying, renovating, and selling property.

Melanie also has first-hand experience of renting out property, owning, and managing six buy-to-let properties in conjunction with her brother and parents. She lives in East London.

Roy Barnhart is a lifelong do-it-yourselfer and former professional building and remodelling contractor. He enjoyed eight years as Senior Building and Remodelling Editor for two national home improvement magazines in the USA. As a freelance writer, editor, and consultant, Roy has contributed articles to more than a dozen home improvement magazines, including *Family Handyman* and *House Beautiful*. He has also contributed to four books.

Colin Barrow has an extensive background in European property and works across a diverse range of related industries. He has researched most international property markets and has first hand experience of buying, building, developing, and selling over two hundred properties in overseas markets. He has written a score of books on property and other wealth creation matters including the best-selling *Starting a Business For Dummies*.

James and Morris Carey, known as the Carey Brothers, are experts on home building and renovation. They share their 20-plus years of experience as award-winning, licensed contractors with millions nationwide through a weekly radio programme in America, daily radio vignette, syndicated newspaper column, and comprehensive Web site (www.onthehouse.com), all titled 'On the House'. Morris and James continue to own and operate a successful home remodelling and construction firm, Carey Bros., and have been named to *Remodeling* magazine's Hall of Fame Big 50, which recognises top achievers in the industry. They've also been honoured as one of the nation's top 500 companies by *Qualified Remodeler* magazine.

Robert Griswold earned a Bachelors degree and two Masters degrees in real estate and related fields from the University of Southern California's School of Business.

Robert is a hands-on property manager with more than 20 years of practical experience, running Griswold Real Estate Management. He hosts a weekly radio show, and has written for the *Los Angeles Times*, *San Diego Union-Tribune*, and *San Francisco Chronicle*. He has twice been named the No. 1 Radio or Television Real Estate Journalist in the Country by the National Association of Real Estate Editors in the US.

Gene and Katie Hamilton have been working on houses and writing about home improvements for over 30 years. They've remodelled 14 houses and write a weekly newspaper column entitled 'Do It Yourself . . . Or Not?' which appears in newspapers across America and on Web sites. The Hamiltons are authors of 16 home improvement books, including *Home Improvement For Dummies*, *Carpentry For Dummies*, *Painting and Wallpapering For Dummies*, and *Plumbing For Dummies*. They're the founders of www.HouseNet.com.

Jeff Howell is a qualified bricklayer, university construction lecturer, and chartered surveyor, with 30 years' experience in the building industry. He writes about building and DIY for a variety of British newspapers, magazines, and construction trade journals, and appears regularly as a guest expert on TV and radio. His Web site is www.ask-jeff.co.uk.

Tony Levene is a member of The Guardian Jobs & Money team, writing on issues including investment and consumer rights as well as on taxation. He has been a financial journalist for nearly thirty years after a brief foray into teaching French to school children. Over his journalistic career, Tony has worked for newspapers including *The Sunday Times*, *Sunday Express*, *The Sun*, *Daily Star*, *Sunday Mirror*, and *Daily Express*. He has written seven previous books on money matters including *Investing For Dummies* and *Paying Less Tax For Dummies*. Tony lives in London with his wife Claudia, 'virtually grown up' children Zoe and Oliver, and cats Plato, Pandora, and Pascal.

Don R Prestly is a former senior editor for HANDY Magazine for The Handyman Club of America, as well as a former associate editor for Family Handyman magazine. In addition to his nearly 20 years of writing and doing home improvement projects, he spent several years as a manager for one of the Midwest's largest home centres.

Donald Strachan is a journalist and copywriter. His articles have appeared in the *Sunday Telegraph*, *Independent on Sunday*, *Observer,* and *Sydney Morning Herald*, among others. He edited *Job Hunting and Career Change All-in-One For Dummies,* and co-authored *Frommer's The Balearics With Your Family* and *Frommer's Tuscany and Umbria With Your Family*.

Jeff Strong began creating sawdust at a very young age while helping his father, a master craftsman, build fine furniture. An accomplished woodworker, Jeff has designed and built countless pieces of furniture. He is the author of *Woodworking For Dummies*.

Publisher's Acknowledgements

We're proud of this book; please send us your comments through our Dummies online registration form located at `www.dummies.com/register/`.

Some of the people who helped bring this book to market include the following:

Acquisitions, Editorial, and Media Development

Project Editor: Steve Edwards

Content Editor: Nicole Burnett

Commissioning Editor: Samantha Clapp

Compiled by: Donald Strachan

Text Splicer: Helen Heyes

Technical Editor: Tom Entwistle, `www.landlordZONE.co.uk`

Executive Editor: Jason Dunne

Executive Project Editor: Daniel Mersey

Cover Photos: Getty Images/Image Source Black

Cartoons: Ed McLachlan

Composition Services

Project Coordinator: Erin Smith

Layout and Graphics: Elizabeth Brooks, Carl Byers, Carrie A. Foster, Stephanie D. Jumper, Christine Williams

Indexer: Ty Koontz

Publishing and Editorial for Consumer Dummies

Diane Graves Steele, Vice President and Publisher, Consumer Dummies

Joyce Pepple, Acquisitions Director, Consumer Dummies

Kristin A. Cocks, Product Development Director, Consumer Dummies

Michael Spring, Vice President and Publisher, Travel

Kelly Regan, Editorial Director, Travel

Publishing for Technology Dummies

Andy Cummings, Vice President and Publisher, Dummies Technology/General User

Composition Services

Gerry Fahey, Vice President of Production Services

Debbie Stailey, Director of Composition Services

Contents at a Glance

Table of Contents

Introduction

*H*ello! Welcome to *Property Investing All-in-One For Dummies*, your launch pad to realising your ambitions in the wonderful world of bricks and mortar. Buying a property is one of the most wallet-draining and stress-inducing things you're ever likely to do in life – and as a property investor you might go through the process more often than most – so the more clued up you are in advance, the better prepared you'll be when a great investment opportunity comes along.

About This Book

Property Investing All-in-One For Dummies gathers information on the key areas you need to be aware of as an investor – housebuying, finance, tax, renovation and property improvement, becoming a landlord, managing tenancies, making a profit, and the law. This book is your one-stop shop for information about taking on the property market and making sound investments through buying, selling, renting, and renovating. Think of this book as your first important investment.

We've written this book in a way that we hope you find useful, easy to work your way around, and fun to read. You'll wear many different hats as a property investor – researcher, buyer, advertiser, bookkeeper, handyman, landlord, salesman, and others besides – and this book is overflowing with advice and information to help guide you along through all those roles.

Property Investing All-in-One For Dummies draws on information from these other For Dummies books (published by Wiley) that you can refer to for greater detail on the subjects we cover here:

- *Buying and Selling a Home For Dummies* (Melanie Bien)
- *Buying a Property in Eastern Europe For Dummies* (Colin Barrow)
- *DIY & Home Maintenance All-in-One For Dummies* (Jeff Howell)
- *Paying Less Tax 2006/2007 For Dummies* (Tony Levene)
- *Renting Out Your Property For Dummies* (Melanie Bien and Robert Griswold)

Conventions Used in This Book

To make your reading experience easier and to alert you to key words or points, we use certain conventions in this book:

- *Italics* introduces new terms, and explains what they mean.

- **Bold** text is used to show the action part of bulleted and numbered lists.

- Monofont is used to highlight Web addresses, showing you exactly what to type into your computer.

Foolish Assumptions

This book brings together the essential elements of knowledge that are essential for understanding the world of property investment. As a consequence, to keep the book down to a reasonable number of pages, we've made a few assumptions about you (we hope you don't mind!). Maybe you're someone who is:

- Harbouring great ambitions of becoming a property tycoon but have yet to take the first step

- Looking to rent out a second home but don't know where to look for advice

- Lured by the potential rewards of becoming a buy-to-let landlord but unaware of the legalities involved

If any (or all) of these assumptions accurately describe you, or if you just want to gain a better understanding of the world of property investment, you've come to the right place!

What You're Not to Read

You can read this book whichever way suits you best. You can go from cover to cover, or hop, skip, and jump through reading the sections that interest you the most. You can also glean plenty of information from this book without reading the sidebars (the grey boxes) – the detail in our sidebars is interesting but not crucial to understanding the rest of the book's content.

How This Book Is Organised

We've divided *Property Investing All-in-One For Dummies* into six separate books, and this section explains what nuggets of information you'll find in them. Each book is broken into chapters tackling key aspects of property investing and the things you'll need to be aware of. The table of contents gives you more detail of what's in each chapter, and we've even included a cartoon at the start of each part, just to keep you smiling.

Book 1: Housebuying Basics and the Law

Book I is the one most people will want to start with, and takes you down the long and winding road of buying a property to start with. This Book helps you navigate the tricky waters of viewing properties, making offers, buying at auction, and conveyancing, and takes a look at researching European property markets.

Book II: Finance, Tax, and How to Organise Them

Practically no-one escapes the tax inspector's net, and this Book is designed to help you get your taxes right as a property investor. Here you can also find help in working out which mortgages work best for you, and some handy hints about being a good recordkeeper.

Book III: Renovating a Property

Book III is primarily about carrying out work on your property yourself, but offers advice on when to consult the professionals, too. When undertaking serious renovation work, many things need to be considered. This Book shows you the way.

Book IV: Becoming a Buy-to-Let Landlord

Leaving no stone unturned in preparing to become a landlord is the aim of Book IV. The chapters within outline the different things you need to do to prepare yourself and your property for this step. It's never too early to start planning, and this Book aims to give you a head start.

Book V: Managing a Tenancy

This Book provides you with the nitty-gritty about having tenants in your property. Finding the right tenants is key, and maintaining a good relationship with them is important, and this Book overflows with information about how to do this. We give you information, too, on what to do if things go pear-shaped.

Book VI: Selling Up at a Profit

To realise the value of your investment, going about things in the right way when it comes to selling up is vital. If you're not sure whether to use the services of an estate agent or go it alone, or how to go about presenting your property in the way that will be most likely to bring about a successful sale, this Book can help you to get it right.

Icons Used in This Book

When you flick through this book, you'll notice little icons in the margins. These icons pick out certain key aspects of personal development:

This icon highlights practical advice to get our personal development methods working for you.

This icon is a friendly reminder of important points to take note of.

This icon covers the boring stuff that only anoraks would ever know. You can safely skip paragraphs marked by this icon without missing anything vital, or you can read it and improve your wealth of knowledge even further!

This icon marks things to avoid in your enthusiasm when trying out personal development skills.

Where to Go from Here

This book is set up so that you can dip in and out of it in a number of ways depending on your situation. If you're most interested in tenancy agreements (for example), head straight over to Book IV, or if you need information about how to negotiate the sale of a property, check out Book VI. However, if you're not sure which type of help you're most interested in, or just fancy an overview of the entire subject, turn the next page and get stuck into Book I.

Good luck to you in your property investment adventure!

Book I
Housebuying Basics and the Law

'The high ceilings, the wooden beams, the leaded
windows – this old house is absolutely <u>steeped</u>
in history.'

In this book . . .

This book walks you through the process of buying a property. From knowing what to look for when viewing a property and how to follow up on making an offer, to conveyancing throughout the United Kingdom and overseas, this books helps to get your property investment plans rolling. What are you waiting for?

Here are the contents of Book I at a glance:

Chapter 1

Step One: Getting the Most from Viewings

In This Chapter

▶ Deciding which properties are worth viewing

▶ Working out the best time to view a property

▶ Knowing the questions to ask and how to interpret the answers

Mike Leigh's film *Career Girls* captures the best bit of the house-buying process – poking around other people's homes. One of the main characters is looking to buy a place in London. Instead of viewing flats within her price range, however, she prefers to look at glamorous pads well beyond her budget. She may not be able to afford them, but seeing how the other half live is far more entertaining.

True, viewing properties can be fun, but, more importantly, it's a vital part of the buying process. You can't make a decision about whether you want to buy a property by only looking at a picture or reading a description. You have to have a good look round and ask the seller various questions and thoroughly research the local rental market if you intend to rent the property out.

If you are buying your first property, the viewing process can seem daunting. But if you know what to ask, how to interpret the answers, and what else to look for, you'll have a successful viewing. In this chapter, we show you how to do just those things.

Finding Suitable Properties

Before you can view a property, you have to find one that interests you and as an investor, one that you know will attract tenants. You can do this in several ways: you may simply come across one you like as you are walking down the street or a friend knows someone who's planning to sell. More likely, you've contacted an estate agent or have been looking at agents' Web sites.

For investors looking to rent out the property, bearing in mind the tenant market you'll be aiming at, and not just your personal preferences for a residence, is vital. Estate agents, letting agents, and the local newspapers are perhaps your best sources of local rental market knowledge and these sources can be extremely useful.

While you may want to see as many properties as possible, viewing those that aren't suitable is a waste of time. The trick is to eliminate unsuitable properties *before* arranging a viewing because the house-hunting process is exhausting enough as it is.

Property particulars: Seeing past the hype

Property particulars are provided by estate agents. These particulars give you details of the property such as how many bedrooms it's got, what size the rooms are and whether there's parking and a garden. It's against the law for an agent to make false or misleading statements about a property. So if the agent says the property has double-glazing, it should have double-glazing.

Even though property particulars mustn't contain false or misleading statements, you still need to take a lot of what is said with a pinch of salt. Agents are well-practised at making something sound much better than it actually is: They have to if they're going to shift some of the properties that come onto their books. Try reading between the lines. 'Traditional' could mean old-fashioned and in need of renovation; 'contemporary' may be too radical for some tastes, etc.

The property particulars may include terms you don't understand, such as *freehold* or *leasehold*. If you're unsure, ask. Don't worry about looking stupid; if it isn't clear to you, chances are it's confused many buyers. If you don't ask, you could make a costly mistake.

Checking out the property yourself

The best way to see whether a property suits you is to drive or walk past it before arranging a viewing. Often, a picture in an ad doesn't tell the full story. It won't indicate, for example, how much traffic passes by or whether you'll be able to get a parking space in the street if there isn't a garage. A quick drive by, without stopping to go in and look around, gives you a preliminary impression, which might be enough to cross the property off your list. If you like what you see, you can arrange a viewing.

Arranging a Viewing

As soon as you come across a property you like, make an appointment with the estate agent or, if the property is being sold privately, with the seller to view it. Moving quickly is important, particularly if the property has just come onto the market; if it's desirable, you can bet that other buyers will be interested.

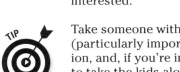

Take someone with you on viewings, Not only will this increase your safety (particularly important if you're a woman), but you also get a second opinion, and, if you're inclined to get carried away, someone to stop you. Try not to take the kids along however, as they'll just get in the way and distract you from the task in hand.

Arranging good viewing times

Most people view properties after work, or at weekends (usually a Saturday as most agents don't work Sundays). Which is fine. The key is to arrange to view the house in daylight so that you can see how much natural light it gets: In winter, therefore, viewing on the weekend is better than after work.

Following are some other tips for making the most efficient use of your time:

✔ **Work out how many properties you can comfortably view in one go.** Try not to book in more than a handful or you'll get tired and irritable and be less capable of making the right decision. The maximum I have viewed in one day when house hunting is five, and that was exhausting. Any more than that, and you may find yourself ready to keel over, particularly if you have to travel between properties.

✔ **Consider taking a day off work to view several properties in one go.** This offers a few benefits – the agent will be less busy than at the weekend, you can get a good number of properties out of the way in one hit, and the task won't cut into your leisure time.

✔ **Go as early in the day as you can:** If a flat in a desirable area goes on sale on a Thursday, for example, and you can't see it until Saturday evening, you may have missed the boat. But if you view it first thing Saturday morning, you can beat the prospective buyers lined up to see it during the day. And if you like it you can make an offer, which the seller may accept before anyone else gets the chance to make one.

Once isn't enough: Repeat viewings

If you are interested in a property after the first viewing, revisit it several times. Don't be afraid to make as many repeat appointments as you need to help you make up your mind. The second viewing is useful for measuring up and checking whether your sofa will fit into the lounge. Feel free to take a tape measure and notebook to jot down these details.

On follow-up viewings, ask to look round on your own without the agent or seller watching your every move. This will help you feel less harassed.

Arrange follow-up viewings at different times of the day and night (within reason!) so you can assess how noise and traffic levels affect the property. If, for example, the house is opposite a school, the road will get very busy around 9 a.m. and 3.30 p.m. When you arrange follow-up viewings, try to time them so that you can be at the property during potential problem times.

- **If the property is on a major road:** Make sure your second viewing is during the rush hour. If the noise is incessant, opening the windows on a warm summer evening and still being able to hear the TV may be difficult (if not impossible!). If you have cats or small children, see the road at its busiest to assess whether it's too dangerous for them.

- **If the property is close to a train station:** Make an appointment to visit the property during the day to see whether commuters clog up the street with their cars and make it difficult to get in and out of the drive or to park in the street. With a train track nearby you should also be wary of the potential noise (see 'Not forgetting the exterior', later).

- **If the property is next to a pub or above a shop:** Visit during opening hours. Are the premises noisy or intrusive? Be particularly wary of off-licences, nightclubs, and 24-hour corner shops where people may hang around outside and cause a nuisance.

What to Look for During a Viewing

Before you view any properties, it's important that you're clear about what you're looking for. This may sound blindingly obvious, but until you ask yourself what features a property *must* have and what features you'd quite like but aren't essential, you can't work out whether a property is suitable for you. With your criteria in mind, you can view a property and objectively compare it with your criteria.

Using your criteria as a basis, write a list of 'must haves' and 'would likes' before viewing any properties. As long as you can tick off all the 'must haves', the property is suitable. And if you have several ticks next to the 'would likes' as well, consider it a bonus.

Not forgetting the exterior

Your viewing of the property starts before you even set foot inside the front door. Before entering the property, check the exterior and make sure you're satisfied with the answers to the following questions:

- ✔ Do the neighbouring houses appear clean and well cared for? Are the neighbours' drives clear of old bangers and rubbish? The type of neighbours you want are those who take pride in their homes. This can also be an important factor when you come to sell the property.

- ✔ Is the road noisy and busy? Is there room for parking (and how easy is it to find) if the property doesn't have a drive? Would it be safe for children (if you have any) to play in the street or for the cat to wander about outside?

- ✔ How safe does the street appear? If it is night-time, is it well lit? Would you feel safe walking home late at night? Would you feel happy leaving your car in the street at night?

- ✔ Does the roof look sound, or are tiles missing? Don't forget to check the guttering and drains, particularly if it's raining.

- ✔ Does the exterior of the property need a lick of paint? If so, you may be able to negotiate with the seller over the purchase price.

- ✔ If wood is on the front of the property, is it in good condition or does it need replacing? Again, this may give you room for negotiation over the price. See Chapter 2 for more details on how to do this.

- ✔ Have any extensions been added to the property?

Walk round the exterior of the property if possible, and check the garden, if there is one. If you view the property at night, come back during daylight.

Look out for anything that might make selling difficult, such as mobile phone masts or electricity pylons in the immediate vicinity, aeroplanes roaring overhead or intercity trains hurtling past at all hours of the day and night. Check train timetables and arrange several viewings at different times to make sure aircraft noise isn't intrusive.

Poking about in the cupboards

Once inside the property, the agent or seller usually takes the lead and guides you round, pointing out certain features. Go along with them, but don't allow them to rush you no matter how busy they are. Potentially, you are going to spend a lot of money on that property, so take as long as you need. Use the checklist (Form 1-1) to ensure you don't forget anything.

Property Checklist

Date of viewing: ....

Address of property: ....

....

Type of property and age: ....

Freehold/leasehold? ....

Seller's name: ....

Estate agent: ....

Asking price: ....

Likelihood of negotiation over price: ....

(Put a tick next to room that exists, plus add comments as to general condition or anything that strikes you about it)

Kitchen ....

Lounge ....

Dining room ....

Bedroom one ....

Bedroom two ....

Bedroom three ....

Bathroom ....

Downstairs toilet ....

Car parking ....

Garden ....

Central heating ....

Double glazing ....

Fixtures and fittings included? ....

....

Has seller made any structural changes? ....

....

Running costs

Gas ....

Electricity ....

Water rates ....

Council Tax ....

Cable? ....

Form 1-1: Property Checklist (Page 1 of 2).

Give the following a score out of 10 (10 is excellent; 0 is poor)

Traffic: ....

Noise: ....

Condition of paintwork: ....

Guttering: ....

Roof: ....

Wiring: ....

Windows: ....

Any repairs needed? ....

Does the area feel safe? ....

Local amenities

Schools: ....

Pubs, restaurants, and takeaways: ....

....

Cinema/theatre: ....

Swimming pool/sports centre: ....

Shops/newsagent: ....

Parks: ....

Is seller part of a chain? ....

Comments: ....

....

....

Date of second viewing: ....

Form 1-1: Property Checklist (Page 2 of 2).

If you are looking at several properties, make several copies of this checklist – one for each property – and make notes as you go round otherwise, you'll forget which problem belonged to which house. You could also take photos to jog your memory further.

If you want to poke about in the kitchen cupboards, you should be able to do so without feeling that's unreasonable. In fact, opening and shutting kitchen drawers and fitted wardrobes will reveal whether the quality is good. You may find that you'll have to replace them as soon as you move in (which could mean you offer less than the asking price; see Chapter 2 for tips on making an offer). Likewise, have a good look at the boiler and fuse-box; if you need to replace the former or rewire the property, it'll cost thousands of pounds.

Look out for damp patches, mould or cracks in the walls indicating subsidence. Ask the agent or seller what is causing the problem, how long it has been like that, and whether any work has been done to rectify it. Be suspicious of new paint or wallpaper as this could hide a problem.

Take a torch and go up into the loft, if possible. Check for any holes, leaks or running water and make sure the roof is properly insulated.

Asking All the Right Questions

You probably have a hundred and one questions to ask. I suggest jotting them down before the viewing so you don't forget them. And remember to make a note of the answers, particularly if you are viewing several properties. Questions you might want to ask the seller include:

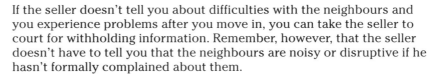

- **Why are you moving?** People move for many reasons: usually because they've outgrown the property with the arrival of children, or it's now too big for them because the children have left. But if the seller is moving because the noisy neighbours are making her life hell, you need to know about it.

- **What are the neighbours like?** If he's made a formal complaint about the neighbours to the council or the police in the past, the seller has to inform you of these problems. (Your solicitor will also ask the seller this question via the seller's questionnaire that he sends to the seller's solicitor during the conveyancing process.)

If the seller doesn't tell you about difficulties with the neighbours and you experience problems after you move in, you can take the seller to court for withholding information. Remember, however, that the seller doesn't have to tell you that the neighbours are noisy or disruptive if he hasn't formally complained about them.

- **How long have you lived here?** Moving house is so stressful that if the seller has only been in the property for six months and can't give a good reason why she's moving, alarm bells should ring.

Be wary, too, of sellers who have lived in a property for 20 or 30 years. The chances are that a lot of work is needed to update the property. Many people put up with problems over the years and learn to live with them. You may not be able to.

- **How long has the property been on the market?** If the property has been for sale for only a couple of weeks, you may have to make a decision quickly in case someone else snaps it up. But if the property has been on the market for months (or years!), there could be a problem. The price may be too high, there may be major structural problems, or the property may be at severe risk of flooding – all making it difficult for a buyer to get a mortgage. Or maybe the problem is that the seller is difficult and messes people around. If the problem is with the property – and not an uncooperative seller – think carefully before you buy. You, too, may experience problems when you come to sell.

✔ **Have many people viewed the property and has anyone else made an offer?** The answer to these questions gives you an indication of how much competition there is and how quickly you have to move if you want to purchase the property. But be wary that sellers and agents may exaggerate interest from other prospective buyers, although it is difficult to find out whether this is the case or not.

✔ **Is the property freehold or leasehold?** If it is freehold, as many houses in the UK are, there is no problem, as you will own the property outright. But many flats are *leasehold,* which means you simply purchase the right to live there for a certain number of years. You must pay service charges and ground rent every year to the freeholder, or landlord, and abide by certain rules. The landlord is also responsible for repairs to the communal areas (see Chapter 4 for more details on the differences between leasehold and freehold). If the property is leasehold, ask the seller for evidence of the service charges and what the landlord is like. Is he reasonable or has the seller had problems with him?

✔ **Are you in a chain and when do you want to move?** Most sellers are also buyers. If your seller is buying another property, there's a strong chance that the seller of that property is also a buyer. This is known as a *chain,* and the longer and more complicated it is the greater the chance of something going wrong. A hiccup with one property can break the entire chain. What's more, resolving the problem could take months. Don't get caught up in a complicated chain if you can help it.

✔ **How much are the utility bills and council tax?** Ask to look at the sellers' gas, electricity, and water bills. Ask what council tax band the property comes under and look at a bill, if possible.

✔ **Has any work been carried out on the property?** If so, when and how extensive was it? Ask to see receipts or guarantees. You should also mention the work to your solicitor so that she can check that any necessary permission was obtained beforehand.

✔ **What fixtures and fittings are included?** Some sellers leave the carpets or curtains because they're buying new or can't face the hassle of taking them: Others strip the property to the bare bones. Find out what the seller's intentions are so that you don't get a nasty shock when you move in. If there's anything you'd like, negotiate with the seller to leave the items for an extra sum. Make sure what you agree is stated in the contract; otherwise, if the seller takes items she agreed to leave, it will be difficult to prove this after you have bought the property.

✔ **Has the property ever been burgled or the seller's car stolen from outside?** If the answer is 'yes, several times', you may rethink buying the property. But if an isolated incident occurred, the seller may have tightened up security since then, so you'll benefit from secure locks and maybe a burglar alarm. Also ask whether the property is situated in a Neighbourhood Watch area; if so, you'll know that the neighbours look out for each other's homes, which can act as a deterrent to burglars. Being in a Neighbourhood Watch area also means lower insurance premiums.

✔ **How easy is finding a parking space?** This is a concern if you have a car and the property doesn't have a garage or off-road parking. Ask the seller how much you have to pay for a permit (if required). Glance at the other cars parked in the street. If they're valuable and their owners are happy to park them there, it should be fairly safe for you to park your car there, too. But if only old bangers are in sight and a couple of burnt out cars for good measure, ask yourself whether you'd be comfortable parking your car in that road (unless you drive an old banger yourself!)

Decision Time

After you view the property several times and don't think you'd gain anything else in viewing it again, you're ready to make a decision. Do you like the property enough to make an offer? If you decide to make an offer, keep these tips in mind:

✔ Don't rush into making an offer. Even if you're really excited, curb your excitement in front of the seller or agent. If they can see how thrilled you are, they'll be delighted because it means you're more than likely to offer the asking price.

✔ If you can get away with offering less than the asking price, try. Mask your excitement; show interest by all means, but remain guarded. Once you've saved a few thousand pounds on the asking price you can celebrate with an even bigger bottle of champagne. Carefully assess whether this is a good strategy first, however. See Chapter 2 for more details on making an offer.

✔ While you can save yourself money by containing your excitement and haggling over the price, you should still make an effort to convince the seller of your seriousness.

✔ Whatever you do, be friendly towards the seller. It doesn't cost you anything and may act in your favour if you and another buyer are competing for the property. If you created a favourable impression, the seller may decide to go with you – even if your offer isn't as high as the other buyer's.

Once you've made an offer, you will have to instruct a solicitor and arrange a survey. See Chapter 4 for more on this.

Chapter 2

Making an Offer

*O*nce you've found the property of your dreams and the seller has accepted your offer, it's all too easy to get carried away. Even if the seller does accept your offer, there's no legal guarantee of ownership or that you'll eventually be successful in purchasing the property. Consider this sobering statistic: one in three agreed sales don't make it to exchange of contracts, according to the National Association of Estate Agents. No wonder buying a property is one of the most stressful things you will ever do.

Although the buyer's offer is binding in Scotland (see Chapter 5), in England, Northern Ireland, and Wales, which we look at in this chapter, this isn't the case. Either side – the buyer or the seller – can pull out up until the time that contracts are exchanged, resulting in financial losses, time wasted, and much inconvenience. One of the main reasons for agreements falling through is when the seller accepts a higher offer from a buyer even though he has already accepted another offer – a practice called *gazumping*. The Government has pledged to reform the system, but until laws are introduced to stop this happening, it's up to you to protect yourself. In this chapter, we look at how you can reduce the chances of being gazumped.

And because finding the right solicitor to oversee the purchase and commissioning a survey (rather than relying on the lender's valuation), are crucial parts of the house-buying process, we look at how to go about both of these.

Making an Offer

Buying a property is a nerve-wracking experience: it's no wonder it is rated as one of the most stressful things you're ever likely to do. And making an offer on a property is no exception.

Once you've found the property of your dreams and have worked out that you can afford it, the next step is to put in an offer on the property. An offer is not legally binding but demonstrates your interest in buying the property. You usually make the offer verbally to the estate agent, if one is handling the sale, or directly to the vendor if the house is being sold privately. You may prefer to make the offer in writing although doing so isn't strictly necessary.

The offer should be subject to survey and contracts – you are not obliged to proceed with the purchase until you are happy with the findings of the survey and contracts have been exchanged.

If an estate agent is involved, he will put your offer to the seller and act as go-between, letting you know whether the seller is prepared to accept it or not. In an ideal world, your offer would be accepted straightaway but in a *sellers' market* – where there are more buyers than there are properties for sale – there's a strong possibility that another buyer will have his eye on the same property as you. If this is the case, you could get caught up in a bidding war. If you have your heart set on the property, upping your offer to outbid the other potential buyer means that it will cost you more in the long run.

Remember that the estate agent is working for the seller, not you. The seller pays the agent commission for achieving a sale; therefore, the more you pay for the property, the bigger the agent's commission. For this reason, treat everything the estate agent says with a healthy dose of scepticism.

Offering below the asking price

It always used to be the case that buyers would try and knock a bit off the asking price, and sellers, expecting lower offers, would add a few thousand pounds on in the first place to allow for it. But the situation has changed in recent years as demand for property – and the price of houses – has rocketed.

For over 10 years, there have been far more buyers than sellers in the UK, thanks to an unprecedentedly long boom period in the housing market. The south-east has been most affected, but in other areas as well, such as the north and west, you couldn't have risked haggling with the seller either when two or more other buyers were prepared to pay the full asking price.

In July 2007, a Royal Institute of Chartered Surveyors survey of the UK housing market hinted that things might be about to change in favour of the buyer in some areas, and in the short term. More unsold property remained on surveyors' books than at the beginning of the year, and the number of new buyer enquiries decreased faster than at any time since August 2004.

The housing market is governed by supply and demand. At times, there are more buyers than sellers; at other times, the reverse is the case. Assess carefully what sort of market it is before you make an offer, or you could face losing out on the property of your dreams – or paying well over the odds for no reason. The best way to find out whether the market is favouring buyers or sellers is to do some research. Chat to estate agents to find out how long properties hang about before being sold. And keep up to date with house price movements by reading the national newspapers, which are always full of tales about the British obsession – the housing market!

When to offer less

Even if the property is fairly priced, you don't want to pay more for it than is absolutely necessary. In some situations, you may want to offer below the asking price:

- **If you're purchasing in a *buyers' market*.** In a buyers' market, where there are more properties for sale than people willing to purchase them, it is often worth offering below the asking price. If properties are taking a while to shift, the seller runs the risk of having to wait weeks, or even months, for another buyer to come along if he rejects your offer.

  In a sellers' market, where there are more buyers than properties for sale, the reverse is the case. And if several buyers are interested in one property a bidding war could break out – a seller's dream but every buyer's nightmare.

- **If the property has hung around on the market for several weeks or the vendor is keen to sell immediately.** Either of these situations could be a good opportunity to offer a few thousand pounds below the asking price. Ask the estate agent how long the property has been advertised and keep an eye on the estate agent's window and local 'For Sale' signs when a property goes on the market to see how long it's been up for sale.

- **If the property needs a lot of work.** If the property is in need of repairs that are not reflected in the price, obtain estimates as to how much the work will cost and then use these as a bargaining tool to get the seller to reduce the price. You may well have a strong case for doing this, particularly if you are buying a dilapidated property in need of a lot of work. Head to Book III, Chapter 1 for information on buying property requiring renovation.

If the seller calls your bluff and refuses to reduce the price, you have to decide how much you want the property. If you firmly believe it is overpriced and you are not really bothered about buying it, stick to your guns. There'll be another property around the corner. And chances are the seller may well decide to lower the price anyway once he realises that you aren't going to budge.

If you have your heart set on a property and don't begrudge paying a little over the odds to get what you want, you may decide to go back to the seller and agree to pay the asking price. Otherwise, if both of you refuse to budge, another buyer may snatch your dream property from under your nose.

Holding your nerve

If you are haggling with the vendor and have offered below the asking price, some time may pass before you hear the verdict, especially if the seller is prepared to accept some reduction but doesn't want to appear too desperate. Once you've decided to offer less than the asking price, try not to panic and bombard the agent with calls, saying you've changed your mind and will pay the asking price after all. Wait for the agent to report back to you: if he sees your desperation, you'll be playing right into his hands, and you can kiss goodbye to any bargaining tool you thought you had.

Assess the situation rationally. If you have thought about your offer carefully, believe the property to be overpriced, and are not prepared to pay more than it's worth, stick by your decision. A rational decision is often the right one. If you aren't sure you did the right thing because you didn't really think your decision through in the first place and you subsequently think you may have made a mistake, you won't be able to hold your nerve.

When it's wise to meet the asking price

If the property is fairly priced, you've decided you want to buy it, and the agent has several other potential buyers lined up, trying to haggle over the price is foolish. It is likely that another buyer is prepared to pay what the seller wants, and by the time the estate agent has got back to you, the seller may have accepted the other offer. If you like the property and can afford to buy it, don't start messing about. My advice is to offer the asking price – and quickly.

My first property purchase was a one-bedroom flat in a new development in the East End of London. I arrived for the viewing having psyched myself up to offer £5,000 below the asking price, not because I felt it was overpriced but because that's what everyone told me you did when buying a property. I instantly fell in love with the flat and decided to make an offer. The agent told me that only four flats were left for sale in the block (out of 42), so if I didn't put a non-refundable £500 deposit down within 24 hours to demonstrate my interest, chances are by the weekend they'd all have gone. I realised there wasn't much point trying to haggle considering the situation and had to make a quick decision: Was I prepared not only to pay the asking price but also to stump up a deposit? The answer was yes, and I visited the agent's office the next day to pay the deposit to secure my flat. I also discovered that the remaining flats had already been sold. My decision turned out to be the right one.

Instinct can be a useful tool when purchasing a property. If you go with your gut feeling, you will make the right decision a lot of the time.

Sealed bids

When several buyers are after the same property it may go to sealed bids, which are standard in Scotland and becoming increasingly popular elsewhere. With sealed bids, the seller's solicitor or estate agent will fix a closing date and time by which all prospective buyers must make an offer for the property, in writing. As well as the price you're prepared to pay, you should include details of when you want to move and whether you would like any carpets or curtains included in the sale.

Once the deadline has passed, it is too late to submit a bid. The seller's solicitor or agent will open all the bids and inform the seller what they are. The seller then gets to choose the winning bid, which isn't always the highest. If she wants to sell her curtains, for example, and one buyer is prepared to pay extra for them, this may swing it in his favour.

Sealed bids speed up the process. The seller knows that by a certain date she will have a number of serious offers on the table to choose between.

If the seller has two identical bids from buyers but one of them can move quicker than the other, she is likely to opt for the buyer who can complete first.

Once the seller has made her decision, it's final. You can't negotiate so make sure you bid high enough if you have your heart set on the property. Instead of bidding a round number, try to go just above this in order to see off any competitors who are also bidding around this mark. For example, instead of bidding £180,000, try £180,101.

Avoiding Being Gazumped

Once your offer has been accepted, there is still no binding commitment on either side, except in Scotland (see Chapter 5). To make matters worse, under the Estate Agency Act, agents are obliged to pass on *all* offers received on a property to the seller, even if an offer has already been accepted. So if the property has been taken off the market because the seller has accepted your offer, there is still a risk that someone else, perhaps someone who viewed the property before you, will make a bid which the agent has to pass onto the seller. In some cases, buyers bypass the agent and go straight to the seller anyway. If the seller accepts the later offer, this is known as *gazumping*.

Gazumping can be quite common in England, Northern Ireland, and Wales, when the housing market is buoyant. The dragged-out process of buying a property in these countries – the process can take as long as 10 to 12 weeks, sometimes even longer – is a prime reason why gazumping happens. And in a buoyant housing market, where prices increase at an incredible rate, the property could well fetch several thousand pounds more by the time the sale comes to completion. So if a desperate buyer offers more than you, the seller may well be tempted to take their cash.

Gazumping can be heartbreaking for a buyer. The financial cost tends to be high because you could have forked out hundreds of pounds for a survey, instructed a solicitor, and paid a mortgage application fee. You will also have to decide whether you are prepared to get involved in a bidding war for a property you thought was practically yours. The trouble is that many buyers feel they have to stick with the purchase because they have already invested so much money – and end up paying over the odds so that they don't lose that cash.

Although gazumping is frowned upon, it isn't illegal. And a higher offer can be very tempting to a seller, particularly if the sale is dragging on. You can reduce the likelihood of being gazumped by pushing the sale through as quickly as possible. Follow these tips:

- ✔ Make sure that all your finances are sorted out before you make an offer and that you have pre-appointed a solicitor. That way, as soon as the offer is accepted, you can move forward with the purchase, and it needn't take months to sort out a mortgage or get the local searches completed. Your efficiency will keep the seller happy, reducing your chances of being gazumped.

- ✔ If you drag your heels over the property purchase and seem to be delaying things unnecessarily, the seller may lose patience and accept another offer. Don't let your actions leave you open to being gazumped.

- ✔ Use an agent who has an anti-gazumping policy. Some agents have a policy on gazumping and ask clients to sign a contract stating that they won't let it happen. Use one of these agents and it could save you hundreds of pounds.

Lock-out agreements

One of the best ways of ensuring that another buyer doesn't outbid you at the last minute is to ask the seller to keep the property off the market for a certain period of time after a price has been agreed. You then agree to adhere to a strict timetable to complete the purchase.

If you have offered the asking price and the seller accepts it, a lock-out agreement is not an unreasonable request. If the seller does agree, an 'Under Offer' sign should replace the 'For Sale' board outside the property or in the estate agent's window. Check that this has been done and if it hasn't, get the situation rectified.

If the property is advertised with more than one agent, make sure all of them know that it is 'under offer' and no longer on the market.

Pre-contract deposit agreements

One way of minimising the chances of either party pulling out once an offer has been accepted is to establish a pre-contract deposit agreement. You can ask the agent to arrange this: Buyer and seller each hand over a small percentage of the agreed purchase price – typically 1.5 per cent – to a third party such as a solicitor. Either party that subsequently pulls out of the deal forfeits this sum to the other party, unless there is a very good reason behind it, such as the survey indicating that the property is not worth what the buyer offered for it. As part of the agreement you also arrange to exchange contracts within a set period of time.

Both buyer and seller benefit from a pre-contract deposit agreement. As a buyer, you know that the seller isn't going to accept a higher offer after you've shelled out hundreds of pounds on a survey and legal fees. And the seller knows that you are serious and not about to change your mind on a whim after her property has been off the market for several weeks.

Buyer and seller insurance

If you're really worried about being gazumped, you can buy insurance to protect you in the event of this happening to you. A number of insurance schemes are available; these pay out if the purchase falls through after your offer has been accepted. For a one-off premium of around £40, buyers and sellers can take out a protection policy, which provides around £500-worth of cover for legal and valuation costs if the other party causes the deal to fall through.

Several insurers, mortgage lenders, and brokers offer buyer and seller protection policies. If you're interested, ask your lender or broker for more details. But remember: to ensure your legal fees are covered if the sale does fall through, you must take the policy out before you instruct your solicitor.

In a strong housing market, buyer and seller protection policies can be very attractive because they offer a lot of cover for a relatively small premium. But if money is too tight to mention and the market is sluggish or the property you're buying has languished on the market for several months, you may come to the conclusion that such a policy is an unnecessary extra.

Making the seller your new best friend

The best way to ensure you don't get gazumped is to get the seller on your side. There are several ways of doing this:

- **Offer the full asking price and prove you have the cash *and* that you can move quickly.** That way you won't look like a timewaster.

- **Be easy going and don't fuss over minor points.** If the seller won't leave you the curtains, for example, let it go and buy your own.

- **Listen to the seller.** Instead of imposing your timeframe on her, make it clear you will complete on her timescale.

- **Don't underestimate guilt.** Establish a friendly relationship with the seller so that she would feel bad about doing the dirty on you and accepting an offer from a rival buyer.

- **Stay in regular contact with the seller or the estate agent.** You want to know exactly what is going on and whether other buyers are sniffing around. Establish a regular flow of information so that they know when your survey is completed or you've received a formal mortgage offer.

After Your Offer Is Accepted: Let the Conveyancing Begin!

Once the seller has accepted your offer, you receive a letter confirming the agreed price, address of the property, and the name, address, and contact number of the agent handling the sale. The letter also includes details of your solicitor and the seller's, so you must have a solicitor lined up in advance. Now it's time for the whole conveyancing process to begin.

Conveyancing is the legal process of transferring ownership of a property or land from one person (the seller) to another (the buyer). During conveyancing, all the legal documents such as title deeds need to be checked and the signing of documents and filling in of forms needs to be organised. Land registry and local searches are also vital to find out whether any long-term plans exist that could affect the value of the property.

Conveyancing can take a frustratingly long time, which is why HM Land Registry and the Lord Chancellor's office are working on plans to speed the process up over the next decade. With the planned introduction of electronic conveyancing, or *e-conveyancing,* the legal process will be faster and more efficient. No more will endless reams of paper be passed back and forth between solicitors. Instead, contracts and deeds will be signed electronically. But until e-conveyancing is introduced, you'll just have to put up with a laborious process.

Head to Chapter 4 for details about conveyancing

Instructing a solicitor

Although you may already have a perfectly good solicitor, he may not be suitable to handle your house purchase unless he is also experienced in conveyancing. If you don't know a conveyancing specialist, ask friends and family for recommendations. And if all you hear is bad reports about various solicitors, at least you'll be able to cross them off your list.

If you are serious about property investing, finding a solicitor with good expertise in property matters and developing a close and trusting relationship with him is important. Speed is often of the essence when purchasing (and selling), so a solicitor who knows you and expects more business in future from you is good to have on board.

Hundreds of solicitors are listed in the Yellow Pages, but this gives you no idea of their quality. Rather than go down this route, ask your agent or mortgage broker (if you use one) to suggest one if you don't have a personal recommendation to go on. They deal with solicitors every day, so they're likely to know someone who may be suitable. And you may even get a discount on the fees if you use one recommended by an agent or your broker.

If you are really stuck, try the Law Society (www.lawsociety.org.uk) or call 0870 606 2500, for a database of solicitors in England and Wales. In Northern Ireland, try the Law Society of Northern Ireland (www.lawsoc-ni.org) or call 028 90 231 614. A licensed conveyancer doesn't have to be a solicitor, however. Try the Council for Licensed Conveyancers (CLC) on 01245 349599 or www.clc.gov.uk, for a list of specialist conveyancers.

Many lenders won't accept a solicitor who is a sole practitioner – that is they don't have any partners in their firm – so bear this in mind when choosing a solicitor.

You don't have to opt for a local solicitor. In most instances, you won't have to go to the solicitor's offices at all; in this day and age, everything can be sorted out over the telephone, by e-mail, fax and post, and your passport is taken as proof of identification. If you live in London, for example, you are bound to find a cheaper solicitor if you look beyond the City.

All solicitors in England and Wales have to be registered with the Law Society. In Northern Ireland, they must be registered with the Law Society of Northern Ireland. This means there is an established complaints system if something goes wrong. The CLC also has a complaints system and will refer you to the Legal Services Ombudsman if it can't deal with it. If your complaint is upheld, you could be in line for compensation.

Understanding the costs

Solicitors' charges vary, so be sure to get a couple of quotes in writing before instructing one. As a general rule, expect to pay around £600 plus VAT (value-added tax) in solicitor's fees if you're purchasing a £100,000 property, for example. If the property is leasehold, where a third party owns the freehold of the building, add on another £100 plus VAT to cover the extra work involved in checking the lease.

As well as the solicitor's fee, which is payable just before completion, you have to pay for disbursements as you go along (although some solicitors will add the cost of these onto their final bill). These are local authority and Land Registry searches that are vital for ensuring that the property had planning permission in the first place and for discovering whether any buildings are planned nearby, such as a supermarket, which could affect the property's value. The cost of these searches varies depending on the size of the property, but for a £100,000 house expect to pay in the region of the following (all plus VAT):

- Local authority search fee: £100
- Land Registry fees: £200
- Water authority water and drains search fee: £40
- Mining search (some areas): £30
- Environmental search (optional): £35

✔ Electronic money transfer fee: £35

✔ Mortgage admin fee: £75

✔ Miscellaneous fees: £25

A number of Internet sites offer a fixed price for conveyancing. This may well work out cheaper than using a high street solicitor, but remember that this is a bit like sticking a pin in the list of solicitors specialising in conveyancing who are listed in the Yellow Pages. Stick to recommendations to minimise the chance of problems down the line.

If you are selling a property at the same time as buying, you'll save money by using the same solicitor to do the conveyancing on both properties.

Chasing up your solicitor

Solicitors can get very busy. But you probably want to move as quickly as possible, especially if you want to avoid being gazumped. The only way to make sure your solicitor does get his finger out is by applying the pressure and keeping your finger on the pulse. Although nobody wants to be a pest, call your solicitor on a regular basis, particularly as you approach exchange of contracts, to ensure you aren't holding up the purchase without realising it.

We have ways of getting round a solicitor

A friend of mine got very frustrated because the purchase of her flat was taking so long, so she called the seller to find out what the hold-up was. The seller revealed that her solicitor was waiting for my friend to sign some documents and return them to him, although these hadn't even been passed onto my friend by his solicitor. Convinced of his solicitor's incompetence and fed up with not being able to speak to him personally, my friend took matters into his own hands and befriended the solicitor's secretary.

This tactic worked brilliantly as the secretary always answered the solicitor's phone and seemed to know more about what was going on in that office – what documents were lying in the in-tray, for example – than the solicitor himself. The secretary also wasn't used to clients being polite to her, so she was happy to chat with my friend. As a result, the hold-ups vanished, everything was done promptly, and my friend grew to enjoy his daily chat with the secretary who lacked the patronising, hurried air of her boss.

If you can't get the organ grinder to give you what you want, don't write off the monkey.

Arranging Your Finances

Make sure that your finances are arranged in principle before you have made an offer, doing so ensures that you can move quickly. Book II, Chapter 1 deals with the ins and outs of mortgages, but if you haven't arranged anything by the time you've made an offer on a property, you'll have to move really quickly if you don't want to annoy the seller and delay the process.

Getting a mortgage application approved can take a couple of weeks, sometimes longer if yours is not a straightforward case. But many lenders will supply you with a certificate saying they are prepared to lend you a certain amount of money in principle, and you can get one of these certificates before you even step foot inside a potential property.

Once you've made an offer and it's been accepted, you can fill out the mortgage application form and return it to your lender. You'll be asked for details of your address, job, income, and any outstanding debts. If you're buying the property with another person, that person also has to supply this information. Depending on the lender's particular requirements, you have to supply pay slips for the last three months, six months' worth of bank statements, and your P60, revealing how much you earned in the last tax year.

You can save time and hassle by having all this information ready before your offer is accepted. If you haven't kept your bank statements and have to order replacements, do this before you find a property you want to buy. Likewise, if you have lost your P60, contact the Inland Revenue to order a replacement. If you leave all this until you need to send off your application, you could hold the purchase up by several weeks.

Arranging a Survey: The Full Monty or the Bare Minimum

Before your lender agrees to let you have a mortgage, it will insist on a valuation of the property. At this stage, you must decide whether you are happy with just this valuation or want a survey, and if so, what type. What you decide depends on the condition of the property, your own buildings knowledge, and the amount you can afford to spend.

Opt for the most extensive survey you can afford. When the cost of the survey is compared with the amount you're spending on the property, it looks like money very well spent.

Basic: Lender's valuation

The valuation report is compulsory, and the lender arranges a local surveyor to carry it out. You have to pay for it – around £250 or so, – but it benefits only the lender. It doesn't tell you anything about the condition of the property, only whether it's worth what you're hoping to borrow. The valuation ensures that the lender is assigning its money wisely.

If you rely solely on the valuation and serious structural problems are discovered after you purchase the property, you only have yourself to blame. Yet despite the obvious risks, around 75 per cent of buyers rely on the valuation and don't bother commissioning a survey.

Better: Homebuyer's report

It is well worth commissioning a homebuyer's report – the next step up from a valuation (see the preceding section) but not so detailed or expensive as a structural survey (see the next section). A surveyor tells you whether the purchase price is reasonable and whether there's anything you should know about the condition of the property. He also suggests what decisions and actions should be taken before exchange of contracts.

If you have a specific concern, you should mention this to the surveyor before he undertakes the survey. Most surveyors will look at a particular aspect of the property if asked, although you may have to pay extra for this. Confirm the cost beforehand.

Choose a homebuyer's report if the property:

✔ Is in good condition – that is, doesn't require significant renovation

✔ Is conventional in type or of traditional construction

A homebuyer's report costs from £300 plus VAT for an average-sized property. This is on top of the cost of the lender's valuation.

Best: Full structural survey

A structural or building survey is the most comprehensive type you can get and is vital if the property:

✔ Is very old – that is, built before 1914

✔ Is in poor condition and needs a lot of renovation

> ✔ Is not of traditional construction – for example, is a thatched or listed building
>
> ✔ Has been extensively altered
>
> ✔ Is going to be significantly altered by you
>
> ✔ Is very expensive

Expect to pay between £500 and £1,100 plus VAT for a building survey, depending on what you want to know and the size of the property. It's money well spent if a problem is unearthed. Sometimes the surveyor suggests that you get a specialist survey done if he thinks a particular issue needs more investigation, such as whether trees on the property will affect the foundations and need removing by a tree surgeon.

If you opt for a homebuyer's report or structural survey, you can often get this done at the same time as the mortgage valuation. Doing so saves time and hassle because only one surveyor needs to get access to the property. But remember that not all surveyors can carry out both types of survey, so be sure that the surveyor you hire can perform a survey as well as a valuation.

Dealing with problems uncovered in the survey

If your survey reveals that the property is fine, that's great news and it's all systems go. Quite often, however, the survey reveals that a problem may exist, and the surveyor may recommend that further investigations are required. Before you panic, remember that this happens quite a lot and is often just the surveyor covering her back. But the specialist survey may well reveal a significant problem, which could affect your decision to purchase the property.

If the surveyor calls for further reports, the lender will insist upon them.

When the property is valued at less than the asking price

Sometimes the lender's valuation assesses that the property is worth less than the asking price, which is bad news if you need to borrow the full amount in order to purchase it. Lenders aren't in the habit of letting buyers have more cash than a property is worth. But if you can find the extra cash from your savings to make up the difference, there's nothing to stop you from going ahead with the purchase, even if you're paying more than the surveyor thinks the property is worth.

Even if you haven't got enough cash to cover the shortfall and don't fancy taking on any more credit, all is not lost if the property is valued at less than the asking price. The surveyor has handed you a useful bargaining tool: go back to the seller and inform him that your lender doesn't believe the property is worth what he's asking for it. And if your lender thinks that, the likelihood is that other lenders will take a similar view so the seller will have trouble flogging the property to another buyer. If the seller won't budge, you may have to accept that the property isn't going to be yours. You may even have had a lucky escape.

Coping with structural problems

If the survey reveals problems with the property, such as subsidence or a condemned boiler, all is not necessarily lost. Your lender may still be prepared to let you have a mortgage but will insist on holding back some of the funds until you have rectified the problem to the surveyor's satisfaction.

The downside in this scenario is that you need to have enough cash saved to fund the repairs out of your own pocket because you won't get the funds from the lender until after the work has been done. If you don't have enough saved, you will have to extend your overdraft, take out a personal loan, or pay for the work by credit card. Make sure you shop around for the cheapest rate before using one of these methods.

If you opted for a building survey, the surveyor will give you an idea of the cost of the work needed: it's up to you to decide whether you can afford to get it done. In this situation, try haggling with the seller. He might be persuaded to knock a couple of grand off the purchase price. But if the seller won't shift and you can't afford the repairs, you may have to give this property a wide berth and find one that doesn't require extensive building work or renovations.

Exchanging Contracts

As soon as both solicitors have completed their work, the survey's findings are satisfactory, the searches haven't unearthed any problems, and your mortgage application has been approved, a date is set for completion. You also have to sign the contract. Once this is done, your solicitor exchanges contracts with the seller's solicitor.

At the point of exchange, you must electronically transfer the deposit to your solicitor's bank account, along with any outstanding solicitor fees and stamp duty land tax.

This is the point of no return: You can't back out after exchange of contracts unless you are willing to incur significant financial penalties.

Don't forget the stamp duty

Stamp duty land tax (formerly Stamp Duty) is a tax imposed by the Government on all property purchases above £125,000, so you can't avoid paying it if your property is more expensive than this. It is banded according to property price at these rates:

- ✔ 0 per cent up to £125,000

- ✔ 1 per cent on properties worth between £125,000 and £250,000

- ✔ 3 per cent on properties worth more than £125,001 and less than £500,000

- ✔ 4 per cent on properties costing £500,001 and above

If you buy a property in an area designated by the government as 'disadvantaged', you don't pay any stamp duty land tax if the purchase price is £150,000 or less.

Stamp duty land tax is due when contracts are exchanged, so make sure you have the funds available to cover it.

Buildings insurance

Once you've exchanged contracts, the property is your responsibility from an insurance perspective. In some cases, the seller cancels his buildings insurance from this date. Your solicitor will insist that you take out buildings insurance for the new property before you exchange contracts in case anything happens to the property before completion.

Even if you haven't completed on the purchase, if the house burns down after you've exchanged contracts, you still have to complete on it. Buildings insurance covers you if any such problems occur. And make sure you arrange buildings insurance well in advance so there are no hold-ups at this stage.

Completion

This is it: the day the property legally becomes yours. Completion can happen the same day as exchange of contracts, or it can happen several months later, depending on what you and the seller agree. Usually though, completion takes place one to four weeks after exchange of contracts.

In the run-up to completion, you should arrange for the meters in the property to be read and ensure that all the utilities – gas, electricity, water, and telephone – are transferred over to your name from the date of completion.

If you buy an investment property that already has a tenant living there, make sure your solicitor has properly checked the tenancy agreement. If you need to regain possession at some point, he needs to make sure that you can easily do so. You also need to check that any deposit paid by the tenant is properly accounted for and find out whether the deposit is in the hands of the vendor landlord, an agent, or one of the new Tenancy Deposit Schemes.

Book I

Housebuying Basics and the Law

Chapter 3

Going, Going, Gone: Buying Property at Auction

*T*he auction scene in *Only Fools and Horses* in which Del Boy and Rodney Trotter are set up for life after flogging an antique watch for millions of pounds is one of hundreds of auction scenes that have appeared on television. As a result, even if you've never set foot in an auction-room, you probably think you have a fair idea what an auction is like – you can get caught out if you so much as scratch your ear and end up with a hideous vase costing thousands of pounds; there's always a bidding war (usually between people who know each other); and the sale price is nearly always a complete surprise to all involved. Oh and when it comes to art, there is always a forgery or two.

Fortunately, auctions in real life are quite a bit different, and few people actually spend serious amounts of money as a consequence of mistakenly scratching their nose! If you're buying a property, checking out the auction-room for real may be worth it. An increasing number of buyers – first-time and experienced alike – find property bargains at auction.

You need to be careful, however. Although auctions are a quick way of buying a property – cutting out weeks of heel dragging and the chance of being gazumped – some sellers use this speed as an opportunity to get rid of a property quickly, hoping the buyer won't ask too many questions. If you don't know what you are doing, you could easily make a big mistake.

In this chapter we guide you through the process of buying a property at auction and identify the pitfalls you need to watch out for.

Pros and Cons of Buying at Auction

Some 5 per cent of all property sales are now done at auction, according to the Royal Institution of Chartered Surveyors (RICS) – and increasingly property developers aren't the only ones who go down this route. In the following sections, we look at the advantages and disadvantages of buying a property at auction.

Why you'd want to: The pros

An increasing number of buyers and buy-to-let property investors are purchasing property via auction for several reasons:

- **A quick sale is guaranteed:** Once the hammer comes down, the sale is binding and you have up to 28 days to complete (when the property is legally yours and you get the keys). There's no chance of being gazumped – when the seller accepts a second, higher offer from another buyer after already accepting your offer.

- **Bargains galore:** When people think of auctions, they think of bargains and there are certainly plenty to be had. Quite often, properties going under the hammer are in need of extensive refurbishment, and the price reflects this. So if you're prepared to put in a bit of hard work, you may well stumble across a bargain.

- **Free and fair competition:** If you're not the only bidder interested in a property, at least you have a fair chance of successfully bidding because the playing field is open. You know exactly how much someone else is prepared to pay – not always the case when you're buying through an estate agent who plays one buyer off against another in order to push up the price.

Why you wouldn't: The cons

You also need to be careful. Buying at auction is fraught with potential pitfalls:

- **Getting the wool pulled over your eyes:** Many sellers use auction because they want a quick sale. Their motivation may well have something to do with the fact that the property has major structural problems. These sellers hope that you won't bother with all the necessary surveys, perhaps because time is short or you don't want to 'waste' money on a survey for a property if you then lose out during the bidding and someone else ends up buying it. To avoid such problems, be wary of cutting corners and *always* get a survey done.

✔ **Not doing your research:** If you buy an investment property (one with a tenant already living in it), be particularly careful with your pre-purchase research (known as *due diligence*). Make sure you've had the lease or tenancy agreement, the rental payment amounts and arrangements, and any deposit arrangements checked by an expert so you know exactly what you're taking on in terms of a legal commitment with the tenant.

✔ **Changing your mind is not an option:** Once the hammer has come down, the sale is binding and neither buyer nor seller can pull out without paying a financial penalty. As the successful bidder, you will exchange contracts on the day of the sale so you must be 100 per cent certain that's what you want. Properties are sold unconditionally, not subject to contract, survey, or finance.

If you change your mind and back out of the deal, you lose your deposit and may face legal action from the seller if he can't sell his property or has to sell it to someone else for less money than you had agreed to pay.

Although buying at auction does have potential pitfalls, if you put in enough preparation *before* the sale, you can get a bargain and reduce the chances of it turning into an expensive mistake. In the following sections, we show you what steps to take to protect yourself.

Getting Started – Action to Take before the Auction

Unlike buying almost anything else at auction, when you buy property, you have to do some legwork first – and quite a bit of it in some cases. If you turn up on the day without having seen the property you're planning to bid for or without having organised your finances, you're likely to run into trouble. Several steps are essential if you're going to successfully bid for a property at auction.

Registering interest with an auction house or estate agent

If you don't know when an auction is taking place, you haven't a chance of even getting there to put in your bid. So you need to get yourself registered with as many auction houses and estate agents specialising in auctions as possible.

Look in your local paper and the property press, such as *Estates Gazette* and *Property Week*, for details of property auctions; contact those auction houses running these and get yourself on their mailing lists. This ensures you are notified of an auction weeks before it occurs and can apply for an auction catalogue detailing all the different lots for sale. And if you have Internet access, check for details of auction houses in the area where you are hoping to buy.

Reading the catalogue

Getting hold of the auction catalogue that lists all the properties for sale is vital. The auction house usually publishes it several weeks before the sale. Most auction houses charge an annual fee if you want the catalogue sent automatically to you. Each catalogue contains a number of houses, flats, and plots of land. It also contains all the details of the property, including any Special Conditions of Sale and any planning restrictions. Make sure you understand how the property is described:

- **Vacant possession:** Empty properties. Ideal if you're buying somewhere to live. Also suitable are those with tenancies due to expire shortly because the tenants are moving out.

- **Tenanted properties:** Properties with existing tenants living in them. Ideal for investment purposes. If you're looking for a property to rent out and you buy one of these, you may not have to bother looking for another tenant (depending on the length of the current tenant's tenancy agreement).

Getting your feet wet without buying

Attend several auctions to see what happens. You shouldn't intend to bid this time around; instead you just want to get a feel of what's required. Most big auction houses run several property auctions a year around the country. Check in local and national newspapers and the property press, such as *Estates Gazette* and *Property Week*, for details.

The Internet is also a useful source. The Essential Information Group works with 150 auction houses, providing a list of coming auctions on its Web site (www.eigroup.co.uk). The RICS also has a list of auction houses on its Web site, along with links to their Web pages so you can apply for a catalogue (www.rics.org/property_auctions).

Most auction houses have priority lists you can join for an annual fee; you are then automatically informed of upcoming auctions and sent a sale catalogue. Auctioneers Allsop & Co (www.allsop.co.uk) charge £45 per year, for example, for subscriptions to their priority list.

Each lot should also have a guide price, which is different from the *reserve price*. The *guide price* is not the asking price, but it is indicative of the minimum price the seller expects to get for his property. Only a guide, this price can be exceeded at auction (see sidebar) – which is exactly what the seller hopes will happen. The guide price can also increase during the marketing period. The guide price is always higher than the reserve price, which is the minimum the seller will accept for the property. The reserve price isn't published; only the seller and auctioneer know what it is, and it's usually set just before the auction.

Viewing the property

Viewing a prospective property is essential. Just as you wouldn't buy a house through an estate agent without seeing it first, you shouldn't rely on the description in the catalogue, or the picture, when making your decision. Even if you think you're getting a bargain, you're still spending a lot of money, so view before you bid.

If you don't make the effort to view the property, you may end up paying far more than it's worth or having to pay for structural repairs you haven't budgeted for because you didn't realise they were needed.

The auctioneer often arranges group viewings on popular lots; contact him and find out what the arrangements are, then go and take a look at the property. Handle this viewing in the same way you would if you were buying a property through the estate agent. Make sure you check the property carefully – both inside and out – and find out why the owner is selling. For more details on viewings, see Chapter 1.

Time is likely to be short – you may have only a couple of weeks between receiving the catalogue and the auction, so arrange to view the property as soon as possible.

Arranging a survey

As well as asking a builder to give you a quote, get a survey done before the auction. Many buyers don't bother because they see it potentially as money down the drain; after all, there's no guarantee that their bid at auction will be successful. But if you don't have a survey and subsequently discover major structural problems that potentially cost a fortune to correct, it's too late. Once the hammer has come down, you can't pull out.

The guide price isn't always a good guide to the sale price!

Convinced that this was the best way to get a bargain, a friend of mine was keen to buy at auction. She sent off for a catalogue and spotted a derelict property, with a guide price of £110,000. Much work was required but this wasn't likely to be a problem as her husband is in the building trade and could do most of it himself.

My friend arranged a mortgage in principle and sat back and waited for the auction. But on the day, everything went horribly wrong: A bidding war broke out between her and two other buyers who were just as keen to buy the property. Although she knew she might be able to get a bigger mortgage and had some savings (originally for refurbishment and new furniture), she couldn't keep up and decided, regretfully, to pull out when the bidding reached £180,000.

It's just as well she did. The hammer finally came down at £276,000. It was later revealed that the reserve price was just £100,000, a third of the bid price – resulting in one very happy seller. My friend believes that the location of the property, near Teddington High Street, and the fact that the house was part of a pretty row of well-maintained cottages, with lots of potential, had a lot to do with such a high sale price.

She was wise to pull out when she did, as she'd never have been able to cover the purchase price and pay for refurbishment, even with her husband doing the work. This is a classic example of how the guide price can wildly differ from the asking price. Remember, you need to know when to bow out gracefully.

The cost of the survey depends on how detailed it is, which in turn depends on the condition of the property and how large it is. The bigger the property, the more expensive the survey. You can find a chartered surveyor to carry out the survey by contacting the Royal Institution of Chartered Surveyors (www.rics.org.uk). See Chapter 2 for more details on the different types of survey available and how much you should expect to pay. Try to get a survey done at least a week before the sale so that you have time to think about the findings and investigate further, if necessary.

If you don't arrange a survey, you risk bidding far more than the property is worth. But if you do commission a survey, and major problems are unearthed, you can make an informed decision as to whether to give the property a miss or put a limit on your bid. You can then use the remainder of your budget to pay for the extra repairs.

Setting a budget for renovation and other stuff

When you buy a property at auction, don't forget to factor into your budget the other costs you'll incur. You'll have to pay fees for any professional advice you obtain from builders, surveyors, solicitors, and a mortgage broker, if you use one (see 'Arranging your financing in principle' later in this chapter). You also have to pay stamp duty land tax on properties costing more than £125,000 (see Book II, Chapter 1 for more details).

In addition, most properties sold at auction need some work, which varies from property to property. Some lots are complete wrecks that need total gutting and rebuilding; others need complete internal refurbishment. Factor the cost of renovations into your budget.

The best way to get an accurate estimate of the work needed is to take a builder or surveyor along when you view the property before auction. He can give you an accurate assessment of the work needed to get the property up to scratch and the likely cost. While you won't get a definitive quote, you will have a good idea of how much it will cost.

Unless you are a property developer or builder, working out how much a new roof is likely to cost is near impossible. And if you drastically underestimate the costs, you could run well over budget, which could hold the project up for weeks or months while you raise extra cash.

Be realistic. If refurbishment is likely to cost more than you can afford or more work is involved than you feel comfortable taking on, you might need to find a less challenging project.

Getting your solicitor on the case

Another task *before* the auction is to inform your solicitor that you're planning to bid for a property. Send her the auction catalogue so that she can inspect the details of the lot you're interested in. She will then be able to contact the seller's solicitor (their details are usually at the back of the auction catalogue) to get hold of the various legal papers that you need to make an informed decision about whether you should bid for a lot. These papers include:

- ✔ Special conditions of sale
- ✔ Title deeds
- ✔ Searches
- ✔ Details of the lease (if it's a leasehold property)
- ✔ Planning permissions

Legal documents are available to view at the auction-room just prior to the sale. But as your solicitor is unlikely to attend, she won't be able to go through them. Make sure you sort out the legalities before the auction; otherwise, you could end up buying a property that never had planning permission or has a lease with oppressive conditions.

Arranging your financing in principle

If you need a mortgage it's important that you have the necessary finances in place *before* auction. If you wait until you've successfully bid for a property before applying for a mortgage, there's a chance that the funds won't be approved before completion, which is non-negotiable. Finding out you've got adverse credit problems once you apply for a loan, for example, could hold the process up by several months. And this isn't ideal if you have to complete within 28 days!

The solution is to get an agreement in principle from a lender, stating that it has approved you for a mortgage, provided that it can verify your earnings. Most lenders instruct a surveyor to complete a valuation before the auction, so you need to give them as much notice as possible.

Arranging insurance

If you successfully bid for a freehold property at auction (see Chapter 4 for the difference between these and leasehold properties), you are responsible for buildings insurance from exchange of contracts (which happens on the day of the sale). So make sure you arrange this in advance of the auction.

Getting the deposit together

If you successfully bid for a property, you're expected to put down 10 per cent of the sale price there and then. Some auction houses ask for £1,000 or £1,500 instead, if this is greater than 10 per cent of the sale price. How you pay depends on the auction house's policy. Some require that you pay by banker's draft, while others accept cash, building society cheque, or personal cheque. Check with the auction house as to what it prefers before the sale.

Because you pay the deposit *before* you get a mortgage, you must have the funds available. The best way to pay the deposit is out of your savings; alternatively, ask the bank to let you have an overdraft (or extend your existing one), take out a personal loan, or get a cash advance on your credit card. Whichever route you take, shop around for the lowest rate of interest and pay it back as soon as you can to avoid paying a fortune in unnecessary charges.

The Day of the Auction Dawns

By the time the auction comes round you should have your finances in place, your survey completed, and your solicitor happy for you to bid for the property.

You should also have attended at least one auction to ensure you know what you are letting yourself in for. Now you reach the nerve-wracking part – the bidding itself.

A lot can change between an auction catalogue being published and the day of the sale. The seller may have pulled out or the guide price may have increased, for example. Give the auction house a call on the morning of the sale to check that the property you're interested in is still going on sale. Otherwise, it could be a wasted trip. If your lot is still up for sale, find out whether there are any last minute amendments or alterations to the catalogue. These will be printed as an addendum and available at the saleroom on the day of the auction.

Getting there early

If you're attending the auction (you can also bid by proxy over the telephone or Internet if you can't make the sale; see the section 'Bidding by proxy', later) arrive half-an-hour early. This gives you time to register if necessary (some auctioneers don't ask you to), find a good seat where the auctioneer can see you, and calm your nerves. It also helps to watch the bidding for a while to get a feel for how it's going and whether properties are meeting their reserve price.

Bring your auction catalogue, cheque book, and some identification – such as a driver's licence or passport. Also bring your solicitor's contact details; the auctioneer will require these if your bid is successful.

Controlling your nervous tic

Mistaken bids at auction are the bread-and-butter of sitcom plots, but in real life, thankfully, they are rare, as most auctioneers require that you raise a paddle with a number on it when making a bid. But waving your arm in the air if you don't intend to make a bid is foolish so sit on your hands if you are worried about catching the auctioneer's eye.

The wrong bid could mean you spend thousands of pounds on a property you didn't want. And as the sale is binding, claiming that it was a mistake is not an excuse. If a mistake is made, let the auctioneer know straight away: don't wait until the end of the sale.

Making sure you don't get carried away

Once you've experienced the frenetic atmosphere of the saleroom, you can see how people get carried away and spend far more than they intended.

Auctions attract many wealthy property developers who bid literally millions of pounds on property, so your £120,000 upper price limit may seem piddling in comparison.

But you've got a budget you need to stick to just as they have, although admittedly theirs is much bigger than yours. You can bet your bottom dollar, though, that nothing would persuade them to pay more than they can afford – developers are too shrewd for that.

If you can't trust yourself to stop when you reach your limit, ask a friend, relative, solicitor, or surveyor to bid on your behalf. Explain what your upper limit is and ask them to stick to it. Someone who's bidding for you is less likely to get carried away; she won't be emotionally involved (her heart isn't set on the property), and she's using someone else's money – yours.

If you bid more than you can afford, you will struggle to finance the purchase. Your lender won't let you borrow more than the property is worth, so you'll have to find the shortfall somewhere else. And if you chip away at the budget you've set aside for refurbishment, you could set back your repairs and renovations by many months.

Going, going gone: Handling the bidding

Once your lot is called, it's your turn. The auctioneer reads out the lot number, full address, and a short description of the property. Then he invites bids at a certain level; bid by raising your hand or catalogue. The property is 'knocked down' to the highest bidder, and the lot is sold once the auctioneer has said 'Going, going gone'. Following are some tips to keep in mind:

- ✔ If you're bidding, don't leave it to the last minute. If you do, you may miss out.

- ✔ Make sure the auctioneer can see you – in a crowded room, this may be difficult. Try not to sit in the front row, however, because you won't be able to see what's happening behind you to gauge how well the sale is going.

- ✔ Make sure you're bidding for the property you *think* you are bidding for. It might sound obvious but it's worth double-checking. You don't want to end up with one you don't want.

- ✔ To bid, put your hand or auction catalogue purposefully in the air and make sure the auctioneer sees it. Some auction houses have a paddle bidding system with a number on it, so check whether this is the case beforehand.

What to do when your bid is successful

If your bid is successful – congratulations! Now you have to do the following
things:

- ✔ **Pay the deposit:** This is usually 10 per cent of the sale price – or a minimum of £1,500. You will also be told when you have to complete – usually
  within 28 days.

  This deposit makes the sale binding. If you don't pay the remaining 90
  per cent of the purchase price within 28 days, you forfeit your deposit
  and lose the property.

- ✔ **Sign a *Memorandum of Agreement*:** This document confirms the sale
  and acknowledges the receipt of a deposit.

- ✔ **Provide identification:** You'll be asked for some ID and your solicitor's
  details.

When these things are done, you're given a signed copy of your contract.
Pass this onto your solicitor as soon as possible. Make sure you don't leave
the saleroom without it.

As soon as you exchange contracts at the sale, you're responsible for insuring
the property. Set this up before the sale and then confirm with the insurer that
you want to proceed with the policy. If you are buying leasehold rather than a
freehold property, you don't need to take out cover, as this is the freeholder's
responsibility.

Bidding by proxy

If you can't make the sale, you can bid by proxy, if you arrange this in
advance. To bid by proxy you can do any of the following:

- ✔ **Bid over the phone during the sale:** In this arrangement, someone in
  the auction-room bids on your behalf.

- ✔ **Bid in writing:** In this situation, you specify a maximum bid, and the
  auctioneer bids on your behalf.

- ✔ **Bid over the Internet:** Contact the auction house for more details.

However you bid, you need to provide a cheque to cover your deposit in full;
this won't be cashed if your bid isn't successful.

Chapter 4

Conveyancing for Buyers and Sellers in England, Wales, and Northern Ireland

In This Chapter

▶ Understanding what happens during the conveyancing process

▶ Finding a solicitor or licensed conveyancer

▶ Making sure you don't unwittingly hold up the transaction

*F*inding your dream property or a suitable buyer can feel like a big achievement after all the hard work and effort you've put in to get this far. But it's just the beginning. Once an offer has been accepted, the next step is *conveyancing*: the legal transfer of a property from seller to buyer. Not only do both parties' solicitors have plenty to do to achieve this goal, but the buyer and seller themselves have their own roles to play. If you know what happens, and in what order, it will reduce the chance of you unwittingly holding up the transaction.

A lot could go wrong between an offer being accepted and exchange of contracts – when buyer and seller are legally obliged to go through with the deal – because there is so much work to be done. It is an extremely stressful time. In this chapter, we offer tips to make everything go as smoothly as possible and to reduce the chances of the transaction falling through.

The Offer Has Been Accepted: Let the Conveyancing Begin!

Once buyer and seller have agreed on a price for the property – subject to contract and survey – the conveyancing can begin This transfers 'good title' – the legal right to possession – from one person to another. A lot of detective work is involved and it can take many weeks to gather all the necessary information. Even though each party's solicitor does the bulk of the work, hold-ups and delays make for an incredibly stressful time.

During conveyancing, several things happen:

- ✔ **You appoint a solicitor or conveyancer to act on your behalf.** Some buyers and sellers prefer to do their own conveyancing in order to avoid paying legal fees. However, it is very risky (see the sidebar 'Do-It-Yourself Conveyancing' later in this chapter). For more details on locating a solicitor or conveyancer, hop to the section 'Finding a Solicitor or Licensed Conveyancer.'

- ✔ **The solicitors get busy.** The seller's solicitor draws up the draft contract, including details of the particulars and conditions of sale; the buyer's solicitor conducts the local searches and contacts the Land Registry. The buyer's solicitor also goes through the draft contract and raises any questions he has with the seller's solicitor. Once they come to an agreement, the seller's solicitor can draw up the final contract. For more details on what the solicitors get up to, see the 'Role of the Buyer's Solicitor' and 'The Role of the Seller's Solicitor' later in this chapter.

- ✔ **You make yourself available to answer questions.** If you are the seller, you must complete the seller's questionnaire, if you are the buyer, you want to ensure that everything you agreed with the seller is included in the contract. For example, if you agreed to purchase certain fixtures and fittings, these should be included. (For more info on your obligations, see 'The buyer's role' or 'The seller's role', later in this chapter).

- ✔ **When all necessary tasks have been completed and the final contract accepted by both parties, contracts are exchanged.** Now there's no going back, you can celebrate! Go to 'Exchange of Contracts' later in this chapter for details of what happens in the final stages.

Following are things you can do to make the conveyancing go more smoothly:

- ✔ Find a solicitor before making or accepting an offer – ideally before you start looking for a property or put yours up for sale. Otherwise you may hold everything up while you find one (see 'Finding a Solicitor or Licensed Conveyancer' later in this chapter).

- ✔ If you're buying and selling a property at the same time, get one solicitor to handle both transactions. This saves you money and lets your solicitor coordinate the sale and purchase so they happen simultaneously.

- ✔ Complete and return the necessary forms and documents to your solicitor as soon as you can. Part of the reason why it can take 12 weeks between an offer being accepted and exchange of contracts is that people sit on documents for days before they return them.

- ✔ If your solicitor tells you that the other party is dragging her heels, contact her to find out what is causing the delay. And while you're at it, make sure you aren't responsible for hold-ups.

The buyer's role

Once your offer has been accepted, there are several things you need to do to ensure your purchase goes through as quickly as possible:

- ✔ Instruct a solicitor
- ✔ Apply for a mortgage
- ✔ Commission a survey

We cover these steps in more detail below.

Instructing a solicitor

When you make the decision to purchase a property, you must inform your solicitor of the seller's contact details and those of her solicitor, the address of the property, and the purchase price.

Applying for a mortgage

If you need a mortgage – and let's face it, most people do! – apply without delay. If you have an agreement in principle (which we highly recommend), inform the lender that you have found a property. Complete and return a mortgage application form, along with a cheque for the lender's arrangement fee, if required.

If you haven't found a lender yet, don't delay. The best way of obtaining a mortgage simply and quickly is to use an independent mortgage broker (see Book II, Chapter 1 for more details on this). She can help you find the best deal on the market. The broker also supplies the lender's mortgage application form; once you've completed this, return it directly to the lender, along with the fee (if applicable).

The advantage of using a broker, apart from not having to wade through the multitude of available mortgages on the market, is that she can apply pressure to the lender if it seems to be dragging its heels over processing your application.

Once you have received a formal written mortgage offer from your lender, you should pass this onto your solicitor. He will need the formal offer in order to exchange contracts with the seller's solicitor.

Commissioning a survey

Your lender instructs a local surveyor to value the property you intend to buy to ensure it is worth the money you intend to borrow. Although you have to pay for this valuation, it is wholly for the lender's benefit, ensuring that, if you default on the loan, the lender can recoup its investment by repossessing and selling your property.

The basic valuation doesn't tell you anything about the condition of the property and whether any potential problems exist. To find this out you must commission a survey. There are two types: the one you opt for depends on the condition and age of the property, your own expertise in assessing potential problems, and how much you can afford to spend. Most buyers need no more than a Homebuyer's Report – which is more detailed than a simple valuation and will point out glaring faults. If the surveyor thinks further investigation is necessary, you should obtain a more detailed report. If the property is very old, however, the likelihood of potential problems is much greater so you should opt for a full structural survey. (For more details on surveys and cost, see Chapter 2.)

The seller's role

You have two major tasks after you accept an offer from a buyer:

✔ Tell your solicitor that you have accepted an offer

✔ Complete the seller's questionnaire – a list of questions from the buyer's solicitor.

We cover these tasks in more detail in the following sections.

Informing your solicitor that you've accepted an offer

When you accept an offer, you need to inform your solicitor in writing, along with contact details for the buyer and his solicitor, the price you accepted, and whether fixtures and fittings are included.

Your solicitor draws up a draft contract using this information and passes this onto the buyer's solicitor who examines it and queries anything he disagrees with or doesn't like the look of.

Completing the seller's questionnaire

Your solicitor passes on a standard list of questions from the buyer's solicitor for you to answer. These questions are known as *preliminary enquiries, enquiries before contract*, or simply *the seller's questionnaire*. They're designed to find out more details about your property; for example, you will be asked the following:

✔ What is included in the sale?

✔ What the boundaries of the property are

✔ Who is responsible for the upkeep of hedges, fences, or walls?

✔ Whether there are any guarantees on any structural work that's been done on the property

✔ Whether you've had any disputes relating to the property

✔ If you have a leasehold property as opposed to a freehold, you will also be asked for contact details for the landlord and whether you have paid up any outstanding service charge bills or ground rent (see the sidebar 'Understanding the contract: differences between freehold and lease-hold' later in this chapter).

You must complete and return the questions as soon as possible – or you risk delaying the sale.

The buyer relies on the answers you give in the seller's questionnaire when deciding whether to purchase your property. You must answer as truthfully as possible; incorrect information provides the buyer with a good case for compensation from you. Or if the buyer finds out you lied before exchange of contracts, he could pull out completely. If you don't know the answer to a question, say so. Don't take a guess. If your guess turns out to be incorrect, you're still held responsible.

Finding a Solicitor or Licensed Conveyancer

If you already have a solicitor that you're happy with, you may think he is the perfect choice to do your conveyancing. But while the legal work involved in transferring a property from seller to buyer is often regarded as one of the more mundane jobs in the legal profession, it is nevertheless a very exact science.

Most lenders insist that you use a qualified solicitor to carry out your con-veyancing and that the practice has at least two partners who are members of the Law Society. The rest is down to you, but we suggest you choose a solicitor who specialises in conveyancing. In England and Wales you can use a licensed conveyancer instead of a solicitor. These people offer the same services as a solicitor but are limited to house purchasing.

The buyer and seller must use a different solicitor to ensure that both parties are dealt with completely fairly. Your mortgage lender insists upon this to eliminate the possibility of conflict of interest. If, by some strange twist of fate, you both happen to have the same solicitor, one of you may be able to use a different partner from the same firm. But it may be better for one of you to just retire gracefully and find another solicitor to use for this transaction.

General advice for locating a solicitor

Personal recommendation is the best way to choose a solicitor or licensed conveyancer. If someone you know still speaks highly of the solicitor who helped them with a property purchase, she is probably alright. Likewise, if someone tells you that he's had a bad experience with a solicitor, you may want to give that solicitor a wide berth.

As a property investor, you'll use a solicitor more than the average house purchaser. It's a good idea to find a recommended solicitor with good property expertise, as not all solicitors have this, and to develop a close working relationship so that your solicitor will go the extra mile when you need her to.

If you don't have a personal recommendation to go on, you can find a solicitor experienced in conveyancing by contacting the following:

- ✔ The public enquiry line of the Law Society in England and Wales (0870 606 6575). This society can provide you with details of up to three solicitors working in your area. You can also try www.lawsoc.org.uk.

- ✔ Alternatively, try the Council for Licensed Conveyancers (www.conveyancers.org.uk) or 01245 349599.

- ✔ The National Solicitors' Network provides details of solicitors experienced in conveyancing in England, Wales and Scotland (www.tnsn.com or 020 7370 0245).

- ✔ In Northern Ireland, contact the Law Society of Northern Ireland (028 90 231 614 or www.lawsoc-ni.org).

Your estate agent or mortgage lender may recommend a solicitor or licensed conveyancer to you and may offer a special rate if you use his services. If you're considering following your agent's or lender's advice in this regard, keep the following in mind. You're under no obligation to use this person, and if the agent or lender insists you do, take your business elsewhere. Even if the charges seem attractive, compare them with what other solicitors are charging to make sure they truly are competitive.

Checking the solicitor out

Find out as much as you can about a solicitor and his practice before instructing him. Although nobody can say for sure how long conveyancing will take, you should try to get some idea. If the solicitor is extremely vague or off-hand, find somebody else. But if he seems eager, he's more likely to get on with the job. When you contact a solicitor find out about the following:

✔ **Who will be dealing with your case on a day-to-day basis?** Quite often it's an office junior. If this is the case, find out how involved your solicitor will be – whether he will be overseeing this person closely, for example.

✔ **When your solicitor is away on holiday who will take over his case-load in his absence?** This is good information to have just in case something goes drastically wrong at the last minute.

✔ **If you're selling your property, is the solicitor signed up to the Law Society's TransAction Protocol?** If he is, you can save a lot of time because, under this protocol, certain documents automatically accompany the draft contract when it's sent to the buyer's solicitor; he doesn't have to apply for them. These are copies of the title deeds; the property information form, which contains preliminary enquiries answered by the seller; and a fixtures and fittings form, detailing what is included in the sale price. The TransAction Protocol speeds up the tortuously long conveyancing process. If you're in a hurry, choose a solicitor who is signed up with this scheme.

Your aim is to assess how professional and efficient the solicitor is because you'll be dealing with him on a regular basis over the next few weeks and how he does his job directly affects the outcome of your property transaction.

Local isn't always necessary

Select a solicitor who is local to the property you're buying. Such a solicitor should have a good knowledge of the area and any planning restrictions. The other advantage of the local solicitor is that you can speed up the whole process by popping into the office with forms and documents or to sign paperwork rather than relying on the post.

You don't *have* to use a local practice as you won't have much face-to-face contact, if any, with your solicitor. Modern communications mean that conveyancing is carried out over the telephone, by e-mail and fax, and via the post. This is good news if you live in an area where conveyancing is expensive – such as a city – as you will almost certainly get a cheaper deal if you use a solicitor who is based further afield.

Cost isn't everything . . . but it's worth considering

Cost is a major consideration when you choose a solicitor; some homebuyers end up spending hundreds of pounds more on conveyancing than others. You inevitably pay higher charges if you're buying a six-bedroom mansion than if you're purchasing a studio flat, or a leasehold property rather than freehold. But shop around and get a couple of quotes for the work, in writing, before you instruct a solicitor to ensure you aren't paying over the odds.

While you don't want to pay too much for your conveyancing, beware of paying too little. The cheapest quote may be attractive, particularly as money is likely to be tight, but this solicitor's charges may be low because he doesn't offer very good service. He may cut corners in order to offer this price or take on more work than he can cope with in order to make up his money. A very expensive solicitor isn't necessarily a better choice. That big, bustling, expensive City firm may be too busy to treat your case as a priority. You could end up pushed right to the bottom of the pile.

As a general rule, if you pay a little more, you're likely to get better service. Avoid the solicitor offering the cheapest quote, as well as the most expensive. A small practice dedicated to conveyancing, with moderate charges, may produce much quicker results for you.

The cost of conveyancing is divided into solicitor's fees and disbursements, both of which are explained in more detail below.

Fees

Both buyer and seller have to pay their solicitor a fee for all the work done liaising with the other party's solicitor, sending out forms and contracts, and giving you advice and guidance. Solicitor's fees can cost anything from £300 to £1,000, plus disbursements (fees for searches, and so on), all plus VAT, depending on the complexity of the case and your individual solicitor.

Some solicitors base their fee on the size of your property: the more expensive the house, the bigger the fee. Other solicitors have a set fee regardless of property size. If you're buying a leasehold property, expect to be charged more than if you're buying a freehold property because of the extra work involved in checking the lease.

Don't rely on a verbal quote over the phone or a rough estimate. Whatever the fee, make sure you get a detailed, fixed quote in writing; then if complications arise, you shouldn't be landed with a huge, unexpected bill upon completion.

Disbursements

The buyer's solicitor incurs a number of costs or disbursements when making various enquiries, known as local searches, on the property. Expect to pay a Land Registry fee, local authority search fee, water authority search fee, and land charges search fee – and there may be others.

You must pay all outstanding charges and fees to the solicitor before completion can take place. Check out Table 4-1 for an example of the breakdown of the actual costs incurred on the purchase of a three-bedroom house in Guildford, Surrey for £190,000; this should give you an idea of the sort of sums you can expect.

Table 4-1	Solicitor's fees, Disbursements and Stamp Duty Land Tax on a £190,000 Property
Item	*Typical Costs*
Property purchase price	£250,000
Solicitor's fees	£600 + VAT
Stamp duty land tax at 1%	£250
Land Registry fee	£200
Bank fee for electronic transfer	£35.25
Official search fee	£8
Bankruptcy search fee	£4
Local search fee	£150
Drainage enquiries	£47
Mortgage administration fee	£75 + VAT
Mortgage valuation fee	£200 + VAT
Environmental search fee	£35 + VAT
Total cost	**£251,763.50**

The buyer also has to pay stamp duty land tax to his solicitor – at the same time as he pays the solicitor's fees. Your stamp duty land tax bill depends on the value of your property, starting at 1 per cent on properties costing £125,000, rising to 4 per cent on properties of £500,000 or more (for more details, go to Book II, Chapter 1).

All property vendors (sellers) will soon be faced with the additional cost of providing a Home Information Pack, which could add something like £600 to £700 to the cost of selling.

Home Information Packs

In spite of much gnashing of teeth from many people, Home Information Packs (HIPs) became law in England and Wales on 1 June 2007 and are being gradually phased in, with 3-bedroom properties coming under the rules from 10 September 2007.

Under the old house purchase process, much of the important information about the property was only made clear weeks after the seller has accepted the offer. If problems showed up, buyers could pull out at the last moment, usually after paying hundreds of pounds in legal and survey fees. This was disappointing for both seller and buyer. Buyers also lost out if, at the eleventh hour, the seller switched to another buyer for a higher price, or simply decided not to sell after all, due to the long delay in the whole process.

The Government has now passed HIPs into law in England and Wales to put an end to this situation. The big change is that the seller now has to pay for the cost of the pack, instead of the previous system where the buyer had to pay his conveyancer and mortgage lender/surveyor for the collection of all the relevant information. The Government reckons the pack will cost £500 to £600 to put together, and slightly more in

London. This breaks this down into around £280 for a 'home condition report', £200 for local authority searches, and £135 in legal fees. However, the Law Society suspects the true figure will be nearer to £1,000.

The following **compulsory** documents *must* be included in a Home Information Pack:

- Home Information Pack Index
- Energy Performance Certificate
- Sale statement
- Standard searches
- Evidence of title
- Additional information for leasehold and commonhold sales, where appropriate

Some documents in the Home Information Pack are **optional**. These include:

- Home Condition Report
- Legal summary
- Home use/contents forms

You can find out more information at the Web site www.homeinformationpacks.gov.uk/.

The Role of the Buyer's Solicitor

If you are buying a property, your solicitor's job is to ensure that there is nothing that can cause you any problems either in the contract or lease (if there is one), or revealed by the local searches. Your solicitor should do the following:

- Check the legal jargon in the title deeds
- Find out the property's background via planning and title searches
- Make sure there is nothing in the lease (if it is a leasehold property) that affects your ownership of the property

~ Ensure that the contract is legal

~ Help you renegotiate the price if problems crop up

Your solicitor doesn't have to take any action until he has received the draft contract, which is drawn up by the seller's solicitor. Before he receives the draft contract, however, he may send out a list of questions to the seller to obtain more information about the property (see 'Completing the seller's questionnaire' earlier in this chapter).

Working through the draft contract

There are two parts to the draft contract your solicitor gets from the seller's solicitor:

~ **Particulars of sale:** A description of the property, what fixtures and fittings are included, and details as to whether the property is freehold or leasehold.

~ **Conditions of sale:** Details of the proposed completion date and the deposit you have to pay when contracts are exchanged.

The contract may also include a provision for you to purchase certain fittings such as carpets and curtains, if you want to, for an extra sum. A copy of the title deeds usually accompanies the draft contract. Your solicitor needs this so that he can check that the seller actually owns the property and has the right to sell it to you.

Your solicitor works his way through the draft contract and raises any questions he has with the seller's solicitor. He also sends you a copy of the contract. Check this carefully to ensure that everything you agreed with the seller is included. If the seller promised to throw in the carpets, for example, and that's not been noted, inform your solicitor before you sign the contract, or you won't have any comeback.

The draft contract can go back and forth between solicitors for some time.

Local searches and Land Registry search

If you are buying a property, your solicitor needs to establish that the seller is actually in a position to sell it to you and that there are no conflicting rights to the land that the property is built upon. These may not be immediately obvious because these rights can go back hundreds of years. It is not unheard of for there to be ancient ecclesiastical or common rights to the land, which could affect your rights to the property. Your solicitor's job is to discover whether this is the case by conducting local searches and contacting the Land Registry.

Understanding the contract: differences between freehold and leasehold

The contract states whether the property is freehold or leasehold. Freehold is much more straightforward: you own the property and the land it stands on, up to its boundaries. As long as you act within the law, you can do what you like on your property. Most properties in England, Wales, and Northern Ireland are freehold.

Buying a leasehold property is more complicated. There are 2 million such homes so you may end up with one. You don't have the freedom of a freeholder; instead, you're buying the right to live in a property for a fixed number of years – the length of the lease. Leases vary in length. Many have more than 99 years left to run, while some have 999 years left on them. Once the lease has expired, the property reverts to the landlord.

The landlord retains ownership of the building and the land the building stands on during the term of the lease. He imposes an annual service charge for the upkeep of the communal areas and structure of the building, as well as ground rent.

The conveyancing process on a freehold property is much more straightforward than on a leasehold because there are fewer potential problems. Keep in mind, however, that most people buying flats have no choice but to buy leasehold, and in the majority of cases, this doesn't cause a problem. As long as the lease has at least 75 years left to run (mortgage lenders generally won't lend money on shorter leases), and your solicitor has studied it closely to ensure it doesn't include any nasty clauses likely to affect the value of your investment, you should be okay.

Local searches

If you've set your heart on a cosy cul-de-sac, you'll be devastated if you discover that there are plans for a motorway to run right through it. Local searches are designed to reveal whether such plans are in existence *before* you buy your new property. If something is planned that would be detrimental to your enjoyment of the property, you'll probably be gutted. But at least you can pull out before exchange of contracts so that you won't have to put up with traffic roaring past your living room window.

Local searches reveal the following:

- ✔ Whether the council has plans for a motorway at the end of the road.

- ✔ Whether any planning restrictions affect your ability to renovate or extend the property.

- ✔ Whether planning permission was received for the property before it was built. Otherwise the council may insist you have it knocked down.

✔ Whether any extensions or conversions in need of planning consent were actually received before building work started.

✔ Whether the water drainage system is working as it should be and who owns the drains.

✔ Whether the sale includes covenants associated with the property and its land.

The location of the property determines whether other searches are necessary, such as commons searches or coal mining, for example.

Local searches aren't comprehensive – there are plenty of things they don't unearth. They only cover the property itself and the areas immediately next to it, as well as roads. They don't check the surrounding area. Your property may be built on contaminated land, but not all councils keep a detailed register of this so you may not find out. Or if a waste disposal plant or block of flats is planned for the adjoining land, you won't find this out either. If your prospective property is close to vacant land, ask your solicitor to check whether anything is registered against it – such as planning permission for a supermarket.

Your solicitor won't visit the property you are buying, so if you have any concerns about adjoining land, mention them to him so he can investigate further.

The cost of local searches varies between local authorities but you should expect to pay in the region of between £90 and £200. The amount of time it takes also varies, anywhere from a couple of weeks to a couple of months, depending on how efficient and busy the local authorities are when your solicitor applies for the information.

You can speed up the searches by paying an extra fee to a private search company to gather the information. Onesearch Direct (www.onesearchdirect.co.uk) is one such company, which guarantees to complete a standard local council search within five days in England and Scotland for a flat fee of £100, including VAT. Your solicitor may be prepared to use the services of such a company if you are happy to pay the extra fee. Such an arrangement may be worth considering if you are in a hurry.

Local searches become invalid after about three months so your solicitor may need to do them again if the sale drags on for longer.

Land Registry search

Your solicitor will also apply to the Land Registry to check that the property is registered in the seller's name and that she is in a position to sell it to you. Expect to pay around £200 for this.

The Role of the Seller's Solicitor

The seller's solicitor has a number of tasks to carry out. These include:

- Drawing up the draft contract
- Negotiating with the buyer's solicitor over the terms included in the draft contract
- Drawing up the final contract
- Finding out how much you owe your lender
- Getting you to sign the transfer deeds ahead of completion
- Receiving the purchase price from the buyer's solicitor and releasing the title deeds to the buyer's solicitor
- Paying off your mortgage, subtracting his fee and the estate agent's and transferring the remaining cash to you (or your new lender if you are taking out another mortgage)

As soon as you notify your solicitor that you have accepted an offer, he contacts your lender and requests the title deeds to the property. He then prepares a draft contract setting out the terms of the sale.

The draft contract is a starting point and is altered as the solicitors haggle over the terms. The purchase price may also be reduced if the survey throws up unforeseen problems. Both solicitors negotiate the contract to their satisfaction. Once this is done and the buyer's solicitor has completed the local searches (see 'Local searches and Land Registry' for details), the draft contract is sent to you for your approval. If you and the buyer are both happy, you both sign. Contracts are then exchanged, and neither of you can pull out.

Your solicitor will then find out how much you owe your lender. He asks you to sign the transfer deed ahead of completion, when he will receive the rest of the purchase price (minus the deposit which has already been paid) from the buyer's solicitor, usually by electronic transfer. On receipt of this money, the title deeds are released to the buyer's solicitor.

Once your mortgage has been paid off and your solicitor has subtracted his fee and paid the estate agent what she is owed, any money left over is transferred to you (or directly to the lender supplying the mortgage for your new property, if you are buying one).

Dealing with Problems Arising from the Survey: Advice for Buyers

It's not for nothing that buying a house is regarded as one of the most stressful things you'll ever do. So much can go wrong that you shouldn't be surprised if you have a hiccup or two along the way. How big these hiccups are, however, and how you deal with them can have an impact on whether your purchase goes through – or not. The following sections explain two types of problems that may come from the survey and give you strategies for overcoming them.

The property isn't worth what you need to borrow

The mortgage lender's valuation states whether the property is worth what you want to borrow to pay for it. If the surveyor gives the thumbs up, you and the seller can breathe a huge sigh of relief because your mortgage is likely to be approved – unless other problems exist and you're seen as a credit risk (see Book II, Chapter 1 for more details on why this might happen).

Sometimes, however, the surveyor doesn't think the property is worth the amount of money you want to borrow on your mortgage; that is, it thinks the property is overpriced. In this case, the lender may agree to lend you as much as it thinks the property is worth and you have to find the remainder. Which is all well and good if you have that sort of money. If you don't, you have a couple of other options:

- ✔ **Ask the seller whether he will reduce the price:** You are in a strong position because the property is overpriced. If the difference is just a couple of thousand pounds, he may be willing to negotiate. However, you have to be prepared for him to refuse and pull out of the sale altogether.

- ✔ **Raise the cash by other means:** Use a bridging loan from your lender, take out a personal loan, extend your overdraft, or use a credit card.

  Think carefully about whether you can afford to take on this extra debt, as bridging loans in particular can be very expensive.

If your appeal to the seller is turned down and you have no way of raising the extra money, you may have to give up on the property.

The surveyor discovers big problems with the property

If you opted for a Homebuyer's Report or full structural survey (refer to Chapter 2 for a description of these surveys) and the report unveils problems, you have to assess whether you still want to buy the property. Your decision depends on the extent and cost of the work to be done and the willingness of the seller to put things right.

If severe damp or subsidence is found, for example, get a clear idea of the cost of repair by talking to your surveyor, who can give you an estimate of the cost involved in putting it right. Alternatively, you can get quotes from two or three builders. Armed with this information, you're in a strong position to renegotiate the price with the seller.

The seller may decide to get the work done himself *before* you buy the property. In this case, the price remains the same. But you may worry about whether the job gets done properly: You may have to send your surveyor back to check the completed work.

If the job is sizeable, however, the seller may not want to go to the trouble of getting the builders in, which means you will have to get the work done after you move in. In this case, ask for a reduction on the purchase price. To strengthen your case, give the seller a copy of the surveyor's report because he may try to downplay the problem.

Before you make any big decisions about the property based on the survey, try to assess how grave the situation really is. You may want to commission another report to look specifically at the problem, particularly if the surveyor recommends this. Although you may be reluctant to spend the extra cash on an additional survey, doing so can save you in the long run. If the problem is serious, you have the opportunity to pull out before making an expensive mistake.

Your lender will insist that you arrange for any extra investigations to be done if the surveyor recommends them. And if you still want to proceed with the purchase, be prepared for the lender to hold back part of the loan until it's happy that you've rectified the problem.

The Final Contract: Vetting and Signing

After both solicitors approve the draft contract, the seller's solicitor draws up a final contract for buyer and seller to sign. Legal documents tend to be full of complicated jargon and can be hard to understand. Although you may be tempted to leave it all to your solicitor, don't. A lot of money – yours – is at stake, so read the final contract very carefully.

If, after you pore over the contract, there's anything you're still not clear about, ask your solicitor to explain it to you.

When you're satisfied with the contract and all its provisions, sign it and return it to your solicitor. When everyone's in agreement and the contract has been signed by both parties, you're ready for exchange, as explained in the next section.

If you're buying a property, as soon as you sign the contract you must arrange for the deposit – usually 10 per cent of the purchase price, although sometimes lower – to be transferred to your solicitor's account. This is non-refundable and subtracted from the amount you must pay at completion. Solicitors may accept a cheque but most insist that the money is transferred electronically by BACS (Banks Automated Clearing Service), which takes a couple of days, or, if it's urgent, by CHAPS (the Clearing House Automated Payments System), which occurs on the same day. Expect your bank to charge you around £25 for this. Your solicitor forwards the deposit to the seller's solicitor, who holds onto it until completion.

Exchange of Contracts

After both parties sign the final contract (as explained in the preceding section), contracts are exchanged, usually over the telephone. The deal is then legally binding on both sides. Now you can relax, confident that the sale will go through. A completion date is also set (see the next section for information about completion).

Here are some important things to remember about exchange of contracts:

- ✔ **After exchange of contracts, you can't back out without significant penalties.** Make sure you don't exchange if you're not 100 per cent sure.

- ✔ **If you're selling your property and buying another, exchange contracts on both properties on the same day (make sure the completion date is the same on both transactions as well).** Otherwise, you could end up homeless if one sale goes through more quickly than the other.

- ✔ **If you're the buyer, as soon as contracts are exchanged, you're responsible for taking out buildings insurance on the property.** The reason is that the sale is binding at this point. Even if, heaven forbid, the property burnt down before completion, you're still legally obliged to go through with the purchase.

Arrange buildings insurance before exchange of contracts – you can ask the insurer to cover the property from the date of exchange.

Completion

A completion date is set when contracts are exchanged. On this date, the seller must move out and the buyer takes possession of the keys to the property. But there is still some work to be done before completion can take place.

Setting the completion date

There are no set guidelines for when completion must take place. On average, it tends to follow exchange by up to four weeks. The date you choose should suit both parties and give you time to notify various utility companies.

Don't pick the nearest date for completion, particularly if it's a Friday. Although moving just before the weekend seems sensible, it can become problematic. If you have problems with the property, such as a water leak, you'll have to wait until Monday to get someone out to fix it – unless you are prepared to pay exorbitant call-out fees to get someone out over the weekend.

Gathering the rest of the money

If you're buying, you must ensure that the funds are ready to pay to the seller on the day of completion. Your solicitor prepares the mortgage documents and arranges for the loan to be available on completion. If you're putting down any funds yourself in addition to the mortgage, ensure that your solicitor gets this money in time (electronic transfer can usually be done by the following day). Your solicitor then transfers funds equal to the purchase price to the seller's solicitor.

Preparing the transfer document and other stuff

The seller's solicitor prepares the document to transfer ownership of the property and the seller must sign this. The buyer is sometimes required to sign it as well. The buyer's solicitor carries out last-minute searches and enquiries to ensure that nothing, such as undisclosed mortgages or disputes, is registered against the seller at the Land Registry.

Do-it-yourself conveyancing

If you fancy a challenge – not one we'd recommend – you can have a go at doing your own conveyancing. An increasing number of buyers and sellers are doing this to save themselves solicitor's fees. But think very carefully before taking on such a daunting project. If you have no prior experience of conveyancing or are buying a leasehold property (which can be particularly complicated), steer clear. And if the other party is doing his own conveyancing, think twice. A whole lot of legal problems could arise which neither of you are capable of dealing with.

Conveyancing is complicated, time-consuming, and lots of hassle. If you have a busy full-time job you may not be able to cope. And if you cut corners and mess up, the penalties are severe.

Even if you do your own conveyancing, your mortgage lender is likely to insist that you pay its legal fees for preparing the mortgage deed (usually a lender allows the buyer's solicitor to do this on its behalf). And some lenders won't agree to you doing your own conveyancing at all so check before taking the plunge.

 Try not to go on holiday so that you're available to answer any last-minute questions your solicitor may have, sign documents, or hand over any money. If you decide to head off to the sun for three weeks and aren't contactable, don't be surprised if problems await you when you return. If you're buying a property where the seller has agreed to do some remedial work, you should check whether this is done before completion.

Paying up

If you're buying, this is what you have to look forward to on completion day. You pay the balance of what you owe for the property (minus the deposit) to the seller, via your solicitor. You also have to pay your solicitor's fees plus VAT, stamp duty land tax, and other outstanding charges. Your lender will transmit the mortgage funds electronically to the seller's solicitor. Then you get the keys to the property. The tortuous house buying process is over! Congratulations! Crack open the champagne.

If you're the seller, here's what you can expect. You receive a completion statement, stating all the outstanding fees and monies that you need to pay, including the estate agent's fee. This is usually paid out of the money your solicitor receives from the buyer and his lender. Your solicitor pays off any outstanding mortgage you had on your property and gives your agent (if you used one) her fee. He then transfers the balance to you – or, if you're buying another property – puts this money towards that purchase.

Alas, the solicitor's job still isn't finished. He must stamp the transfer (and pay stamp duty land tax) and put the title deeds in the buyer's name and send the deeds to the mortgage lender, if the buyer has taken out a mortgage. For a leasehold property, the solicitor also ensures that the freeholder is informed that the sale has been completed, and the buyer's name is put on the lease.

Chapter 5

Buying a House in Scotland

In This Chapter

▶ Arranging a mortgage and instructing a solicitor before searching for a property

▶ Making an offer and successfully outbidding other buyers

▶ Checking that all is as it seems before completion

*W*hen you buy a house or flat in Scotland, the legal process is very different from the rest of the UK. Not only is it different; the home-buying process in Scotland is also considered far superior to the outdated practice in England, Wales, and Northern Ireland. In Scotland, everything happens much quicker, and gazumping is virtually unheard of because the contract is binding once the seller accepts an offer.

But no system is perfect, and the Scottish way of doing things has its problems. You have to be absolutely sure when you make an offer because you can't pull out. And because you pay hundreds of pounds for a survey before making an offer (it plays a part in deciding how much you bid), you lose that money if your bid is unsuccessful – and then you have to start all over again with another property.

In this chapter, we highlight what you need to bear in mind to achieve a successful purchase in Scotland – the first time you try.

Becoming an Owner-Occupier

Nearly every property in Scotland – whether a house or flat – used to be sold on an *owner-occupier basis,* which meant that you owned the property absolutely and could dispose of it as you would have done a freehold property in England, Wales, or Northern Ireland. This system was known as *feudal tenure.*

Scotland has no freehold or leasehold properties as there are in England, Wales, and Northern Ireland (see the sidebar in Chapter 4 for more details on these). The absence of leasehold property is good news because a lease tends to slow down the house buying process considerably.

Feudal tenure could be restrictive. Once you bought the property, you could not extend it or run a business from home without the permission of the original landowner or developer – known as *the superior* – for example. Getting these conditions altered was complicated. If the superior refused to budge, you had to appeal to the Lands Tribunal for Scotland after buying the property.

Luckily, this situation has changed. Feudal tenure has been completely abolished under the Abolition of Feudal Tenure (Scotland) Act 2000, so property owners now have much more freedom. After November 2004, superiors disappeared and homeowners – known as *vassals* – now own their property outright. The superior had to be compensated for his loss though. For more details of these changes, check out the Scottish Executive's Web site (www.scotland.gov.uk).

Few remaining *feuduties* (annual cash payment to the superior) exist. After 28 November 2004, feuduty ceased to be payable, but during the period 28 November 2004 to 28 November 2006 former superiors had the right to serve notice on former vassals requiring a 'compensatory payment' in respect of feuduties abolished at 28 November 2004.

If you are buying a flat, you also need to:

✔ **Watch out for the communal areas, the roof, stairs, and hallways.** These are owned equally by the proprietors of the flats in a block or converted house. If you buy a flat, you're responsible for the joint maintenance of these areas. When you view the property, pay close attention to them (your surveyor should check them out as well).

✔ **Remember that you own the external walls of your own flat and are responsible for their maintenance, but the proprietors of the other flats have an interest in this being done because if you neglect this, it could affect the value of the whole building.** Make sure the title deeds spell out how maintenance and repair costs are split between flat owners.

Getting the Order Right: Finance First

As soon as your offer is accepted, you're committed to the purchase so it's important that you have your finances arranged first. Get them agreed in principle *before* you arrange your first viewing; that way, you won't lose out on the dream property you've just found because you couldn't get a mortgage in time to make an offer.

The first thing you must do is check that you can afford to buy a property. The best way of finding a lender prepared to let you have a mortgage is to shop around. To make this easier, use an independent broker (see Book II, Chapter 1 for more details on finding a mortgage).

When you arrange for financing so early in the process, you don't need a firm offer because you'll have no idea of the price of the property you're going to buy – you haven't even started looking yet! What you need is an *agreement in principle* where the lender promises to let you borrow a certain amount. With this certificate, you can hunt for a property safe in the knowledge that you can afford to spend a certain amount of cash.

Finding a Solicitor

You will need the help of a solicitor, or an independent qualified conveyancer, fairly early on in the process. (Conveyancers only specialise in *conveyancing* – the legal transfer of property from seller to buyer – unlike solicitors, who can usually handle other aspects of the law in addition to property transfer.)

The solicitor has a much greater role than he does in the rest of the UK. He's involved from the start, informing the seller's solicitor that you're interested in the property, advising you on what price you should offer, and negotiating a deal with the other party. And this is on top of all the conveyancing he does, explained in the later section 'When Your Offer Is Successful'.

Although you can do your own conveyancing, we don't recommend that you do so unless you're *absolutely sure* you know what you're doing.

Most buyers use a solicitor because independent qualified conveyancers are still rare in Scotland – although they are slowly becoming more common. To find a licensed conveyancer, contact the Scottish Conveyancing and Executory Services Board on 0131 556 1945.

Personal recommendation is the best way to find a good solicitor. But if you don't have a recommendation to go on, contact the Law Society of Scotland, which provides a list of solicitors in its Directory of General Services (Telephone 0131 476 8137 or try the Society's website: www.lawscot.org.uk). Alternatively, try the SiteFinder directory for a list of solicitors. You can find this in your local solicitors' property centre (see the next section, 'Finding the Perfect Property').

When you look for a solicitor, keep these things in mind:

- ✔ **Solicitors don't charge fixed fees for conveyancing, and prices can vary a great deal.** Be sure to shop around and get two or three quotes for the work. Also find out from the solicitor how much the _disbursements_ – known as _outlays_ – are likely to cost for the searches he carries out on your behalf; these can be substantial.

  Because you instruct a solicitor at such an early stage, you have no guarantee that your purchase will be successful. So find out what your solicitor charges if it falls through.

- ✔ **You cannot use an English solicitor in Scotland (they're not permitted to practice north of the border).** If you're buying in or moving to Scotland, ask your English solicitor to recommend a practice in Scotland.

Buyers tend to make an offer through their solicitor because it's the safest way of doing so. Find a solicitor before you start viewing properties then, when you find a property that you want to buy, you'll be ready to move quickly and make an offer.

Finding the Perfect Property

The process of finding a house or flat in Scotland is not dissimilar to the rest of the UK. Properties are advertised in estate agents' windows and brochures, newspapers, and on the Internet. The difference is that solicitors, as well as agents, sell properties. In fact, the most common way of finding property in Scotland is through a solicitor's property centre.

Solicitors' property centres

Solicitors' property centres tend to be located in shopping centres in major towns and cities, even though they don't actually sell anything, least of all property. All they do is provide information to buyers, with staff able to give only general advice. Properties are displayed and described in the same way as in an estate agent's window, along with the name of the solicitor handling the sale. If you want further information on a property, you must contact the solicitor handling that sale.

Big cities often have several solicitors' property centres at different locations. The Edinburgh Solicitors' Property Centre (ESPC), for example, has showrooms in Edinburgh itself, Dunfermline, Kirkcaldy, Stirling, and Falkirk, and has grown to become an important residential property marketing organisation throughout east central Scotland. They advertise thousands of properties for sale on its Web site and in its showrooms. Go to www.espc.co.uk. The Web site also includes tips on arranging a mortgage or finding a solicitor.

The big advantage of solicitors' property centres is that you can view thousands of properties for sale across the region – not just those on the books of one solicitor, thus saving shoe leather and time. The ESPC, for example, has 265 member solicitor firms. The service is free to buyers and you can register online for e-mail alerts should a property that suits your requirements become available. Alternatively, arrange for your local centre to post you its weekly list of properties for sale.

For a list of solicitors' property centres, contact the Law Society of Scotland or visit the Scottish Solicitors' Property Centres' Web site (www.sspc.co.uk), where these centres are listed by location.

Estate agents

Agents work in much the same way as they do in England, Wales, and Northern Ireland, and you should bear the same things in mind when dealing with them. Only use an agent who belongs to the National Association of Estate Agents (NAEA) as this organisation gives you a comeback if you have a complaint against a member (www.naea.co.uk or call 01926 496800).

Agents are legally obliged to treat buyers fairly and not deliberately mislead you, but keep in mind that they act for the seller, not you (the seller pays the agent's commission). So take everything an agent tells you with a large pinch of salt. If you feel that you've been misled, complain in the first instance to the agent involved. If he's part of a chain, contact the head office instead. If the problem isn't resolved or you're still unhappy, contact Citizens' Advice Scotland at www.cas.org.uk or on 0131 550 1000. If the agent belongs to the NAEA, complain to this body (call 01926 496800 or e-mail info@naea.co.uk).

The agent writes the description of the property, known as the *property particulars,* which include the number and type of rooms, their size, and any other details she feels may be of interest. If you don't understand anything, ask.

Get hold of a copy of *Real Homes*, a fortnightly list of properties for sale compiled by the biggest estate agents in Edinburgh. You can obtain a copy from the office of any agent who contributes to the list.

Newspapers

All the big Scottish papers, such as *The Scotsman* and the *Herald,* have size-able property sections on certain days of the week. They also have extensive property Web sites, which they update regularly. You can search through hundreds of properties for sale by price, size, and region on *The Scotsman*'s *and Scotland on Sunday*'s Web site: `http://property.Scotsman.com`. The sister Web site of the *Sunday Herald* also offers a virtual tour of properties for sale (`www.s1homes.com`).

Don't forget local newspapers. They often carry a good selection of proper-ties for sale in the area you're interested in.

Viewing properties

When you come across a property you like the sound of, you must view it before you even contemplate making an offer (see Chapter 1 for more details on what to look for during a viewing and what questions to ask).

As you view properties, remember that an offer is binding. So if you *think* you want to make one but aren't absolutely sure, go back again and again until your mind is made up – one way or the other.

Make sure you don't agree to anything or sign any documents before contact-ing your solicitor (see the next section). Otherwise you could be committing yourself to a purchase before you are in a position to do so.

Found the Property? What to Do Before You Make an Offer

Once you've found a property you want to buy, there are several things you must do before you make an offer, because it is binding. Below, we run through the order you should follow to make sure everything goes smoothly.

Get your solicitor to note interest

Once you find a property you want to buy, your first phone call shouldn't be to family and friends to tell them how excited you are but to your solicitor.

Your solicitor's response may be less enthusiastic (he won't, after all, jump up and down at your good news), but he will telephone the seller's solicitor or agent to *note interest* in the property. This means you will get the chance to make an offer.

Complete your mortgage application

After your interest has been noted, you can apply for your mortgage. If you have an agreement in principle from a lender (refer to the earlier section 'Getting the Order Right: Finance First'), request an application form. Complete this without delay and return it to the lender, with a cheque for the arrangement fee (if applicable).

If you haven't got an agreement in principle, there is no time to waste. Contact an independent broker (see Book II, Chapter 1 for more on how to find one) to help you locate a home loan. You will have to fill out an application form (as above) and pay the arrangement fee.

The lender arranges for the property to be valued to ensure it's worth what you're planning to borrow. This valuation isn't a survey and doesn't give any indication of the condition of the property; it simply covers the lender's back, although you have to pay for it. You need to arrange for a survey yourself, as explained in the next section. (You can find additional information on valuations and surveys in Chapter 2.)

Don't make an offer on a property without your lender's approval. Otherwise, you could commit yourself before you have the funds to pay for it.

Survey first, offer later

Unlike in England, Wales, and Northern Ireland, you arrange a survey *before* you make an offer because the offer is binding, *not subject to contract and survey.* If structural faults are discovered after you've made an offer – tough.

We recommend that you pay for a survey. You may be tempted to reduce costs but skipping the survey is not the way to do it. True, there's no guarantee that your offer will be successful, but if you discover serious structural faults only after you have made an offer, you will regret it.

The best way to find a surveyor or valuer is through personal recommendation. But if you don't have a recommendation to go on, and even if you do, make sure you use one who belongs to a professional body so that you have some comeback if things go wrong. Your surveyor should belong to the Royal Institution of Chartered Surveyors (RICS); look out for the letters ARICS (associate) or FRICS (fellow) after his name. For a list of RICS-registered surveyors in your area, contact RICS Scotland on 0131 225 7078. Alternatively, membership of the Incorporated Society of Valuers and Auctioneers (now merged with RICS) or the Incorporated Association of Architects and Surveyors, is also acceptable.

RICS Scotland publishes a helpful leaflet explaining the different types of surveys available, called *Buying Property? Then you need a survey.* For a free copy, contact RICS Scotland (on 0131 225 7078). You can also read the leaflet on its Web site at `www.rics-scotland.org.uk`.

The types of survey available are more or less the same as elsewhere in the UK. Most buyers opt for a homebuyer survey and valuation (known as a homebuyer's report elsewhere in the UK) as this is cost-effective – usually upwards from £300 – standardised and compact. It tells you what condition the property is in and how much it is worth. Few buyers bother with a full structural survey – also known as a building survey – which costs between £600 and £1100 plus VAT but if the property is very old or unusual, it may be worth considering.

If your survey reveals potential problems, instruct a surveyor to investigate further (it's worth the extra expense). More details on what's involved in each type of survey can be found in Chapter 2.

If you're buying a flat, you're jointly responsible for the upkeep of common parts, such as the hallways and stairs, with the rest of the flat owners in the purpose-built block or converted house. Ask your surveyor to check the whole building – not just your flat. If the building desperately needs redecorating or a new roof, you'll have to pay part of the bill. Be sure you're prepared to do this and can afford it.

Making an Offer

If the survey is satisfactory and your lender is happy with it, it's time to make an offer. Even if the survey has raised problems, you may still be prepared to make a lower offer.

If significant building work is required, get a couple of quotes from builders before you make an offer. Once you know the extent of the problem, you can make an informed decision as to how much you are prepared to pay for the property.

After you make an offer, you can't retract it. If the seller accepts your offer, it's legally binding. So don't make an offer unless you're absolutely sure you want to buy that property – and can do so.

Offering above the asking price: Why you should

In England, Wales, and Northern Ireland, sellers expect bids below the asking price. To allow for this, sellers often set a higher asking price than the property will realistically fetch. But in Scotland, the opposite is the case: bids are invited *above* the asking price. The asking price is also known as the *upset* – the minimum that will be considered.

In a very small number of cases, the price is *fixed*, usually when a builder or developer is selling a property. There is very little chance of negotiation and the first buyer offering the asking price gets the property.

Discuss how much you are going to offer with your solicitor, taking into account the upset, the survey's findings, and what similar properties are fetching in that area. You don't have to follow your solicitor's advice but it may be helpful. Also keep the following in mind:

- ✔ The seller may have set the asking price low to generate interest among buyers, in which case you could find that the actual purchase price could be as much as 20 or 30 per cent higher. If the housing market is strong, or you are bidding for a popular property, expect to pay significantly more than the upset to secure it.

- ✔ If several buyers note interest in a property, it will go to sealed bids (see Chapter 3 for more information on how these work). The seller's solicitor sets a deadline by which date bids must be submitted, and you're notified after it has passed as to whether you have won.

Once you've decided how much you are prepared to offer, your solicitor informs the seller's solicitor in writing. This is the first of a number of letters – known as *missives* – that go back and forth between solicitors if your bid is successful. As well as your bid, include the following:

- ✔ Details of when you want to take possession – the *date of entry* – and what fixtures and fittings you want included in the sale. (A list of what the seller is happy to leave behind is included in the *property particulars*, which you should have received before viewing the property).

- ✔ A number of *qualifications* or conditions, which enable you to withdraw your offer if the property turns out to be subject to local authority proposals or notices that adversely affect it.

The seller may give a qualified acceptance to your offer – accepting some terms and rejecting others, such as the date of entry. You then discuss with your solicitor whether you are happy to accept the seller's terms. Missives go back and forth until an agreement is reached.

Offering below the asking price: When to consider it

As a general rule, if you offer below the upset, you've got little chance of being successful – except in the following situations:

- ✔ **The property is proving difficult to shift.** Test the water first so you know this to be the case (your solicitor should have a good idea of how the land lies) before making a lower offer.

- ✔ **Your survey has unearthed a lot of problems with the property, and it turns out to be worth less than the upset.** If this is the case, you are justified in offering below the upset. (You certainly don't want to offer more than the property is worth if you're going to face a sizeable repair bill after you move in.)

When Your Offer Is Successful

If your offer is accepted, it's tempting to start celebrating. But you're not quite ready to pop the cork, so keep the champagne on ice for a little longer. Several missives must pass back and forth between your solicitor and the seller's solicitor as all the clauses in your offer are discussed. The aim is to *conclude missives* – a bit like finalising contracts in the rest of the UK – once everything has been agreed. The fixtures and fittings included in the sale will also be finalised, along with the date of entry.

Once missives are concluded, a *bargain* is made – the equivalent of exchanging contracts. The purchase can now be completed in a few days, unlike the four to six weeks it takes in the rest of the UK. You have now entered into a binding contract with the seller. Unless the conveyancing process throws up some complications, you can't back out unless you're prepared to pay thousands of pounds in compensation.

Conclusion of missives can occur quickly, leaving you little time to get your finances arranged. So it's vital that you complete your mortgage application *before* you make an offer. You must also ensure you have enough cash to cover solicitor's fees, charges for searches, stamp duty land tax, and the deposit.

You're responsible for insuring the property once missives are concluded, so be sure to arrange buildings insurance beforehand. This covers the cost of rebuilding the property should it burn to the ground or some other disaster befall it before you have even moved in. Lenders insist upon it.

The conveyancing process begins

Once missives are concluded, your solicitor checks a number of documents to ensure that the property can be legally sold to you and that the local authority doesn't have any plans adversely affecting it. The items he checks include the following:

- ✔ **Title deeds:** The solicitor checks whether he is happy with the title you are being offered. The deed tells him whether the seller actually owns the property and is therefore in a position to sell it, and that there are no problems with rights of way.

- ✔ **A Search:** This is a document provided by the seller detailing the history of the property. It states when each sale occurred and whether there are any outstanding charges on any loans taken out to purchase the property.

- ✔ **Property Enquiry Certificates:** Like local authority searches in the rest of the UK, Property Enquiry Certificates are provided by the seller and list any planning proposals that are in existence that could affect the property.

- ✔ **Building warrants or certificates of completion:** A building warrant is issued to provide permission for the building of the property, and the builder must obtain a certificate of completion once the work has been satisfactorily completed, in line with building regulations.

If your solicitor is happy with the findings of the searches, he drafts a *disposition*, which transfers ownership of the property to you.

If you're taking out a mortgage, you should have completed your application form by this stage. Your solicitor normally acts for the lender as well as you, informing the lender about the title on the property and preparing the *standard security* – the lender's mortgage deed. She also arranges for the loan money to be ready at date of entry and gets you to sign the loan documents.

Make sure you draw up a will. If you aren't Scottish and purchase a property there to use as your main residence, you acquire Scottish domicile. And if you die without making a will, Scottish law regulates the distribution of the land and buildings you own in Scotland. To avoid any confusion, consult your solicitor about drawing up a will.

Preparing for the date of entry

A couple of weeks before your date of entry, your solicitor sends you a letter telling you how much cash you need to forward to her to complete the transaction. You need to pay the following:

- ✔ **The deposit:** This is the amount you put down when you take out a mortgage. How big the deposit is depends on your savings and your lender's requirements – some require a minimum of 5 or 10 per cent, while others require no deposit at all.

    The bigger your deposit, the better mortgage rate you're likely to get. You could also avoid paying a mortgage indemnity guarantee (see Book II, Chapter 1 for more information).

- ✔ **Solicitor's fees:** In addition to the fee you negotiate with your solicitor, you must pay VAT – at 17.5 per cent – on top.

- ✔ **Stamp duty land tax:** Stamp duty land tax is payable on properties costing more than £125,000and is calculated on a sliding scale. The rates in Scotland are the same as the rest of the UK. No stamp duty land tax is payable on properties costing less than£125,000; one per cent on properties between £125,001 and £250,000; three per cent on properties between £250,001 and £500,000; and four per cent above£500,001. Properties under £150,000 in disadvantaged areas may qualify for exemptions. To see a list of areas that qualify, go to the HMRC Web site at www.hmrc.gov.uk or call 0845 603 0135.

- ✔ **Search and registration charges:** You have to reimburse your solicitor for various charges, such as drawing up the disposition or transfer of ownership from the seller to you. There is also a charge for registering the title in your name.

Completion

This is it – the day you've been waiting for! The date of entry is quite often the same as the date of settlement, when the sale is completed and you take possession of your new property. The day before the date of settlement, ensure you have passed onto the solicitor all the money that you're stumping up including your deposit and his fees and disbursements.

In order to get those all-important keys, your solicitor must transfer funds equivalent to the full purchase price to the seller's solicitor on the date of settlement. In return, your solicitor receives the title deeds, which are sent to your lender to keep for as long as you have that mortgage, the disposition – proving the property has been transferred to you – and the keys.

Your solicitor registers the disposition and standard security in the General Register of Sasines or the Land Registry of Scotland, depending on where the property is, and passes your stamp duty land tax onto HMRC.

Chapter 6

Researching European Markets

- -

In This Chapter

▶ Planning your background research

▶ Exploring potential properties abroad

▶ Establishing what you're willing to pay for – and what you're not

▶ Extending and using your network of contacts

▶ Getting estate agents and others to do the legwork for you

- -

*E*urope is too big and varied a region to start looking for a property without setting some boundaries to your search.

Early on in the process, ask yourself (and your partner) probing questions to figure out exactly what you want from your new property. Your answers can save you a lot of wasted time and effort. Your responses can lead you to:

✔ Research specific areas to find out what they're like in different seasons, what facilities are available, and travel times to and from the UK.

✔ Look for estate agents in a specific region and find out property prices.

✔ Consider how difficult an area is to get to and from. (In the early months and years, you are likely to spend a lot of time travelling to and fro.)

All these factors and more are important parts of your research of the area. This chapter gives you strategies for conducting your research and locating houses that you can afford and that you find appealing.

Researching from Home

You will find no shortage of different types of property on the European market – from ruined farms in Bulgaria at one end of the spectrum to posh palaces in Puglia at the other. Fortunately, you can discover properties by conducting research at home before ever setting foot abroad.

Unless you have a clear idea of what type of house you want and where you want it, start with wide search criteria. After you do a broad sweep, perhaps by attending an overseas property exhibition and spending a few evenings visiting Web sites, you can begin to narrow your search to a particular area and property type. Then you can head for the airport!

This section guides you through some excellent research options that you can utilise without ever leaving the comforts of home – or at least the comforts of the UK.

Attending exhibitions

You can now attend literally hundreds of exhibitions all over the UK – and indeed the world – that focus on various aspects of overseas house and property buying, including in countries in Europe.

Some exhibitions focus on a particular country, such as France, while others group together a clutch of neighbouring or similar (at least in the eye of the organiser) countries. So Hungary, the Czech Republic, Slovenia, and Croatia are often bundled together, as are Malta, Cyprus, and Turkey. Though administratively convenient, from a property buyer's perspective these countries have as much in common as chalk and cheese.

Other exhibitions, such as EMIGRATE, the Emigration Show run by Outbound Publishing, start from the supposition that attendees are planning a new life in a new country. These exhibitions typically have immigration officials on hand from a number of countries to explain the relocation procedures and to actually process applications.

At many exhibitions, you see firms specialising in building and renovation, removals, insurance, overseas mortgages, medical and health services, pet passports, and transportation. You may even be able to enjoy food and wine from the region, which adds to the overall experience of the event.

Although a useful starting point for research, exhibitions run by a single selling agent or by a particular developer showing its portfolio of properties should never be seen as the only research you need to do.

Following are some of the major overseas property exhibitions throughout the UK. In addition to these, look in the press for details of other exhibitions – more are being launched every year and many national exhibitions now run regional road shows.

✔ **Daily Mail Ideal Home Show** (020-8515-2000; www.idealhomeshow.co.uk) usually runs at Earls Court, London, in March.

✔ **Evening Standard Homebuyer Show** (020-8877-3636; www.homebuyer.co.uk) runs at ExCel, London, usually in March.

✔ **Homes Overseas Exhibition** (020-7939-9888; www.homesoverseas.co.uk) runs at Olympia, London, usually in March.

✔ **International Property Show** (01962-736-712; www.international propertyshow.com) runs several times a year in London and Manchester.

✔ **Property Investor Show North** (020-8877-3636; www.property investor.co.uk) runs at the G-MEX Centre, Manchester, in June.

✔ **World Class Homes** (0800-731-4713; www.worldclasshomes.co.uk) runs local exhibitions monthly around the UK.

✔ **World of Property Show** (01323-745-130; www.outboundpublishing.com) is held three times a year, once in the north of England and twice in the south.

✔ **EMIGRATE: Emigration Show** (01323-726-040; www.outboundpublishing.com) runs at Sandown Exhibition Centre, Esher.

Aside from these major exhibitions, you can attend hundreds of smaller property shows, usually run in hotels, taking place throughout the year. Look for advertisements in local newspapers.

Using the Internet

The Internet can be a great way to find out a little about the property market in a particular area relatively quickly from the comfort of your own home. Hundreds of Web sites offer (or claim to offer) comprehensive details on property in Europe.

While the Internet is a useful starting point for your research, do not consider it the end of your process.

As you search online, you're sure to encounter many sites promoting properties *off plan*, which means that building work may well not even have started and a completed apartment or villa may be years away. Often off-plan Internet sites show a convincing computer image of the property on offer and invite you to 'reserve' your villa or apartment for a mere £500, usually payable online using your credit card. You must understand that you are getting *absolutely nothing concrete* for your money and that you have little chance of recovering any investment if the property is not completed for years or – worse – never completed.

The following Internet property sites cover Europe. However, this is not an exhaustive list; sites come and go all the time.

- ✔ www.europerealestatedirectory.net is a portal with links to about 60 brokers selling property throughout Europe.

- ✔ www.oliproperties.com/oliproperties accepts registration from any individual or agent who has property to sell or let, both residential and commercial. The site lists more than 9,000 properties in countries including Bulgaria, Croatia, Cyprus, Czech Republic, Hungary, Malta, and Turkey.

- ✔ www.primelocation.com/international-property was launched in 2001 by a consortium of more than 200 leading independent estate agents across the UK who wanted to be in the vanguard of online property marketing. In 2006, the company was bought by Daily Mail & General Holdings Limited as part of its further expansion into the online business sector. The site's international section carries more than 50,000 properties from estate agents in more than 40 countries. The site has a search engine for filtering property by country, price, and for sale or for rent.

- ✔ www.propertyfinder.com/property/international has links to 270,000 properties for sale or rent.

- ✔ www.propertiesabroad.com (which is not to be confused with the less helpful www.property-abroad.com) offers strong listings, primarily in Turkey and Cyprus, but its scope is extending fast.

- ✔ www.property-abroad.com is a family-run business set up by Les Calvert and features more than 28,000 properties in more than 42 countries.

- ✔ www.themovechannel.com was founded in 1999 by Dan Johnson. The site started life as a simple guide to the buying procedures for residential properties in the UK, but with 200 partners it now covers buying guides and property listings for nearly 100 countries. The site has an amazing filter allowing you to pre-select properties to view by a host of specialised criteria, including ski property, golf property, renovation projects, and commercial property.

- ✔ www.remax.com is a franchised estate agent network with 5,400 offices in more than 50 countries.

Talking to international property agents

Almost certainly one of the first people you will come across in your property quest is an estate agent. Estate agents play a pivotal role in matching supply and demand. Despite appearing to sit between buyers and sellers in the housing supply chain, estate agents are in fact appointed by the sellers to look after their interests. Not only do sellers choose the estate agents, but also the sellers pay them, by way of a percentage of the price realised on the property.

Agents have hundreds of villas, apartments, and plots of land on their books. They also have links with dozens of other estate agents, who in turn have hundreds more properties for sale.

Getting agents to work for you

The really neat aspect of working with an estate agent is that, if you handle the process right, the agent can be working for you in your team, while being on the payroll of someone else. In other words you have a free resource. If you handle the agent right, they can take much of the sweat out of the job.

To get an estate agent on your side, utilise the following strategies:

✔ Only contact an estate agent after you do some initial spadework and establish a firm idea for yourself of the sort of property you're looking for. You need to appear serious in order for an agent to take you seriously.

✔ Keep in regular contact with the agent so you stay at the forefront of their mind. The more contact you have with the agent, the more likely he or she is to think of you first if something suitable comes on the market.

✔ Keep a record of your dealings with the estate agent. Record details of any telephone conversations you have with them, including who you spoke to, on what date, and what was said. This record demonstrates your professionalism and keeps the agent on his or her toes. A record can also help to avoid any disputes further down the line if something that you thought was agreed is later denied.

✔ Try to have the money in place *before* you start to look. Estate agents take you more seriously if they know that you are a cash buyer or at least have a 'decision in principle' from your lender that indicates you can borrow a specific sum. Also, having your money in place before working with an agent may give you the edge over other potential buyers.

✔ Ask lots of questions. Far from being an irritation, questions serve only to reinforce your interest in doing the deal. The questions closest to an estate agent's heart are those related to how quickly the sale can wrap up. So ask at the outset how quickly the seller wants to sell or how soon the seller can vacate the place. Make sure that this schedule fits in with your timing, but generally anything that speeds up the process and moves money into the agent's coffers more quickly endears you to him or her.

Assessing an agent's qualifications

Not every country has its own regulations, code of conduct, or professional association for estate agents and brokers. But for nations that do have such associations, stick with their members. The advantage of dealing with licensed agents is that they, like lawyers and other professionals, are regulated and you can claim against the governing body if you are dissatisfied in any way. Working with an unlicensed estate agent is more risky.

Many UK-based international estate agents have jumped on the overseas property bandwagon, some with little or no previous experience dealing in international property. Try to deal only with *established* estate agents with a strong track record in the country or countries you are most interested in.

The international professional association connected with British professionals is the Federation of Overseas Property Developers, Agents and Consultants (0870-350-1223; www.fopdac.com). Other useful resources include the Confederation of European Real Estate Agents (+31-70-345-8703; www.webcei.com) and the International Real Estate Federation (www.fiabci.com), which offers a full A–Z listing of members.

Working with a house hunter

If you can't spend much time travelling around Europe, you may consider employing the services of a person or organisation to do some of the legwork for you. *House hunter* seems to be the common descriptive term for this sort of service. They don't replace the estate agent; rather, their work is complementary. House hunters may or may not be affiliated with a specific estate agent. You want a house hunter who works with *every* estate agent so that you can be sure of getting unbiased help.

Usually house hunters ask you to fill in detailed questionnaires designed to capture your needs precisely. They then set to the task of finding properties in the area you want, at your price, and that they believe correspond to your needs. They personally visit properties, take detailed notes and photos, and send information to you for viewing before you make the trip to visit their selections.

After you're in the country, they set up viewing appointments and even accompany you on visits. If you decide to buy one of the properties, you deal directly with the estate agent. The fee structure depends on the type and level of service you decide on, but the following gives you an approximate idea of the cost range of house-hunting services:

✔ **Retainer fee:** €1,500–2,000 ($1,030–1,370) to search for a property to purchase or rent. You can deduct this fee from the final completion fee if your search is successful. This fee retains services for a period of usually 13 weeks.

✔ **Completion/success fee:** Between 1 and 2 per cent of the final purchase price, with a minimum fee payable of €7,000–10,000 ($4,800–6,800).

✔ **Search for rented accommodation:** Typically one month's rental fee.

✔ **Orientation tour:** Beginning at €1,000 ($860), this service involves taking you around a chosen region, highlighting important factors such as roads, schools, building projects, and anything that may make an area more or less attractive.

✔ **Area review report:** Around €400 ($275). If you can't visit an area or want an overview of several areas, house hunters can write you a report that covers much the same ground that an orientation tour provides.

Useful Web sites for locating house hunters include WNM International Property Search (07786-081-027; www.wnm-int.com), Elite and VIP (01737-366-986; www.eliteandvip.com), and Second Home (01937-590-574; www.secondhome.uk.com).

Reading papers and magazines

Almost all the British Sunday newspapers and many of the dailies have overseas property sections. The newspapers also carry articles on most aspects of living abroad, ranging from getting medical cover to pension rights and finding a mortgage. From time to time, you can also find detailed coverage of particular regions in a country. You can also find a number of glossy magazines that tend to feature new resorts, often adjacent to ski resorts, golf courses, or marinas.

Make the following papers and magazines part of your regular reading list while researching the property market:

✔ *Dalton's Weekly* is available as a hard-copy version as well as a new Web site (www.daltonsholidays.com). Both carry advertisements for properties in Europe.

✔ *Homes Overseas* (020-7939-9888; www.homesoverseas.co.uk) is a monthly worldwide magazine and Web site with property listings.

✔ The *Daily Telegraph* property section on Saturdays.

✔ The *Financial Times* on Saturdays.

✔ The *Sunday Times* property section.

✔ *World of Property* (01323-726-040; www.outboundpublishing.com) is a bi-monthly publication covering international locations; it features periodic sections on specific countries.

A growing number of English-language papers and news sheets are published and distributed across Europe. These publications target both the expat communities and property buyers in general. Look out for them in your chosen locations.

Working up your network

After you narrow down your search area, you can consider bypassing estate agents and try connecting directly with sellers. Sellers are almost certain to find the idea of selling direct to you appealing because doing so cuts out about 5 per cent of estate agent fees.

Start by seeing whether you can find a foreigner like yourself who wants to sell up. Don't panic: Just because someone is selling up doesn't mean that he or she has had a bad experience. In many cases, buyers are trading up after putting their toes in the water.

Start by asking your friends and acquaintances to see who has a property for sale. Even if you don't know anyone with a house in one of the countries you are interested in, by the time you do some preliminary research, you can uncover a veritable army of second-home owners in that country.

To widen your pool of contacts, draw on your skills as a networker. Everyone you find with a property abroad knows a couple of others, and they in turn know a couple more. Pulling on that thread soon leads to hundreds of people with whom you have some connection, however tenuous. Someone along the line probably knows someone else who is thinking of selling a home abroad.

Doing Hands-on Research: Rest, Recreation, and Reconnaissance

After you do all your background research, you're ready to see what the countries on your narrowed-down list are really like.

When you make appointments with estate agents, make sure that you leave yourself plenty of time to wander around on your own. Agents want to keep you focused on their properties, but you want to get a broad appreciation of the whole property market in your chosen area.

Taking short breaks

The advent of low-cost airlines means that you can reach much of Europe within a few hours from a dozen or so British airports. For less than the cost of a modest weekend in a British holiday resort, you can get a four-day break in Sofia or a long weekend in Pisa.

Check for bargain short breaks on Web sites such as Lastminute.com (www.lastminute.com), Travelocity.com (www.travelocity.com), and Expedia.com (www.expedia.com). Consider trying several new travel-focused search engines, including Kayak.com (www.kayak.com), Mobisso.com (www.mobisso.com), and Sidestep.com (www.sidestep.com).

Keep in mind that *when* you visit can be as important as *where* you visit. For example, the buzz of a seaside resort in the summer months may not be replicated in the winter and autumn. Not only are the tourists gone, but also many restaurants, cafés, and perhaps even the cinemas may have pulled the shutters down.

Tackling the tourist office

The people behind the counter usually speak English – an invaluable asset when you are seeking out useful information in a foreign land. Also, a tourist office is a reassuring indication that you may well have a holiday rental market for the property you plump for.

Following are a few subjects to probe those in the tourist office about to help you decide whether an area is worthy of your attention:

- ✔ **Accommodation:** Tourist offices normally maintain a database of local hotels, guesthouses, and private landlords willing to put you up. These recommendations are almost certainly cheaper than the places being plugged on the Internet or by travel agents.

- ✔ **Local attractions:** The more leaflets on display, the larger the office, and the more staff at work, the more certain you can be that the area is popular for visitors – a fact that you can't be quite so confident about just by reading a guidebook or searching the Internet. After you know just how popular an area is, you are more able to build a forecast of likely rental income.

✔ **Quality assessment:** Many tourist offices rate local properties using a star or other measurement system. Understanding how an area's tourist office assesses quality is the key to knowing how to pitch a rental for any property you may buy.

✔ **Transport:** This is a topic that tourist office personnel are well geared up on. First, find out the routes, frequency, and rates of buses and trains. These answers give you a feel for how easily you can live in the area without a car – as well as how likely you are to attract potential business or holiday renters.

Driving the area

The optimal way to size up a region is to drive around it. Of course, driving in a new area is not always that easy, or for that matter safe for an unaccompanied foreigner. For example, in some countries the road signs are not only in a foreign language but also in a near-indecipherable alphabet such as the Cyrillic used in Bulgaria.

When you drive yourself, you can expand your search beyond the well-established developments. Get a good detailed map of the area you are interested in and systematically travel everywhere you find a cluster of buildings.

Contacting the locals

Start talking to local builders, lawyers, and surveyors and see whether they know of any properties about to come on the market. Take care not to be sucked into parting with any money until you have taken legal advice.

Be careful: Freelance *introducers* hang around estate agents' offices, banks, hotels, and bars in many European countries. These individuals watch and listen to visitors, searching for foreign people who are obviously in the country on property-hunting visits. Introducers typically wait until an opportunity arises to introduce themselves – often as an obliging English speaker who just happens to know of a special bargain dream house that is not listed on the market at large. Of course, no one works for nothing. These people have arrangements with various estate agents who can load the deal to pay off the introducer's fees.

You do not need the services of an introducer. No vendor in his or her right mind is likely to surround the sale of a property in a veil of secrecy. By diligently ploughing round the estate agents yourself in your chosen area, you can do – for free – absolutely everything that introducers typically offer to do.

Narrowing Down Your Choices

After doing desk research and perhaps visiting one or two of the most promising countries on your radar screen, you may find your head swimming with a mass of decisions and choices. Don't worry – that's a good sign. It means that you are on the right track.

Your next task is to focus down to a handful of properties that are worthy of further investigation. Start by making the big decision first: Are you primarily out to make money, or are you hunting for something that you and your family will enjoy?

Then decide how much you are prepared to spend, taking account of extra costs that are certain to be involved, including brokers' fees, local property taxes, the costs of renovation, and so forth. Take time to consider what type of property and facilities (swimming pool, sea views, and so on) are essential to your needs. You may have to bounce back and forth between what is desirable in terms of a property and what is affordable.

Your decisions may even influence the country you end up choosing. For example €30,000 (£25,850) can buy you a pool, a view, and three bedrooms on the Black Sea coast, but you'll need at least ten times that in most of Tuscany. Decisions, decisions!

This section gives you tools and tips for winnowing down to the best locations for you.

Refining your search

Before you head out to the airport, you need to have a handful of specific destinations in mind.

- ✔ Your first decision is whether your main goal is to find a property as an investment or as somewhere for R&R (rest and recreation, or perhaps rest and retirement someday).

- ✔ The next factor to take into account is your appetite for risk. Whatever your intentions, buying a seaside apartment in Sebastopol, Ukraine, or anywhere in Northern Cyprus is a whole lot riskier than going for one in Spain, for example.

Figuring out your needs

Soon into your property search, you are likely to discover a wealth of attractive places to buy, but they all have something slightly different to recommend them. One may have a great garden and fantastic views but be located hours from a beach or airport. Another may need masses of work but have plenty of space for a bed-and-breakfast location so you can generate an income. You need to work out exactly what you really need – and are prepared to pay for.

The following questions can help you assess your basic personality and identify your most important needs in a new property. Take time and ask yourself – and your partner and family, if appropriate – the following questions. Consider writing down your answers to serve as a reminder and a tool for further planning:

- **Are you a town or country person?** No right answer here, but you need to know yourself before you splash out money for a sprawling farm or a hip urban loft.

- **Do you want to be inland, in the mountains, or on the coast?** Again, no right answer, but some nations in Europe are landlocked, have a limited coastal area, or lack significant residential development in mountainous regions.

- **Do you want to be isolated or have neighbours close at hand?** Keep in mind that being in the wilds with a partner may be fine, but consider what a property would be like if for some reason he or she wasn't there.

- **How important is outside space to you?** Urban dwellings have little outside space and what they do have, you probably have to share. By contrast, country properties may have too much space for you to maintain yourself.

- **How close do you want to be to shops, bars, and restaurants?** If you like to go out frequently, you probably want a property located in or near an active neighbourhood or town centre.

- **How important is public transport to living in a particular area?** If you plan to rely on public transport, find out your public transport options, including which are nearest, how much they cost, and how often they run.

- **How far away are leisure attractions?** While the distance to the beach or other sports facilities (golf, tennis, swimming, fitness centre, or riding) may seem like a minor issue for you, renters and visitors are likely to want to partake in these activities.

- **What arts, cinema, and other entertainment are available in the area?** You may not need a property near museums and galleries, but a few intriguing entertainment options are usually necessary.

✔ **What are your potential neighbours like?** Do they have children and constant visitors? How much do you have to see them? Are they locals or foreigners? Does anyone speak English?

✔ **How far away is the nearest airport?** Also, find out whether budget airlines travel to the airport, region, or country.

✔ **Do properties in the area tend to sell quickly?** You may want to move up or out. Choosing an area with wide appeal and an active property market gives you options.

Deciding your budget

OK, so you are sold on a particular country in Europe. But before you start to think seriously about looking at properties, you need to set your budget. You can waste an awful lot of time racing around a country looking at properties only to find that they cost more than you are prepared to commit. (Even searching on the Internet is frustrating when you haven't established a budget for yourself.)

Adding up how much you have

The average cost of a house in the UK is €257,000 (£180,000), and the average cost of a property in Country A is €130,000 (£89,200). (You have to take averages with a pinch of salt, as by definition almost nothing is average. The great mass is above or below!) So if you intend to sell up and either downsize in the UK or abandon ship altogether and move abroad, in theory you need to have plenty of money to spare.

But if you do the sums carefully, you may not have quite as much as you would expect. The €127,000 (£87,100) you thought you may have as a result of selling in the UK so that you can buy abroad is more likely to be €99,990 (£68,500) when you take purchasing and moving costs into account (see Table 6-1).

Table 6-1	Calculating How Much Money You Really Have If You Sell Up and Move Abroad		
Item	*Cost*	*Actual Cost*	*How Much You Have Left*
Sale price of UK home	€257,000	€257,000 - €7,710 (3%)	€249,290/£
Sale price of buying abroad for	€130,000	€130,000 + €14,300 (11%)	€104,990
Moving furniture	€5,000	€5,000	€99,990

So unless you are bringing other savings or reserves to the party – or you intend to take out a mortgage – going through the sums in a fashion similar to that shown in Table 6-1 is necessary to give you an idea of how the big numbers stack up. If you are seriously conservative with your money, then you can expect to earn interest on the €99,990 (£68,500) difference between selling in the UK and buying abroad, which amounts to around €3,000 (£2,050) a year. You will have to find an obliging friend or relative to live with, rent a house in your home country, or rent in your prospective country for the period in question, so you will also need to factor in that cost too.

Finding out how much you can borrow

If you intend to sell up in the UK and buy a similar property abroad, you probably don't need to borrow any money. However, if you have the income to support a loan, you can change the whole scenario.

Consider again the idea that you own an average €257,000 (£180,000) house in the UK. The UK has 11.5 million mortgages, totalling around £800 billion, which makes for an average mortgage of £69,560. That means that the average mortgagee has about £110,440 of equity available to borrow against.

Consider this situation another way: If you happen to be somewhere near the average figures, you can raise around 80 per cent of the amount of equity by remortgaging in the UK. That gives you €126,217 (£88,353) in funding from your British property, which is a very large slice of the €149,300 (£102,400) you need to buy an average house in Country A, pay all the legal expenses, and move your belongings.

In buying a property abroad, you acquire a new chunk of property equity against which you can borrow more. In theory, you can probably raise 70–80 per cent of the cost of your second property by way of a mortgage secured on that property. But before you get carried away and rush and buy a yacht, remember that any borrowing has to be serviced. That means that every month you get a bill from the mortgage company to pay for borrowing the money and to repay a slice of the borrowings. We look in detail at mortgage options in Book II, Chapter 6.

So if you feel you can afford – or can generate from your overseas and British properties – about £9,000 of extra income, then you should have little difficulty in raising all the money you need to keep your home in the UK and buy a house abroad. You also give yourself the flexibility to return to the UK at a later date by not getting out of the British property market.

Setting your budget

Now for the $64,000 question: How much do you set aside for your purchase? The answer depends on your age, objectives, and appetite for risk. For example:

✔ If you and your partner are over 50, risk-averse, and plan to take up residence in the country you are buying into and live there for the rest of your life, then sell up in the UK, buy abroad for less, and bank the difference.

✔ If you and your partner are both under 50, want to keep your options open about returning to the UK, and don't want to take much of a risk, then downsize properties in the UK, buy an average house abroad, and take out just enough of a mortgage to fund the deal.

✔ If you are both under 50, want to keep open the option to return to the UK, and are happy to take a fair amount of risk, then keep your present house, rent it out, and buy a house abroad by taking out a sizeable mortgage.

Factoring in rental income

If you have properties in both the UK and abroad, you can rent out the location you're not living in, meet your mortgage costs, and perhaps even turn a small profit.

For example, if you have an average house in the UK worth £180,000 and an average mortgage of around £70,000, you want your rental income to exceed your costs:

Income	Expense	Cost
Rent £7,800	Mortgage on £70,000	£5,000
	Insurance	£500
	Agent's fees at 15%	£1,170
	Wear and tear, 10% of rent	£780
	Total expenses	£7,450

Given this scenario, your profit from renting is £7,800–£7,450, or £350. Okay, so you aren't going to get rich on the rent, but you do get to keep your British property and any capital appreciation.

However, adopting the strategy outlined in this section means that you must raise all the money you need from a source other than by selling up your British home. That may mean less time on the beach and more in the bar – your bar, that is, pouring out the beers for paying punters.

After you decide on your strategy and set a budget, stick to it. However appealing a property is, you can't exceed your budget unless you can see a way to increase some other aspect of the equation, such as being able to rent out one of your properties for part of the year or earning additional money in some way (such as by taking a job or starting a business).

To renovate or not to renovate – that is the question

If you buy a property in need of renovation or extension to turn it into something that meets your needs, you need to be prepared for some significant additional costs.

Carrying out large-scale building work, even in your own country, is fraught with problems and dangers. Doing so with all the attendant problems of working in a foreign language, with an alien currency, and probably having to operate at a distance with only periodic site visits being possible, makes overseas remodelling work even more difficult. Add to the mix the people and organisations you have to deal with – an architect, a builder, perhaps a plumber, and an electrician too. Plan to have your hands full for several months, dealing with the town hall, getting planning permission, and making sure that you can obtain the necessary building licences to cover the changes or designs you have in mind. Of course, there is always the option of hiring a project manager to supervise the renovation.

Aside from the strict legal aspects of planning and usage, renovation work may not be economically viable for several reasons. The most obvious, particularly in country areas, is the cost of providing usable water – and to a lesser extent power, sewage facilities, and telephone. Geographic reasons may render your plans unviable – the property may be too far from a good road, be on a steep slope, or have foundation issues.

Always keep in mind that one day you may want to sell your property, so it has to be both appealing and economically viable to someone else who may not be quite so enamoured with it as you are.

Book II
Finance, Tax, and How to Organise Them

'It's nothing to do with the full moon — he always goes through a change when he tries to reorganise our finances.'

In this book . . .

Knowing how to navigate your way around the world of finance and tax is important in any business – especially so when your game is investing in property. The chapters in this book help you to get to grips with this side of property investing, from tracking down the best mortgage for you to moving your money around.

Here are the contents of Book II at a glance:

Chapter 1

Getting a Mortgage

*U*nless you are a Premiership footballer, a film star, or can call upon a sizeable trust fund or inheritance, it's unlikely that you'll be able to buy a property outright for cash. More likely, you'll have to borrow the money – and that means taking out a mortgage. Securing a mortgage can be daunting because of the vast sums of cash involved. Nevertheless, the proliferation of mortgage deals in recent years makes getting a home loan that suits your circumstances easier than ever. And with interest rates still at relatively low levels, you don't have to sell your soul to the devil to get one.

But this proliferation of choice has its downside. With so many lenders offering a range of different, and sometimes complex, deals, it can be hard to see the wood for the trees. For most homeowners, their mortgage is their biggest single outgoing every month, so finding the right one is crucial. Yet the British public pays £3.5 billion more than necessary for their mortgages each year, according to research from independent financial adviser The MarketPlace at Bradford & Bingley. In this chapter we will guide you through the different mortgages available and help you avoid paying more than you should.

Finding a mortgage doesn't have to be scary. With the right advice and by doing your own careful research, you can find a decent deal that you aren't going to regret 10 years down the line.

How Mortgages Work

A mortgage is a loan for the express purpose of buying a flat or house. The majority of homebuyers take out a mortgage for 25 years (the length of the mortgage is the *mortgage term*). The aim is to pay back the money you borrow, plus interest, by the end of the term – and the property will be yours. Because homebuyers are so used to hearing about a 25-year timeframe, many assume that you have to take a mortgage out for this length of time. But that's not the case.

You can vary the mortgage term to suit your circumstances; most lenders will let you take your mortgage over as few or as many years as you want, although there are a couple of restrictions. Most lenders require that you take out a mortgage for a minimum of five years and that you pay it back by the time you retire.

If you are 20 years old and want to take out a mortgage over 40 years, for example, most lenders will be happy to let you do this. Or if you are expecting to receive a lot of money over the next couple of years, you can take a mortgage out for two or three years if you wish, although the repayments would prove prohibitive for most people. Likewise, most people pay off their mortgage by the time they stop working but in some cases you can continue your mortgage into retirement as long as you can demonstrate to your lender that your retirement income will cover the mortgage repayments.

There is a growing trend towards longer mortgage terms, particularly for first-time buyers. The advantage of paying your mortgage over 30, 40, or even 45 years is that your monthly repayments are significantly reduced, which is ideal for those on relatively low incomes. But the downside is that there will be many more of these repayments so you will end up paying a lot more interest in the long run. While a longer term might enable you to get on the property ladder while you're still on a moderate income, it's worth working out exactly how much it is going to cost you. This is why the 25-year mortgage term is so popular, because the repayments tend to be the most manageable for the majority of borrowers.

Table 1-1 shows how much you'd end up paying back if you took out a £120,000 repayment mortgage over 15, 20, or 25 years at a rate of 5.85 per cent. Note that over the longer term (25 years), you may pay less every month but you end up paying more over the term of the loan than if you'd opted for a 15 year mortgage term.

Table 1-1	Cost of a Mortgage Over Different Time Scales	
Mortgage Term	**Monthly Repayment**	**Total Amount Payable**
15 years	£990.08	£178,214.40
20 years	£835.66	£200,558.40
25 years	£747.69	£224,307.00

Source: London & Country Mortgages

Mortgages come with age restrictions. You must be at least 18 and should finish paying back what you've borrowed before you retire, unless you can prove retirement income sufficient to cover the repayments. So if you are 50 and plan to retire at 65, most lenders will let you take out a mortgage over 15 years – but no longer.

Who offers them

Mortgages are offered by banks, building societies, and specialist lenders – which tend to be offshoots of major building societies and concentrate on niche markets, such as the self-employed or those with credit problems. As their name suggests, building societies were established with the original intention of providing the opportunity to purchase properties to those whose needs were not met elsewhere. And with more than 7,000 mortgages available from over 100 lenders, finding one that suits you shouldn't be impossible. It might just take a little time!

Don't assume that the bank you have your current account with should be your first port of call when applying for a mortgage. Banks have different strengths. Even if you chose yours because of its excellent current account, it doesn't follow that it will also have the best mortgages.

Shop around for the best mortgage by using an intermediary, such as an independent financial adviser or mortgage broker if necessary (see 'Using a middleman' later in this chapter). Remember how much cash you are spending. Getting the best deal at this stage is vital if you don't want to pay over the odds in the long term.

How much should you borrow?

What the lender is prepared to lend you and what you should borrow are two different things. The Department of Trade and Industry (DTI) identifies the question 'How much can I afford to borrow?' as one of the most important a homebuyer should ask herself before applying for a mortgage.

Typically, lenders let customers borrow three or three times their salary or two and a half times joint salary if they're buying a property with a partner or friend. So if you earn £20,000, you can borrow £60,000 on your own or £100,000 if your husband earns the same amount as you. But this isn't going to get you very far when you consider that the average national house price in the UK was £151,467, according to the Halifax House Price Index at the time of writing.

Book II

Finance, Tax, and How to Organise Them

Times are changing, though, with more and more lenders now using an affordability score tied in with a credit check. Applicants receive overall scores of A to F, with A being excellent and F indicating potential problems. In practice, this system may result in some borrowers being approved for larger loans than with the old salary system.

In an effort to bridge the gap between what you can afford and what you can borrow, some lenders have increased their *income multiple* – the number of times your salary you can borrow – to four, five or even six times income, depending on your particular circumstances. This will enable you to buy a more expensive property.

Four times income is the usual maximum income multiple and is becoming increasingly common. While you may think you can cope borrowing this much, if interest rates shoot up, your repayments could rocket. Rates may be at historically low levels but in the early 1990s they were as high as 15 per cent and repossession was common. And if history repeats itself, and there are signs that it could, this might spell disaster for your budgeting.

How mortgage rates are set

Before taking out a mortgage it helps if you understand a bit about how they work. The mortgage rate – the amount of interest you pay the lender in return for borrowing money to buy your property – reflects the Bank of England base rate. The Bank of England's *Monetary Policy Committee* (MPC) sets the base rate on the first Thursday of each month. The decision to cut, raise, or leave the base rate alone depends on several factors, including inflation, consumer confidence, and the state of the housing market. If there are signs that inflation is rising, for example, the MPC raises rates in an effort to curb consumer spending. However, if the economy is showing signs of slowing down, the MPC cuts rates in order to boost consumer borrowing.

Often within minutes of the MPC meeting, lenders adjust their mortgage rates accordingly. So if the base rate is raised by 0.25 per cent, most lenders' standard variable rate (SVR) also increases by this amount. This affects those on every type of mortgage rate apart from fixed and sometimes capped rates (see 'To fix or not to fix?' later in this chapter). However, nothing prevents lenders raising rates more than the base rate increase, or not raising them as much. Market forces mean lenders tend to stick together and follow the same pattern. But if a lender wants to buck the trend and attract some extra business, there's nothing to stop it doing so – except perhaps its profit margin!

If you are on a variable, discounted, or tracker rate, you are exposed to movements in the base rate, with a strong chance that your mortgage repayments will change straightaway. This is great if the base rate is falling because it means that your mortgage repayments will fall as well, but it can make things very difficult for you if it's going the other way.

If you are on a fixed rate deal or, in some cases, a capped rate, you won't be affected by an increase in the base rate until you come to the end of that offer period. However, the downside is that you won't see the benefit of a base rate cut either.

It's important not to overstretch yourself. Even if you find a lender who is willing to lend you four times your salary – or more – ask yourself whether you would be happy with that level of repayments every month. Remember: you still have to eat!

Choosing between Repayment and Interest Only

There are two ways to repay your mortgage – by paying a slice of the capital plus interest every month (*repayment*) or by just paying the interest each month (*interest-only*). With the latter, you have to set up an investment vehicle to pay off the capital at the end of the mortgage term. Whether you choose a repayment or interest-only mortgage largely depends upon your attitude to risk.

Book II

Finance, Tax, and How to Organise Them

Repayment loans

If you want a guarantee that all the capital you borrow is paid off by the end of the mortgage term, a repayment loan is the only option. Each month, you pay a proportion of the interest on the loan plus a slice of the capital. If you keep up with the repayments, at the end of the mortgage term, all the capital will be paid off and the property will be yours.

Although the monthly mortgage payments are higher than with an interest-only loan, most people opt for a repayment mortgage because they don't want to take a gamble on the roof over their head.

If you want peace of mind, the only way you get any guarantee that the mortgage will be paid off at the end of the loan period is by opting for a repayment loan.

Interest-only loans

An interest-only mortgage does exactly as it suggests: each month you pay back just a chunk of the interest on the loan. You don't repay any of the capital until the end of the mortgage term when you must pay it back in full; otherwise, your lender can repossess your property.

Although an interest-only mortgage may seem risky, they used to be extremely popular as the monthly mortgage payments are lower than with a repayment deal. For example, if you borrowed £80,000 on an interest-only basis at 5.65

per cent over 25 years, your mortgage repayments would be £376.67 per month. But if you took out a repayment loan instead, you would end up paying £498.46 per month.

While interest-only mortgage payments are obviously lower than with a repayment deal, you must also set up an investment vehicle to pay off the capital at the end of the mortgage term. Most people use endowments (although these are very unpopular now), individual savings accounts (ISAs), or pensions to do this. The following sections explain these options.

Endowment mortgages

You've probably heard about endowment mortgages during the past few years. It would be impossible not to notice that they've come in for a lot of stick because many could potentially fail to provide enough cash for home-owners to pay back their mortgages. The question about whether endowment policies were mis-sold continues to rumble on.

Two types of endowment policy exist – with-profits and unit-linked:

- ✔ **With-profits endowments:** Your monthly payments are pooled with those of other investors. At the end of the year – and depending on investment performance – bonuses are paid out by the insurer you invest your money with. At the end of the mortgage term, you get a one-off *terminal* bonus, which can be a large proportion of your final payout but isn't guaranteed.

- ✔ **Unit-linked endowments:** Your premiums buy units in stock-market linked investments. The value of these investments goes up and down on a daily basis. Unit-linked endowments can grow quicker than with-profits, but as is usually the case, an investment promising greater returns also involves higher risk.

Equities can go down as well as up. Don't gamble on the roof over your head unless you have enough cash in reserve to cover any potential shortfall.

ISA mortgages

ISAs are tax-free investment vehicles, which replaced personal equity plans (PEPs) and tax-exempt special savings certificates (TESSAs) in April 1999. Three types of ISA exist: cash, insurance, and stocks and shares. For the purpose of mortgages, equity ISAs are used. You invest a monthly sum into an ISA, either through a personal portfolio of ISA investments or through a specialist ISA mortgage package. The money (hopefully) increases over time, tax-free. If your ISA does well, you may be able to repay your loan before the end of the term.

The advantage of an ISA is that you don't have to pay the high levels of commission that you do on endowments and pensions. They are also far more flexible because switching investments and stopping or re-starting payments is easy. You also have more say over where your money is invested and your returns are free of tax.

But before you sign on for an ISA mortgage, keep these things in mind:

- ✔ ISA mortgages are linked to the stock market. The bear market that has had such a crippling effect on endowments has also affected ISAs. In fact the volatility of the stock markets since March 2000 has been such that the popularity of ISA mortgages has dropped dramatically and many lenders no longer offer them.

- ✔ If you use an ISA as a repayment vehicle, you're limited to how much you can invest each tax year (between 6 April and 5 April the following year). This limit is £7,000, so you may find it difficult to generate the capital you owe during the mortgage term.

  Everyone aged 18 and over is allowed to invest up to £7,000 tax-free in an ISA each tax year. If you buy your property with another person, you can each utilise your allowance and invest up to a total of £14,000 each year in ISAs.

Book II

Finance, Tax, and How to Organise Them

If you take out an ISA mortgage, don't forget to insure your investment contributions in case you lose your job or have an accident and can no longer work. Any of the usual protection products should be suitable. You can find more information about ISAs from the HMRC Web site at www.hmrc.gov.uk/leaflets/isa-factsheet.htm.

ISA mortgages are extremely high risk. Don't take one on unless you're sure you know what you're doing.

Pension mortgages

Backing your interest-only mortgage with a pension is another good way of maximising the tax breaks available. Instead of investing in an endowment or ISA, your extra monthly payments go into a personal pension fund, and you also pay premiums into a life assurance scheme.

The idea is that when you retire, you end up with a tax-free lump sum – up to 25 per cent of your pension pot – which you use to pay off the capital you owe. You use the rest to purchase an annuity, which is a guaranteed income for life and forms your pension. Because you can't get hold of your cash lump sum until you retire, pension mortgages tend to run for a lot longer than endowment mortgages – they can be as long as 35 or 40 years.

Pensions are a highly tax-efficient way of saving. For every 60p a higher rate taxpayer invests in his pension (78p for basic rate taxpayers), the Government tops up this contribution to £1. This tax relief should lead to higher investment returns than investing in an ISA or endowment simply because you have more money going into your pension fund.

Pension mortgages have their problems. There are no guarantees, and what you end up with is linked to market performance and the skills of the fund managers who handled your investment. For this reason, pension mortgages can be risky. Pension rules also tend to be very complicated, so you are likely to need professional advice if you opt for a pension mortgage. If you have a pension mortgage, keep a close eye on the performance of your fund to ensure it's on track to pay off your mortgage. If it isn't, you have to think about alternative arrangements to cover any shortfall.

 Pension mortgages are extremely tax-efficient, but they are linked to the stock market and highly complicated. For these reasons, they're ideal for sophisticated, self-employed higher-rate taxpayers. Everyone else should give them a wide berth. In addition, if you're a member of an occupational pension scheme at work, you can't have a pension mortgage anyway.

To Fix or Not to Fix?

Once you've decided on how you are going to repay your mortgage, you need to choose which type of home loan you're going to take out. The type you choose depends on your circumstances and attitude to risk. Your main options are:

- ✔ Variable
- ✔ Fixed
- ✔ Discount
- ✔ Capped
- ✔ Tracker
- ✔ Flexible
- ✔ Offset or current account
- ✔ Family offset

In the following sections, we explain in detail how each type works, along with the pros and cons.

Variable rate mortgages

Every lender has a standard variable rate (SVR), which is linked to the base rate and used as the basis for calculating many of its other deals – such as fixed or discounted rates. You can have a mortgage on the lender's SVR but it is expensive – it costs more than a fixed or discounted deal, and the rate moves up and down in line with the base rate. So if the MPC increases interest rates, the lender will usually raise its SVR accordingly, perhaps within minutes. (See the sidebar 'How mortgage rates are set' earlier in this chapter to understand the impact that MPC decisions have on interest rates.)

Many homeowners end up on their lender's SVR when their fixed or discounted deal comes to an end. When this happens you should remortgage to another deal to cut costs. The advantage of being on the SVR is that, in most cases, you are not tied in and can switch to another deal at any time without penalty. This could be useful if you are thinking of moving in the near future. But you will have to pay a higher rate of interest for this flexibility. And some lenders may charge you a penalty for switching if you have recently come to the end of a fixed or discounted deal and there are overhanging redemption charges for a number of years. If this isn't the case, find a fixed, discounted, or capped rate deal pretty smartish.

Although SVRs vary from lender to lender, they tend to be fairly similar because the market is so keenly priced. But while a mortgage on the lender's SVR isn't the most competitive deal to have, the SVR is a useful indication as to whether the lender is competitive in its fixed and discounted rates. If a lender's SVR is very high compared to the base rate and other lenders' standard rates, you can probably assume that the lender's fixed or discounted rates are not competitive either. Give this lender a wide berth and find one with a lower SVR – and better deals.

Six out of ten UK homeowners are on their lender's SVR. This is alarming because it means many people aren't getting the cheapest mortgage they could be. Your lender's SVR, even if it is competitive, is almost certainly likely to be higher than a fixed or discounted deal. So once the special offer on your mortgage has come to an end, make a point of remortgaging to another deal, otherwise you end up paying over the odds.

Fixed rate mortgages

Fixed rate mortgages are exactly as they sound. For a set period of time, your mortgage payments are guaranteed, no matter what happens to the base rate. If you take out a five-year deal fixed at 3.99 per cent, for five years, you'll be charged interest at 3.99 per cent.

Because your mortgage payments are fixed, budgeting is a lot easier than it is if you're on a variable rate. For this reason, fixed rate deals are ideal for first-time buyers and those who are on tight budgets.

Mortgages are usually fixed for two, three, or five years, but you can take out a 10-, 15-, 20-, 25- or even 30-year deal. Relatively few people are keen to fix their mortgage for this long, though, because circumstances can easily change over such a length of time. At the end of the fixed rate deal, you automatically revert to your lender's SVR for the remainder of the mortgage term and it's time to shop around for another offer.

The longer the fixed rate you opt for, the higher the rate of interest you pay. Therefore, a two-year fixed is bound to have a lower rate than a five-year deal. If interest rates are very high, and there's a possibility that they'll come down within a couple of years, you may want to opt for a two-year fixed and then take out another fixed rate deal at the end of that period. If, on the other hand, rates are exceptionally low and, therefore, more likely to go up than down, a five-year fixed is a good bet. (And besides, if rates do actually fall slightly during this time, you still get a cheap deal.)

Before you sign on for a fixed rate deal, consider these things:

✔ Most fixed rate deals carry stiff penalties if you redeem them during the offer period, which could amount to as much as a few thousand pounds. To avoid paying a penalty, don't fix for five years, for example, if there's a possibility that you'll be moving in three. Some deals are portable though and you can take them with you if you do move during the fixed rate period.

✔ While a fixed rate cushions the volatility in the market and protects you if interest rates rise, the downside is that you don't benefit if interest rates fall. Over the course of five or more years, rates could drop significantly.

If you're worried about budgeting, opt for a fixed rate deal. Be prepared to move quickly, however, as some lenders offer competitive rates for a very limited period of time. Delay – and you are likely to miss out.

Discount rate mortgages

Most lenders offer discounted deals, which tend to be a couple of percentage points below their SVRs. Discount rates are usually taken over two or three years. As with fixed rate deals, the shorter the term, the lower the rate.

The big advantage of discount deals is that they tend to be lower than fixed rate deals initially. You also benefit from any cut in the base rate because your rate is directly linked to your lender's SVR. But here also lies the problem: if the base rate goes up, your mortgage payments increase accordingly. If there's a lot of volatility in interest rates, your mortgage payments could fluctuate dramatically from month to month.

Only opt for a discount rate if you can afford to be wrong – in other words, if you can cope with an increase in your mortgage repayments. If you can, a discount rate will give you a better initial rate than a fixed rate deal, plus you'll benefit from any interest rate cuts during the discounted period.

Capped rate mortgages

With a capped rate mortgage, you know the absolute maximum you'll be paying each month. Your mortgage rate can rise but only as high as the cap. If the base rate continues to rise after the cap has been met, your mortgage repayments aren't affected. Capped rate deals are usually offered over 3, 5, or 10 years.

Because the rate is capped rather than fixed, it can fall, allowing you to take advantage of any cuts in the base rate. This makes a capped rate deal attractive because you can benefit from the best of both worlds.

Capped rate deals come at a price. They tend to be more expensive than fixed rate deals, and fewer are available so you have less choice.

Book II

Finance, Tax, and How to Organise Them

Index tracker mortgages

An index tracker mortgage tracks a set margin above the base rate, usually 1 per cent. If the base rate is 4 per cent, you pay 5 per cent until the rate changes. The advantage to index tracker mortgages is that the lender can't widen the margin and charge you more than 1 per cent above the base rate.

As an incentive, many lenders offer substantial discounts on tracker deals for six months or more. These discounts can result in very attractive rates and, given that tracker deals don't carry penalties after the offer period, you can then switch to another deal when the discount comes to an end.

As with a mortgage on the lender's SVR, tracker mortgages go up and down – there is no certainty. And as they usually track *above* the base rate, you end up paying more than if you'd opted for a fixed or discounted deal.

Flexible mortgages

A number of lenders offer flexible mortgages, although terms and conditions and benefits vary considerably. All flexible mortgages have a facility for varying repayments, so you can pay more or less than your mortgage payment

A year to the day: A comparison

Old-fashioned loans – quite a few of which are still in existence – charge interest on an annual basis, which works out much more expensive than loans for which interest is calculated on a daily basis. The main difference between daily and annual calculation of interest is as follows:

✔ **Daily calculation of interest:** At the end of every day your mortgage lender calculates how much you owe on your loan. The great advantage of this is that when you make a mortgage repayment, your money gets to work straightaway, reducing your mortgage debt – and the amount of interest you pay over the term of the loan. As mentioned earlier in this chapter, the interest is the killer in terms of mortgage costs.

✔ **Annual calculation of interest:** If your lender calculates the interest you owe on an *annual* basis, your mortgage payments are knocked off the total you owe once a year, rather than when you make them. So if your interest is calculated on 1 January, nothing you pay during the rest of the year is used to reduce your mortgage. You end up paying more interest (because you owe more capital for longer) even though you have actually paid the cash to the lender.

Some lenders calculate interest on a *monthly* basis; this works in the same way as annual calculation but a repayment doesn't make a difference to the amount you owe until the following month. So for around 30 days, your lender benefits more from you paying off a chunk of capital than you do.

Here's the thing to remember: Calculating interest on an annual basis is an arcane, outdated method. Avoid lenders who still adhere to this practice, where possible.

each month, or nothing at all. This ability to overpay, underpay, or to take a payment holiday depends on how much money you have built up in your mortgage 'account'; if you have overpaid by several hundred pounds, you can take payment holidays, but you can't miss a payment completely if you haven't built up anything in reserve.

Flexible mortgages are ideal for the self-employed or anyone whose income fluctuates. When you're flush, you can pay more than required so that when finances are tight, you can miss a payment or two – and not be penalised for doing so. The other advantage of overpaying is that you reduce your interest payments, enabling you to pay your mortgage off more quickly.

Interest is calculated daily on flexible deals, which makes a big difference in how much interest you pay over the term of your loan; essentially, you end up paying less. See the sidebar 'A year to the day: A comparison' to find out why.

Flexible mortgages tend to have the same rate as the lender's SVR, making them more expensive than fixed or discounted deals. If you don't use all of the flexible options, you may be better off steering clear of a flexible mortgage.

If you're drawn to a flexible mortgage simply because you want the ability to overpay when you can afford to, remember that many standard mortgages with offer periods, such as fixed and discounted deals, enable you to overpay a limited amount – usually around 10 per cent of the outstanding mortgage – without penalty each year.

Offset and current account mortgages

A relatively new innovation is the offset mortgage or the current account mortgage (CAM). These mortgages are fairly similar although they differ slightly on a number of points:

Book II

Finance, Tax, and How to Organise Them

- ✔ **Offset mortgages:** Offset mortgages enable you to use your savings to reduce the amount of interest you pay on your mortgage. It works like this: You open a savings account and/or current account with your mortgage lender. You make your monthly mortgage payment each month, as usual, but your savings and current account are counted against your mortgage balance in order to reduce the interest you are charged, while remaining separate. If you owe £60,000 on your mortgage, for example, but have £12,000 in your savings account and say, £500 in your current account, you'll be charged interest at your mortgage rate on £47,500. By leaving money in your current or savings account for as long as possible each month, you reduce the interest you owe on your mortgage further still, because the rate is calculated on a daily basis.

- ✔ **Current account mortgages (CAMs):** CAMs work in a similar way to offset mortgages although your home loan, current account, savings, and even credit cards and personal loans are all lumped together in one account rather than everything kept in separate pots. On your monthly statement you get one overall figure – usually a minus – telling you how much cash you have after all your savings are offset against your debts. You pay a set monthly amount from your account to cover the mortgage and your savings are used to reduce the amount of interest you owe.

    Even a small amount of money can make a big difference to the amount of interest you owe. Consider this example: If you take out a £100,000 mortgage over 25 years at 7.5 per cent interest and spend all your salary every month except £100, which you leave in the account, you will pay off your mortgage six years and nine months early, saving £40,263 in interest. The residue of money left in the account every month may not seem much, but the key thing is that it eats away at the capital you owe.

Because the interest on offset mortgages and CAMs is calculated daily, you pay what you owe on that day. If you have just been paid, it doesn't matter that you'll soon spend all that cash; for several days, a large chunk of money has been offset against your mortgage. In the long run, this enables you to repay your loan a lot quicker.

Critics of offset mortgages and CAMs argue that they are so flexible that borrowers who aren't disciplined won't pay their mortgages off on time. For example, some CAM providers let you borrow the difference between your mortgage (say, for example, £62,000) and the value of your house (say, £150,000), so in this example, you could get your hands on an additional £88,000 to do with what you like.

Another problem with CAMs is that everything is lumped together into one statement each month. While seeing all your debts and savings on one piece of paper is handy, it means your grand total will be in the red by a serious amount. Many people can't cope seeing that they are £120,000 overdrawn, for example. Others prefer not to switch their current account to their mortgage lender, preferring to stick with their existing bank.

Although offset mortgages and CAMS are a great way of reducing your interest payments, they tend to be more expensive than fixed or discounted deals because they're usually on the lender's SVR. However, lenders have started offering fixed rates on offset mortgages to make them more attractive to buyers. Watch out for penalties, however, which are likely to be charged during the offer period. A variable offset mortgage or CAM doesn't have any exit penalties.

Unless you have several thousand pounds in savings, which can be offset against your mortgage repayments, it probably isn't worth opting for an offset mortgage or a CAM. Offset mortgages and CAMs tend to be more popular with mature borrowers as they are more likely to have various savings lying around, or buyers who regularly receive substantial bonuses which they can put towards paying off their mortgage.

Why APRs aren't key to picking a mortgage

With so many different types of mortgage to choose from, working out the best value deal can seem impossible. Sometimes it feels like even mathematicians would struggle to compare deals with different rates of interest once offers and charges have been taken into account.

To make this job easier, annual percentage rates (APRs) were introduced. Under the Consumer Credit Act, lenders must provide the APR next to the headline mortgage rate in order to enable borrowers to compare the cost of different loans. The APR takes into account the total cost of the mortgage, including setting up costs, valuation fees, when interest is calculated, and any discounts or special offers in the early stages.

However, APRs can be unreliable so don't rely on them. You're far better off getting an individually prepared quote listing all upfront and ongoing costs.

Family offset mortgages

The success of offset mortgages has led some lenders to introduce a family offset loan, whereby a buyer can offset savings belonging to their parents and/or other family members against their mortgage. For example, you may have a mortgage of £70,000 but no savings. Yet your parents have £25,000 in savings, which they are happy to offset against your mortgage. This means your parents' savings stay in their name and they can get their hands on the money when they need to, but they receive no interest on it. Instead, they count against your mortgage so you only pay interest on £45,000. Few lenders offer this option, so you'll have to shop around for the best deal.

Book II

Finance, Tax, and How to Organise Them

How Your Deposit (or Lack Thereof) Affects Your Mortgage

The deposit is the cash down payment you make on your mortgage, and the general rule is the bigger the better. Not only will your mortgage repayments be lower, you'll also qualify for a cheaper rate and won't have to pay mortgage indemnity guarantee (MIG) – insurance taken out by lenders (but paid for by you) if you have a limited, or no, deposit. (See 'Mortgage indemnity guarantee' later in this chapter.)

Long gone are the days when buyers saved up until they had a 10 per cent deposit, however. Nowadays, you may get away without any deposit at all because 100 per cent and even 125 per cent mortgages have been available. Things are tightening up now, though, as a result of rising interest rates and the knock-on effects of the sub-prime (high risk borrower) lending problems being experienced in the USA.

Ideally every buyer would have a sizeable deposit to put down. Most people, in fact, use their savings to raise a deposit of between 5 and 10 per cent of the purchase price (although your deposit can certainly be higher if you have a lot of spare cash or have sold a property to buy a new one). But not everyone has several thousand pounds lying around to use as a deposit. And if you don't want to waste valuable time saving up for a deposit when you'd rather buy here and now, you'll have to try to get a mortgage without one.

Getting a mortgage for the whole purchase price – or more

A growing number of lenders have been offering 100 per cent or even up to 125 per cent loan to value (LTV) mortgages – this is the size of your mortgage in relation to the property value, so you may not need any deposit at all. These mortgages have been particularly popular among first-time buyers because they enable them to get a foot on the property ladder before prices rise even further instead of 'wasting' several years trying to save up for a mortgage.

With a 100 per cent mortgage (or larger), you won't qualify for the most competitive deals that are open to those with a sizeable deposit. The higher rates are the lender's way of covering the risk in taking you on. If house prices fall, you also risk going into *negative equity*, which means you owe more than the property is worth. And if you had to sell the property quickly, for whatever reason, being in negative equity could be a big problem.

Mortgage indemnity guarantee

Mortgage indemnity guarantee (MIG) is a one-off insurance premium paid for by borrowers who don't have much of a deposit. If you need to borrow at least 90 per cent of the LTV of the property, you will almost certainly be charged several thousand pounds worth of MIG, which is added on to your loan. MIG protects the lender in case you default on your mortgage payments, and it has to repossess your property and sell it at a loss. It doesn't benefit you at all, yet you have to pay for it.

MIG is expensive and outdated. Avoid lenders still charging MIG where possible and opt for a MIG-free deal. If this isn't achievable, it may be worth saving up for a bigger deposit and putting your house purchase off until you can avoid MIG.

Negotiating the Maze: Where to Find the Right Mortgage

Many people apply to the lender directly when taking out a mortgage. But with so much choice, it is hard to know which lender to choose. In our opinion, if you really don't know what you're doing, you should use an independent mortgage broker to help you find the best product for your needs. Whatever you do, don't rely solely on your bank to come up with the best deal.

Why your bank might not be your best bet

Most people are governed by inertia when it comes to their financial affairs, which is why so many stick with the same bank year in, year out even though they would almost certainly get a better deal elsewhere. And if this is true of current accounts, it is almost certainly true of mortgages.

In the past, if you approached your bank for mortgage advice, you would likely end up with a mortgage from your bank. This is because, under Financial Services Authority rules, your bank was only licensed to sell its own products. This situation is changing, however, so your bank will be able to offer mortgages from other providers. But at the very most, these other options will simply represent a very limited panel of lenders.

Why is this a problem? Well, you are unlikely to get the best mortgage rate, may incur a penalty for switching your mortgage even after the offer period, and will generally have limited your choice from the start. In other words, you are not giving yourself the best chance to find the best deal. Seeing that you're spending so much money, limiting yourself from the start is a rather foolish approach.

Book II

Finance, Tax, and How to Organise Them

Using a middleman

Do yourself a favour and shop around using an intermediary – we suggest an independent mortgage broker is your best bet. Why should you do all the leg-work yourself? A broker spends all her time following the mortgage market, knows the best deals at that particular time (they are ever-changing), and can talk you through the whole process. If you need your hand held by an expert, a broker is the expert to do it.

If you decide to use a broker, make sure you use a truly independent one. The best broker is one with access to the whole mortgage market, not just a hand-ful of lenders. That way, he can do a full search and find the best available deal at that time.

Some estate agents provide their own mortgage service, which is likely to be far more limited than the broad market view offered by an independent broker. Give your estate agent a wide view when it comes to financing your house purchase.

Using the Internet

The Internet is the most comprehensive source of information on mortgages, providing you with a wealth of information. Even if you aren't planning on actually applying for your mortgage online, you can still research the various loans and deals out there before you sign up for anything.

Researching online

The Web is great for researching the mortgage market. Several Web sites offer free calculators that enable you to quickly work out how much lenders will let you borrow and what your monthly repayments will be. For those who already have a mortgage, some sites also have calculators that let you work out whether remortgaging is worth your while.

Although these calculators are general guides and no guarantee of whether a lender will actually let you have the cash, they're a great place to start. Many of the big independent mortgage brokers also have tables of mortgage 'best buys' on their Web sites, which enable you to see the best available deals at a glance. When you're ready to sign on the dotted line of your mortgage application form, it's worth double-checking these tables to ensure you have the best deal.

Here are some of the best sites, all of which are offered by big independent brokers:

- ✔ **Charcol:** www.charcolonline.co.uk
- ✔ **London & Country:** www.lcplc.co.uk
- ✔ **Savills Private Finance:** www.spf.co.uk
- ✔ **The MarketPlace at Bradford & Bingley:** www.marketplace.co.uk
- ✔ **Chase De Vere Mortgage Management:** www.cdvmm.com

Another excellent Web site worth looking out is www.moneysupermarket.com. At this site, you can compare over 7,000 mortgages, as well as home insurance policies and mortgage protection plans. Finding the right mortgage is very straightforward. You'll be asked several questions, such as the purpose of the mortgage – first-time purchase, self-build, or raising capital – as well as the location, price, size of your deposit, details about the property, and your earnings and outgoings. As long as you have this information to hand, completing all the details shouldn't take longer than 10 minutes or so. Moneysupermarket then provides details of all the suitable deals for you, along with links so that you can click through to the lender's home page to apply.

Moneysupermarket also offers a guide explaining mortgage terms. And even though the site is very clear and easy to use, if you get stuck, you can contact moneysupermarket's financial team over the phone. You can also arrange a face-to-face consultation if you prefer.

Do yourself a favour and save yourself some money by using a broker's Web site for research and then applying online through the site. By doing this, you can take advantage of all the available know-how but you won't have to pay the fee (if it's a fee-charging broker) you would have been charged if you'd had a face-to-face consultation.

Applying for a mortgage online

The Internet is certainly changing the way the home-buying process works. It is possible to save time and jump the queue by applying for a mortgage online. In fact, mortgage broker Charcol reveals that one customer in three now applies for a mortgage via its Web site.

Many homebuyers don't realise that applying for a mortgage online is possible. If you're confident that you have found the right deal and don't want mortgage advice, you can fill in an on-screen application form and submit it to the lender. You'll receive an e-mail back informing you that the lender is processing your application.

 Applying online can be quicker than filling out a hard copy of the form and posting it to the lender because the advantage of e-mail applications is that they are processed automatically as soon as they are received. Post, on the other hand, is opened and processed when someone is available to do it. With e-mail applications, you don't have to wait for an application form to arrive in the post and for the postal service to deliver the completed form to your lender. Additionally, some lenders waive their application fee if you apply online.

Filling in a mortgage application form online is not for everyone. Mortgage application forms can be complicated, and many people like being guided through them by a lender or broker. If you don't feel ready to fill out a form online, stick to pen and paper and asking for advice!

Self-Certification Mortgages for the Self-Employed

When you apply for a mortgage, most lenders require three months' worth of wage slips to prove that you earn as much as you say you do. But not everyone can provide three months' worth of wage slips from an employer. If you're self-employed, you won't have this evidence of income. Yet with around 3.2 million self-employed people in the UK, the industry has found ways around this problem. As long as you have two years of audited accounts to prove your income, a mainstream lender (as opposed to a specialist lender) will usually let you have a standard mortgage.

But if your business hasn't been running for at least two years, you won't have enough accounts to satisfy a mainstream lender. And even if you have been going longer than two years, the problem for many self-employed people is that their accounts don't adequately reflect their income. If you employ an accountant, part of his job is to ensure you don't pay more tax than is absolutely necessary, which is perfectly legal but means you may have a problem convincing a mortgage lender that you can actually afford to repay more than your accounts indicate.

If you fall into this category, you may have to opt for a *self-certification mortgage*. This enables you to certify your own income, by signing a document stating how much you earn. You don't need to prove audited accounts.Most specialist lenders judge each case on its own merits rather than use strict income multiples, but as a general guide, many let you borrow up to three and a quarter times your stated income. If you state that your earnings for last year were £40,000, for example, the lender will let you borrow up to £130,000.

It might be tempting to lie about how much you earn in order to get a bigger mortgage. But resist this temptation because you may have problems meeting your repayments if you overstretch yourself.

While rates on self-certification loans used to be much higher than on conventional mortgages (because of the perceived extra risk of lending to the self-employed), they have come down in recent years. However, they still tend to be higher than the rates for standard loans (although some lenders have started offering mainstream deals to self-certifiers). You can choose between the same types of deal, although flexible loans may be most useful to the self-employed whose income might fluctuate.

You also have to stump up a bigger deposit in most cases – some lenders even want as much as 25 per cent of the purchase price. However, some specialist lenders are happy with a 10 per cent deposit, so all is not lost if you can't afford such a substantial downpayment. You'll just have to shop around for a deal you can afford.

Miaow! Cat-Mark Mortgages

The Cat-mark is awarded to mortgages that are low-cost, easy access and have simple terms. The Government introduced Cat-mark (also known as Cat-standard) mortgages in order to give consumers an idea of the most straightforward products on the market. Cat-standard mortgages are guaranteed not to charge MIG, for example, and interest has to be calculated daily rather than annually. The lender must also mention all other fees and costs up front so that the borrower knows exactly what the mortgage is going to cost him. Other criteria for Cat-standard mortgages include the following:

- You can take your mortgage with you should you move property, as long as you stay with the same lender.

- You can choose which day of the month you make your mortgage repayments.

- You are allowed to make early repayments, and there are no tie-in periods.

- The maximum variable interest rate is no higher than 2 per cent above base rate, and there are no redemption fees.

- If you find yourself in arrears equivalent to three months' repayments, you will pay standard interest charges only on the outstanding debt.

- If you take out a fixed or capped rate Cat-standard mortgage, redemption fees must be no more than 1 per cent of the loan for each remaining year of the fixed or capped period and reduced each month.

- There is no redemption charge once the fixed or capped-rate offer period has finished.

Cat-standard mortgages are hard to find. Few lenders offer them because there isn't much in these mortgages for them. And Cat-standard mortgages won't suit people looking for a discounted mortgage because this type of mortgage doesn't qualify for a Cat-mark.

We often come across people who wrongly think that a Cat-standard mortgage is in some way guaranteed or recommended by the Government. In other words, it is one of the best on the market. However, there is no element of recommendation involved.

Cat-standard mortgages sound great in theory. But they've largely been a failure because the rates aren't competitive enough. If you pick a mortgage with a good rate, that doesn't charge MIG, and has no overhangs (redemption penalties after your offer period has ended), you won't go far wrong and won't need a Cat-standard deal.

Buyer Beware: Things to Watch Out For

Mortgages can be such a minefield because many products come with a sting in the tail, usually hidden somewhere in the terms and conditions. And if you don't spot this before you sign on the dotted line, you could end up with a deal that is not as competitive as it first appears.

Read the terms and conditions carefully. If you are using a broker, he should point out any potential nasties. But you can help yourself by watching out for the main things to avoid.

Penalties for early redemption

Most mortgage deals (other than standard variable rate loans) have some sort of redemption penalty if you cash your mortgage in within a certain period of time. If you take out a five-year fixed rate deal, for example, the only way the lender can offer you such a deal is if you stick with it for the five years, at least. If you cashed in your mortgage before then and paid no penalty for doing so, the lender would lose money. This is why lenders charge a penalty – a percentage of the interest owed on the loan – if you decide to switch mortgages before the stated time period is up. This practice is fair enough really and one most lenders follow when offering fixed or discounted rate deals, although not all lenders charge such penalties.

What aren't acceptable, in any situation, are *extended redemption penalties*. These are also known as *overhangs* because they run longer than the offer period. For example, some lenders offer two-year discounts at startlingly good rates. But the payback is that you are then tied into the deal for not two, but five years or even longer; if you try to redeem the mortgage at any time during that period, you face a substantial penalty, which can be in the region of thousands of pounds.

Accepting such a deal is clearly not in your best interests because it ties you to an uncompetitive rate – often the lender's SVR. To make matters worse, this sort of deal tends to be offered by a lender with a high SVR. So any of the earlier savings are lost by paying higher interest for years after the offer period has come to an end. So never take out a mortgage with an extended redemption penalty. The rate will undoubtedly look more attractive than loans without overhangs but there is a good reason for this – afterwards you are stuck on a higher rate for what can seem forever.

Compulsory insurance

Compulsory insurance, where a lender forces you to take out its insurance as a condition of taking out one of its mortgages, is a big rip-off; avoid it at all costs. Certain forms of insurance are essential when taking out a mortgage, such as buildings insurance; others, such as home contents insurance, are optional. The only way to get the best deal on this is to shop around. Taking what the lender offers is unlikely to produce the best deal.

Many lenders, particularly building societies, offer two mortgage rates: a really cheap deal and a higher rate. The catch with the cheap deal is that you have to sign up to the lender's buildings insurance (and in some cases its home contents insurance as well). Yet research shows that you are better off in the long term opting for the higher rate and shopping around for your insurance. That way, you can change insurer every time your premium comes up for renewal – if necessary – rather than stick with an uncompetitive deal that's tied to your mortgage.

Some lenders don't impose compulsory insurance, but they do try to make it as easy as possible for borrowers to take out their insurance because it's such a money-spinner for them. Often, on the mortgage application form they include a reminder that you must take out some form of cover and provide a box that you simply tick if you want to take out the lender's buildings insurance. Lenders are counting on the fact that you'll be so stressed by the whole mortgage application that one less thing to worry about is welcome. But even though some lenders offer competitive rates, you can't assume that this is the case.

Not Forgetting the Not-So-Little-Extras

If the mortgage rate were the only thing you had to worry about, the finance side of buying a property would be fairly straightforward. Unfortunately, this isn't the case. You need to think about lots of little extras, explained in the following sections.

Some lenders or mortgage brokers refund the cost of certain fees as an inducement to taking out a mortgage with them; others offer free buildings and contents insurance or mortgage payment protection for a limited period of time. Such offers can add up to a saving of several hundred pounds. As you shop around for a lender, be sure to ask about these incentives.

Lender's arrangement fee

Practically all lenders charge borrowers an upfront fee, known as an *application*, *arrangement*, or *booking fee*, to reserve the mortgage. This fee is non-refundable. You may also have to pay a completion fee once you receive the money. Expect to pay up to £650, although some lenders can charge double this, depending on the deal.

When the mortgage market is very competitive, that is, lenders are doing all they can to attract borrowers, you may get these fees refunded, so be on the look out for those deals. However, don't choose a mortgage solely because your fees are refunded.

Some deals don't have arrangement fees. But if the lender charges a higher interest rate in order to make the money back, you'll probably end up paying a lot more in the long run than you would if you'd just paid an arrangement fee in the first place. Many lenders let you add the arrangement fee onto the mortgage, so you don't have to pay a lump sum up front. This can make cash flow a little easier and even though, in theory, you will pay interest on it, it's a negligible amount.

Mortgage valuation fee

The lender charges you a fee for having the property valued – which seems a bit cheeky if you consider that the valuation is done to satisfy the lender, who wants to make sure the property is worth what it's being asked to lend you to buy it. You don't benefit at all from this arrangement, apart from the fact that it brings you closer to getting your mortgage. The amount you're charged depends on the size of the property (see Book I, Chapter 2 for more details), but expect to pay £350 or more.

The valuation fee is unavoidable although in competitive mortgage markets, or if you are remortgaging, some lenders refund it. The lender sends a surveyor to value the property. You don't have to do anything at all; the valuation fee is added onto the money you borrow from the lender.

Mortgage broker fee

If you use a mortgage broker to help you find your home loan, you may have to pay a fee, depending on how the broker works. Some brokers are paid by commission, which means that the lender who supplies your mortgage pays the broker a sum for passing on your business. The amount varies but is usually in the region of a few hundred pounds. If the broker receives more than £250 from the lender, he has to inform you of this.

However, if you use a broker who doesn't take commission, you have to pay him a fee for his time and expertise. The broker's fee varies from broker to broker but is usually in the region of 1 per cent of the value of the mortgage, which can translate into several thousand pounds.

Make sure you know from the outset whether your broker is paid by commission or is expecting a cheque from you after she has arranged your mortgage. Whether you choose fees or commission depends on whether you are unduly concerned that a commission-paid broker will be influenced in the choice of lender that she recommends to you. We really don't think the majority of professional independent brokers would be influenced in this way – and it could mean saving yourself thousands of pounds if you opt for a broker who is paid by commission.

Survey costs

Getting a survey is always wise. So expect to pay for a survey on top of the valuation (which doesn't really tell you anything about the condition of the property). As explained in more detail in Book I, Chapter 2, two different types of survey are available: a basic homebuyer's report or a full structural survey. Which one you go for depends on the condition and age of your property and how much money you want to spend. A homebuyer's report starts at around £300 a building survey can cost anything between £500 and £1100, plus VAT, depending on the size of the property and exactly what you want investigated.

Skimping on a survey may seem like an easy way to cut costs. But think about how much money you're spending on the property – and how expensive it would be if you made a mistake.

Book II

Finance, Tax, and How to Organise Them

Legal fees

Unless you do your own conveyancing or legal work, you have to pay a solicitor to do it for you (see Book I, Chapter 4 for more details on using a solicitor and legal costs). Again, costs vary, but expect to pay around £600 in legal fees for the purchase of a £100,000 property. Legal fees are usually payable on exchange of contracts.

Land Registry and local searches

As well as paying the solicitor a conveyancing fee, you also have to pay him for the Land Registry fees and charges for local searches, which he undertakes on your behalf. These uncover whether the property had planning permission or not in the first place and whether any major works such as a supermarket are being planned for the empty plot next to your property.

The solicitor may bill you for these searches as he commissions them or he'll add the cost onto his final bill. Expect to pay in the region of £500 for these.

Stamp duty land tax

You pay stamp duty land tax to the solicitor at the same time as exchange of contracts (which means you can't pay the stamp duty land tax out of the mortgage advance). The amount you pay depends on the value of your property, but it starts at 1 per cent on properties over £125,000, rising to 4 per cent for properties over £500,000. Stamp duty land tax can, therefore, be quite a sizeable chunk of your budget, so don't forget about it or you could be in for a nasty shock when the solicitor sends you his bill.

Completing the Mortgage Application Form

Once you've decided on the mortgage you want, you have to complete a mortgage application form and supply several items to prove that you are who you say you are. Identification proving who you are and information stating where you got the deposit from, for example, is necessary to crack down on fraud. Lenders take this very seriously.

As soon as you start looking at properties, start gathering together the information that your lender is going to want to see. Keep hold of wage slips, your most recent P60, bank statements, and some recent utility bills. These are all examples of the sort of things the lender wants to see. Getting them ready now can save you time – and stress – later.

Every lender has its own version of the mortgage application form, so it isn't possible to tell you exactly what information you'll be required to provide. But most lenders follow the same pattern. Most forms run to several pages, and you're required to give the following information:

- **The name, current address, and date of birth of each applicant.** If you have not lived at your current address for at least three years, you have to provide the address(es) of where else you have lived.

- **The address of the property you intend to buy and how much you want to borrow.** You're also asked for a contact name and number for someone who can give the lender access to the property to arrange the valuation. This person is usually the estate agent handling the sale, but where the owner is selling privately, you have to give the owner's name and contact details.

- **Your solicitor's name, address, and contact number.** The lender wants evidence that you have instructed a solicitor because it will be dealing with him during the application process.

✔ **The size of your deposit and where you got the money from.** Again, the source of your deposit is important in order to reduce the risk of money laundering. Beyond that, the lender doesn't really care whether you saved up your deposit, got it as a present from a relative, or took out a loan. All are considered to be acceptable sources.

✔ **Each applicant's job title, employer's name and address, salary, and length of employment.** This information is necessary in order to convince the lender that you earn enough to meet the mortgage repayments each month and aren't overstretching yourself.

✔ **Each applicant's bank account details, including name and address of branch, sort code and account number, and number of years you have banked with them.** This information enables the lender to check your basic creditworthiness.

✔ **Whether either applicant has any county court judgments (CCJs) against them or has ever been declared bankrupt.** This information allows the lender to find out whether you have defaulted on any loans or mortgages in the past – in other words, whether you're likely to meet your repayments each month.

✔ **Details of any personal loans, outstanding credit card debts, or other monthly outgoings.** By finding out about your current commitments, the lender can work out whether you can afford to finance your mortgage.

✔ **Whether you want to take out the lender's buildings insurance or not.** If you do, tick the box. But we recommend that you don't take out the lender's insurance until you have shopped around and made sure it is the best deal available at the time. If you get your insurance elsewhere, make sure you have it arranged by the time you exchange contracts, or your solicitor won't let you go ahead.

✔ **Each applicant's signature and the date.** The signature is an important declaration that all the information you have provided is correct, so don't forget to autograph the application form!

Problems Getting a Mortgage

Once you've completed your mortgage application form and returned it to the lender, you can't do much apart from sit back, cross your fingers, and wait to be approved. And if everything is in order, it will be.

But sometimes the lender rejects your mortgage application because the information you gave doesn't stack up. One in four applicants is rejected, so you're not alone. The main reasons for a mortgage being rejected are the following:

✔ Unstable job or income history

✔ Missed repayments on some form of credit

✔ County Court Judgments (CCJs)

✔ Bankruptcy

✔ Not being on the electoral roll

✔ Not having a bank account

✔ Mortgage arrears

✔ Repossession

✔ Unemployment

Even with a bad credit record, you should be able to get a mortgage although you will have to pay more for it. Non-standard borrowers (also known as *sub-prime* or *credit-impaired*) are often charged a higher rate of interest than on a mainstream loan. Instead of automated credit scoring, specialist lenders look at each case on an individual basis. However, they are likely to lend you less and require a bigger deposit than on standard loans. There can also be very severe early redemption penalties.

Given that rates are higher with non-standard mortgages, your aim should be to try and get back on track with a cheaper mainstream product within three years or so. Of course, the way to do this is to keep up with your mortgage repayments.

Credit scoring

Financial problems in your past could well come back to haunt you when you apply for a mortgage. But many people who think they have a clean slate aren't prepared for it when their mortgage application is rejected – although this is quite common.

The reason for this rejection is probably to be found on your credit file. These are records of all your financial affairs and are held by the main credit reference agencies: Equifax (`www.checkmyfile.com`) and Experian (`www.experian.co.uk`). If you have missed a payment on a credit card or loan, for example, this is recorded on your credit file.

Before applying for a mortgage, get a copy of your credit file so that you can have any mistakes corrected. (You're charged £2 for accessing your file.) It may be that you haven't done anything wrong at all; your records could have been confused with a family member of the same name. By checking your file, you can have simple mistakes like these corrected.

Every time you apply for any form of credit, it leaves a 'footprint' on your file. So even if you're rejected for a credit card, for example, a record of this application appears on your file. The more footprints you have, the more credit hungry you appear, and the louder the warning bells sounding for the mortgage lender. Footprints remain on your credit file for six months only. So if there are lots of them, it might be worth waiting a few months before trying again to get a mortgage.

County Court Judgments (CCJs)

Every mortgage lender wants to know whether you have any county court judgments (CCJs) against you and most will reject your application if this is the case. A CCJ is an adverse ruling against someone who has not satisfied their debt payments with their creditors. Once recorded against you, it stays on your credit file for seven years. Usually, you have to satisfy any CCJs against you before you can get a mortgage.

All is not necessarily lost, however: some specialist companies accept applicants with CCJs. The bigger the problem and the greater the number of CCJs against you, the higher the mortgage rate you can expect to pay. But if you have a sizeable deposit, many lenders won't load the interest rate significantly.

Book II

Finance, Tax, and How to Organise Them

Chapter 2

Financing with a Buy-to-Let Mortgage

In This Chapter

▶ Making sure you can afford a rental property

▶ Negotiating the buy-to-let mortgage maze to find the best deal for you

▶ Renting out your home in order to buy another property to live in

*F*inding the right rental property is just the beginning. Financing your purchase is a big consideration, and there are many ways to go about it. Few of us are lucky enough to be in the position to have enough cash to buy a property outright – and even if you are, that might not be the best way of doing it. Luckily, scores of mortgage lenders now offer competitive buy-to-let loans specifically for this purpose for investment landlords. But be warned: This can be a double-edged sword. Landlords are spoilt for choice: Deciding whether a fixed rate or discounted deal is best for you can be difficult, because much depends on the future movement of interest rates (which can be very difficult to predict). We recommend that you use an independent mortgage broker to help you source the best deal.

In this chapter, we look at the various ways that you can buy your rental properties and the different types of buy-to-let mortgages available. We also cover how to calculate whether your rental income will be good enough to pay the mortgage, and what criteria the lender judges you on. The financial side can be a bit of a pain to sort out, but to ensure it doesn't become a burden later on, you need to take a good look at your finances and plan your purchases very carefully.

Making Sure You Can Afford to Buy a Rental Property

Buying property to rent out is a very fashionable step to take. Newspapers regularly feature tales of housewives and retired teachers who have made thousands of pounds speculating on the property market. These stories have great appeal because they are about ordinary people who, without much prior know-how, take the plunge and decide to become landlords.

Despite these media stories, property remains a big investment risk because so much money is involved. Becoming a landlord might be appealing, but you need to think carefully before taking the plunge. If you are in a lot of debt with a big overdraft, owe thousands of pounds on credit and store cards, have an outstanding personal loan or two, or a massive mortgage on your own home, think twice before buying a rental property.

Even with detailed tenant-screening criteria (see Book V, Chapter 1), landlords can end up with tenants who don't pay their rent some months or with an empty property for a period of time because of a temporary shortage of suitable tenants. Ask yourself whether you could cover the rent and associated costs for several months if you had to. If the answer is no, you are likely to be overstretching yourself – and buying a rental property might not be for you.

Buy-to-Let Mortgages

You must be between the ages of 18, 21, or 25 and 65 to 75 (depending on the lender and your particular circumstances) to qualify for a buy-to-let mortgage. The minimum term for borrowing tends to be five years, the maximum can be anything up to 40 years, as long as the landlord hasn't retired during that time. And the lender will also demand that the property is ready to rent before it lets you have a buy-to-let mortgage.

Many lenders offer a good range of competitive deals with rates of interest not that much higher than you'd typically pay on your main residence, rather than the commercial rates landlords paid in the past. In addition, buy-to-let lenders take into account the rental income of a property when deciding whether to lend you the money to purchase it, rather than your own income.

Before 1996, when the buy-to-let scheme was introduced, most landlords were cash buyers, as they weren't allowed to rent out a property on which they had an outstanding mortgage. Some lenders gave permission for the property to be rented out if there was a mortgage on the property – but certain conditions had to be satisfied first. But the buy-to-let mortgage scheme has changed all that.

Generating enough rental income

Buy-to-let loans are calculated differently to normal mortgages (where you might expect to borrow between three and four times your income). The lender decides whether or not to lend you the money to buy the property

---

Think before committing your funds

We know one accountant who spends 90 per cent of his time dealing with clients who want to invest money for their retirement but don't want to use a pension to do this. Often they have thousands of pounds to invest and prefer to put it into property instead.

One client who came to visit him had £200,000 in cash. This client wanted to use this money to buy a rental property. He was convinced that the best course of action was to buy one large property outright because he didn't want to take on another mortgage.

But our accountant friend advised otherwise. He told his client that dividing the sum to pay four deposits on four rental properties was a much better use of his cash. He pointed out that taking out a buy-to-let mortgage on each property would not be increasing his risk, because the rental income would cover the mortgage payments. It could also work to his advantage because each property would generate a little bit of extra income and he could reduce his tax bill by offsetting his mortgage interest repayments against the rental income.

The client took his accountant's advice and ended up buying four properties with his cash, thereby spreading his risk and maximising his potential income. Think twice about how you invest the money you have before taking the plunge.

Book II

Finance, Tax, and How to Organise Them

according to the likely rental income the property will generate, known as the *rental cover.*

The rental cover is the proportion of the mortgage payment that the lender requires the rent to cover. Because you are likely to have your own home already, you're probably already making payments on a mortgage based on your income. Thus you'll use the rental income from your tenants to pay the buy-to-let loan. For this reason, the lender needs to know that this amount will be enough to cover the mortgage.

The average minimum rental cover lenders require can be anything from 100 to 130 per cent. If we take the highest amount – 130 per cent – if the monthly mortgage payments on your rental property are likely to be £500, you should be looking at generating rent of £650 a month from your tenants.

When deciding whether to allow you a buy-to-let loan, some lenders still take your income into account, in addition to the potential rental income of a rental property. The amount you have to earn from a source other than your rental income varies from lender to lender.

You must calculate your rental income carefully. When you apply for a buy-to-let mortgage, most lenders ask for some evidence, in writing, of what the rental property is likely to generate. You can get an estimate of what rent the property can generate from a letting or estate agent who has some knowledge of the local rental market. Ask local agents with similar properties in the area on their books what rent you can expect from your prospective property. If agents estimate that the rent you can reasonably expect is much less than what you need, you may as well stop wasting your time and look for another rental property.

Raising a deposit

As with the purchase of your main residence, when you buy a rental property you need to put down a deposit. The deposit tends to be bigger than that required by the mortgage lender on your main residence, because the risks are thought to be that much greater. Most lenders require a deposit of at least 15 per cent.

The bigger the deposit, the smaller the mortgage. If you have, say, £60,000 in savings, you may be tempted to put this all down as a big deposit on one property. But ask yourself whether this strategy is the best way of doing things. Dividing this deposit between two rental properties may be better because, as long as the mortgage payments are adequately covered, how high they are doesn't really matter. Having two properties, rather than one may work out much better for you financially in the long run; in other words, put down the minimum deposit the lender requires from you and then keep the remainder until you see another rental property you like the look of. By following this strategy, you can grow a property portfolio and avoid putting all your eggs in one basket.

Never invest money in a rental property that you may need in the short term. Property is a very illiquid investment that you should plan to hold for the long term. There's no point overstretching yourself on the deposit if you haven't got enough spare cash in the bank to fix your car if it fails its MOT.

Finding the right buy-to-let mortgage

Getting the right deal can be the difference between making a go of your rental property business or not. Interest repayments that are too high will significantly eat into your profits.

Scores of mortgage lenders offer buy-to-let loans, and hundreds of different deals are available. Theoretically, you should be able to find a buy-to-let mortgage that's suitable for you. Finding the right one requires that you take the time to think about what you want from your mortgage – and what you don't.

Extra fees

Don't forget that a valuation fee needs to be paid, based on the value of the property, but usually around £350. You also have to pay a fee of anywhere from £650 to £1300, although this varies between lenders, for setting up the mortgage, which is added onto your loan on completion of the deal. If you use a broker, you may also have to pay a fee for their services.

You can find a wide choice of buy-to-let mortgages designed to fit all sorts of circumstances. Some are geared to the purchase of one property, others to the creation of a portfolio of up to five properties. Generally speaking, loans of £15,000 to £1m per investor are available, repayable over five to 40 years.

Some lenders offer *staged payment loans.* These types of loans are ideal if the rental property needs a lot of work before you can rent it to tenants. The lender's surveyor agrees to the value of a fully refurbished property, and the mortgage offer is based on this value. A proportion of the loan is made available up front to buy the property, with the rest of the cash paid in stages as work progresses. In other cases, the lender holds back a chunk of the money until the landlord has completed essential work, such as employing a tree surgeon to remove a tree growing close to the property whose roots could affect the foundations. In such cases, you have to ensure you have enough cash on hand to cover the required work until the lender releases the funds.

Some buy-to-let mortgages allow you to buy up to five properties with one loan. This option can be the simplest way of extending your property portfolio, so ask your mortgage lender or broker for more details.

Decision 1: Interest-only or repayment mortgage

As a prospective landlord you first have to choose between an interest-only and a repayment mortgage.

The following sections explain the features of each type of mortgage.

Interest-only mortgages

Interest-only buy-to-let mortgages are the most popular among landlords, with nearly two-thirds opting for this type of loan, according to the Association of Residential Letting Agents (Arla).

Interest-only loans do exactly what they say on the tin: You pay only the interest on the loan each month. At the end of the mortgage term, you still owe the mortgage lender the capital you borrowed in the first place. The onus is on you to set up an investment vehicle into which you save enough cash each month to repay the capital at the end of the loan period.

Landlords don't need to take out an investment product to back an interest-only loan on a rental property. This is because you are likely to already have a main residence and aren't relying on your rental property to provide a roof over your head once you retire. You can plough the money you would have put into an investment vehicle into other rental properties – the idea being that when you need to repay the capital on one of your rental properties, you can simply sell one to pay back the lender what you owe.

All of your monthly mortgage payments can be offset against the rental income of the property for tax purposes. If you opt for a repayment loan, it is possible to claim the interest part against the rental income for tax purposes, but not the capital portion.

Repayment mortgages

Repayment mortgages are less popular than interest-only mortgages for buy-to-let purposes, but may still be worth considering. With a repayment mortgage, you pay not only the interest on the loan each month, but also a slice of the capital. The idea is that at the end of the mortgage term you will have paid off the loan in full and the property will be yours.

Of course, your monthly repayments are higher than if you had opted for an interest-only deal. The calculation as to what percentage of the monthly repayment is interest and what is capital needs to be done when offsetting rental income against your mortgage repayments on your self-assessment tax return. Your mortgage lender should provide you with these figures.

Decision 2: To fix, discount, track, or be flexible?

Once you've decided to opt for an interest-only or repayment deal, you must choose between the various types of mortgage available: fixed rate, discount flexible, or tracker. The following sections explain.

Think very carefully about what sort of mortgage would best suit your requirements before signing on the dotted line. What suits one landlord quite often doesn't suit another. Consult an independent mortgage broker for more advice.

Tracker mortgages

Many landlords opt for tracker rate mortgages with no penalties at any time for switching because they like their flexibility. Their mortgage repayments track interest rate movements – the Bank of England base rate or LIBOR (the rate of interest at which banks borrow funds from other banks).

The advantage of tracking a rate of interest is that if your mortgage rate is one per cent above it, you always pay one per cent more than that rate – no more and no less. While the rate your mortgage is tracking can fluctuate, you are not at the whim of your mortgage lender. Instead of dictating rate movements as, and when, it likes, the lender is instead committed to following the movement of the rate being tracked.

Fixed rate mortgages

An increasing number of landlords opt for fixed rate buy-to-let mortgages as they also bring peace of mind: You can't guarantee that your tenant is going to pay the rent on time every month, no matter how good your tenant-screening criteria are (although you should make sure that your tenant screening _is_ good anyway – see Book V, Chapter 1) but if you fix your mortgage rate, you at least know exactly how much you have to pay the mortgage lender each month.

The most useful fixed rate deals for your purposes are likely to be _short term_ – of three or five years' duration. You can get fixed rate deals for one, two, 10, 15 and even 30 years, but it isn't much use if the fixed period is too short or indeed too long. You don't want to think about remortgaging in a year's time and a lot can happen in the next 30 years!

Discount mortgages

A discount mortgage is a popular choice for landlords. You need to be comfortable with the fact that interest rates can go up as well as down, so while you might be getting a discount of around 3 per cent off the standard variable rate, it could go the other way as well if the Bank of England decides to raise interest rates.

Discount mortgages can work out cheaper than fixed rate deals if the base rate is low, but keep in mind that the rates go up as well as down, and you have no protection against a rise in your mortgage repayments – unlike a fixed rate mortgage. Discount mortgages can be a good deal, but they also add an extra layer of risk that most landlords could do without.

Flexible mortgages

Many landlords choose a flexible mortgage because it actually helps them manage their rental property business. Flexible deals allow you to overpay or underpay when you want. This flexibility can be useful when dealing with tenants because sometimes even the most reliable ones can forget to pay their rent on time, or the property could lie empty for a couple of months in between tenancies. If you paid slightly more than you needed to during those months when the rent was on time or the property occupied, these overpayments count towards the total you owe, allowing you to pay less when the property is empty or when your tenants are struggling to pay the rent one

Book II

Finance, Tax, and How to Organise Them

month. The advantage of overpaying and then underpaying is that you aren't penalised for flexibility.

Alternatively, you can take a payment break and make no monthly mortgage repayments at all for a certain period of time – as long as you have built up your credit with overpayments when times were better.

Most flexible deals have interest calculated on a daily basis, which is a real bonus because it means you aren't paying over the odds as you are with monthly or annual calculations.

Remortgaging to a better deal

Once you've carefully chosen your buy-to-let mortgage, that shouldn't be the end of the financial decisions you have to make. Even if you opted for a fixed rate deal for three or five years, after that time, your mortgage reverts to the lender's standard variable rate (SVR), which will inevitably be considerably higher. Likewise, once landlords with discount mortgages come to the end of the offer period, they find themselves on their lender's much higher SVR.

If you are on your lender's SVR, you are almost certainly making higher monthly mortgage repayments than you need to. When this happens, it's time to remortgage to a better deal.

Remortgaging is when you switch from your current deal to another provided by the same lender or another lender if yours can't offer you a better deal. The first step to remortgaging is to approach your current lender and ask whether they can offer you a lower rate. Remind them that you are a loyal customer. If you have more than one rental property mortgaged with them, remind them of that fact, too. If your current lender can't offer you a cheaper deal, shop around, using a mortgage broker if necessary.

Switching to another buy-to-let mortgage could save you hundreds of pounds a year in interest. An increasing number of landlords are cottoning on to the fact that remortgaging is a relatively painless, straightforward way to save cash and help them grow their business. Many landlords take advantage of any increase in the equity in their property to release this cash when they remortgage to put down as a deposit on another rental property.

The process of remortgaging is fairly straightforward. Once you have chosen the deal you want, approach the lender and fill out an application form. Your property will have to be surveyed again, and you'll have to pay legal fees, but some lenders refund these on certain remortgage deals. You may have to pay a penalty for switching however, and a fee on the new mortgage so do the sums, and work out whether it is financially viable before taking the plunge.

Releasing equity

One way of raising finance to buy a rental property is to release money from your own home. With property appreciating so much in value, many home-owners find they are sitting on tens of thousands of pounds worth of equity in their homes. One way of buying rental property is to remortgage your own home to release some of this equity and put it towards the cost of a rental property.

The more the merrier

While you might think that the more properties you take on, the greater the risk, in fact the opposite is the case. As your property portfolio grows, your risks are reduced. For example, if you own ten rental properties and have problems with one of your tenants who is late paying her rent, more than likely things will be running smoothly with your other nine properties, let to good, reliable tenants who pay on time. The bad tenant is just a tiny percentage of the whole and seems like less of a big deal when you look at the bigger picture.

Owning more than one rental property is also useful when it comes to calculating your income on your tax return. Your property portfolio is considered as a single whole, rather than as a number of individual properties, so if you made losses on one rental property you can balance them against the gains made on another one when filling in your self-assessment tax return. Landlords can significantly reduce their tax bill and minimise their losses at the same time by doing this.

Don't run before you can walk. A large property portfolio may be your dream but a slow start is the best strategy to employ. Familiarise yourself with how the system works, what to look for in a property, and how to deal with tenants before taking on another rental property. And never forget to do your research carefully before buying another rental property – no matter how experienced you think you have become.

Renting Out in Order to Buy Again

Let-to-buy is growing in popularity. In let-to-buy, homeowners decide that instead of buying another property to rent out, they'd quite like to move somewhere else and rent out their existing home instead. You may want to do this if you have spent a lot of time and effort doing your current property up, and while you and your family may have outgrown it, you think it would make an excellent rental property.

If let-to-buy is your plan, you must notify your mortgage lender and inform them that you want to switch your mortgage over to a buy-to-let loan. (Most landlords then take out a 'regular' mortgage to buy the property they are going to live in similar to the one they had on their first property.)

The mortgage lender is not the only company you have to notify. Insurers often have different policies for rental properties, so don't assume that your current insurance company will continue to offer the same buildings cover on your home as before. You may subsequently find that the insurer refuses to pay out in the event of a claim. It is far better to come clean and make sure you are adequately covered. For example, ensure that your insurance covers you for landlord's risks, which can run into hundreds of thousands for an injury claim.

Not everyone will want to live in a home decorated or furnished to your individual taste. In addition, being dispassionate about a property is harder if you've lived there for many years and spent a lot of time and effort doing it up. Tenants might want something quite different, so if you want to be successful in letting your former home, try to look at it from their point of view.

Chapter 3

Saving Tax on Your Bricks-and-Mortar

*D*eath and taxes: the two things in life that are said to be impossible to avoid. And when it comes to investing in property, there are plenty of taxation rules that you need to get to grips with. These are far more complex than those regarding homeownership but they can work in your favour – as long as you have a general understanding of the basic concepts.

While taxes may be unavoidable, you can reduce them in several ways – completely legitimately – when it comes to investing in property. In this chapter, we look at the taxes you must pay as a property owner and how you can avoid these, saving your hard-earned cash and ensuring your business is as profitable as possible.

Tax is, of course, a taxing subject, and you may find it helpful to have a copy of Tony Levene's *Paying Less Tax 2006/2007 For Dummies* (Wiley) to hand in addition to the information included in this chapter.

Paying Stamp Duty Land Tax and Council Taxes

The UK has two specific property ownership taxes. You have to pay stamp duty land tax on the purchase price of the property. And then there is council tax each year (most pay in monthly instalments). Council tax varies according to where you live as each local authority sets its own rate. How much you pay also depends on the value of your property – the more it's worth, the more you pay.

Stamping on stamp duty

Stamp duty, nowadays more properly known as stamp duty land tax (SDLT), is an extra cost you pay when you buy property. There is no escape. You have to pay stamp duty land tax whether you want to live in the property yourself or are purchasing the property as an investment.

The tax authorities like stamp duty land tax because it is almost impossible to dodge completely as it's all part and parcel of the conveyancing routine that you follow when you purchase property.

The amount of stamp duty land tax you pay depends on the purchase price of the property. Table 3-1 shows the threshold levels and percentage of stamp duty land tax payable.

Table 3-1	Stamp Duty Land Tax Percentages
Purchase Price	*Per Cent Due as Stamp Duty Land Tax*
Up to £125,000	0
£125,001 to £250,000	1
£250,001 to £500,000	3
£500,001 plus	4

Stamp duty land tax is calculated on the price of the property so you pay the rate for the purchase value on the whole sum, not just on the amount over each tax threshold. Buy a house for £250,000 and you pay stamp duty land tax of one per cent, or £2,500. But go up £1 to £250,001 and the whole deal is charged at 3 per cent giving a bill of £7,500 (plus three pennies to be exact). Wherever possible, look for properties priced just below thresholds. House-sellers tend to know there is no point in asking for £251,000, let alone £250,001.

Buying in disadvantaged areas for stamp duty land tax advantages

There are not too many UK properties changing hands at £125,000 or under. But if you buy a house or flat in one of the UK's 2,000 most disadvantaged postcodes, there is no stamp duty land tax payable on properties selling up to £150,000. This can save you up to £1,500. HMRC's Web site at www.hmrc.gov.uk/so has a full list of these areas. Whether you are really better off or whether prices adjust to the stamp duty land tax freedom is not clear.

Seeking advantages without going too far

If you're interested in a property priced a few thousands over the stamp duty land tax threshold amount, look to see if there are items that can be sold separately outside the main property deal so you can bring the price of the house or flat itself below the threshold. Anything portable can fit in this separate category, including curtains, carpets, moveable furniture, washing machines, dishwashers, fridges, pot plants, and some garden sheds. But you can't include fixtures such as fitted kitchens, bedrooms, and bathrooms, or, as some have tried, fuse-boxes, or blades of grass!

The taxman pays especial attention to home purchases just below thresholds to prevent arrangements between buyer and seller to hand over cash so that the purchase price on paper looks lower or to pay ludicrous sums to purchase moveable items. She will be happy with prices that reflect a balance between a willing buyer and a willing seller. Pricing a nearly-new washing machine in good condition at £300 is probably fine. Putting a £3,000 tag on a clapped-out dishwasher is definitely not, even if you claim it's so old that it's a collector's item.

Contributing council tax

Council tax pays part of the cost of local authority provisions such as schools, parks, libraries, and refuse collection. The rate varies widely from area to area but is based on the worth of your property. This value decides which band is used to calculate the amount you pay. In many cases, the band has little connection with the real value of the property. My own home, for instance, was last valued in 1990, although in 2005, the government announced that a new round of valuation will take place . . . some time!

The system sorts out properties into the right order treating small, low-cost properties in the lowest band and huge houses in the highest band. However, if the local authority valuation of your property appears widely inaccurate, you can appeal against this. Your local authority can explain how to do this. Note that few appeals are successful, however.

If you're renting out your property, under the Local Government Finance Act 1992, the tenant is obliged to pay this tax for living in the property. When the property is empty or between tenants, the landlord is responsible for footing the bill. If you rent out a house with multiple residents in their own rooms (a *House in Multiple Occupation*) you may find yourself responsible for collecting

Book II

Finance, Tax, and How to Organise Them

and paying the council tax for your tenants. However, if the house residents are all students, the house will be exempt from this tax.

Council tax is charged on a daily basis, so your tenants are liable for it from the day they move into the rental property until the day they move out. Ensure that when tenants move in that they contact the local authority and get the council tax bill put into their names, so that you don't continue to be liable. You may want to write this letter and send it yourself to ensure it gets done.

If the property is empty, you may be liable for the council tax, depending on whether or not it is furnished. If the property is furnished and empty, you get a discount on the full amount; the size of this depends on the local authority. If the property is unfurnished and empty, no council tax is paid for the first six months. After this time, if the property is still empty, you have to pay the discounted charge – whether the property is furnished or not.

While tenants are responsible for council tax in most rental properties, this is not the case when a house is in multiple occupation (HMO). Check out Book V, Chapter 1 for more details on properties that are defined as being HMOs. If the property is an HMO, the owner is responsible for paying the council tax rather than the tenants. For council tax purposes, the definition of multiple occupation includes any dwelling inhabited by persons who do not constitute a single household, all of whom have the right to occupy only part of the house. Working out whether people sharing a house constitute a single household or not can be difficult. If in doubt, include a provision in the tenancy agreement allowing you to increase the rent by the amount of any council tax you might end up paying on the rental property.

Avoiding Capital Gains Tax

Capital gains is income generated when possessions, including property (which is not your main residence), are sold for a profit. You won't have to pay capital gains tax (CGT) until you actually come to sell your property.

Every person has a CGT allowance – £9,200 in 2007–08 tax year – so any profits above this amount are taxed. Each person has their own annual allowance so if you own a property jointly with a spouse, you can subtract a total of £18,400 (2007–08) from the profits you make before any tax is due.

There are other allowances and expenses which can be deducted from this profit, thereby reducing the CGT you have to pay. For example, you can legitimately set against tax all the costs incurred in the purchase of the property, such as:

    ✔ Stamp duty land tax.

    ✔ Legal fees.

    ✔ Cost of capital improvements – renovating and furnishing the rental property.

    ✔ Accountancy fees.

When calculating the CGT you owe, inflation also plays a part. This is known as *taper relief* and is based on how long you have owned the property. The longer you own the property, the less you are taxed on any profit you make from the sale because the indexed gain is tapered. There is no taper for the first two years, but after that, the taxable gain is discounted by 5 per cent per year up to a maximum of 40 per cent for properties owned for 10 years or more.

CGT is calculated at the same rate as income tax. So if you are a higher rate taxpayer, CGT is paid at a flat rate of 40 per cent. If you are a basic rate taxpayer, what remains of your lower and basic rate tax bands is used up (£34,600 for 2007–08) in total, with tax on any remaining amount at the higher rate of 40 per cent.

For example, if you bought a property for £200,000 and sold it for £300,000, your profit would be £100,000. You then subtract your annual allowance – £9,200 – leaving a profit of £90,800. Say the cost of purchasing the property amounted to £15,000, this leaves you with a taxable profit of £75,800. Assuming you pay CGT at 40 per cent, this will leave a tax bill of £30,320.

CGT can be incredibly complicated and very expensive if you aren't sure what you are entitled to and what allowances you can offset against income. It is well worth getting an accountant or tax adviser to advise you before you come to sell one of your rental properties.

Avoiding Income Tax for Landlords

The main tax you must pay is on your income. When calculating what tax you owe, HMRC takes all sorts of income into account, including your wages, bonuses and commission, rents, dividends, and interest. This income is taxed at various rates up to 40 per cent.

Landlords have to pay income tax on any profits they make from their rental property. But you can reduce the tax you pay – completely legitimately – by deducting all operating expenses from rental income. Operating expenses that can be deducted include:

Book II

Finance, Tax, and How to Organise Them

- Cost of maintenance and repairs.

- Management fees.

- Advertising costs.

- Accountancy and legal fees (although not those incurred on the sale or purchase of property).

- Service charge and ground rent (where applicable).

- Travelling expenses.

- Insurance.

- Interest paid on mortgage debt and other finance costs.

The initial cost of buying the rental property is a *capital outlay*, not an allowable expense. Sometimes there's a very fine line between capital outlay and expenses that are allowable deductions from income so the situation can become confusing. For example, if your rental property is in a lettable state when you buy it and you give it a lick of paint, such redecoration costs are allowed against rents received. However, if the property was dilapidated when you bought it so you got it cheap but then had to spend several thousand pounds on renovations, you wouldn't be able to claim the cost of these against the rent.

Many capital expenses will be deductible at a later date – when you come to sell the property (see 'Avoiding Capital Gains Tax' earlier in this chapter). Be sure to keep receipts for when the time comes.

Many landlords opt for interest-only mortgages. There are two advantages in doing this. The first is that monthly payments are lower than on a repayment mortgage – where some of the capital is repaid each month along with the interest – although you will need to pay the capital back at the end of the mortgage term (you can always sell the property to do this). The other advantage of an interest-only deal is that the total monthly amount can be offset against the rental income for income tax purposes. If you opt for a buy-to-let mortgage on a repayment basis you can deduct only the interest portion from the rental income when calculating how much tax is due: it is a more complex calculation and you will have to pay tax on the repayment part. See Chapter 2 for more information on interest-only and repayment mortgages.

If you let more than one property, these are treated as a single property business for tax purposes. The advantage of this is that if you make profits on one property and losses on another, these will cancel each other out. It is also much easier to complete your tax return as you do one for all your properties and are spared the effort of filling in one for each property.

Tax on deposit money

You don't have to pay tax on deposits you receive from tenants until these deposits become income. When received, the deposits are a liability that must be paid back to the tenants at a later time, after deductions are made for damage to the property and your furniture, or cleaning. However, after your tenant vacates the property and you withhold a portion of the deposit, it may be classified as income. Essentially, the deposit isn't taxable as long as you have an expense for the same amount as the deduction. Under the Tenancy Deposit Protection legislation that came into effect in April 2007, landlords no longer have control over how much money is deducted from the deposit, particularly in the custodial scheme. Therefore, money approved for deduction from the deposit is of necessity equal to the actual cost of any repairs. If this stuff about Tenancy Deposit Protection is new to you, take a look at Book 4, Chapter 3.

Book II

Finance, Tax, and How to Organise Them

Allowances on furnished property

If your rental property is furnished, you can claim a deduction for the net cost of replacing a particular item of furniture or furnishings. However, you cannot claim for the cost of the original purchase of the item.

Alternatively, you can opt for an annual allowance for wear and tear, which is offset against your income. This allowance is 10 per cent of your annual rental income after deducting charges or services that would normally be borne by a tenant but are actually being borne by the landlord, such as council tax (see 'Contributing council tax' earlier in this chapter).

You must choose whether you want to opt for a deduction for a specific item or an annual wear and tear allowance. Once you've made your decision you must stick with it; HMRC does not allow you to chop and change between the two.

Advanced Tax Avoidance Tips

The best way of ensuring you don't pay more tax than is absolutely necessary is to plan ahead. Seeking professional advice is worthwhile long before you reach the stage where you have to pay tax to ensure you don't miss any opportunities. If you leave it too late, it may cost you.

Making the most of interest deduction

Here's a tip that can get you a tax-deductible loan to use in your life outside of buy-to-let. Very few people know about it as those that do are paranoid HMRC will stop it if it becomes widely publicised.

It's known to the tax cognoscenti as *Paragraph 45,700* after the number in an HMRC internal manual. It enables you to remortgage a property for a greater sum than the original loan and use the cash released for any purpose whatsoever, not necessarily for the property. This means you can be getting tax relief on your highest personal tax rate for cash you use to buy a yacht or a car or a round-the-world cruise.

The one proviso is that the new loan cannot be greater than the market value of the property when it was first used in the letting business.

Here's how it works. Suppose you bought a house 10 years ago for £100,000. It is now worth £250,000 and you decide you want to move to another town and to a better property but let out this house. The market value is £250,000 so you can borrow up to £250,000 and offset the interest against rental income. You repay the original £100,000 mortgage leaving you with £150,000 to spend where the interest is tax-deductible.

A more common scenario is where you bought a buy-to-let for £100,000 but were restricted to an 80 per cent loan. The property is now worth £125,000 so you can take out a remortgage for £100,000 (80 per cent of £125,000). This remains within the rules, as you have not borrowed more than the value of the property when it became a buy-to-let. You now have £20,000 to spend as you wish, with the taxman picking up part of the interest payments.

A third possibility is where you buy 'off-plan' (that is purchasing before the property is built) at a discount. If the off-plan cost is £150,000 you will borrow against that. But once complete, and hence available for letting, the property is worth, say, £200,000. The taxman will allow tax-deductible interest on a loan up to £200,000.

Although these strategies may work well in rising market, obviously they won't work so well when the market is static or declining. You can obtain useful mortgage and tax advice at the Mortgage Trust Web site (www.mortgage trust.co.uk).

Share and share alike: owning property with someone else

Owning property jointly with one or more other people can have a positive impact on your tax bill. However, the extent of the savings you make depends on how you are related to the person you are buying with. Below, we look at the tax advantages of joint ownership, as well as the specific advantages of buying with a spouse or civil partner.

Joint ownership

There are a number of tax reliefs and bands that every person is entitled to. So when you buy a property with one or more people, you have double, triple, or even more the value of these.

For example, everyone has a personal allowance; an annual CGT exemption; a lower rate, basic-rate tax band; as well as a nil-rate band for inheritance tax purposes. So if you are a higher-rate taxpayer and buy a property with a basic-rate taxpayer, it is assumed that you own it 50:50. So instead of 40 per cent tax payable on the total profit, half the profits will be subject to tax at a rate of 22 per cent.

It is not just income tax where joint ownership can result in savings. When you sell the rental property, each person has their own annual CGT allowance so both count towards any profit made. Thus, if each person has an annual CGT allowance of £9,200, £18,400 can be deducted from profits before any tax is payable.

Several tax reliefs and bands don't necessarily make it advantageous to purchase property with another person. Stamp duty land tax is still payable in full, for example, no matter how many of you are buying the property together, although of course you should be able to split the cost between you.

You can save income tax by ensuring the property is in joint names or even in the sole name of the person with the lower overall income. If one of you pays tax at 40 per cent and the other 22 per cent, it makes sense for at least half (if not all) of the property to be in the lower taxpayer's name so less tax is due. If you don't decide this initially at the time of purchase it is possible to transfer a share later on – by consulting a solicitor – but it makes sense to plan ahead and do this from the start.

Buying with a spouse or civil partner

Spouses and civil partners who buy property together can benefit from the same advantages as those of joint owners. But the main additional advantage of being married or having a registered civil partnership is that you can transfer assets between the two of you without incurring CGT or other charges. In some instances, an outright transfer of the whole property to your spouse – if they don't work or pay less tax than you – may be beneficial. But if you have bought with someone who isn't a spouse or civil partner, tax must be paid.

Taking on holiday homes

If you have a furnished country cottage that you rent out to holidaymakers, or a city centre flat desirable for tourists, or a caravan you're willing to rent out, then you can be in the furnished holiday accommodation game and set up for tax savings.

Don't worry if your property is not in the midst of a national park or does not enjoy stunning views of the Thames or Edinburgh Castle. To qualify, the property can be anywhere, not just in an area desirable to holidaymakers.

The tax inspector will see your property as a spare-time business provided you follow these 'furnished holiday lettings' rules.

- ✔ The property must be in the UK – anywhere.

- ✔ It must be furnished so it can be used immediately (but you don't necessarily have to provide sheets and towels).

- ✔ The rent charged must be commercial, with a view to profits.

- ✔ The accommodation must be available to the public for at least 140 days a year. And it must be occupied by paying customers for at least 70 days each year.

- ✔ For at least 7 months each year, the property cannot be occupied by the same people for more than 31 days continuously.

   If you own more than one property, you can average the occupancy periods.

Looking at what you get from a holiday let

You can offset loan interest against the rental income. The cost of the furniture and other items such as washing machines and crockery can be set off against tax. You can also claim tax against costs such as advertising, agents' fees, insurance, and council tax. If you make a loss, you may be able to deduct that from your other income.

And, of course, there is no rule to prevent you enjoying a few weeks in your own property. Always assuming you want to because it's somewhere attractive!

Running a furnished holiday let is counted as a trade. It's taxable under Schedule D, similar to most other self-employment activities but unlike buy-to-let. This means you can save tax by buying a personal pension with part of your holiday let earnings.

If you sell your furnished holiday let at a profit, you can claim business taper relief on any Capital Gains Tax (CGT) bill.

Dealing with your overseas holiday home

Money you make from renting out a house or flat outside the UK is treated in much the same way as a holiday let in this country. You can offset your costs, including interest, against the rental income.

But non-UK letting activities have to be kept separate from those within the UK. And you may have to pay tax in the country where your property is situated. Such tax payments can generally be counted as credits against UK tax payments so you won't have to pay twice.

Moving in tenants over your shop

There are special tax incentives for converting unused or storage space over shops into habitable accommodation. These *flat conversion allowances* come with rules. They are intended for tenants whose agreement runs from one to five years, the flats must not have more than four rooms (excluding hallway, kitchen, and bathroom) and the property must be accessible directly from the street and not through the downstairs business. Needless to say, you can't live there yourself.

You can set all the renovation costs against the rent you receive from tenants in the first year. But you can carry over the costs into following years so you may not have to pay any tax on the rent for some time!

And the rules cease to apply if the rental is very high. HMRC publishes weekly rent limits for London and outside London, adjusting them from time to time.

Moving into big-time property ownership

Serious property investors who are prepared for a long haul (and taking quite a bit of risk) can save tax through Enterprise Zone schemes. *Enterprise Zone schemes* involve buying new (or up to two years old) commercial buildings such as factories, office blocks, and shops in certain designated areas with a view to owning them for 25 years. You can do this on your own if you are really rich, or through specially set-up syndicates known as *Enterprise Zone Property Trusts*. You get full tax relief on the investment in the buildings but not on the cost of the land. And you can offset any interest payments against other income.

This type of property ownership is strictly for top-rate taxpayers who are happy to invest for up to the next 25 years. In practice, however, they carry high risks and many of them have failed to meet investor expectations.

Thinking about Inheritance Tax

Many people don't realise that inheritance tax (IHT) is payable on their estate after their death. This is because IHT is no longer a tax on the rich: any estate worth more than £300,000 (2007–08 tax year) is liable, as the threshold hasn't kept in line with house price growth. IHT can create quite a dent in what you leave your beneficiaries as it is payable at a rate of 40 per cent. But with a bit of forward planning it is possible to avoid paying this tax – or at least reduce the amount you pay.

If your estate passes to your spouse or civil partner, there is no IHT to pay. But this is not particularly tax-efficient. Each person has a nil-rate band, so it is worth utilising both of these to reduce the tax payable. For example, if a husband leaves his share of the property to his wife on his death, she pays no IHT. But when she dies and leaves the property to their children, only her nil-rate band can be utilised (meaning the first £300,000 (2007–08) is tax-free). However, if he had given his share direct to the children, they could have utilised his nil-rate band (meaning the first £300,000 would be tax-free and then when their mother died, the first £300,000 of her share would also be tax-free). Therefore, they inherit £600,000 in total before they have to pay any tax.

Writing a will – and keeping it updated

The most important step you can take is to make a tax-efficient will. This sets out who gets what when you die. Make sure you take into account both your own nil-rate band and your partner's when doing any IHT planning.

Writing a will is fairly straightforward; contact a solicitor (look in the Yellow Pages for details of one near you) to do this. For more on wills, grab a copy of Julian Knight's *Wills, Probate & Inheritance Tax For Dummies* (Wiley).

Giving it away

If your estate exceeds the nil-rate band it may be necessary to give some of your belongings away during your lifetime – rather than waiting until you die. You can give away as much as you wish, without paying any tax, as long as you live for seven years after making the gift. Keep a record of such gifts and ensure it is in a place where it is easy to find.

Establishing a trust

A trust is a legal arrangement enabling you to give away assets, such as property, in a tax-efficient and controlled way for the benefit of nominated individuals. It can be set up during your lifetime or on your death, as stated in your will.

Many people use a discretionary trust to hold property for the benefit of stated people, such as their spouse, children, and other relatives. Trustees have control over the funds but you can direct them as to when beneficiaries can get their hands on the assets.

Many tax benefits can be derived from a trust but make sure you understand exactly what you are getting into. Seek advice from a trust specialist.

Chapter 4

Using a Company to Hold Your Property

In This Chapter

▶ Recognising the advantages of using a company to purchase property

▶ Avoiding the pitfalls

▶ Setting up a company

Many property investors want to know whether they should use a company to purchase their property or buy it as an individual or via a partnership. This isn't as straightforward a question as it seems. Many factors need to be taken into account; otherwise you could find you are making a huge mistake by choosing one option over another.

The tax regime for companies is very different to that for individuals or partnerships. This chapter examines the pros and cons of using a company so that you understand what's involved. We also give help on setting up a company – if you decide it's the right course of action for you – and details on how to place property you already own into a company.

Understanding the Pros of Using a Company

Using a company to purchase property rather than as an individual or via a partnership has several advantages. Much depends on your investment strategy, ambitions, and how long you intend to hold onto the properties for. The main advantages are explained in more detail in the following sections.

For more information on your setting up as a company, and on your tax responsibilities, pick up a copy of Tony Levene's *Paying Less Tax 2006/2007 For Dummies* (Wiley), and Colin Barrow's *Starting A Business For Dummies* (Wiley).

Beneficial tax regime

The main reason investors use a company to purchase property is to save tax. A limited company pays corporation tax on all its profits, including income and capital gains. Corporation tax is charged at lower rates than higher-rate income tax. The maximum effective corporation tax rate is 30 per cent, compared with 40 per cent for a higher-rate taxpayer holding property outside a company. The Small Companies Rate (SCR) is currently 20 per cent rising to 22 per cent over the next two years.

Companies choose their own year-end accounting date, unlike individuals who must use the end of the tax year (5 April). Opting for the conventional tax year to bring your company tax conveniently in line with your personal tax is often a good idea, though.Companies must also work out their own tax liability and must pay any tax owed to HMRC within nine months of their financial year end. Interest is charged at a commercial rate on late payments.

The corporation tax self-assessment form must be filed to HMRC within 12 months of the company's financial year-end or you are liable for penalties.

Deciding to use a company to purchase property simply on the basis of corporation tax rates may turn out to be extremely short sighted. Look at the bigger picture and avoid making a snap decision.

Limited liability

One of the biggest worries facing landlords is what might happen if a tenant sues after having an accident in their rental property. For example, if a tenant falls down the stairs, which are later found to be faulty. If the tenant sues the landlord, the cost could be prohibitive. It may result in the landlord having to sell the rental property, or even their own home, to raise the compensation payable to the tenant. However, it should not be too difficult to ensure that you are adequately insured with landlord's Insurance to fully cover this risk. Other major risks with property investing exist, however, which it is not possible to insure against.

The advantage of a limited company is that it is a separate legal entity, responsible for its own debts and other liabilities. Your liability is strictly limited to your direct investment in the company: you are not personally responsible for any liabilities, debts, or charges for which the business is liable. So if your tenant does fall down the stairs, the limit of your liability is the amount you have invested in the company. The tenant can't come after any of your assets that are held outside the company, such as your own home. If you buy property as a sole proprietor or via a partnership there is no protection for your own assets or your partner's, and all your assets are potentially at risk.

Flexible ownership

Property held outside a company is generally in the names of two or three people at most. If you are the sole owner of a property, transferring ownership to others is complicated. But if a company owns the property, getting more investors involved is easier. Many people start their business small but then want to involve family members or others later on. A company structure makes this far easier to achieve.

If you want to pass a property onto a family member, a capital gains tax (CGT) is paid if the property is held outside a company. But if the property is inside a limited company, that family member can subscribe for some shares. The ownership can then pass from you to someone else tax-free, because the value of the transfer is held over for CGT purposes.

A limited company can also be advantageous in retirement. You may decide you want to stop working but want the business to keep going. Using a company structure means you can retain ownership as a shareholder but still pass on the day-to-day management to someone else.

Status

Creating the right impression is a vital part of business and a company sounds more professional than a business in your own name. Putting 'Limited' after your name tends to make people think you are perhaps a bigger organisation and more professional than a one-man band. This may be helpful in encouraging potential tenants to rent one of your properties or persuading investors to take a stake in your company.

Spotting the Cons of Using a Company

Using a company to hold your rental property isn't all plain sailing – otherwise, all property investors would do this instead of owning it as an individual or via a partnership. The company framework tends to mean increased bureaucracy, paperwork, and expensive accounting administration compared with holding property outside a company.

Considering whether the financial savings are sufficient to compensate for the time running a company inevitably takes up is vital. Although corporation tax rates appear attractive compared to personal tax rates, these may be outweighed in the longer term by the difficulty in extracting gains from the company. If you sell property you own outside a company, once you have paid any CGT you owe, the remaining cash is yours. You also get an annual exemption for CGT purposes, so are not liable for tax on the whole amount – which isn't the case if you sell property owned by a company. But if you sell property owned through a company, corporation tax is payable on any gain.

There is no *taper relief* (which reduces CGT) for capital gains purposes either if it is held in a company. For individuals, the longer you hold an asset, the more taper relief you get, reducing the CGT you owe.

If you, or any member of your family, are planning on using any of the properties held by the company for personal use, severe tax consequences could arise. Compare this with the CGT benefits of personal use when investing in property directly.

Obtaining relief for certain administrative expenses, such as using your home as an office or motor expenses, may also be more difficult when investing through a company.

Consulting a tax planning specialist before you make any changes to your financial position is a good idea. He can help you consider your overall financial position in relation to your property assets and family tax planning.

Setting Up a Property Company

Setting up a company is fairly straightforward and probably easier than you might think. Companies House (`www.companieshouse.gov.uk`) can advise on the basics of registering, but can't give detailed advice. Most solicitors and accountants can set up a company on your behalf, with some providing off-the-shelf companies. Alternatively, you can use a company formation agent, who will advise you and carry out the process for you. Look in your local Yellow Pages or on the Internet for details of these. You can also look at company formation by using one of the do-it-yourself legal kits at `www.Lawpack.co.uk`.

You could handle the registration process yourself but it is worth seeking professional advice to ensure you don't make any mistakes.

Before you can begin operating as a limited company, you must register with Companies House or the Companies Registry for Northern Ireland, depending on where you live. You will need:

- ✔ **A Memorandum of Association:** This gives details of the company's name, location, and states what the company will do, such as borrow money, buy or sell land and property, and rent out property. It also sets out the framework for the share structure.

- ✔ **Articles of Association:** This describes how the company will be run, shareholders' rights, and the power of the directors of the company.

- ✔ **Form 10 (Statement of the First Directors, Secretary, and Registered Office):** This details the company's registered office, as well as names and addresses of the directors and company secretary.

- ✔ **Form 12 (Declaration of Compliance with the Requirements of the Companies Act):** This states that the company meets all the legal requirements of incorporation.

Book II

Finance,
Tax, and
How to
Organise
Them

For downloadable forms relating to company registration in England and Wales, go to the Companies House Web site at www.companieshouse.gov.uk or if you're in Northern Ireland, the Web site of the Department of Enterprise, Trade and Industry online at www.detini.gov.uk.

Private or public?

You must decide whether you want your company to be a private limited company or a public limited company (PLC). Most small businesses opt to become a private limited company because they have no intention of being quoted on the stock market.

PLCs also require share capital of at least £50,000, while such companies must also have two shareholders, two directors, and a qualified company secretary. If you opt for a private company, you must appoint at least one director and a company secretary. The same person can't undertake both roles.

Choosing a name

It may sound a simple enough task but you can't call your company the same name as another company. You may also want to avoid names that are similar to those of existing companies. It may be worth getting 'Property' somewhere in the title so that prospective tenants and investors know exactly what the company does.

The company will need a registered office address, where the name of the company should be prominently displayed. The name should also be displayed on your stationery, letters, receipts, invoices, and cheques.

Registering to pay tax

Once you have registered your company, and decided on a registered office address, Companies House passes on your details to HMRC. But you must ensure that you also contact your local tax office to let them know that your company exists. If you don't you may be fined.

HMRC sends you form CT41G. This must be completed and returned in order to get the company into the Corporation Tax system. You must do this within three months of starting your business activities or penalties are imposed. You must also register the company as an employer for PAYE purposes or for VAT, if either is applicable.

Placing Existing Property into a New Company

While you may have set up a company to buy property in the future, you may already have property that you would like to transfer over. The problem is that as you already own the property you are trying to place in your company, you could potentially be liable for a huge CGT bill if you transfer it over. Careful timing and the use of annual exemptions and taper relief might make it possible to do the transfers without having to pay any, or much in the way of, tax. Seek specialist tax advice to ensure you don't pay more tax than you need to.

If the property has been your main residence at any time in the previous three years it may usually be transferred tax-free into a property investment company.

While certain reliefs minimise potential CGT bills incurred when transferring property you already own into a company, avoiding a hefty tax bill entirely is difficult. In most cases you should keep the company for future investments and leave your existing properties as they are.

Chapter 5

Recordkeeping and Financial Management

In This Chapter

▶ Setting up a filing system to keep track of your paperwork

▶ Hanging on to the records you need for the right amount of time

▶ Taking advantage of computer software to help you with your accounting

*I*f you ask a group of property investors what their least favourite part of the job is, you'll probably hear 'the paperwork' more than any other response. Most owners don't mind the hands-on aspects of managing their properties, like cleaning or painting; many of them even enjoy it. And meeting prospective tenants and showing the property is fun compared to recording when the rent is paid, sending out late notices, and writing out cheques to pay the bills. But the financial management aspects of accounting for all the funds you receive and expend are critical elements of running your rental housing venture. In this chapter, we show you how to do it.

Organising Your Files

If you have an aversion to keeping track of documents, then managing properties may not be for you. If you own property, you need to prepare many important written records and keep them ready for prompt retrieval. Every property investor must have a basic filing system with separate records kept for each property.

If you own one or even a few properties, your filing system can be a simple box file with dividers, available at any office supply shop. If you own more properties and your box file is overflowing, moving up to a filing cabinet (preferably one that is lockable) makes sense.

The property ownership file

From the moment you take your first steps towards purchasing an investment property, begin storing your paperwork in a property ownership file. Keep all the important documents relating to the property in this file, including purchase offers and contracts, structural surveys, mortgage loan, insurance policies, pest control reports, and correspondence. Also keep a photocopy of your deeds in the property file and place the original in a fireproof safe or bank safety deposit box.

Separate files for each property

Each of your properties should have its own file with separate folders for income items, as well as a separate folder for each of the property's expenses. Keep copies of all receipts in the expense folders so that when you come to file your tax return, you can easily locate the information you need.

We recommend keeping a master maintenance file for the records and receipts for all maintenance and capital improvements of each property. Doing so gives you a history of the physical condition of each property throughout your ownership of it.

Tenant files

In addition to having a file for expenses and income, landlords should create a tenant file for each rental property containing all the important documents for each specific tenant, including his rental application, tenancy agreement, and all other legal notices, tenant maintenance requests, and correspondence. Always keep the original of each document and provide the tenant with a photocopy.

You may opt to keep many of these files on your computer, but for owners of only a few properties, a manual system is fine.

Use a system for recording all significant tenant complaints and maintenance requests. This will provide a valuable paper trail if a dispute ever arises regarding your conduct as a landlord in properly maintaining the premises. Failing to have good records could very well result in a court dispute being determined solely on your word against your tenant's word – and the odds aren't good under such circumstances.

When your tenants move out, attach a copy of their Deposit Itemisation report (of which more details can be found in Book V, Chapter 5) and bind the entire tenant file together. Transfer it to a separate file for all former tenants, filed alphabetically by property.

Insurance file

Insurance is such an important issue that you should have a master insurance file that contains current policies for all types of insurance cover on all your properties (you can find out more about insurance in Book IV, Chapter 5). This file should also have a calendar on which you can track the expiration or renewal dates for each policy and ensure that you have requested competitive bids well in advance of the policy expiration date. Keeping accurate records of any incident reports or claims made on your insurance policy is critical as well.

Book II

Finance, Tax, and How to Organise Them

Maintaining Property Records

Maintaining complete and accurate records of all transactions is extremely important in the world of property management. An inventory, for example, is vitally important for landlords to avoid disputes with tenants when they come to move out of the property; you can use the inventory to account for any deductions in their deposit. If a dispute between you and your tenant does end up in court, having documents outlining the understanding between the parties makes life a lot easier. If you can't provide the required records, your tenant will have a stronger case than he or she otherwise would have.

But maintaining proper records is also important because you have to report your income and expenses for each property on your annual self-assessment tax return to determine whether you've made a profit. HMRC requires all property investors to substantiate all income and expenses by maintaining proper records, including detailed receipts of all transactions. You don't want to be in a situation where you can't support the accuracy of your tax return, particularly if the taxman asks to see the evidence.

The following tips should help you to keep on top of your records:

✔ Document your income in a notebook and keep all bank deposit slips and statements. Rental property expenses, even if you write a business cheque, should have a written receipt to fully document the expenditure. HMRC may not accept a cheque as proof of a deductible property expense unless you have a detailed receipt to back it up.

- Develop and assign a one- or two-character code for each property you own (if you have several properties) and mark each receipt accordingly. When you have information for several properties on a single receipt, make photocopies and store the receipts in the folders you've set up for your respective properties. This way, you can provide evidence of the expense for each property instead of having to wade through all your folders looking for the information you need.

- Keep all receipts, bank statements, and invoices for at least six years in case HMRC decides to conduct an investigation. For taxation purposes, you need to maintain records regarding the purchase and capital improvements made during your ownership for as long as you own the property. Certain rental property records such as those concerning injuries to children should be maintained forever.

If you are using your car to visit your property, make sure you keep a detailed written log of all your mileage. Your mileage is a deductible business expense as long as it is directly related to your property and you have accurate records to document the mileage. This simple log should indicate the date, destination, purpose, and total number of miles travelled. You may be surprised at the number of miles you travel each year in your investing activities – and the deductible expense can be substantial.

Taking Care of Business: Rental Property Accounting

HMRC does not require you to keep a separate bank account for each rental property that you own, but you do need to keep your rental property activities separate from your personal transactions.

If you only have a few rental properties, you may be able to keep track of your tenants' rent payments in your head. But don't rely on your memory. Always track each rental payment in writing. The best policy is to provide a receipt whenever possible, regardless of the method of payment.

Be sure to accurately record the payment of a tenant's deposit. These funds are typically not considered income; instead, they are a future liability that is owed back to the tenant if the tenant honours the terms and conditions of the tenancy agreement. The deposit may become income at a later date, if you apply any portion of it to cover delinquent rent, cleaning, repairs, or other charges. (See Chapter 3 for details about when the deposit changes from a future liability to income.)

If you manage your own property and do your own accounting, it's important to actually review and analyse your finances in the same manner as a professional property manager would. You may think that you know everything you need to know about your rental property, and setting aside your finances until the end of the tax year may seem harmless, but financial management (and an understanding of your current financial situation) is an important skill for any landlord to master.

Creating a budget and managing your cash flow

Every landlord should have a *budget*. A budget is a detailed estimate of the future income and expenses of a property for a certain time period, usually one year. A budget allows you to anticipate and track the expected income and expenses for your rental property. Many landlords neglect to allocate and hold back enough money for projected expenses, so when the time comes to make a repair, for example, they don't have the money set aside to cover it. But if you set up a budget, you'll be better able to anticipate your expenses.

Although the budget for a small family rental property is fairly simple, a proper budget is essential if you own several properties, which require more careful planning. That planning includes a thorough review of past expenses and the current condition of the property. Trends in expenses, such as utilities, can also be important when estimating the future cash flow of a rental property, so be sure you don't overlook them.

Many landlords rely on cash flow from their rental properties not only to cover their expenses, but also to supplement their personal income. But you need to have a built-in reserve fund set aside before you start taking out any rental income funds for personal reasons, particularly if you're a small-time landlord. Maintain a reserve balance large enough to pay your mortgage and all the basic property expenses for *at least* one month without relying on any rental income.

Set up a bank account in which you set aside money for anticipated major capital improvements. For example, you may own a rental property that will need a new roof in the next five years. Rather than see your cash flow wiped out for several months when the time comes to pay for that new roof, begin setting aside small amounts of money into a capital reserve account over several years.

Don't forget to allocate funds to cover bi-annual and annual expenses such as council tax (if you pay it) and potential income tax due on your rental property net income. You can read about these and other outgoings in Chapter 3.

Book II

Finance, Tax, and How to Organise Them

Using computers for financial management

Most landlords begin investing in property with a small house or flat. At this level, the accounting is extremely simple, and you can do it manually with pen and paper in a simple spiral notebook. But when you expand to a property portfolio comprising several rental flats or houses, you need to look for better and more efficient systems that are geared to the specific needs of rental property bookkeeping. Consider using a computer and a spreadsheet or general accounting software. Doing so can make your life a lot easier because, once set up, using a computerised system makes it quicker to record the information you need and simpler to review it.

Many basic software spreadsheets (such as Microsoft Excel) should handle your needs if you own a handful of rental properties. But you might want to opt for more specialised software, such as a general business accounting package. Good software providing this service is the entry-level Personal Accountz and the more advanced QuickBooks or Peachtree Accounting. This software can handle and streamline all the basic accounting requirements of a landlord managing several rental properties. You can customise the financial reporting offered by software to meet your needs. Monthly reports often contain income and expense information compared to the monthly budget, as well as year-to-date numbers.

While this software is useful, keep in mind that it lacks specific rental-housing industry information and reporting that are invaluable to effective property management.

If you want more help managing and organising your rental properties, *Property Intellect* (Wild Rabbit Software) is an easy software package to use. This includes inventories, space for details of your rental properties, and options to add in automatic tenancy agreement generation and inventory taking. *Landlords Property Tax Manager* (Property Tax Portal) is another powerful software package enabling you to manage your properties, tenants, finances, and even calculate your tax liability.

The US has a much wider range of professional rental accounting software programs for landlords. These programs are aimed at those with scores of rental properties. Recommended programs include *Tenant Pro for Windows* and *Yardi Professional* (yes, we know – this one sounds more like a hitman than a computer program). They typically offer the following:

- ✔ Complete accounting (general ledger, accounts receivable, accounts payable with cheque writing, budgeting, and financial reporting)
- ✔ Tenant management, including many standard rental management forms

✔ Tenant service requests, timetabling maintenance work, and reminder notes

✔ Additional services such as tenant screening and utility billing

As you can imagine, American landlords find these packages very useful. But as they are designed for landlords with at least 100 rental properties, they aren't really necessary for the majority of UK property managers.

Most UK landlords who don't use manual accounting will probably opt for more basic accounting software to ease the process of running your rental property business. Before picking this software, gather as much information as possible. Be sure to talk to actual users of the product, preferably people who have comparable rental properties and similar accounting needs. Determine what features the software offers, how easy it is to operate, the computer hardware requirements, the availability and cost of technical support, and the strength and reputation of the company backing the product. Try to get hold of a demo or trial version of the software that you can use before you buy, just to make sure it's what you want. Or at least ask your landlord friends to give you a quick demo of how the package works. You can find a list of one hundred or so basic and professional UK property management software packages on the www.landlordzone.co.uk Web site directory by clicking on 'Software'.

Book II

Finance, Tax, and How to Organise Them

Hiring a professional number-cruncher

Although rental property accounting is fairly straightforward, you may not have the time or inclination to do it yourself. If you aren't prepared to handle your own accounting and recordkeeping, hire an accountant to handle it for you. Alternatively, try to find a lettings agent who's willing to just perform rental property accounting services for a fee. Your local phone book is a good place to begin your search.

When you use an agent you typically receive several important accounting reports within a couple of weeks after the end of each accounting month. If you review these reports regularly, you can get a lot of information. These reports can provide you with a good understanding of your rental investments and give you the opportunity to enquire about or suggest changes in operations.

Chapter 6

Financing Abroad

*F*inding your dream property may be the first bit of research you have to do, but it isn't the last. Getting the money together to make the purchase go smoothly is every bit as vital as finding the house. Money may make the world go round, but when you are buying a property abroad your main concern is to make your money go round the world, or part way round at any rate.

You need your money to move safely, quickly, and without losing too much value on its travels. We explain how in this chapter.

Moving Money Around

Having money is clearly essential if you are hoping to play any part in the property game – but you also need to have enough of it in the right place at the right time. You have lots of ways to get your money from A to B, but all involve costs and the possibility of the sum shrinking as it travels. In fact, some methods are not only unnecessarily costly – they expose your hard-earned cash to greater dangers than are necessary. This section explores your money-transfer and exchange options.

Understanding exchange rate risks

Any property purchase takes time. The longer a purchase takes, the longer you are exposed to currency market forces that can make your payments unpredictable. Most European countries try to ensure that their local currencies move within a narrow band of the euro. (The pound sterling also moves, informally, in some harmony with the euro.)

But none of these rules ensures that the value of any currency is stable over time. During my first spell of living abroad, which amounted to five years, sterling depreciated by 20 per cent against the currency I paid my bills in. That is like having a fifth sliced out of your monthly pension or pay packet – a very serious sum of money.

Using credit or debit cards

Using a British credit or debit card is probably the easiest and simplest way of moving money from the UK to another country for day-to-day expenses, food, fuel, meals out, and hotel bills. However, you may find in some countries that your card is less than welcome, as the credit card charge may eat up around half the profit the retailer expects to make on a transaction. (Of course, you can usually find one of Europe's many hole-in-the-wall locations with an automated teller machine (ATM) and draw out up to about €300 each day without too much trouble.)

If you do plan to use your card extensively abroad, let your card supplier know in advance. Otherwise your card may be rejected, as banking software is now programmed to rapidly detect any potentially abnormal purchases.

Credit and debit card companies often make a *foreign currency conversion charge* of around 1 per cent on all overseas transactions. Some actually charge as much as 2.75 per cent, though the figures are fairly hard to spot in the currency conversion process. Always build this cost into your thinking when paying for a purchase by card. Remember that you are also dealing in real time, so fluctuations of the euro or the local currency against sterling, or whatever currency your credit card operates in, are reflected immediately in your credit card purchases.

If you have an offshore euro account with a credit card, currency exchange isn't an issue when you make purchases in euros. If you're buying outside the euro zone, you still have the problem of putting money into your offshore account in your domestic currency.

While credit and debit cards are helpful to move small sums around, they are not much use for paying regular utility bills or moving the larger sums needed to buy your property.

Paying with personal cheques

You can potentially receive personal or business cheques, say for interest and dividends, and arrange to have them paid direct into your overseas bank account. Likewise, you may be able to find a creditor abroad brave enough to take a personal cheque. However, such transactions can take a while to clear, involve some additional charges, and expose you to the vagaries of the bank's rate of exchange for the currencies in question.

A banker's draft is another option – this is a bit like a cheque but as it is drawn by the bank itself, anyone receiving a banker's draft can usually rely on it as being as good as money after it's in their hands. The problems with banker's drafts are much the same as with personal cheques – they can be slow and costly tools for getting money from A to B, and if you lose one the money could be lost forever.

Book II

Finance, Tax, and How to Organise Them

Trying traveller's cheques

Traveller's cheques are a secure means of moving money, but they're more appropriate while you are visiting overseas rather than living there.

Traveller's cheques are an expensive way to move money. Charges can be as high as 13 per cent, with a small amount of government tax added on. You also still have the worry of exchange rate fluctuations, unless you take euro traveller's cheques to a country in which the euro is a standard local currency.

You must complete a bit of paperwork to acquire traveller's cheques. You also need to have your passport handy when you use them and you must keep a record of their numbers in order to report them as stolen or lost if necessary. Receiving replacement cheques can take some time, though American Express offers a three-hour replacement service at its offices.

Transferring between banks

Having your British bank transfer funds electronically to your bank overseas is fairly quick. The entire process can be done with relative ease in 24 hours (in theory at least). If you give your British bank instructions before noon, the money will appear in your overseas bank by close of business the following day. In practice though, allow three full working days for the money to clear.

As a property owner in Europe, exchange rates and money-transfer changes may be leading factors in your choice of British banks. You need to check exactly what your bank charges for its transfer service and what rate of exchange it uses. Banks have a great deal of leeway regarding rates of exchange. The tourist rate is the least advantageous to you – and naturally is the one banks favour. You need to insist on the commercial rate of exchange and push for as low a charge as you can secure.

Telegraphic transfers

If you really are in a hurry to get funds abroad, telegraphic transfer is probably the answer, but it comes at a cost. A charge from 5 to 10 per cent on transactions is not unheard of – but if it's that or lose a property or forfeit a deposit, a transfer can be a life saver.

Lots of companies are in the telegraphic transfer game, which is hardly surprising as it is so lucrative. For example, Western Union (www.westernunion.co.uk) operates a Money in Minutes service in which approved transactions are generally available for pick-up right away, subject only to the hours of operation at the receiving agent location. Citibank (www.citibank.com/uk) allows you to transfer up to £10,000 in sterling or in the currency of the recipient account every day. The service also allows you to view the exchange rate before you complete the transaction.

Employing specialist currency dealers

A new breed of firm has sprung up that deals almost exclusively in helping you move currency around the world, either to buy property or complete other business-related transactions. Such firms aim to reduce the cost to you of moving money around, while making good margins themselves.

Currency specialists offer most of the following financial options. You can use one or more of these options, at a per-service cost, to give yourself certainty and security.

- **Spot contract:** Use this option when you need currency now at today's rate. The money is available within two working days of the agreement and can be telegraphically transferred immediately or held on account, pending your instructions. Whatever you do with the funds, the exchange rate is final.

- **Fixed-term forward contract:** Use this option when you have a future commitment to pay monies at a fixed date in the future, for example a stage payment on the purchase of a house under construction or for serious renovation work. The rate is fixed at the time of the agreement and remains constant irrespective of fluctuating exchange rates, for up to two years in advance.

✔ **Forward time option contract:** Use this option if some aspects of your costs have a variable date assigned to them. For example, the final payment on a property being constructed is bound to have a degree of uncertainty about it. Using this contract, you can elect to collect your currency at any time between two predetermined dates, usually with flexibility of 90 days between the two dates. The advantage of a forward contract is that you only need to put down a deposit of 10 per cent of the contract value. This means that you have the comfort of knowing that you have fixed the cost of your future commitment and yet you keep the use of your capital until the stage payments are due.

✔ **Limit order:** Placing a limit order enables you to specify a defined better rate of exchange that you want to buy at. Use this option if you believe that, for example, the euro is going to weaken against the pound. (Say the euro is currently trading at €1.50 to the pound – you can place a limit order to buy euros if and when they reach €1.52 to the pound.) Limit orders remain valid until they are either executed or cancelled. They can be cancelled at any time.

✔ **Stop loss order:** This option enables you to set a lower level of exchange rate that you are prepared to buy at – in other words, a worse rate than that currently available. For example, if the market is trading at €1.50 to the pound and you think that you may get a better rate by waiting, you can still protect yourself in case the market moves against you by placing a stop loss order at €1.49. If the market improves to, say, €1.52 and you hope for further gains, you can move your stop loss order to €1.51 and thus protect the gains already made. Stop loss orders remain valid until they are either executed or cancelled. They can be cancelled at any time.

Some useful currency dealer Web sites include:

✔ www.currenciesdirect.com

✔ www.currencies4less.com

✔ www.interchangefx.co.uk

✔ www.4xuk.co.uk

Getting a Mortgage

Borrowing money is never a great idea – it's the surest way known to humankind to lose friends and alienate relatives. One exception to the maxim, however, is that borrowing can be useful if the money is used to buy an asset, such as property, rather than a consumable item or experience, such as a luxury holiday.

Even though borrowing to buy property is in principle a good idea, you still have to be able to afford the repayments in practice. Be sure to balance the following two factors:

- ✔ **How much do you need to fund the purchase of the property and carry out any repairs and modifications?**

- ✔ **Can you afford the repayments, bearing in mind that interest rates may change over time?** To work this out, you need to calculate your free income – the money you have that is not earmarked for living expenses and other fixed commitments. To this, you can add any income you expect to get from renting out your home in the UK or your new property.

Table 6-1 shows how much to allow in mortgage costs to cover each €100,000 (£70,000) you borrow, for a range of time periods and at different interest rates.

Table 6-1 Interest and Repayment Expenses per €100,000 (£70,000) Borrowed at Various Rates and Terms			
Interest rate	*10-year mortgage*	*15-year mortgage*	*20-year mortgage*
4%	€12,329	€ 8,994	€ 7,358
5%	€ 12,950	€ 9,634	€ 8,024
6%	€ 13,587	€ 10,296	€ 8,718
7%	€ 14,237	€ 10,979	€ 9,439
8%	€ 14,903	€ 11,683	€ 10,185

A number of mortgage options are available today, many of which we explore in the following sections. However, as far as your budget is concerned, depending on time and interest rates you need to budget for between €7,358 and €14,903 in mortgage costs per €100,000 borrowed.

Remortgaging at home

Remortgaging is by far and away the easiest and maybe even the cheapest option for raising funds. You get to keep your house in the UK and, lender permitting, you can even let out your house to help cover some or all the mortgage repayments for your property overseas.

All you really need to remortgage your home is a fairly substantial slice of unencumbered equity in the property; that is, the difference between what the property is worth and what you still owe the mortgagor. You don't even need to demonstrate an income in the UK, as you can go through a buy-to-let type scheme. You also want to avoid any exchange risk exposure after you complete the deal on your home. (See the earlier section 'Understanding exchange rate risks' for information on dealing with exchange rate issues.)

You can typically borrow up to 80 per cent of the value of your property, with an interest rate about 1 per cent or so more than a conventional mortgage (currently around 6 per cent total), depending on the lock-in term you select. Arrangement fees vary depending on your circumstances but are likely to be a few hundred pounds. The entire process takes a few weeks at the most, often much less. You may even be able to get an agreement in principle in a day or so, which at least gives you the comfort to get on with making an offer on a property.

Talk to your current mortgage provider and also see what brokers such as Charcol Online (0800-358-5560; http://mortgages.charcolonline.co.uk) can provide. Also check out the UK Mortgage Brokers' Directory (0845-061-4282; www.mortgages.co.uk/brokers), which describes the services of more than 50 mortgage providers.

Mortgaging through a British or international bank

If putting your British home on the line with a remortgage appears too risky, consider looking to either British or international banks to put up the readies. Several British banks and building societies lend on homes abroad. But not every lender arranges loans on every type of property, lends the same proportion of the purchase price, or lends in both sterling and euros.

Banks to try for a mortgage include:

- **Newcastle Building Society** (0845-606-4488; www.newcastle.co.uk)
- **Norwich & Peterborough Building Society** (0845-300-6727; www.npbs.co.uk)
- **Lloyds Bank** (020-7374-6900; www.lloydstsb.com/mortgages/own_overseas).

All British banks impose conditions on loans, such as lending only on amounts above £60,000, advancing no more than 75 per cent, lending for no more than

Book II

Finance, Tax, and How to Organise Them

20 years, or restricting use to owner occupation only. They also restrict themselves to places where they have reliable local partners, which does not always follow the same patterns as, say, the coverage of estate agents working in English. For example, it is currently not possible to find any of the major UK banks offering a mortgage for a property in Hungary, even though Budapest has a very strong and growing property market.

International banks also offer mortgage finance for overseas properties.

World Wide Tax.com (www.worldwide-tax.com) has a country-by-country database of all banks with their Web addresses. Visit the Web site and then select the country you want. Most of these Web sites have information in English as well as application forms for opening an account online.

Trying the locals

UK-based mortgages still offer loans on a larger proportion of the purchase price, interest rates closer to the prevailing bank rate, and a faster service than the loans you can obtain from many European countries. But the big plus of having a mortgage in a local currency is that you don't have to worry about exchange rates. The money you borrow in this way will be a set sterling amount, sufficient to cover the purchase price of your property whatever currency the property is being sold in. Your liability remains to repay a sterling amount, which if your income is also in sterling eliminates the currency risk.

Shop around for a mortgage abroad; interest rates and terms vary considerably depending on the bank, the amount, and the period of time. Mortgages are generally available for up to 70 or 80 per cent of the mortgage valuation, repayable over up to 20 years, with interest rates 2–3 per cent above the local base rate.

Buy Off Plan

Buying off plan is a strategy to make your money go further in situations where your research convinces you that the property market is a sure-fire winner.

Buying off plan, in essence, is simple. A developer normally has a long lead time between buying the land, getting planning permission, building the property, and finally getting it sold. The time between shelling out initial cash and getting it all back (plus a bit more) can be years. In the meantime, the developer has to find new sites to develop, which in turn requires more money. If a developer waits for a development to sell out before buying another, he or she has workers hanging around doing nothing, and in the process misses out on some potentially good opportunities through lack of cash. (Sure, a developer can go to a bank, but that means paying interest every month.)

The alternative to bank financing is to use a property buyer as a bank of sorts by offering the buyer some inducement to break a cardinal rule of investing: Never give a builder money up front. In return for up-front money, the builder typically discounts the final purchase price by up to 20 per cent and perhaps throws in some furnishings for good measure.

Off-plan buyers can typically stage payments over the building process, which helps with cash flow. For a two-year building project, expect to pay out around 20 per cent in the first year, another 20 per cent halfway through the second year, and the remaining 60 per cent on completion. This formula is not hard and fast – but it is a reasonable rule of thumb with which to work.

The real attraction of buying off plan is the ability to make your money go further. For example, say you have a kitty of £100,000: Rather than buy just one apartment for that sum, you can put the same money towards buying five apartments off plan. By the end of year one (halfway through the building process), you have paid out just 20 per cent of the total asking price of £500,000 (5 units x £100,000). And you still have six months to sell, say, four of the apartments before the next payment is due. If your market estimates are correct, your properties may now be worth 5–25 per cent more than you paid a year earlier. If you factor in the 20 per cent discount you received for taking the risk in the first place, you may have sufficient profit to end up with one apartment that costs you absolutely nothing.

Buying off plan is not without risks, for various reasons:

✔ First and foremost, prices may not rise as you hope.

✔ When you buy off plan, all you have to go on is an architectural drawing, which shows the layout from above but doesn't tell you important features such as how high above the floor the windows are, for example. (If windows end up being above 1.2 metres in a sitting room, you can't see out of them when sitting down; below 1.2 metres in a bedroom, and you lose privacy.)

✔ No matter how realistic the computer image of a proposed site may look, it cannot tell you about the environment *around* the proposed property – for example, the refuse tip, quarry, scrap-metal yard, or building site next door or just down the street.

✔ The project may not be completed (or it may be shelved for years) if the developer goes bust or if insufficient interest exists for the project. In such circumstances, your chances of recovering any deposits and stage payments are slim. Even should another developer take over the project at a later date, you have no guarantee that the new developer will take on the liabilities of the bankrupt developer.

Many off-plan developments are offered by companies with little experience of this type of project. Check out companies offering off-plan deals carefully. Ask to see details of previous projects, and try to talk to a number of their clients who have bought through them. Ask several estate agents for their opinions of the company, and get local professional advice to make sure the builder has obtained planning permission and proper title to the land, which can be passed to you.

Book III
Renovating a Property

'Let's face it, Malcolm, I don't think we've cured our damp problem.'

In this book . . .

You may decide to invest in a property with potential for a facelift, or one in need of some serious work. This book gives you easy-to-follow advice and instruction on how to approach home repairs and renovation, from simple jobs like bleeding the radiators to knowing when to call for the professionals.

Here are the contents of Book III at a glance:

Chapter 1

Renovating Wrecks: Property in Need of Work

A property that is perfect in every way, needs no work doing to it, and is ready to move straight in to is many buyers' idea of hell. Instead, they want a blank canvas, something they can make their mark on and do up to their own taste. For these people, the ideal is often a derelict property in need of extensive renovation. Two bonuses: Property that needs gutting often costs less than property in pristine condition, and a renovated property can increase its value by thousands of pounds if you get the renovations right.

Not everyone is cut out for property renovation. TV home makeover shows are fuelling interest, but the reality is that renovation is time and labour intensive and mistakes can be costly. A nicely done renovation is rewarding, true, but you need to think carefully before taking the plunge. In this chapter, we help you figure out whether buying and renovating a dilapidated house is for you. We also look at the pitfalls to watch out for when buying a listed or thatched property and how to make sure you don't fall foul of any building regulations. And because getting a full structural survey is vitally important when you buy a house to renovate, we explain why you can't afford to scrimp on the survey and examine the false economy of cutting corners and trying to get by without one.

Can You Stomach Renovation?

The first thing you need to do is assess whether doing up a property is a job you feel comfortable with. Property renovation and development may be booming, but many of the people making a killing are experienced. Those who aren't trained architects, surveyors, or builders know of architects, surveyors, or builders they can call upon. And as you discover with property renovation, having good contacts is vitally important to the success of your project.

Calculating the amount of work you're comfortable with

No two renovations are the same. When you choose a property, carefully assess whether the work required is realistically something you can handle or out of your league. Because nothing is worse than feeling out of your depth, you must be really honest with yourself. Ask yourself these questions:

- ✔ **How skilled are you at DIY jobs?** If your own property has the scars of several botched DIY jobs – the result of your own handiwork – thinking that you can renovate an entire property on your own is madness.

  If you lack the skills and time to do the work yourself but find your heart still set on property development, we recommend that you resign yourself to calling in the experts and stick to a consulting role. See the section 'Knowing when to call in the building experts – and where to find them' for the people you'll need to contact.

- ✔ **How much time do you have to devote to the project?** And if you also have a busy, stressful job with long hours, it's unrealistic to think that you can do all the work at weekends and during the evenings. Be critical of your personal skills and the amount of time you have to devote to the project. A good self-assessment can make the difference between a successful renovation and a costly disaster.

- ✔ **How much cash is the project likely to cost you?** You may be getting the property on the cheap because it needs a lot of work doing but the renovations could work out to be very costly. Work out your budget *before* buying a property and be wary of committing yourself to a project that you simply can't afford. Otherwise you'll be stuck with a half-finished property for months (or even years!) while you try to raise the necessary cash.

If you have a little building experience or DIY expertise and have time on your hands, a less extensive renovation project – such as a property that needs interior refurbishment rather than a new roof and completely gutting – may be more realistic. Taking on a smaller project may be a better place to start for these reasons:

✔ You can save a lot of money by doing some of the 'easier' work – such as chipping old plaster off the walls or grouting tiles in the bathroom or kitchen – yourself.

✔ You can develop and become more confident in your skills. Building up your own experience and knowledge is invaluable even if you plan to hire experts to do the work for you. After all, you still need to make sure they don't pull the wool over your eyes and do a good job.

Figuring out how extensive the renovation is

Once you know how much work you're comfortable with, you need to be able to judge whether a particular property requires just what you can provide – or more. In other words, you need to be able to determine how much work – and what type – needs to be done in the property you're considering. Make sure you have a survey done and if you don't have the necessary experience to judge what work is needed from this, ask a builder or surveyor for advice.

Something that looks like a straightforward renovation may not be. You may think the crack in the living room wall is simply a bad plaster job only to discover that the cause is bad subsidence and that the foundations need extensive underpinning. Don't buy any property – particularly one that needs a lot of work – without a full structural survey.

Book III

Renovating a Property

Knowing when to call in the building experts – and where to find them

If you lack the skill and time to do a renovation yourself, you're going to need skilled professionals to do the job for you. Even if you have some building experience, you may need to hire help for the areas you don't have experience in. The following sections explain who some of these pros are that you're likely to be working with.

Project managers

Renovating a property is a full-time job because you need to be on site several hours a day to ensure everything is running as it should be. If you haven't got the time or inclination to do this, you need to hire a project manager to oversee the renovation.

The project manager is responsible for hiring all the necessary people to complete the job – the contractors, see the following section – ordering the materials, and generally running the site to ensure the project finishes on time and to budget. She needs to be on the site six or sometimes seven days a week to ensure everything is getting done. As a result, a project manager doesn't come cheap and could cost you up to 10 per cent of your total budget, depending on the work involved.

Personal recommendation is the best way to find a project manager. Ask friends, relatives, neighbours, and builders or other contractors you trust whether they can suggest someone suitable.

To save costs, you can be your own project manager. Many people who are new to property development give this a go – and are actually very good at it. Keep these things in mind:

✔ If you don't have the time and don't have an eye for it, leave the project management to the experts. Otherwise, it's false economy.

✔ If you've never done any property renovation before, you're unlikely to have a full contacts book of builders, plumbers, and electricians suitable for the job you need done. You'll have to build one up quickly if you aren't using a project manager.

Contractors

Unless you are an experienced builder, electrician, and plumber yourself, you'll need to call in such experts. These are known as *contractors*, because you contract them to do a certain job.

Following are some ideas on locating reputable contractors:

✔ Personal recommendation is the best way of finding contractors. Ask family, friends, and neighbours who've had similar work done whether they can recommend a builder or plumber. Then inspect his work yourself and take up other references.

Don't take on a contractor just because he is a friend of a friend. If anything goes wrong with the job, seeking redress and treating the situation as a business transaction can be a lot harder. In addition, you risk falling out with your friend. Make it a rule to work only with qualified contractors personally unconnected with your friends or family.

✔ If possible, choose a builder who belongs to the Federation of Master Builders (FMB) or Guild of Master Craftsmen. These people are vetted before joining and follow a code of practice. Also, if you are unhappy with a member's work, you can follow a complaints procedure to address the issue. To find a member, look out for the FMB or Guild logo on builders' vans, stationery, and advertising.

✔ Check out www.improveline.com, which enables you to search for contractors working in your area. The listed contractors are recommended by members of the public and have been screened for their credit and legal history and number of years in the business.

✔ The Yellow Pages also lists contractors, but use this as your last resort because you'll have no idea from the entry whether a contractor is good or bad. If you do rely on this source, go and see a couple of past projects and then check out references.

As you narrow your list of contractors, do the following:

✔ Get at least three quotes for the job – and don't necessarily go for the cheapest. Make sure the quote clearly states whether materials are included and what, if any, you are expected to supply. Once you reach agreement, make sure to get the quote and any conditions in writing.

✔ Check out the contractor's last job and ask the employer whether the contractor's work was satisfactory.

✔ Talk through what you want and try to gauge how helpful and cooperative a builder is. If he is at all dismissive or patronising, you may find working with him difficult and might be better off looking for someone else to take on the job.

✔ Ensure your builder has clear instructions about what you want, in writing, *before* starting the job. This should make renovation go much smoother.

Although you can find many reputable contractors who wouldn't dream of conning you, there are also plenty of cowboys – builders who don't do a good job, run over schedule, and try to charge you more than you agreed for the work in the first place. Spotting when you're being taken for a ride is crucial to the success of your project so be on the lookout for shoddy workmanship. With some careful research and management, however, dealing with contractors needn't be a disaster.

Architects

If the property requires a lot of extensive changes, you may decide to hire an architect to draw up plans for these and to call on their technical know-how. Architects can also work as project managers, seeking planning and technical approvals, managing site inspections, and generally sorting out the whole job. It's worth consulting an architect as early as possible and certainly before you start renovating a property.

A consultation can cost between £55 and £95 an hour, depending on how specialised or complex the project is.

Book III

Renovating a Property

When commissioning an architect, opt for one who is a member of the Royal Institute of British Architects (RIBA). Via RIBA's Web site (www.riba.org), you can search for an architect by location, size of project, sector of expertise, or type of service. Members are subject to a code of professional conduct, and while RIBA has no statutory powers to seek compensation if you feel your architect has let you down, it does offer practical assistance.

Finding Your Wreck

As with any property purchase, start with estate agents. Register with several and let them know what you want. Here are other ideas for finding your wreck:

✔ **Go to an auction.** An auction is another great source of properties in need of extensive renovation because vendors know they'll get a quick sale albeit for a knockdown price.

Although the salesroom can be a great source of bargains, always be sceptical about properties for sale at auction. Why does the seller want to get rid of his property so quickly? What is the condition of the property? If you're not careful, you could find yourself buying something that needs a lot more work than you'd bargained or budgeted for. For guidelines to buying a property at auction, head to Book I, Chapter 3.

✔ **Get online.** The Internet is another good source of properties for sale in need of renovation. Register with a number of property sites and take potluck.

✔ **Look at local papers.** Local newspapers are another good source of properties for sale, so make a note of what day they come out. Many often have their own Internet sites as well, which are updated more regularly so check these daily.

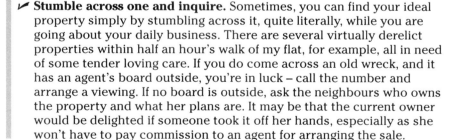

✔ **Stumble across one and inquire.** Sometimes, you can find your ideal property simply by stumbling across it, quite literally, while you are going about your daily business. There are several virtually derelict properties within half an hour's walk of my flat, for example, all in need of some tender loving care. If you do come across an old wreck, and it has an agent's board outside, you're in luck – call the number and arrange a viewing. If no board is outside, ask the neighbours who owns the property and what her plans are. It may be that the current owner would be delighted if someone took it off her hands, especially as she won't have to pay commission to an agent for arranging the sale.

Calculating Costs and Setting a Budget

One of the biggest mistakes people make when renovating property is to go wildly over budget. If you have got plenty of spare cash, getting carried away may not be a problem. But if money is tight, blowing your budget could have a catastrophic effect and put the project months behind schedule.

Estimating how much you need to spend

The first step to setting a budget for the project is knowing how much work needs to be done. If you are new to property development, you have to rely on the experts to guide you. Get three quotes for each job (see the earlier section 'Contractors' for details on what to look for and remember that the cheapest isn't necessarily the best). Although estimates will vary from property to property, the following prices give you a very general idea of cost when fully refurbishing a three-bedroom semi-detached house:

Work	*Estimated Amount*
New roof (tiled)	Around £50 per square metre
Underpinning the foundations	£3,000 to £4,000
Rewiring	£3,000
Plumbing	£3,000 to £5,000
New kitchen	£3,000 to £5,000
New bathroom	£1,500 to £4,000
Loft conversion	£8,000 to £10,000

Book III

Renovating a Property

Figuring out your budget and sticking to it

When you buy a house in need of renovation, not only do you have to pay for the property itself, you also need to budget for the following:

- ✔ **The contractors' fees:** These include wages, materials, fixtures, and fittings. To figure out how much you need to allow for these, add up the quotes you've accepted from the contractors who'll be doing your work.

- ✔ **Your contingency fund:** You use this fund to cover any unexpected expenses or as an emergency fund should something go wrong, which can easily happen, particularly if you are new to renovating property. The contingency fund should amount to 10 per cent of your total budget.

The contingency fund is not an optional extra. Rather, it's as integral a part of your budget as the money you have earmarked for building materials. If something unexpected crops up, this fund ensures your project is completed during the time allotted and is not held up – or abandoned – while you try to find the extra cash.

The purpose of the budget is to ensure you don't get carried away, and you must be ruthless with it. If you opt for marble flooring in the bathroom, for example, when you budgeted for lino, you're likely to run out of cash and end up skimping on the kitchen with cheap cabinets that fall apart within 18 months.

Nearly everyone goes a little crazy in one area or another when developing property. This can be a problem if you're renovating the house only to sell it on for a profit. Even when you plan to live in the property, you still don't want to run out of cash and end up living in an unfinished house while you try to save up to complete the job.

If you do run out of cash, your project will fall behind schedule while you try to find the extra money you need. Tradesmen you've lined up will go on to the other jobs they have lined up, and you may have to wait before they can come back and complete your job. To save yourself the stress and hassle that inevitably comes when a job falls behind because of lack of funds, work out your budget carefully in the first instance – and then stick to it.

Using a Surveyor

The best way of calculating how much work is needed is to get a surveyor to assess the job. She will know what is likely to be causing cracks in the walls, for example, and what remedial work is needed. Cutting corners at this stage in order to save a few hundred pounds is a very risky strategy and strongly inadvisable in the long run.

Locating a surveyor

Personal recommendation once again comes top of the list when choosing a surveyor. But don't forget other sources, such as estate agents and mortgage lenders, who deal with surveyors every day. Keep in mind, however, that the surveyors that mortgage lenders use are more adept at providing basic valuations, which are fine if your renovation is straightforward. But if your project is more complicated, hiring a surveyor who specialises in renovations and can provide an in-depth survey is usually money well spent.

As with builders, not all surveyors are used to working with all types of property. Try to find one who has experience of working on properties similar to yours, especially if it has unusual features. Follow up references and check previous projects to ensure employers are satisfied with the surveyor's work.

Credentials are important; ensure that your surveyor is a member of the Royal Institution of Chartered Surveyors (RICS), the main professional trade association. Members are easy to spot because the letters *MRICS, FRICS,* or *TechRICS* appear after their names. For extra peace of mind, check with the RICS whether the surveyor's qualifications are genuine by phoning 0870 333 1600.

Full structural survey required

There are two types of survey available when you buy a property (as well as the lender's valuation). Of these, the full structural survey is best when you buy a property in need of renovation (for more detail about surveys, go to Book I, Chapter 2).

The full structural survey is the most expensive (anything from £400 to £1,000, depending on your requirements and the size of the property). It is also the most comprehensive, running to many pages. It will uncover any hidden problems and give you a full picture as to what you're committing yourself to. This information is vital in establishing whether you can afford to do all the work required. You can also use the findings as a bargaining tool when making an offer: If there is a lot more work than you envisaged, try haggling with the vendor to reduce the asking price.

Many buyers are put off by the cost of full structural surveys, but it's money well spent, particularly if you're buying a house that needs a lot of work. And given that you could be spending hundreds of thousands of pounds buying and renovating the property, the cost of the survey is small fry in comparison.

When you hire a surveyor, you should receive a full outline of the job in writing, detailing his qualifications, what he will do, and how much the survey will cost. Insist on this before commissioning him.

Although your surveyor won't tell you whether or not you should buy the wreck you have set your heart on, the survey can give you a clear idea as to whether it's a good idea or not. Quite often, the surveyor will recommend that more specialist surveys be carried out: for example, if a tree is situated close to the porch, she may suggest another survey to discover whether its position will affect the foundations and cause problems in the future. You can use this information to determine whether you want to have the tree removed.

The surveyor can also help you understand how serious the survey's discoveries are. If the survey uncovers subsidence, for example, it might not be as bad as it sounds, particularly if the property is in the southeast of England where many houses are built on clay soil. In that situation, the surveyor may feel that underpinning, which is relatively straightforward, will be enough to rectify the problem. If your survey does uncover subsidence or damp, take advice from the surveyor as to what work is needed and how much it will cost.

Buying a Listed Property

Many listed properties fall into disrepair because they tend to be fairly old and more expensive to maintain than a relatively modern property. Because of their listed status, owners of these properties have to get permission for any changes they make. Obtaining this permission can be time-consuming and off-putting. Although listed properties are often charming, they can present all kinds of problems, which you should be aware of before buying one.

Listing bands: what they mean

Listed buildings don't necessarily have to be old, although most buildings constructed before 1840 tend to be listed. Buildings illustrating technical innovation or associated with a famous person or event can also make it onto the register. And we're not talking just about pretty Cotswold cottages either – power stations, football stadia, and barns can all be listed.

English Heritage is responsible for recommending to the Secretary of State for the Environment which properties make it onto the register in England. In Wales, this is the responsibility of Cadw; in Scotland, Historic Scotland; and in Northern Ireland, the Environment and Heritage Service.

There are several different types of listed building. In England and Wales, these are Graded I, II*, and II. In Scotland, grades A, B, and C are used, while in Northern Ireland, where just 2 per cent of properties are listed, it's A, B+, B1, and B2, all of which roughly signify the same thing. In England, 90 per cent of listed buildings are Grade II, and in Scotland, Grade B is the most popular (60 per cent of properties). These grades roughly translate as:

- ✔ **Grade I/A:** Buildings of exceptional interest.
- ✔ **Grade II*/B:** Particularly important buildings of more than special interest.
- ✔ **Grade II/C:** Buildings of special interest that warrant every effort to preserve them.

Finding listed properties

With around 500,000 listed buildings in the UK, there is a strong chance that you'll come across one that you want to buy if you're looking for a property in need of renovation. For information on listed buildings and advice on conservation and renovation work, contact the relevant authority:

- ✔ English Heritage (www.english-heritage.org.uk)
- ✔ Cadw in Wales (www.cadw.wales.gov.uk)
- ✔ Historic Scotland (www.historic-scotland.gov.uk)
- ✔ Environment and Heritage Service in Northern Ireland (www.ehsni.gov.uk).

For a selection of listed properties for sale, try the Society for the Protection of Ancient Buildings (www.spab.org.uk) or Pavilions of Splendour, an estate agent specialising in listed properties (www.heritage.co.uk).

Ensuring you don't fall foul of the law

While you can't install modern double-glazing into a Grade I listed seventeenth-century period cottage, you don't necessarily have to live with something you don't like. Alterations can be possible as long as you get Listed Building Consent from your local planning authority first. This is a bit like applying for Planning Permission and is often granted if your request is reasonable.

Demolishing, altering, or extending a listed building without Listed Building Consent is a very serious offence: The penalty can be an unlimited fine or up to 12 months' imprisonment. It is essential that you familiarise yourself with what is and isn't allowed. In addition to extensions, alterations needing consent include the following:

- ✔ Painting over brickwork
- ✔ Replacing doors and windows
- ✔ Removing external surfaces
- ✔ Installing a satellite dish, TV aerial, or burglar alarm
- ✔ Changing roofing materials
- ✔ Moving or removing interior walls
- ✔ Building new doorways
- ✔ Removing or altering fireplaces, panelling, and staircases

Book III

Renovating a Property

If you're in any doubt about what you can and can't change, contact your local planning office. It's better to be safe than sorry.

To stay on the right side of the law, you must look after your listed building properly. If you don't, your local authority can serve a 'repairs notice' specifying the work it considers necessary for the preservation of the building. If you don't comply with this notice within two months, it may make a compulsory purchase order on the property.

Maintenance costs and insurance

The cost of materials for listed properties tends to be greater than with 'regular' renovations because you may need to source specialist materials, such as reclaimed bricks or tiles, in keeping with the style of the original building. Some grants are available to assist with urgent major repairs on Grade I, Grade II*, or Grade A or B buildings. It is extremely unlikely that you'll be able to get any sort of grant for a Grade II or C listed building, however. To apply for a grant, contact your Conservation Officer via the local council.

VAT (value-added tax) is not payable on alterations – as long as a VAT-registered builder carries out the work and you have Listed Building Consent. But remember that VAT remains payable on repairs and other work not requiring consent.

When it comes to insuring a listed building, a specialist insurer is likely to be your best bet. Buildings insurance covers the cost of rebuilding the property should it be destroyed in a fire, for example, so take professional advice from a surveyor on the rebuilding figures. And listen to recommendations made by your insurer as to ways in which you can reduce the risks, such as fire precautions.

Chapter 2

Dealing with Damp

*T*his chapter tells you how to deal with one of the most common building problems: Dampness.

Is a Fungus Amongus?

One of the most common symptoms of dampness is a white powdery substance that appears on your walls. Although most people mistake the white powder for a fungus (fungus is typically green or black), it's really *efflorescence*, which is a growth of salt crystals caused by the evaporation of salt-laden water.

Efflorescence appears when mineral salts in the masonry, plaster, or mortar leak to the surface. Although efflorescence isn't particularly destructive, it's unsightly and on rare occasions can result in *spalling* – crumbling of the brickwork – or minor deterioration of the surface on which it grows. If your house was built in the last few years, then efflorescence might be simply the result of construction water coming to the surface and drying out. If you've got efflorescence appearing on older brickwork, however, or on internal plastered surfaces, then it is a sign of the passage of moisture, which needs to be diagnosed and rectified.

On outside walls, efflorescence is most likely to be *lime* (calcium carbonate) leached out from the mortar. It's harmless, and in most cases the natural action of the wind and rain removes it over a few years. To hasten its removal, wait for a spell of dry weather, and brush it off gently with a soft brush. Resist the temptation to wash it off with a hose, as this can bring even more lime to the surface and make the efflorescence look worse!

On internal plastered surfaces, efflorescence is probably *gypsum* (calcium sulfate), which you can more easily remove by wiping with a damp cloth. It is common for some efflorescence to appear on newly plastered walls – especially where pink gypsum plaster has been used on the inside of solid brick walls on older houses. Leave the walls to dry out thoroughly for a few months before decorating, wipe off any efflorescence that appears, and seal the plastered surface with dilute PVA solution (such as Unibond) before decorating.

Preventing Moisture from Building Up under Your Property

If you see efflorescence on your basement walls and/or your walls are perpetually damp and mildewy, you've got a moisture problem! A natural spring, a high water table, a broken water or sewer pipe, poor drainage, excessive irrigation, and poor ventilation are some of the most common causes of this problem.

What's a little water around and under the house going to hurt, you ask? Lots! Aside from turning your basement into a sauna, excess moisture can lead to a glut of problems, such as repulsive stinks, rotted timbers, insect pests, foundation movement, efflorescence, and allergy-irritating mould. We can't stress enough the importance of doing everything you can to keep excess moisture out of this area of your property.

Rooting out the cause of moisture

A musty or pungent smell usually accompanies efflorescence and excessive moisture. Start by checking for leaks in water and sewer pipes under your property. A failing plumbing fitting or corroded pipe is often the culprit. Fitting a replacement or installing a repair 'sleeve' around the damaged section of pipe almost always does the trick.

Believe it or not, a wet basement may be the result of a leaking toilet, bath, or valve located in the walls above. When it comes to finding the cause of a damp basement or sub-floor area, leave no stone unturned.

Overwatering plant pots, window boxes, and hanging baskets surrounding the house is another common cause of water down under. Adjusting watering time, watering less often, installing an automatic timer, and adjusting sprinkler heads are the simplest means of solving this problem. Better yet, move the plants!

Dealing with the rising damp myth

The problem with getting builders or surveyors in to diagnose your property's dampness problems is that a lot of ignorance exists about rising damp. Specialist 'damp-proofing' firms are often only too keen to tell you that your property has 'rising damp'. Treat their diagnoses with a healthy dose of scepticism. In most cases these firms use electrical moisture meters on the walls, but these meters are calibrated for use only on timber, and are almost guaranteed to give high readings when used to test masonry, plaster, and wallpaper. In many cases, we've seen rising damp diagnosed in walls that are actually completely dry, simply by misuse of these meters.

If your property really does have dampness problems, the best way of dealing with them is to use traditional good construction practices – lowering raised outside ground levels, and making sure that gutters and rainwater pipes are clear and draining away properly, and that the house is heated and ventilated.

Using gutters to reduce moisture

Rain gutters are more than a decorative element to the roofline of a house. Their primary purpose is to capture the tremendous amount of rainfall that runs off the average roof. Without gutters, rainwater collects at the foundation and eventually ends up in the basement. If you don't have gutters, install them. And if you do, keep them clean.

Book III

Renovating a Property

Make sure that your gutters and rainwater downpipes direct water a safe distance away from your house. Even worse than not having gutters and downpipes is having downpipes that jettison water directly into the ground next to the walls. Ideally, your downpipes should direct water into yard gulleys connected to the main sewer system, or piped to run into a nearby ditch or stream.

Some older houses have downpipes running into *soakaways*, which are basically just holes in the ground next to the house, filled with stone or builders' rubble, and covered over with soil. Over the years, soakaways become silted up, and instead of allowing water to percolate gently into the ground, they become mini-ponds, which can allow water to soak straight back through the footing or basement walls of the house. If your house has soakaways, we recommend digging them out and renewing them, or preferably relocating them three or four metres away from the house. You can dig a trench and add a bend and a length of plastic pipe to the foot of the existing downpipe to direct the water to the new soakaway. You can buy modern soakaways that are plastic cages that you bury in the ground.

Draining water away from the house

Be sure that the soil and hard paving around your property is at least 150 mm (two brick courses) below the level of the damp-proof course, and slopes away from the building. This helps divert most irrigation and rainwater away from the structure.

Lowering ground levels

A patio or path that slopes towards the house discharges water into the basement or sub-floor area, which in turn breeds dampness problems and rot. Unfortunately, the only sure way to correct this problem is to remove and replace the source, and replacing a path or patio can be pricey. If the previous owners of your property were unwise enough to install a new path or patio without bothering to remove the old surface first (a surprisingly common situation), then this will have raised the ground level, and presents you with a big problem. Ideally, you should dig it all up, and lower the ground levels, but we know this can be a daunting prospect.

A possible compromise is to lower the ground level immediately next to the wall, to a width of 300 to 400 mm, and pave this strip at the new lower level. It should be paved with a gradient so that rain water runs away to the nearest existing yard gulley or, preferably, you should fit some new yard gulleys in the lowered strip, connected with pipes that direct the water away from the house or into the main drainage system.

Giving the problem some air

Ventilation is another effective means of controlling moisture in a basement or sub-floor area. Two types of ventilation exist:

- ✔ **Passive ventilation** is natural ventilation that doesn't use mechanical equipment. Terracotta airbricks are often set into the walls below the level of an inside suspended timber floor. They can work well, as long as they're not blocked by raised ground levels (see 'Lowering ground levels' above), and as long as they're positioned to allow a through flow of air below the floor. This means having airbricks in both the front and back walls of a terraced house, and also making sure that you have ventilation gaps in the footings of any intermediate walls running up the centre of the house. Victorian builders often put just one terracotta airbrick or perforated metal vent in each of the front and back walls, so you can add extra airbricks to improve the ventilation. Modern plastic airbricks are the same size as the old terracotta ones (75 x 225 mm and 150 x 225 mm), and are reckoned to have about five times more ventilation area.

✔ **Active ventilation** involves mechanical equipment, such as an extractor fan.

Passive ventilation should be your first choice because it allows nature to be your workhorse and doesn't necessitate the use of energy to drive a mechanical device. You save on your electricity bill and help the environment by not relying on fossil fuel. Having said that, don't hesitate to use active ventilation if your crawlspace or basement needs it.

If you use passive ventilation, you must keep vents clean to allow maximum airflow. Thinning shrubbery, vines, and ground cover may be necessary from time to time. If your vents are clear and moisture is still a problem, you may be able to add vents.

All the passive ventilation in the world may not be enough to dry out some problem basements. In these cases, install an active source of ventilation, such as an extractor fan.

Saying 'oui' to a French drain

Book III

Renovating a Property

If the advice we gave in the previous sections doesn't help and you're still faced with a basement or sub-floor area that looks like a bog, it's time to call in a building engineer to determine whether the condition requires the installation of a French drain. A French drain is a drainage channel dug around the outside of the house, right next to the walls. Some older houses have French drains that are just filled with stone, but the modern version uses perforated plastic land-drainage pipes that are bedded on, and back-filled with pea shingle. The pipes are laid at a gradient to drain water clear of the house or away to the main drainage system.

If you already have a French drain, it still needs occasional maintenance. Clean the inside of the pipe once a year by using a pressure cleaner, which is a high-powered water blaster with a hose and nozzle for use within drainpipes. You can rent this equipment from a tool hire company, or a plumbing contractor or sewer and drain cleaning service can clean a French drain for you.

Chapter 3

Installing Kitchen Cabinets

*C*abinets are expensive. You'll probably spend the biggest part of your remodelling budget on them, so you want to install them correctly.

Although you can measure for your own cabinets, you might want your cabinet supplier to assume the responsibility for measuring up your kitchen to determine the proper cabinet sizes. Include in the order any prefinished *filler strips* that might be required. These narrow boards are installed between stock-size cabinets to make them fit a space, provide necessary clearance around appliances, and sometimes to fill a gap next to a cabinet that abuts a wonky wall.

Plan your work schedule before you begin the installation. Set aside a weekend to install cabinets for a small kitchen and a week or more for a larger kitchen or more complex installation.

These days, most people buy kitchens from large DIY outlets, or stores like Ikea or MFI. The more expensive kitchen units come pre-assembled (which uses up a lot of space in the delivery van), and the cheaper ones come as *flat packs*, meaning that the sides, back, base, and shelves have to be screwed together on site to make up the cabinet. This makes transporting them a lot easier and cheaper, but it does mean you need more time to assemble the units before installation. Kitchen base units are usually supported on screw-adjustable plastic legs that can be used to make up for out-of-level floors, and these are hidden by plinths or kickerboards that are cut to size and clip onto the legs using spring clips.

Many kitchen retailers also provide an in-store design service, and can calculate how many base cabinets, wall cabinets, and how much length of worktop you need to complete your kitchen. So measure up your kitchen space and take a sketch down to the DIY store to see what they can offer you.

Gathering the Right Tools

Gather all the tools you need before you start a project. The tools you need to install new cabinets include:

- One 600 mm and one 1200 mm level (the 600 mm one is good for checking level and plumb in tight areas; use the 1200 mm level for checking level and plumb and to determine the high point of your floor)
- 2-metre or 3-metre aluminium straightedge or length of 100 x 50 mm timber (used with the level for checking the floor's level and high point)
- Chalk line
- Tape measure (5-metre minimum)
- Stud finder
- Stepladder
- Variety of clamps – squeeze, wooden screw, and spring clamps of various sizes
- 5 mm-diameter countersink drill bit
- 75 mm #10 cabinet screws
- Several No. 2 Posidrive screw bits
- 10 mm drill/driver (corded or cordless)
- Hammer
- One or two packages of wood shims (thin strips of wood)
- Jigsaw
- Heavy-duty extension cable for a corded drill or jigsaw (a 10-metre cable is best, especially if you need to draw power from another room)

Marking Reference Lines and Mounting Locations

Marking reference lines is the first and most crucial step in installing cabinets. If you don't have accurate reference lines, your cabinets may become misaligned, which affects their operation and appearance.

Checking your floor for level

Don't assume that your floor is level. Most floors are off by a little bit, but not so much that cabinet installation is impossible for a DIYer. To check your floor for level, follow these steps:

1. **Lay a long straightedge against a wall where you will install the base cabinets and set a 1200 mm level on it as shown in Figure 3-1.**

   The straightedge spans a greater distance of the floor, giving you a more accurate reading with the level. To determine if the floor is straight, sight down one edge and the other, looking for any bends.

2. **Determine the first high point. Lift one end of the straightedge or the other as needed to centre the bubble between the lines in the level's phial.**

   If the phial already indicates level, you're home and dry: This floor section is level. If an adjustment is needed, then the point where the level contacts the floor is your first high point.

3. **Using the level/straightedge, determine if any point along that wall or an adjacent wall where base cabinets are to be installed is higher.**

   Place an end of the straightedge on the first high point and extend the straightedge further along the wall or to any adjacent walls, checking for level as you did in Step 2. To make sure that the highest point along the wall is not lower than a point 600 mm off the wall (rare), check with a 600 mm level perpendicular to the wall. If it is, you need to add the difference to the height of your reference line (see next section).

Book III

Renovating
a Property

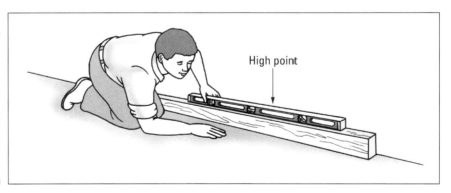

Figure 3-1:
Use a straightedge and level to find and mark the floor's high point on the wall.

High point

Measuring cabinet heights

When you have your measurements marked on the wall, get someone to assist you to snap chalk lines or draw horizontal lines with a spirit level and pencil at the top of where your base cabinets and the bottom of your wall cabinets will sit (see Figure 3-2). These lines give you your reference lines for installation. Perform this procedure on each wall where you plan to install cabinets. Be careful as you chalk the lines – make sure that they stay level around the entire room. To make your measurements accurate, follow these steps:

1. **Measure up 885 mm from the highest point and mark the wall. Using a level, pencil a level reference line on the wall to represent the top of the base cabinets.**

2. **Measure up 1240 mm from the reference line at both ends and mark the wall to represent the top of tall cabinets and wall cabinets.**

3. **Measure up 480 mm from the reference line at both ends to represent the bottom of 760 mm wall cabinets.**

When you have your measurements marked on the wall, snap chalk lines that represent the bottom and top of your wall cabinets. If you have shorter wall cabinets, such as those over an oven or fridge, measure down from the top line a distance equal to the height of the cabinet to determine the bottom edge. These lines are your reference lines for installation. Perform this procedure on each wall where cabinets will be installed.

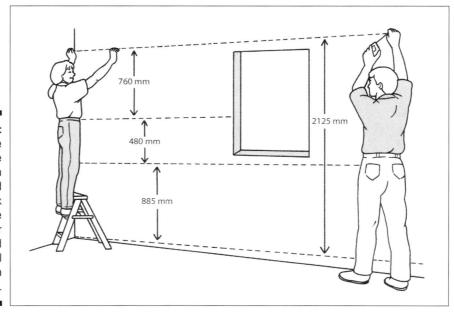

Figure 3-2: Measure from the floor's high point and mark reference lines for base and wall cabinets on the wall.

Adding cabinets before flooring

Should you lay your new flooring from wall to wall and then install the cabinets on the new flooring, or should you install the cabinets first and butt the new flooring up to it? Either method works, but installing new cabinets before new flooring is better. (See Chapter 7 for more on flooring.)

If you choose to install the cabinets first and then lay the flooring, you save money by using less flooring material. Plus, you can work on the subfloor and not have to worry about damaging new flooring when you're installing cabinets. And you can make your flooring cuts close enough to the cabinet so that you can cover any small gap by a kick-space beading strip.

Locating the wall studs for mounting

On timber stud walls you must secure wall cabinets with screws that you drive into wall studs. Hanging cabinets with hollow wall anchors (cavity toggles) is asking for a disaster! Even the most heavy-duty hollow wall anchor can't support the weight of a cabinet plus the weight of all the items stored inside.

Use a stud finder to locate each wall stud. In most buildings, especially in houses built after the 1960s, the wall studs are spaced every 400 or 450 mm. In older properties, spacing can vary. Mark each wall stud along the three level lines wherever cabinets will be installed. You will use these marks to guide where you drive screws that secure the cabinets.

A nifty way to verify your marks and ensure that you have indeed located the wall studs is to hammer in a lost-head nail in an area hidden by the cabinets. If you've found the stud, you'll have trouble driving the nail after it has penetrated the plasterboard.

After you've marked the wall stud locations, attach a temporary *ledger board* to help support the wall cabinets during installation. Use a long 100 x 25 mm timber board. Secure the ledger board along and below the line that marks the bottom of your wall cabinets. Drive a 60 mm-long drywall screw into every other stud to secure the ledger board to the wall (see Figure 3-3). Cut the ledger board to length as needed, depending on the length of your wall cabinet sections.

Figure 3-3:
Attach a ledger board to support wall cabinets temporarily.

Checking your walls for plumb

You need to check to see if your walls are *plumb*, or vertically level. The best way to check is to place a 1200 mm level vertically on adjacent walls at an inside corner. If the wall against which the cabinet end butts is either in or out of plumb (walls can lean slightly inwards or outwards), you will need to *shim* the cabinets (insert thin wooden strips cut from any bit of timber) as you install them to make them plumb. Cabinets that butt an out-of-plumb wall will leave a tapered gap that you will need to address. If the gap is not more than 6 mm wide and you are installing *face-framed* cabinets (American-style cabinets where the doors close onto a timber frame), you can plane the edge of the *stile* (the vertical part of the frame) as needed to close the gap. Larger gaps require that you install a tapered filler strip. Such a strip is best cut on a table saw, so you may want help for this. European-style *frameless* cabinets do not have frames, and the door hinges and catches are fitted direct to the chipboard sides of the cabinets. To fit these cabinets against out-of-plumb walls, the last (exposed) side should be scribed and cut to an exact fit against the wall.

Noting cabinet position

Just as you establish a level horizontal reference line to determine cabinet heights, you must also establish a plumb vertical reference line to locate the cabinet sides. Walls are rarely perfectly plumb. Follow these steps to work out your vertical plumb line:

1. **Starting at an inside corner like the one shown in Figure 3-4 (assuming there is one), use a 1200 mm level to check for plumb.**

2. **If the top of a wall that the end of a cabinet butts into leans in, measure along the wall it will be installed on and mark a point that is equal to the width of the first cabinet.** You can find this dimension on your cabinet order or by measuring the width at the front face of the cabinet.

3. **Using your level, pencil a plumb line from that point to the floor.** If the wall leans out, measure out from the bottom of the wall to locate the reference line; if it bows out at the middle, measure from the middle.

4. **Repeat the procedure on the adjacent wall so you have a line on each wall indicating the location of the first cabinet.**

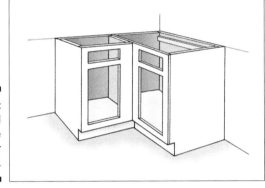

Figure 3-4:
A blind
inside
corner
cabinet unit.

Book III

Renovating
a Property

If you have face-framed cabinets, the frames or faces extend 6 mm beyond either side of each cabinet. Since the initial plumb reference line and the other plumb lines measured from it represent the full width of the cabinet, the back edges of an installed cabinet will be 6 mm away from its line on the wall. If you have frameless cabinets (often referred to as European-style cabinets), the front and rear width dimensions will be the same, so the edge of a cabinet will fall on its line.

Hanging Wall Cabinets

We recommend installing wall cabinets first because you don't have to work above the base cabinets. The open area of the floor allows you, your able assistant, and your stepladder clear access.

Before you mount the wall cabinets, get organised. Unpack each cabinet and remove the doors. Mark each door and cabinet with numbered masking tape so that the door that came off a specific cabinet goes back on the same cabinet. They may look the same, but each door and cabinet box was matched, drilled, and attached to fit only the cabinet it came with. Start with a corner cabinet as No. 1 and then work out in each direction, using the No. 1 cabinet as your starting point.

Note: This section describes installing framed cabinets. Installation instructions for frameless cabinets are similar except when connecting adjoining cabinets, as explained in the next section.

Follow these steps to install your wall cabinets:

1. **Transfer stud locations from the wall to the inside of each cabinet before you lift it into place; and drill clearance holes for the mounting screws.**

   Measure carefully and measure twice. Drill the holes in the upper and lower *hanging rails* of the cabinets (the two horizontal pieces of timber along the top and bottom of the back of the cabinet). Clearance holes, which are the same diameter as the screw, ensure that the cabinet will be drawn tight to the wall by the head of the screw.

2. **Set the first wall cabinet on the ledger strip and 6 mm away from its reference line on the wall; secure the top and bottom of the cabinet to the wall with 75 mm-long #10 cabinet screws, as shown in Figure 3-5.**

   Don't tighten the screws completely. You'll go back later for a final tightening of all the screws after cabinets are aligned with each other, joined together with screws, and plumbed.

Figure 3-5:
Secure the wall cabinet on the ledger strip.

Get your helper to hold the unit in place while you secure it with screws. If you're working alone, cut some lengths of wood and make a V-shaped notch in one end. Use these pieces as braces by placing the notch against the bottom of the cabinet and wedging the wood up to hold the cabinet in place. Put a rag or piece of cardboard over the cabinet to protect it.

3. **Position the second cabinet on the ledger and next to the installed cabinet. Attach it with screws as you did the first one.**

4. **Join the two cabinets with two clamps, located about ¼ the distance from the top and bottom.** Use wooden screw clamps or short bar or sash clamps with padded jaws that won't mar the cabinets. Don't position clamps at hinge locations because this is where you will join the cabinets with screws. As you tighten the clamp ensure that the face, top, and bottom of the two frames are all perfectly flush.

5. **Drill clearance holes through the face frame, countersunk so that the screwheads will be flush with or below the surface, and pilot holes in the adjoining cabinet.**

   Locate the holes at the hinge positions so when the hinges are installed, the screwheads will be concealed. The easiest way to drill these holes is all at once, using an adjustable combination bit.

6. **Drive 60 mm drywall screws into each hole and remove the clamps.**

   If the holes are not properly sized or if you overdrill the screws, they can easily snap off. Use the proper bits and adjust the speed on your drill to limit the drilling to only what is necessary to drive the screws.

7. **Install the remaining wall cabinets along this wall in the same manner and then remove the ledger.**

8. **If the plan calls for a filler strip at a particular location, clamp it to the face frame and attach it as you would attach two cabinets together.**

   Often a filler strip must be *ripped* (cut to width along its length) to suit a particular space, and sometimes it must be tapered as well. As this task should be done on a table saw, you may want to employ a carpenter to help with fillers.

9. **Starting at the corner, plumb the cabinets using the reference line on the adjacent wall and a 600 mm level, and insert shims as required.**

   Install shims behind the cabinet at the bottom or top until the cabinet is plumb and the proper distance from the reference line. Loosen an installation screw, insert the shim until the cabinet is plumb (see Figure 3-6), and drive in the screw again. When all cabinets are plumb, trim off the shims with a very sharp utility knife.

Book III

Renovating a Property

Figure 3-6:
Use shims to make a cabinet plumb.

10. **Similarly complete the installation of cabinets first on adjoining walls and then other walls.**

    Clamp the filler strip in place and drill 5 mm pilot holes through the cabinet face frame and filler strip, using a countersink bit to recess the screw head into the face frame. Secure the strip with 75 mm drywall screws.

11. **Reinstall the doors and check each one for smooth operation.**

    Doors have a tendency to misalign after they've been removed. However, many styles of hinge allow you to make minor adjustments to get doors operating smoothly. Be careful when redriving the screws for the hinges. The screws are generally made from a fairly soft metal, which makes the heads easy to strip and the shafts easy to snap off. A stripped screw can be replaced. A snapped off screw will need to be extracted, because you need to use the same hole that has the broken screw in it. To remove a broken screw, use a screw extractor. Extractor kits are available at home improvement centres and hardware shops for less than £20.

Before moving on to the base cabinets, install a decorative valance over the sink, if your design includes one. You need to position the valance between the two cabinets that flank the sink, secure the valance temporarily with clamps, drill countersink, clearance, and pilot holes through the adjacent cabinet stile into the ends of the valance, and then secure it with 60 mm screws.

The installation steps in this section and those that follow are for face-framed cabinets. Frameless cabinets are installed in much the same manner except when connecting adjoining cabinets. To join frameless cabinets, use wood screws that are just shorter than the thickness of the two cabinet sides. Secure each cabinet with four screws placed about 25 mm in from the front edge of the cabinet. If you drill pilot holes, be very careful not to drill completely through both cabinets.

Adding the Lower Level: Base Cabinets

Now you can fill in the bottom half and install the base cabinets. You start the same way you did with the wall cabinets – unpack each cabinet and remove all doors and drawers, marking each one as you go with numbered masking tape, to make sure that you return the right door or drawer to its intended spot.

Installing the corner cabinet (s)

Start on the same wall and corner where you installed the wall cabinets. The three types of corner unit and installation process are:

✔ A **blind base** installation, where the cabinet on one wall (the blind base) extends almost to the corner, and then a standard base cabinet installed on the adjacent wall butts into it. Install these cabinets as a team and clamp them together as you level, plumb, and attach them to the wall.

✔ A **corner base** single cabinet, which extends 91.5 cm along adjacent walls. You must align it to reference lines on both walls as you level, plumb, and attach it to the wall.

✔ In the third option, **two standard base cabinets meet at their front corners** creating an inaccessible space in the corner. Install these cabinets in pairs to ensure that they meet precisely.

The steps that follow describe an installation that starts with a blind base:

1. **Position the blind base cabinet and then the standard base cabinet on the adjacent wall that butts into it, as shown in Figure 3-4.**

2. **Working on both cabinets, insert shims under the exposed ends and front edges until each cabinet is flush with the horizontal line and 6 mm away from the plumb reference line on its wall.**

   Use a level across the top, from front to back and on the face of the cabinet, while inserting tapered shims. Shim under exposed edges to raise the back to the line; shim under the front to level the front from side to side and back to front (see Figure 3-7).

3. **Clamp the top edges of the cabinets together.**

   Because the face frame overhangs the base cabinet by 6 mm, insert a 6 mm shim between the cabinets near the back edge to maintain that 6 mm space.

4. **Attach the cabinets to the wall with 75 mm screws at each wall stud location.**

   Drill clearance holes in the rails first and don't drive the screw tight just yet. Chances are you'll still need to spend time shimming the cabinets until they are just right.

5. **Check the cabinets again to make sure that they are plumb and level in all directions, and that they still align properly with the two reference lines and with each other.**

   Loosen an installation screw to insert a permanent shim behind the cabinet at each stud location as needed. Tighten the screw to secure the cabinet and keep the shim in place. Spend lots of time getting this corner perfect: Proper installation of the remaining cabinets depends on it.

Figure 3-7:
Use shims
as needed
to level the
blind base
cabinet.

Finishing the base cabinet installation

Installing the rest of the base cabinets is less strenuous than hanging the wall cabinets because the cabinets rest on the floor and don't need to be supported while you secure them to the wall. However, it's still a good idea to have someone nearby to help make adjustments.

Before you install your sink-base cabinet, you may need to make cut-outs for the plumbing pipes if the cabinet has a back (see Figure 3-8). Measure from the side of the adjacent cabinet to the centre of each plumbing supply or waste pipe. Transfer those measurements to the back of the cabinet and use a hole saw or jigsaw to cut out openings for your plumbing pipes to fit through. If you make a mistake in the cutting, stick a piece of 6 mm-thick hardboard or plywood to the botched panel and cut new holes. No one will see the bodge-job!

Figure 3-8:
Make cut-
outs for the
plumbing
pipes in the
back of the
panel.

Follow these steps to finish installing the base cabinets:

1. **Place the next cabinet in position and check it for plumb and level.**

2. **If shims are needed, gently tap them into place with a hammer.**

   Don't trust your eye to check for level. Just because the two cabinets are flush along the top edge doesn't mean that they're both level and plumb. Check it and adjust as necessary. You may need to place shims under the front or exposed side of the cabinet and between the back of the cabinet and the wall.

3. **Attach the cabinets together as you did the wall cabinets. (See the 'Hanging Wall Cabinets' section, Steps 4, 5, and 6, earlier in this chapter, and see Figure 3-9.)**

Book III

**Renovating
a Property**

Figure 3-9:
Connect
the base
cabinets
with 60 mm
screws.

4. **Install the remaining cabinets and any required filler strips in the same way, attaching each one to the previously installed cabinet.**

   Complete the installation of each cabinet and then check all installed cabinets for level, plumb, and alignment before moving on to the next cabinet.

After the cabinets are secured, cut away all protruding shims as you did for wall cabinets. If you have a gap between an end panel and the wall, use a decorative trim to cover the gap, as with the wall cabinets. To cover a gap at the floor along the area called the kick space, install a strip of matching hardwood called the *plinth*, which clips onto the adjustable cabinet legs.

Don't reinstall the doors and drawers on the base cabinets until after you've installed the worktop (see Chapter 4) – they are safer out of the way, and you need to have access to the underside of the worktop to secure it to the cabinets.

Chapter 4

Installing Worktops and Sinks

A new worktop can add a finishing touch to a total kitchen remodel or stand alone as an upgrade that makes an outdated kitchen look fantastic. A new worktop doesn't cost that much, either. Stock worktops cost as little as £15 to £20 per linear metre. Even custom-made and ceramic tile worktops and splashbacks aren't that expensive – at least when compared to the cost of remodelling an entire kitchen.

A moderately skilled DIYer can handle the installation of a post-formed worktop, which is a seamless piece of laminate with a chipboard base that covers the entire splashback, flat surface, and front edge of the worktop. A ceramic tile worktop isn't too far beyond the skill level of most average to experienced DIYers, either, if you take your time and have some patience. However, leave installing solid-surface, granite, and concrete worktops to a pro.

Gathering the Right Tools

We can't stress enough how much easier you make your task by getting all the tools together for the entire project before you start. Set up a pair of sawhorses and a half sheet (1200 x 1200 mm) of plywood to act as a staging area for tools. With that setup, you have all the tools laid out so that they're easy to grab when you need them.

Here are the tools you need for installing worktops:

✔ 13 mm open-end wrench

✔ 10 mm corded or cordless drill

✔ 18 mm spade bit, or flat bit

- 18 mm thick wood strip for support behind the laminate end cap
- Belt sander
- G-clamps
- Compass (no, not the one for finding North)
- Plasterboard screws (25, 30, and 40 mm)
- End-cap kit (for finishing the ends of the worktop)
- Fine-tooth steel plywood blade
- Hand file
- Heavy-duty extension cable
- Heavy-duty work gloves and eye protection
- Household iron
- Levels (both 600 mm and 1200 mm)
- Masking tape
- Package of wood shims
- Phillips/Posidrive screwdrivers (medium-sized, straight-tip, and No. 2)
- Portable circular saw
- Powered jigsaw
- Pressure sticks (short lengths of 1 x 1 or 1 x 2 board or trim)
- Rags or cardboard (to protect your worktop's surface when you use squeeze clamps)
- Sanding belts, sized for your belt sander (coarse, 60 grit; medium, 100 grit)
- Sawhorses (two)
- Scrap 1 x 4 board of short length
- Squeeze clamps (at least one pair)
- Tube of construction adhesive
- Tube of silicone caulk and a caulk gun
- Utility knife

Installing a Worktop

Post-formed worktops are great for DIYers because the laminating step is eliminated and the mitred corners are pre-cut. Stock worktops are available in 1-metre increments, so to complete an installation you have a bit of work ahead of you. First, you need to *scribe* the worktop (this means using a piece of wood and a pencil to copy the shape of the wall onto the end of the worktop) to fit against any end wall. Then cut it to length; if it turns a corner, you'll join the pre-cut 45-degree mitred ends. After you've installed the worktop, you cut out a hole for your sink (if your worktop wasn't already pre-cut for a sink) – certainly enough sawing and drilling to give you that DIYer's high!

Before you begin, remove the cabinet doors as well as the drawers from the base cabinets. Clear access makes worktop installation easier.

Ensuring a perfect fit: Scribing and trimming

Wouldn't it be great if your walls were as straight and true as the edges of the worktop? Fat chance!

The best way to check whether a corner is square is to use this simple geometric formula:

1. **Measure 300 mm along one wall from the corner, and mark that spot.**

2. **Measure out 400 mm along the other wall and mark that spot.**

3. **Measure the distance between the marks.** If the walls are square, the distance between the marks will be 500 mm.

Book III

Renovating a Property

If the corner where the worktops fit is out of square even by as little as 10 to 15 mm, you're likely to damage the worktop by trying to make it fit without trimming it to size. If you find that your walls aren't close to square, hire a professional to do the installation.

To shape the edges of your worktop, you need to transfer the contour of the wall onto the worktop's edge surface. Use a compass to scribe, or transfer, the wall's contour onto the laminate. Follow these steps to ensure a perfect fit:

1. **Set the worktop in place where you plan to install it.**

   When installing any section of worktop, check that it's level. Use a 600 or 1200 mm level. If the worktop isn't level, slide shims between the worktop and the support struts of the cabinet frame to level the worktop. The shims will remain in place and won't move after you secure the worktop to the cabinets.

2. **Set your compass to fit the tip in the widest gap between the worktop and the wall.**

3. **Move the compass along the wall to draw a pencil line on the worktop's surface that matches the wall contour (see Figure 4-1).**

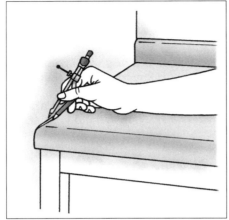

Figure 4-1:
Scribe a line on the worktop surface.

4. **Remove the worktop and set it on a pair of sawhorses.**

5. **Secure the worktop to the sawhorses with G-clamps.**

   Place a piece of hardboard between the clamp jaws and the worktop's surface to protect the surface.

6. **Remove the excess worktop (up to the pencil line) with a belt sander and a coarse (60-grit) sanding belt (see Figure 4-2).**

   A coarse belt works best because it removes laminate and the substrate (base) quickly yet neatly. If you have a lot of excess worktop, say 3 mm or more, cut off most of it with a jigsaw and then use a belt sander to finish up to the pencil line.

   Hold the sander as shown in Figure 4-2. Avoid an upward cut, which might chip or lift the plastic laminate.

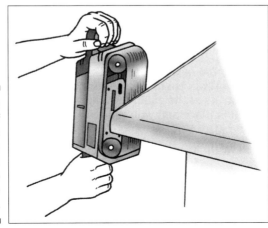

Figure 4-2:
Sand off excess laminate and substrate up to the scribed line.

7. **Reposition the worktop and check for any tight spots.**

8. **Touch up any tight spots with the sander and recheck the fit again before cutting it to length (as described in the following section).**

   You want the worktop to fit, especially if you're installing it during the humid summer months when the wall is fatter with humidity. If you're installing the worktop in the drier winter months, leave a gap of about 1.5 mm along the wall to allow for movement due to changes in temperature and humidity. Fill the gap with a bead of silicone caulk as one of the final steps in the remodel.

Sizing and finishing your worktop

Stock worktops are sold in 1-metre increments, so most people have excess to cut off and end caps to apply.

Cutting off excess

The easiest way to cut off any extra length of a post-formed worktop is with a circular saw and fine-tooth steel plywood blade. Don't use a carbide-tipped blade – those blades have larger teeth, which increase your chances of chipping the laminate. Just follow these steps:

Book III

Renovating a Property

1. **Place the worktop upside down on a pair of 100 x 50 mm timbers on sawhorses.**

   Be sure to extend the 100 x 50s under the entire worktop so that the cut-off is fully supported. You may want to clamp the worktop to the sawhorses for extra security; however, the weight of the worktop should be enough to keep it from moving.

2. **Measure the length of worktop that you need and mark a cutting line on the base.**

3. **Cut and clamp scraps of 100 x 25 to the splashback (if it has one) and to the underside of the counter to guide your cuts (see Figure 4-3).**

   The distance between the guide and the cut line varies according to the saw and blade that you use. Measure the distance from the edge of the saw shoe (base) to the inside edge of the blade to determine proper spacing.

4. **Make your vertical cut through the splashback first and then cut from the rear of the worktop toward the front.**

   Support the cut-off end or have a helper hold it while you cut. Failure to do so causes the piece to fall away before it's completely cut and will break the laminate unevenly, ruining the worktop.

Figure 4-3:
Cut the
worktop
along your
cutting
guide.

Applying end caps

If your worktop has an exposed end that doesn't butt against a wall or into a corner, you need to finish it by applying a laminate end cap – a piece of the laminate surface to cover the exposed end.

Laminate end caps are designed to cover either left- or right-hand counter ends. Kits usually come with one of each. End caps are pre-cut to fit the worktop profile but oversized at the back edge to allow for a scribed fit, so you need to do some trimming with a hand file. End caps also come coated with heat-activated adhesive, which makes installation a doddle. Follow these steps:

1. **Attach the provided wood strips to the bottom and back edges of the worktop with wood glue and brads, which the kit may also provide.**

    These strips support the end cap because the base alone isn't thick enough. Make sure that the strips are flush with the outer edge.

2. **Position the end cap on the cut end of the worktop and align the angle and corner with the contour of the worktop's surface.**

3. **Maintain that alignment as you run a hot clothes iron over the end cap to activate the adhesive.**

4. **After the glue and end cap have cooled, finish the edges.**

    File off excess material that extends past the backing strips. Also, lightly file the top edge so it isn't quite as sharp. A hand file works best. Push the file simultaneously towards the worktop and along its length.

Never remove excess by pulling the file – always push! Pulling breaks the glue bond, and the end cap will come off and may even break.

5. **Reinstall the cabinet doors, put the drawers back in place, and you're done.**

Installing a mitred corner

If your worktop turns a corner, it probably has two pieces, each with a 45-degree angle, or mitre cut. You'll probably have to do some scribing and trimming of the splashback to get it to fit against the wall without leaving gaps and to make the front edges of the two pieces meet without any of the base showing. Follow these steps:

1. **Place the worktop pieces in the corner to assess the fit.**

   Align the two pieces so the mitred edges meet properly. Push the two worktop pieces against the wall and into the corner as far as possible without misaligning the edges. At the same time, adjust the worktop pieces until the overhang at the cabinet face is exactly the same along the entire length of both tops.

2. **Scribe and trim the back edges of each piece (as described in the 'Ensuring a perfect fit: Scribing and trimming' section) so that the rear mitred points fit exactly in the corner of the wall.**

   Typically, excess plaster in the corners requires you to trim some material from this area. Additional trimming may be required to compensate for other wall irregularities.

3. **Before you join the pieces, mark the ends where you need to cut them to length (as described in the preceding section).**

4. **After cutting the tops to length and applying the laminate ends, apply wood glue to both edges of the mitred joint and reposition the two sections.**

5. **Connect the two pieces from the underside with the toggle bolts that came with the worktop.**

   Position the wings of the bolt into the slots on each piece. Tighten the bolt with an open-end wrench. As you do so, check the joint on the surface to make sure that the seam is perfectly flush. If it isn't, adjust the worktop position and retighten the toggle bolts.

6. **To ensure that the joint stays flush while it dries, place a G-clamp on the front edge joint and place pressure sticks on either side of the joint, as shown in Figure 4-4.**

Book III

Renovating a Property

Pressure sticks are simply two equal lengths of board (usually 25 mm square) that are slightly longer than the distance between the worktop and the bottom of the wall cabinets. The sticks need to be longer than that distance so you can wedge them in place to force pressure onto the worktop.

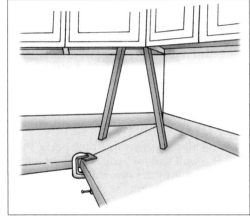

Figure 4-4:
Create a smooth seam with pressure sticks.

Cutting a hole for the sink

The splashback may interfere with making the rear cut for a sink cut-out. In that case, you must make the cut with the worktop upside down – so make the sink cut-out after testing the fit but before joining any mitre joints or attaching the worktop.

You can order your worktops pre-cut, including a hole for the sink, but do so only if you know that all your measurements are absolutely, positively dead-on, with no chance of being off by even a little bit. And if you're like us, that's very unlikely. Cutting a hole in a post-formed worktop isn't difficult. Just follow these steps and take your time for professional-looking results.

Using a template

Most sinks come with a paper or cardboard template to help outline the area you're going to cut out. Quite often, the cardboard template is part of the packaging for the sink. Use a utility knife to cut the template from the box.

If your sink doesn't come with a template, you can make your own:

1. **Place the sink upside down on the worktop where you're going to install it.**

2. **Measure from the back edge of the sink to the splashback to make sure that the sink is evenly positioned.**

   Make sure that the sink is back far enough – typically very close to the splashback – so that when you install the sink, it will fit behind the cabinets with room for the fixing clips.

3. **Trace around the outer edge of the sink with a pencil.**

   Have a helper hold the sink in place or tape it to ensure that it doesn't shift while you're tracing.

4. **Measure the lip on the underside of the sink.**

5. **Mark the dimension of the lip in from the line you traced around the sink.**

   Mark the lip dimension on the worktop at several points inside the traced line and then draw straight lines connecting the marks. You can freehand the corners – just follow the same shape as the corners you traced by using the sink.

   The distance between the two lines forms the lip on the worktop to support your sink. The inner line is the cutting line.

Making the sink cut-out

To cut a hole for a sink, a jigsaw is the easiest, most reliable, and safest saw to use. (**Note:** Always, always, always use a new jigsaw blade. An old or dull blade can chip the laminate along the cutting line.) Some people use a circular saw; however, doing so involves making a plunge-cut with the blade because you don't have a big enough starter hole to work with. Wear heavy gloves and eye protection when making this cut. Follow these steps:

1. **Drill two starter holes in opposite corners just inside the cutting line. Use an 18 mm spade bit and drill through the laminate and base.**

   Don't worry if the cut edge is rough. The rim of the sink will cover it. You're cutting into sections that you'll eventually cut out and discard.

2. **Place the blade of the jigsaw in the starter hole and line up the blade exactly on the cutting line (see Figure 4-5).**

3. **Cut slowly along the line.**

   Don't be in a rush – let the saw do the work. Again, don't worry about any little chips that may occur: The sink lip will cover them.

 If the splashback interferes with the saw shoe and prevents you making the cut, turn the worktop over to complete the cut from the underside. If you choose this method, make this cut first. To make a clean, safe cut, ask a helper to support the cut-out area so that the piece doesn't drop and cause the saw blade to bind. Make sure your helper wears heavy gloves and eye protection.

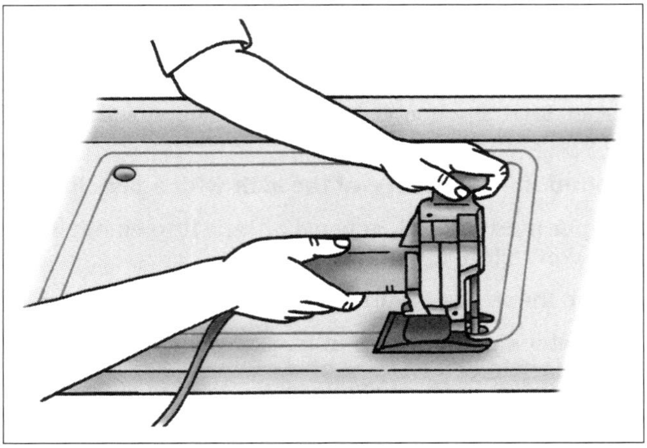

Figure 4-5:
Insert the jigsaw blade in the starter hole and cut around the cutting line.

When it's time to install the sink and taps, move on to the 'Installing a Sink and Taps' section for all the information you need. You'll find it easier to drill for and even install the taps before you attach the worktop.

Securing the worktop to the base cabinets

After you've scribed, trimmed, test fitted, and applied any end caps to the worktop, and the glue has set at any mitred corners, you can begin the job of securing it to the base cabinets. Some chipboard worktops come equipped with nylon brackets that are screwed to the underside of the worktop and into the sides of the base cabinets (from the inside). Other worktop materials have to be glued to the base cabinets.

Don't start securing the worktop to the cabinets until the mitred joint has dried. Allow the glue to dry for at least four hours, or overnight if you have time – it's better to wait a little longer than to rush the job and have the seam break because the glue hasn't set. If the seam does break, you need to remove the old glue – a very difficult task – and start again.

Follow these steps to attach a worktop to the base cabinets:

1. **Position the worktop pieces on the cabinets.**

2. **Screw the nylon fixing brackets in place or, to glue the worktop, apply a bead of silicone caulk or construction adhesive (as specified by the worktop manufacturer) along the top edge of all the cabinet parts that support the worktop.**

   Tip up a straight worktop to apply the adhesive. Insert shims under a mitred worktop rather than trying to tip it up to prevent breaking the glue joint. The caulk or adhesive will hold all the parts in place after it dries.

3. **Lower the worktop back into place or remove the shims.**

4. **Place pressure sticks every 300 to 450 mm to help the adhesive bond the worktop to the cabinets at the back edge, and apply clamps to the front edge.**

   Place pressure sticks along the back corners (where the corner blocks are located) to get the worktop down tight.

5. **Seal any gap between the splashback and the wall or along the edges and the wall with a clear silicone acrylic sealer.**

6. **Reinstall the cabinet doors, put the drawers back in place, and have another cup of tea.**

If you're going to paint the walls and you want to paint the clear sealer, make sure the label says that it can be painted. Most silicone acrylic sealer is paintable, whereas regular silicone sealer isn't.

Installing a Sink and Taps

Installing a sink and taps is easy, whether you're doing a complete remodel or simply updating the look of your kitchen. The information in this chapter, coupled with the manufacturer's instructions for both the sink and the taps, will help you through the steps.

Book III

Renovating a Property

Here are the tools you need to gather for installing your sink and taps:

- ✔ Groove-joint pliers
- ✔ Adjustable wrench
- ✔ No. 2 Phillips/Posidrive screwdriver
- ✔ Medium-sized slotted (straight-tip) screwdriver
- ✔ Caulk gun
- ✔ A tube of silicone caulk/adhesive
- ✔ A small container of plumber's putty
- ✔ Bucket and rags

Setting the stage: Preparing to install your sink

Much of the work of sink installation actually takes place before you set the sink into the worktop. Taking your time with the preliminary work ensures a smooth installation.

If you don't install your sink and taps according to the instructions, you'll have to foot the bill for the replacement even if the product is defective.

Taking the measurements

In most cases, the old plumbing configuration will work with your new sink. But if you're making a major change in the design of the new sink, make sure that the old plumbing fits the new sink's requirements. So, before you buy or order a sink, take a few measurements.

Establishing the drain height

Measure the distance from the underside of the worktop to the centre of the waste pipe that comes out of the wall. This distance is usually between 400 and 450 mm, which allows adequate space for the water to drop into the trap and still leaves enough space below the trap for storing items underneath the sink in the cabinet.

The drain height is usually not an issue unless you're going from a very shallow sink to one that has a very deep bowl (225 to 300 mm deep). Even if you do switch to a deeper bowl, it may only be a problem if your old setup had a shallow bowl coupled with a high drain exit position.

If you do find that you only have a few centimetres of space between the bottom of the bowl and the centre of the drainpipe, contact a licensed plumber to assess the situation and determine if the waste pipe needs to be lowered.

Determining the shut-off valve heights

You should also measure the height of the *shut-off valves*, the small isolating valves that allow you to cut off the water supply to an individual tap or appliance. Measure from the floor of the sink base cabinet to the centre of the valve.

If your sink doesn't have shut-off valves, install them now while you're working on the system.

Attaching the taps before installing the sink

Yes, the heading is correct. The easiest and best way to install the taps is before the sink is in place. If you install the taps before installing the sink, you won't have to strain or reach because everything is completely open.

Most sinks come with factory-drilled holes along the back edge or lip for the taps.

Securing the taps to the sink

Before you begin, create a stable workspace where you can safely position the sink. Put down some cardboard to prevent accidentally scratching the sink surface when it's time to flip the sink over to tighten the tap nuts.

It's time to begin the assembly process.

1. **Place the taps over the holes, with the taps' water supply** *tailpieces* **(threaded pieces located directly beneath the taps' handles) going through the holes.**

2. **Screw the plastic nuts onto the threaded tails (which will later connect to the supply lines) and hand-tighten until snug.**

3. **Use groove-joint pliers to finish tightening the nuts.**

   Be careful not to over-tighten the nuts. Plastic nuts are easy to strip or ruin with pliers.

4. **Seal the area where the taps meet the sink, according to the manufacturer's instructions.**

   Some taps come with a rubber gasket that goes on the bottom of the tap body between them and the sink. Other tap manufacturers recommend applying a bead of silicone mastic on the bottom of the tap body before positioning the taps on the sink. Both methods keep water from getting underneath the taps where it could run down the factory-drilled holes and drip onto the sink base cabinet floor.

Attaching water supply lines to the taps

After the taps are secured to the sink, you can attach the water supply pipes that will eventually be connected to the shut-off valves on the main water supply pipes. Regardless of what your supply pipe is made of, it probably uses a coupling nut to secure it to the tap's tailpiece. Simply screw the coupling nut onto the tailpiece until it's snug and then give it a couple of final twists with groove-joint pliers.

Don't rush when attaching the supply pipes. Tap tailpieces are usually either brass or plastic, and the threads can be easily stripped if the coupling nut is started unevenly. Finger-tightening the nut onto the tailpiece helps ensure that it's going on straight.

Dealing with factory-attached tails

Some taps come with factory-attached soft-copper supply pipes on both the hot- and cold-water tails, which means the only attaching will be directly to the shut-off valves. You should, however, do a little preshaping of the soft copper before setting the sink into position in the worktop.

Book III

Renovating a Property

Measure the distance between the water supply pipes under the sink and then gently bend the soft-copper supply tails until they're about the same distance apart as the water supply pipes – they don't have to be exact, just close.

Be very, very careful when shaping the soft copper. Soft copper is very fragile and kinks relatively easily. You won't be able to get rid of the kink, which restricts water flow and will eventually begin to leak.

The best way to shape the copper into position is to gently slide it through your hands as you gradually move it into position. Don't try to shape the copper in one go. Make two or three passes through your hands for best results.

Installing flexible copper supply tubes

Flexible copper supply tubes are similar to, if not the same as, the factory-attached soft-copper supply tubes found on some taps. The same care is needed to bend and shape the copper tubes that you install. Try to shape the tubes into position before attaching them to the sink's tails. After the tubes have been shaped, secure them to the tailpiece with the coupling nut.

If the supply tubes are too long for your supply setup, cut them to length to fit into the open end of the shut-off valve. Determining how much to cut off is easy:

1. **Position the tube between the tailpiece and the shut-off valve and mark the tube so that it will fit down into the valve after it has been cut.**

2. **Use a tube cutter to cut off the excess.**

3. **Attach the tube to the tail with a coupling nut and use the compression nut and ring to secure the other end of the tube to the shut-off valve.**

Installing braided tails

One of the best new plumbing products to come along is the line of braided steel supply pipes. These pipes are constructed of a rubber supply tube (like a hose) wrapped in a steel-braided outer jacket. They're so flexible you can take the excess length and simply put a loop in it and then connect it to the shut-off valve.

Other sink extras, such as a soap dispenser or spray hose, should be installed now. Follow the manufacturer's installation instructions.

Putting things in position: Finishing your installation

It's time to put the sink in place and see how it looks. After the sink is in place, you can make the supply pipe and waste pipe connections that transform the gaping hole in your worktop into a working sink.

Setting in your sink

If you're installing a stainless steel sink, you can probably handle the lifting and positioning yourself. However, if your new sink is cast iron or cast enamel, get a helper. These sinks are heavy and awkward to handle. Follow these steps:

1. **First, dry-fit the sink to determine exactly the right spot.**

   Set the sink into the opening in the worktop. Centre the sink in the opening and then draw a light pencil line on both sides and along the front edge of the sink.

2. **Lift out the sink and flip it over.**

   Lay a piece of cardboard on the worktop to protect it (and the sink) from scratching and then flip the sink over so that the tap handles hang over the edge of the worktop.

3. **Apply a bead of silicone mastic (about 5 mm wide) around the edge.**

   The mastic prevents water from getting between the sink and the worktop, and it also holds the sink in place. Use a silicone-based bath and basin mastic, which usually contains mildew killers and stands up against the dirt, soap scum, and gunk that you find around the kitchen sink. Silicone mastics also remain somewhat flexible, which is helpful because the sink actually drops very slightly when full of water and lifts when the water is drained. The movement is very slight, but over time this movement would cause a regular oil-based mastic to crack.

   After the mastic has been applied, you need to install the sink quickly so the mastic doesn't dry before you get it in place.

4. **Lower the sink into position using the pencil lines to get it in the same location.**

Connecting the supply pipes

No matter what type of material you use for your water supply pipes, you want leak-free connections. The fastest connection to use is the screw-on nut and washer that's on the end of a steel-braided supply pipe. Simply tighten the nut onto the threaded outlet on the tap tail and the shut-off valve.

Another common connection is a *compression fitting*. It consists of a *coupling nut*, which secures the fitting to the tap tail and the shut-off valve, and a *brass compression ring*, which forms the sealed connection between the supply pipe and the fitting it's attached to. Compression fittings are a tighter connection than a screw-on nut and washer fitting. Here's how to install a compression fitting:

1. **Start by sliding the compression nut onto the supply pipe with the nut threads facing the valve.**

2. **Now slide the compression ring onto the supply pipe.**

Book III

Renovating a Property

3. **Place the end of the supply pipe into the appropriate valve, making sure that it fits squarely in the valve opening.**

   If the supply pipe end doesn't go in straight, the connection will leak, because the angle of the end of the supply pipe won't allow the compression ring to sit properly between the supply pipe and the valve fitting.

4. **Reshape the pipe until it fits squarely.**

5. **Once the pipe is in place, pull the compression ring and nut onto the valve and screw it tight.**

6. **Open the shut-off valve to check the connection for leaks.**

   Keep some rags handy, just in case.

Hooking up the waste pipe

Drain kits come in different materials and configurations, but installing them is a piece of cake. Choose the kit with the configuration for your sink type, and you're halfway home!

Choosing the right kit

You have a couple of choices for drain kits: Chrome and PVC. Both kits work well and are equally easy to use. The main factor on deciding which one to use is cosmetic – will the waste pipe be visible? If it will be visible, you'll want to use the chrome kit. If it's out of sight in the sink base cabinet, which most kitchen drains are, then the good old white plastic PVC kit is the way to go; it's cheaper, too.

Kitchen sink drain kits use nut and washer screw-together connections. As well as being easy to install, these kits also let you easily disconnect the assembly to unclog a drain or rescue that wedding ring that fell down the plughole. A basic, single-bowl kit includes:

  ✔ A **tailpiece,** which connects to the bottom of the waste outlet

  ✔ A **trap bend** (or P-trap), which forms a water-filled block to prevent sewer gas from coming up through the sink drain

  ✔ A **trap arm,** which is connected to the downstream end of the P-trap and then to the waste pipe that leads to the main drainage pipe

A double-bowl drain kit will have everything the single-bowl kit has along with a waste tee connection (a T-shaped bit of pipe) and additional length of waste pipe to connect both bowls to a single P-trap.

If your sink has a waste disposal unit, you need an additional longer section of waste pipe to connect the disposal unit's waste pipe to the bowl waste pipe. The crosspiece that comes in the kit will hopefully be long enough to make the connection between the unit and other sink bowl waste pipes. Follow your unit's installation instructions.

Making the connection

Assembling and connecting the drain kit is fairly simple. Don't expect the horizontal pieces to be in really straight alignment with the tailpieces or the waste pipe. The only thing that matters is that they all eventually get connected together. Follow these steps to assemble and connect your drain kit:

1. **Start by attaching the tailpiece to the sink waste and tightening the slip nut and washer by hand.**

   If you have a multiple-bowl sink, all of the drain tailpieces should be the same length for an easier installation.

2. **Next, slip the trap onto the tailpiece and then position the trap's horizontal piece next to the waste pipe coming out of the wall.**

   The horizontal piece must fit inside the end of the waste pipe. Remove the trap and cut the horizontal section to fit using a fine-tooth saw (a tenon saw or junior hacksaw).

3. **Reattach the trap to the tailpiece and into the waste pipe and tighten the slip nuts and washers.**

Checking for leaks

Before you do anything else, get the bucket and rags ready. Lay some rags directly below each connection so that, if there is a leak, the towels will immediately soak up the water. Leave the rags there for a couple of days, just in case a leak develops over time.

Have your helper turn on the water while you begin inspecting for leaks. Don't open up the shut-off valve just yet. Let the water pressure build up to the shut-off valve so that there's time for any slow-leak drips to occur. Leaving the valves closed for a few minutes should be long enough to know whether any water is leaking. Once you know the shut-off valve connection isn't leaking, open the valve so that the water goes into the supply pipes. Again, let the water pressure build in the supply pipes for a few minutes and then inspect the supply connections at the tap tails.

Don't be alarmed if you have a joint that leaks. Just shut off the water, take a deep breath, disassemble and reassemble the connection, and check again for leaks.

Book III

Renovating a Property

Installing a Ceramic Tile Worktop

Ceramic tile is attractive, durable, and resistant to spills and stains. A ceramic tile worktop is more expensive than a post-formed top and involves considerably more work to install, but the beauty of ceramic tile is usually enough to offset the extra cost and labour. See Chapter 5 for more on tiling.

Gathering additional tools for tiles

In addition to the tools listed at the beginning of this chapter, here's what you need to install a tile worktop:

- 18 mm marine-grade plywood
- 25 x 50 mm board (used for front-edge build-up)
- Framing square
- Grout and grout sealer
- Notched trowel
- Plastic tile spacers
- Rubber grout float
- Tile adhesive (mastic) or thinset mortar
- Tile backer board, such as cement board
- Tile cutter
- Tile nipper (special pliers used for cutting/nipping small pieces)
- Tiles, straight and bull-nose (curved for the worktop edge trim)

Constructing your ceramic worktop

You need two styles of tile for a worktop: Straight-edged (plain) tiles, and bull-nose tiles. Bull-nose tiles come in two styles: A single rounded edge for use along a straight edge, and a double bull-nose (two adjacent rounded edges) for use on outside corners.

You can use worktop edge-trim tiles instead of bull-nose tiles. Using a wet saw, you cut the edge-trim tiles to length and mitre them to fit inside and outside corners. (Your tile supplier can usually make wet-saw cuts for you.) The splashback on a ceramic tile top can be installed over a separate chipboard core (backer board isn't needed) or directly on the wall. The top of the splashback can end with a bull-nose tile or extend to the underside of wall cabinets. Figure 4-6 shows how a ceramic tile worktop fits together.

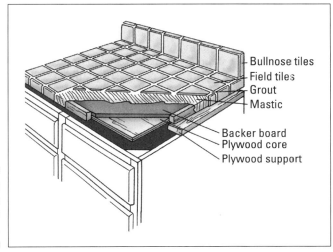

Bullnose tiles
Field tiles
Grout
Mastic

Backer board
Plywood core
Plywood support

Figure 4-6:
The layers
of a tile
worktop.

Follow these steps for building a ceramic tile worktop:

Book III

**Renovating
a Property**

1. **Cut and position the marine-grade plywood so it fits against the wall flush with the face of the cabinets. Secure it to the cabinets with plasterboard screws.**

   Drill pilot holes through the plywood into the top edges of the cabinets. Remove the plywood, apply construction adhesive to the tops of the cabinets, then replace the plywood and drive in the screws.

2. **Cut the tile backer board, such as cement board, and test its fit.**

   To cut cement board, score the surface with a utility knife guided by a metal or wood straightedge; snap along the scored line; and complete the cut of the reinforcing material with your utility knife.

3. **Attach the backer board with cement board screws or exterior-rated plasterboard screws, as suggested by the manufacturer.**

   For a more rigid installation, use a notched trowel to apply mastic or thinset mortar (available where tiles are sold) over the plywood before attaching the backer board.

4. **Fill in the screwhead holes with filler or thinset mortar.**

   Allow the filler to dry and then sand it smooth.

5. **Attach a 25 x 50 mm board to the front edge, making sure it's flush with the top of the backer board.**

   Glue and nail the board to the plywood.

6. **Position bull-nose tiles (or worktop edge-trim tiles) on the front edge.**

   Position a line of plain tiles next to the bull-nose tiles separated by tile spacers (which will be hidden by the grout). Add more spacers on the back edge and place a straightedge against it. Then trace a line along the board to mark the edge of the first course of plain tiles. This is the first line of your centreline.

7. **Mark the centreline perpendicular to the line you just drew, as shown in Figure 4-7.**

   Align one leg of a framing square with the line of tiles and the other side will indicate the centreline.

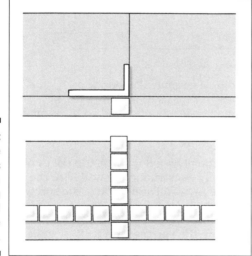

Figure 4-7:
Mark the centrelines using a framing square and dry-fit the tiles.

8. **Dry-fit rows of tile along the lines using tile spacers.**

   On a straight worktop, determine whether it's best to centre a tile on the centreline or align an edge with it. Choose whichever leaves you with the widest tile at the ends. If you have a worktop that turns a corner, lay out the tiles starting at the corner. On a worktop that wraps two corners, lay out tiles starting at the corners and plan the last (cut) tile to fall in the centre of the sink.

9. **Use a tile cutter to make straight cuts on plain and bull-nose tiles (see Figure 4-8).**

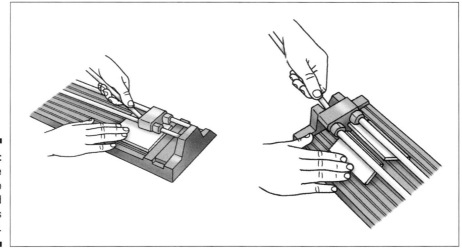

Figure 4-8:
Use a tile
cutter to
score and
cut the tiles
to fit.

10. **To make curved cuts, freehand score the area on the tile to be removed with a glass cutter.**

    Then use a tile nipper to break off numerous small pieces until the cut-out is complete (see Figure 4-9).

Book III

Renovating a Property

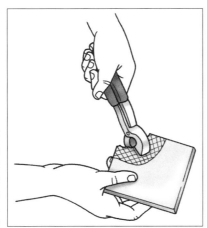

Figure 4-9:
Remove
small pieces
with a tile
nipper.

11. **After you've dry-fit and cut all the tiles, secure them to the base with mastic or thinset mortar.**

    Apply the mastic or thinset mortar with a notched trowel to ensure a uniform coat, and use plastic tile spacers between tiles to ensure even spacing. Allow the mastic or thinset mortar to set for at least 24 hours.

12. **Fill the gaps between the tiles with grout using a rubber grout float.**

   Hold the float at a 45-degree angle to the tiles and use a sweeping motion to force grout into the gaps. Wipe off any excess grout with a damp sponge. Let the grout dry for about an hour and then wipe off any haze on the tile. Don't let grout on the tile dry for too long or you'll never get it off! After you clean the surface, allow the grout to dry for as long as the instructions say on the packet.

13. **Seal the grout with a penetrating silicone grout sealer.**

   Although sealing the grout is a tedious job, it's critical that you do it to keep the grout from staining and to extend its useful life.

Chapter 5

Out on the Tiles: Tiling in Kitchens and Bathrooms

*T*iles are hardwearing, easy to clean, and stylish. Whether you fancy minimalist white, colourful mosaics, or luxurious marble, you can find tiles to suit every taste and budget. Tiled surfaces are also basically waterproof, which makes them favourites for shower enclosures and kitchen splashbacks. Tiling can also be a lot of fun – it's the quickest way we know of transforming a rough old wall into a gleaming 'as-new' sparkling surface.

This chapter shows you how to choose and buy tiles, measure up for quantities, fix the tiles to the wall, and grout them to achieve an attractive, professional-looking tiled finish.

Choosing Your Tiles

For bathrooms and shower enclosures, the classic (and, coincidentally, the easiest and cheapest) tiled finish is achieved with plain 150 x 150 mm square white ceramic tiles. For variation, you can add stripes of 75 mm coloured half-tiles as borders, at skirting or dado height, or to line up with the washbasin or the top of the door frame or shower door. Or, for a different touch of colour, try coloured grout. Plain white tiles with a dark blue or dark red grout can look stunning. You can buy coloured grout ready-mixed, or buy pigment to add to white powder grout. The larger the spacers between the tiles, the more dramatic the visual effect of the coloured grout.

Tile tips

To find out how many tiles you need, measure the height of the wall and multiply it by the width of the wall. This gives you the total surface area. Boxes of tiles are usually marked with the *coverage*, which means the total area you can tile with the contents of the box. To find out how many boxes of tiles you need, simply divide your area by the coverage.

Allow for breakages by counting half-tiles as full tiles when measuring up. Buy 10 per cent extra, just in case. Some shops offer a refund for any unused boxes of tiles, but you should keep a few spares in case you need to replace a cracked tile in the future.

Check that the batch number on each box of tiles is the same, to avoid strong differences in colour. For natural stone tiles, slight variations in colour are normal, so mix the tiles from different boxes before you start tiling.

If white tiles aren't adventurous enough for you, you have plenty of other choices:

- ✔ **Coloured tiles** come in a huge variety of shades and patterns. But always remember that the effect of a whole wall – or a whole room – of coloured tiles will be far greater than the small trial panel you see in the tile shop, and may be overpowering. Many a property purchase has fallen through following the prospective buyers' sight of a bathroom tiled in 1970s brown or avocado – usually with bath, toilet, and washbasin to match!

- ✔ **Mosaic tiles** may look tricky, but don't worry – you don't have to stick all the tiny individual tiles on one by one! Mosaic tiles are sold on larger sheets, held together by a mesh backing. After you stick them on the wall, the grout hides the mesh. Mosaic tiles are great for irregular or curved surfaces.

- ✔ **Glass tiles** are expensive, but look stunning. Used as part of a scheme (such as the splashback behind a washbasin surrounded by ordinary white tiles) they become a real focal point for a room. Glass tiles are available as mosaics or in standard sizes in a wide range of colours. They also make great borders or dados.

- ✔ **Natural stone tiles** can't be beaten for their texture and pattern. Marble and granite add a touch of luxury to any room, and slate is great for that rustic country kitchen look.

To avoid staining, always protect natural stone tiles with a suitable sealant.

✔ **Metal tiles** give an ultra-modern look. In bronze or stainless steel, and with a variety of surface patterns, they can make your kitchen splashback look like something from the Starship *Enterprise*. Use them sparingly, though – a whole wall of metal tiles can make your kitchen look more like a canteen, or a hospital operating theatre.

Ceramic wall tiles are thinner and less durable than floor tiles. You can use floor tiles on walls but you can't use wall tiles on floors!

Preparing for Tiling

Ready to try tiling a wall or splashback? Right then – roll up your sleeves and get your mitts on the following items:

✔ Ceramic tiles

✔ Spirit level

✔ Tape measure

✔ Timber battens

✔ Tile adhesive

✔ Grout

✔ Notched trowel or adhesive spreader

✔ Rubber grout float or squeegee

✔ Sponge and dry cloth

✔ Tile cutter

✔ Plastic spacers

Book III

Renovating a Property

Once you've got your gear, follow these steps to prepare the wall for the tiles:

1. **Make sure that the wall is flat.**

   Fill any holes with plaster or filler, and use a straightedge to check that there are no bumps or hollows.

   You can't correct an uneven surface by using more adhesive, because it shrinks as it dries, pulling the tiles into the hollow.

2. **Use a spirit level and pencil to draw horizontal and vertical lines in the centre of the wall to act as your guides when laying the tiles.**

   Start in the middle of the wall, leaving any cut tiles for the edges. But make sure that any cuts are not too small. Anything smaller than half a tile looks awkward, and is difficult to cut. Your horizontal and vertical centre lines can be used as either the edges or the centres of your first rows of tiles – whichever works out better for your cuts.

3. **Before you start spreading adhesive, dry-space the tiles across the wall to optimise your cutting-in to the edges.**

You can cheat a little by using larger or smaller plastic spacers to make the tiles fit along the wall. Spacers come in 3, 4, 5, and 6 mm widths, but don't use different-sized spacers in the same room, or the eye will be drawn to the different width of the grouting.

4. **Nail or screw a horizontal timber batten to the wall to act as a starter for the last-course-but-one from the bottom.**

This is especially important when tiling above a bath or shower tray. Once the tiles have been fixed, and the adhesive has set, you remove the batten and then fix the bottom course of tiles. If the top edge of the bath or shower tray is out of level, you can then trim the bottom course to fit.

Cutting Tiles

Before you invest in any kind of tile cutter, ask the people in the tile shop which one will come in most useful for your particular job, and ask them to demonstrate how to use it. Lots of different tile cutters exist for every cut you need, for example:

- ✔ **A hand-held glass cutter,** which has a diamond point or steel cutting wheel, is perfect for making straight cuts on one or two ceramic tiles – to replace an individual broken tile, perhaps. After marking your line with a pencil on the back of the tile, you simply use a straightedge to guide the cutter, score a clean line, and then snap the tile along the scored line over the edge of the table or work bench or across two matches laid on a flat surface.

- ✔ **A flat-bed tile cutter** is great for tiling a shower, bathroom, or kitchen wall. These cost around £10 to £20, and make short work of cutting even the toughest tiles. You lay the tile on it, and the cutter slides along on a bar, giving a straight cut every time. You then push down on the handle, and the tile is broken across a central spine. Buy a tile cutter that is long enough to cope with the biggest tiles you are likely to use. For a little more money, you might as well get one that can cope with 300 mm tiles, which enables you to cut most floor tiles as well as 150 mm wall tiles.

- ✔ **A hand-held tile saw** is what you need for anything other than a straight cut – such as cutting around pipes. A tile saw is similar to a coping saw, used in woodwork, but the blade is a tough steel strip coated with diamond grit. It can be used to cut any kind of shape in a ceramic tile, but be warned, it's very hard work. We have been known to spend an hour or more sawing away at the corner of a ceramic tile in order to get an exact fit around a water pipe feeding a washbasin. The worst thing is if you spend 55 minutes on the cut, and then try to hurry it when you get near the end and crack the tile! So be patient. Really patient.

- **A tile nibbler** is a useful tool for cutting off narrow edges, corners, or other awkward shapes. The technique is to score the glazed surface of the tile with a tile cutter, and then nibble away, a tiny bit at a time. If you have only one or two fiddly cuts to make, you may find you can do the same thing with a pair of pincers or pliers.

- **A diamond-disk tile cutter** is the daddy of them all. If you have a really big tiling job to do, or a lot of complicated cuts, then it may be worth hiring one. A diamond-disk tile cutter is an electric-powered table saw with a water-cooled blade that makes short shrift of cutting any ceramic tile. You can even use it to cut a circular hole in the centre of a tile by lowering the cutting disk onto the tile while the table rotates. We've never done it ourselves, you understand, but it looks pretty impressive in the instruction video!

Fixing Tiles

Once you've laid out and cut your tiles to size, it's time to get them on the walls. You can buy tile adhesive as a dry powder to mix with water, or as ready-mix in tubs. Powder is the cheaper option, but if you want to tile only a small area then ready-mix is easier to use. Different types of adhesive suit different surfaces, such as wood, metal, wet areas, plasterboard, and MDF. Always make sure that you use the right type of adhesive for the surface you are tiling, otherwise your tiles may loosen and fall off. Ask the salesperson for advice before you buy, then follow these steps:

1. **Use a notched trowel or spreader to evenly cover a small area of the wall with adhesive.**

   Make sure that the area isn't too large, or the adhesive may dry before you finish tiling. Don't spread adhesive any thicker than 4 mm, and don't use 'dots' of adhesive on the corners of the tiles, as this may cause them to crack as the adhesive dries. Start off by spreading enough adhesive for one or two tiles, and then build up to larger areas as you get the hang of it. Start from the timber batten described in Step 4 in 'Preparing for Tiling' earlier in this chapter.

2. **Slide each tile into place and give it a slight circular twist, to bed it into the adhesive.**

   Insert plastic spacers into the corners between the tiles for even spacing and to aid horizontal and vertical alignment. Make sure that you press the spacers deep into the adhesive, so that the grout will eventually cover them. Wipe off any excess adhesive with a damp cloth before it dries.

Book III

Renovating a Property

Lay a batten or straightedge across the face of each course of tiles, and push gently, to make sure that all the tiles are bedded to the same depth.

Grouting

After the tile adhesive has set hard – usually after 24 hours – make sure that the tiles are clean, and that there are no stray bits of hardened adhesive sticking out from the joints. Ensure that the plastic tile spacers are well below the surface of the tiles, and that the grout will bury them. If any spacers are too close to the surface, or standing proud of it, flick them out with a blade or the point of a thin screwdriver. Then follow these steps:

1. **Use ready-mixed grout straight from the tub, or mix powdered grout with clean water to a stiff paste, and rub it all over the surface of the tiles with a grout float, squeegee, or sponge.**

   Work the grout back and forth across the tiled surface, pushing it into the joints as firmly as you can.

2. **Wipe off the surplus grout with a damp cloth or sponge.**

3. **As the grout dries, keep wiping the faces of the tiles clean with a damp cloth or sponge, but take care not to drag the grout out of the joints.**

4. **Finally, finish off with a soft dry cloth, buffing the tiles until they shine.**

Finishing Off

After 24 hours the tiles might have a slight haze of dried grout on them. Buff it off with a clean dry cloth.

Stone tiles and some unglazed terracotta tiles need to be sealed to prevent staining. Check with the manufacturers' instructions to see whether this sealing needs to be done before or after grouting.

Chapter 6

Heating, Ventilating, and Insulating Your Property

*M*ost grown-ups would never admit it, but their boilers frighten them. A boiler is a big, mysterious piece of machinery. Plus, as every kid knows, monsters live behind it.

We're here to tell you that a boiler is nothing to be afraid of and is less mysterious than you think. Your heating system simply heats up water and then moves that heated water around the house, through pipes and into radiators – it's really that simple. However, the technology behind this process is pretty complicated, which means that a professional must perform most of the maintenance tasks that are associated with your heating system.

The maintenance that a do-it-yourselfer can do is easy and non-threatening – we're confident that you can do it without difficulty.

Looking After Your Central Heating

Routine annual inspection and cleaning by a qualified heating engineer keep your central heating system running for many years without trouble. Don't be penny-wise and pound-foolish. A dirty, inefficient boiler costs you far more than a service call. The service-person will catch little problems before they become big trouble. And a neglected system fails years sooner than a well-maintained one.

Gauging the pressure

Most traditional central heating systems work off *indirect* pressure – meaning the pressure that comes from the weight of water in the header tank (also called the feed-and-expansion tank) at the top of the house, or in the roof space. Systems like this heat the radiators and also heat a separate tank of hot water for bathing and showering. This indirect pressure is fixed, and doesn't require any attention.

However, some newer systems have combination boilers (usually known as 'combi' boilers) and don't have a separate hot water tank. These combi boilers heat the central heating radiators just like a traditional boiler, but provide hot water to the shower and taps by 'instantly' heating water from the mains supply as it passes through the boiler. Combi systems work off *direct* pressure to provide hot water, and they also have to be pressurised in order for the central heating side of the system to function.

Sometimes the pressure drops due to tiny leaks in the system that you wouldn't otherwise notice, or after you have bled a radiator (see 'Bleeding the radiators' later in this chapter) and then the boiler refuses to fire up. If this happens, don't panic. Check the pressure gauge on the front of the boiler (it may be hidden behind a fold-down hatch or panel) – it should be reading around 1 atmosphere (check the boiler manufacturer's customer instruction booklet for the exact figure). If the pressure reading is almost down to zero, then that explains why your boiler doesn't want to fire up.

Re-pressurising the system is something you can easily do. Follow the instructions in your boiler's customer instruction booklet, which explains how to connect the *filler loop* – a flexible braided pipe that connects your boiler to the incoming mains cold water supply. You open the valve on the end of the filler loop that allows water to flow into the boiler and pressurise the system. Keep an eye on the pressure gauge, and turn the valve off when the pressure reaches 1 atmosphere (or whatever your boiler's specified pressure is). The filler loop may be hanging loose below the boiler, or the installer may have left it connected, for just such an event. Once the system has been re-pressurised, the boiler should fire up when you turn on the heating, or open a hot water outlet.

Bleeding the radiators

Bleeding a radiator is sometimes necessary in even the best of systems. If you have a radiator in your system that is cold at the top, chances are it's air-logged. Bleeding the air out of the radiator relieves the pressure and enables the system to fill normally.

To bleed the radiator, turn the *bleed valve* (a tapered screw in one top corner to let the air out) about a quarter-turn counterclockwise and keep the screwdriver or radiator key in the valve. If you hear a hissing sound, that's good – it's air escaping. As soon as the hissing stops and you see a dribble of water come out, close the valve.

Don't open the valve more than necessary; hot water will come rushing out before you can close it. At the very least, you'll make a wet mess. At worst, you could be scalded. You can help avoid this by bleeding the radiator when the heating system is off.

Ventilation: Letting Your House Breathe

When we talk about ventilation, we're actually talking about two different things: Interior ventilation and structural ventilation. Proper interior ventilation is vital for health and comfort – it helps a house rid itself of moisture, smoke, cooking smells, and indoor pollutants. Structural ventilation controls heat levels in the loft, and moderates dampness below suspended ground floors and in the basement.

Interior ventilation

Book III

Renovating
a Property

Kitchens, bathrooms, and utility rooms are the biggest sources of moisture and odours. The secret to having a non-stinky house is to have three key exhaust units: An exterior-venting cooker hood, and bathroom and utility room extractor fans.

Many kitchens have a cooker hood that doesn't actually vent anything – it just 'filters' and recycles air. To get rid of the greasy, smoky, steamy air requires ductwork to an exterior vent. If your kitchen is perpetually stinky and the walls are covered with a thin film of grease, you need to stop eating so much fried food, and you need an exterior-venting extractor fan.

Airborne grease makes extractor fans sticky, which in turn attracts dirt and dust. Clean the grill and fan blades twice a year, or whenever they start to look bad. The filters in recycling cooker hoods need cleaning every couple of months or so (depending on how and what you cook), and the fan and housing need a good cleaning every six months. If the filters have charcoal pellets inside, they need to be replaced annually. You can clean your cooker hood filter in the dishwasher. For the grill and fan blades, use a spray-on degreaser. (Test the degreaser first to make sure that it won t remove paint.) Follow with a mild soap and water wash. Finally, flush with fresh water and towel-dry.

Mould and condensation

Unless there is a specific cause for dampness such as faulty gutters, drains, water pipes, leaking roof or rising damp, mould is often caused by condensation (airbourne water vapour). Condensation often stems from too much steam being generated in the house from cooking and washing, coupled with too little heating and ventilation in the house. Tenanted properties are often more affected by mould than owner-occupied ones, sometimes being left all day with little or no heating. Occupants return in the evening to literally blast the building with moisture from cooking, washing, and breathing while providing little ventilation for the moisture. The longer a house has been subjected to this, the more the dampness and mould takes a hold in the fabric of the building and the quicker these conditions reappear when conditions again encourage it.

The answer to mould and condensation is to keep the building thoroughly dried out and warm by heating adequately, and to keep the building well ventilated. Vent out steam production in the room it comes from instead of letting it spread throughout the house.

In rented properties, this can be a very complex area, and you should be wary about jumping to conclusions about whose fault the mould is. When cases have come to court, judgement has as often been against the tenant as it has the landlord.

Bathrooms generate huge amounts of moisture and some unpleasant smells. If you have incurable mildew in the shower, paint peeling off the walls, or a lingering funky smell, you need to install an extractor fan or get a bigger, higher-capacity fan. Extractor fans can vent the bad air through the wall or through the ceiling and loft. Call an electrical contractor to do the work.

Steam, hairspray, and other grooming products create a tacky surface that attracts dust, dirt, and fuzz at an alarming rate. Clean the housing, grill, and fan at least twice a year. Use the same techniques for cleaning that we suggest for cooker extractors.

Structural ventilation

To keep heat and moisture from roasting and rotting your property over time, having adequate ventilation in the loft and below the suspended ground floor (and the basement, if it's unfinished) is important.

In the loft, the idea is to create an upward flow of air. Cool air flows in through vents in the eaves and out through vent(s) nearer to, or at the peak of, the roof. Below the floor, cross-ventilation is utilised.

If insulation, crud, or dead mice block the vents, or if there aren't enough vents, the loft and subfloor area can become humid. Rot can develop. Condensed water can soak insulation, making it ineffective. Condensation from above and below can make its way into the house, ruining ceiling, floor, and wall finishes and short-circuiting electrical wiring. If you notice that your vents are clogged, clear them immediately.

Building regulations specify how much ventilation you need. As a general rule, have 1,000 square centimetres of vent area for every 15 square metres of loft area or subfloor. We think more is better.

Roof ventilation

If your loft is hot and humid in the summer, you may need to install additional vents at the eaves and at the ridge of the roof. Assuming you're not a trained carpenter, we think it's best to leave this kind of work to a professional, someone who knows his or her way around the roof structure and knows how to install leak-free roof penetrations.

Even venting must be maintained. Make sure that each vent and screen is painted (to prevent deterioration) and that the screens are secured to the frame of the vent. Animals, tennis balls, and other common household missiles have a way of dislodging vent screens. Badly damaged vents should be replaced. Solid vent screens prevent vermin of all sorts from settling in your loft.

You can staple cardboard baffles to the rafters inside the attic adjacent to the vents. The baffles prevent loose-fill insulation from being blown into piles, leaving bare spots.

Extra vents are difficult to install and might require special tools to cut through timber, concrete block, and brick. Don't go poking holes in your foundation on your own – call a carpenter or builder to do the work. These professionals have the know-how, tools, and experience to do the job properly.

Underfloor ventilation

Moist air can cause rot in the subfloor space, too, attacking your property from below. Just like a loft, a subfloor area needs a good flow of fresh air. If your subfloor area is always overly damp, or if you see mildew on the walls or structure, you may need better ventilation.

Subfloor vents can be damaged in the same way as eave vents. In fact, because these vents are closer to the ground, the potential for damage is greater. Creatures that can't get into your loft will settle for the area beneath the floor. Establish a no-holes policy. Maintain subfloor vents in the same way that we suggest for eave vents.

Book III

Renovating a Property

Upgrading Loft Insulation

The longstanding popularity of fibreglass and mineral wool insulation is based on several important features: They are excellent insulators, vermin resistant, and fireproof.

The problem with loft insulation is that handling the stuff is like hugging a hedgehog: The fibres produce an irritating itch when they contact bare skin. Plus, medical experts suspect that inhaling airborne fibres can be hazardous to the lungs. Yikes! In our experience, mineral wool insulation (such as 'Rockwool') is more irritating than fibreglass, but both should be treated with respect. This means wearing a good-quality disposable dust mask, work gloves, long trousers, and a long-sleeved shirt. If you find you are especially sensitive to the fibres, then get someone to seal the gap between your gloves and shirtsleeves with masking tape before you get to work.

Energy Performance Certificates

As a home owner or investor landlord, you'll soon need to pay more attention to the energy efficiency and insulation of your property. UK Government regulations and EU directives are being gradually introduced which will demand higher environmental standards.

Soon, Energy Performance Certificates (EPCs) will be required when a building is constructed, rented, or sold, and with some types of conversion. EPCs allow prospective buyers, tenants, owners, and occupiers to see energy efficiency and carbon emission information about the building, so that they can consider energy efficiency and fuel costs as part of their investment.

The EPC is similar to the labels now provided with domestic appliances such as refrigerators and washing machines, and will be produced following an energy assessment of the property by a trained assessor and incorporated into the Home Information Pack (HIP). EPCs are valid for 10 years, except for sales of homes which are subject to the Home Information Pack Regulations 2007, where a HIP is required. In these cases, an EPC must be no more than 12 months old when the property is first marketed.

Homes require an EPC on construction or conversion from 1 January 2008. Commercial buildings require an EPC on construction or conversion from 6 April 2008. Rented homes will require an EPC on from 1 October 2008, and landlords are responsible for ensuring a valid certificate is made available to all prospective tenants. Commercial buildings over 500 square metres require an EPC on rent from 6 April 2008 and all remaining commercial buildings will require an EPC on rent from 1 October 2008.

It's a good idea to consider EPCs whenever you work on a property so that you can take the opportunity to improve energy efficiency.

To eliminate these problems, some manufacturers have developed a product called *polywrapped* or *encapsulated* insulation. The batt insulation is encapsulated in a perforated polyethylene or fabric covering that prevents airborne fibres and protects the skin from fibre contact. The product looks like a fibreglass sausage.

The perforations in the polywrap allow moisture to pass through, so the poly does not form a vapour barrier when applied over existing insulation. This feature makes the polywrapped insulation ideal for upgrading a loft insulation blanket. For areas where a vapour barrier is desired, insulation is available with the perforated polywrap on one side of the batt and a solid polyfilm on the other side. When using the vapour-barrier type of poly, you apply the vapour barrier side with the barrier facing the wall or ceiling. A vapour barrier – as its name suggests – stops moisture vapour travelling from one place to another. You usually use a vapour barrier to prevent warm, moist air finding its way from warm places (like living rooms) through to cold places (like unheated lofts) where it can cause condensation problems.

If your ceilings lack adequate insulation, choose polywrapped insulation. You can install polywrapped insulation on top of any type of existing insulation. The usual practice is to install the new polywrapped insulation at right angles to the existing insulation, as shown in Figure 6-1. You can cut the insulation with a sharp trimming knife or large scissors.

Figure 6-1: To add insulation to a loft, install polywrapped insulation at right-angles to existing insulation.

Chapter 7

Flooring: Keeping a Leg Up on Foot Traffic

*T*he most used and abused interior surface of a house is the floor. No matter what type of flooring material your property has, it takes a beating every day.

This chapter shows you how to refurbish, repair, replace, and install new flooring. We also discuss where to use and where not to use specific flooring types. From hardwood to carpet and from sheet flooring to ceramic and vinyl tiles, this chapter's got you – well, your floor – covered.

The Subfloor: A Solid Base

Whether you're installing flooring in a room for the first time or tearing out and replacing old flooring, a solid, smooth subfloor is critical for successful installation. So it all starts at the bottom: The subfloor.

The subfloor is the material – either wood or concrete, depending on where it's located in the house – that serves as the bottom layer of support for the flooring. Properties built from the 1970s on generally have plywood or chipboard subfloors. Older houses, say from the early 1960s and before, often have individual 25 x 150 mm boards as subflooring. Both types form a solid base, and both can be damaged and require repair. The following sections take a look at the problems you might run into when inspecting and prepping a subfloor.

Fixing low spots in the subfloor

A new floor should be smooth and level. But over time, houses shift and settle, and low spots in the subfloor sometimes develop. The best way to check for low spots is twofold:

- ✔ Do a quick visual inspection; you can usually see any significant low spots.
- ✔ Lay a 1200 mm level in various places over the entire floor, get down on your hands and knees, and look for spots where the subfloor and level don't touch.

To eliminate a low spot, fill the area with ready-mix self-levelling compound, which you can get from a DIY shop. This stuff is easy to use because it's pre-mixed; you simply spread it on the floor and smooth it with a floor trowel. Feather the edges of the patch. After the patch dries, use a spirit level to make sure that you've levelled the low spot. If the level is still off, fill in with additional compound until you get it right.

Making repairs to subflooring

Water can damage a kitchen or bathroom floor beyond the repair of an under-layment patch. Water can cause the subfloor to rot or, in the case of plywood subflooring, *delaminate*. Delamination occurs when the individual layers of plywood separate. Water can also damage board subflooring by warping it.

A damaged subfloor results in an uneven finished floor surface. If you find rot, delamination, or warping, you must replace the damaged areas.

To replace damaged single-board subflooring, remove the damaged section of the board. You may be able to get away with replacing a small length of the board, or you may have to replace the entire board. Replacing the entire board makes the repair easier because the joints at the end of the board will fall directly over the floor joists, and you can screw them (or nail them, although screwing them is easier) in place. If you're replacing only a section of the board, cut out the section so that the ends of the new board's length fall over the middle of the floor joist. If they don't, the ends will be hanging free, and you won't be able to secure the joints to anything below. This setup creates weak spots in the subfloor.

Replacing damaged plywood subflooring is fairly easy. Most of the damage we've seen has required replacing an entire piece of plywood, although you can cut out a smaller section and replace it. When replacing an entire sheet of subfloor, you need to remove the nails or screws that secure it to the joists. If the fasteners are screws, you're in luck: Simply remove them with a powered drill/driver. If the subfloor is nailed down, a little more work is involved, but it's doable for most people.

Use a claw hammer or nail puller to get under the head of the nail and loosen it slightly from the floor joist into which it's driven. You won't be able to pull the nail out completely by using the claw hammer. The nails used for securing subflooring, called *ring-shank* or *cement-coated* nails, are meant to be driven into wood but not to be removed easily. A ring-shank nail has a series of rings on the shaft or shank that hold the nail in the wood. To pull up these nails, you need a tool called – surprise! – a *nail puller*. Its design gives you enough leverage to pull out even ring-shank nails.

Installing board or plywood subflooring is the same. Set the material into position and secure it with 75 mm-long plasterboard screws. We recommend using screws because doing so is easier and faster than using nails, and you can remove screws more quickly and easily, too.

Understanding underlay

All types of flooring require an underlay to be installed over the subfloor. The subfloor provides overall structural support and strength, and underlay creates a level surface and helps prevent squeaks and uneven wear on vinyl or sheet flooring, and even keeps the finish on wood floors from cracking.

For most wood floors and vinyl or sheet flooring, a 3 mm- or 6 mm-thick plywood underlay is adequate. Check your flooring's installation specs to see which thickness of underlay it requires. If you use the wrong underlay, you void the warranty on the flooring.

Book III

Renovating
a Property

Underlay for ceramic tiles is completely different Because of the weight of the tiles, grout, and adhesive, a stronger, thicker underlay is needed. For most installations, tile backerboard (most commonly cement board but also gypsum and other materials) is recommended. Cement boards are made of cement-based materials and are usually 12 mm thick. They come in 900 x 1200 mm sheets, not 1200 x 2400 mm sheets like plywood does, so one person can handle them. However, even the 900 x 1200 sheets are a handful, especially in tight quarters, such as a bathroom. Cement board is secured to the subfloor with cement board screws, roofing nails, and ring-shank nails specifically made for use with cement board. Be sure to use the recommended nails.

If you plan to use an existing underlay, make sure that it's in good shape – free of loose pieces, low spots, and damage. You inspect underlay the same way you inspect subflooring, and make repairs the same way, too. Look for low spots and fill them with an underlay patch. Secure any loose spots and get rid of those squeaks now!

Check to see what the flooring manufacturer's installation instructions say about how to deal with joints between pieces of underlay. Most flooring companies recommend, and in some cases require, that you fill every joint with underlay patch to eliminate gaps between pieces of underlay, especially if you're installing sheet flooring. Filling the gaps creates a single, smooth, flat surface for the flooring and reduces the likelihood of high or low spots.

Hardwood Flooring

Something about the beauty and warmth of a hardwood floor just can't be topped. Whether it's a natural or synthetic wood floor, the rich colour and grain of the wood really add class to a room.

Refurbishing: When hardwood only needs a touch-up

Regular dusting or vacuuming keeps most wood floors looking good for years. Occasionally, however, the flooring needs an extra boost to gets its original look back. We're not talking about stripping and refinishing a wood floor or even a light sanding and recoating with finish; we're talking about simply using the cleaning product recommended for your flooring.

Before you delve into stripping your hardwood floor (covered in the next section), try this technique:

1. **Rub a small area with 0000-grade steel wool dipped in methylated spirit.**

2. **Wipe it dry to remove any wax.**

3. **Damp-mop the area and apply a coat of paste wax.**

If this process brings the floor back to life, do the rest of the floor in the same manner. This three-step process may seem like a lot of work, and it does take time, but it's easier and neater than sanding and stripping and may make your floor look the way you want it to.

Don't try this method with synthetic wood flooring. The finishes on these products aren't designed for rubbing with an abrasive, such as steel wool, or cleaning with common cleaning products such as soap, floor polish, or scouring powder. Damp-mop the synthetic wood floor with a bit of vinegar in water. Just be careful not to flood the floor. A wrung-out damp mop will do the trick.

Refinishing: Making your floor look new again

If you tried refurbishing and your floor still looks less than great, you probably need to refinish the floor. This process involves removing all the old finish (wax and stain). To do so, you need a walk-behind floor sander, which you can hire. Also hire a handheld power edge sander for sanding tight against walls and in corners and doorways. Both units have a vacuum and dust bag system to minimise the amount of sanding dust left behind.

A walk-behind sander has a large rotating drum that evenly removes the finish – if you use the correct series of sandpaper grades and operate the sander properly. Tool hire shops have the three grades of sandpaper you need for successful floor refinishing: coarse, medium, and fine. The large sheets are designed to fit tight against the drum. Some sanders have a slot into which you tuck the sandpaper; other models have a screw-down bar that secures the paper. After the paper's in place, you tighten the drum with a wrench (supplied with the sander). For safety, wear a dust mask and eye and ear protection.

Some rooms may have a small piece of concave or convex moulding along the base of the skirting boards. For best results (and the least damage), we recommend removing the moulding. Doing so gives you maximum access when sanding and refinishing where the floor meets the wall.

Sanding off the old stuff

The most important idea to remember when sanding hardwood floors is to sand with the grain of the wood, maintaining an even pace. Sanding across the grain leaves gouges that not only look horrible but also are almost impossible to remove. Use the sandpaper in successively finer grades: Start with coarse to remove the toughest of the nasty finish and work your way to fine.

 When operating the floor sander, lift the drum of the sander off the floor and then turn on the power. If you start the sander with the drum resting on the floor, it's likely to damage the floor, and it could take off and shoot forward almost uncontrollably.

When you get to the end of the section you're sanding, or if you need to stop before that point, raise the drum and turn off the power. Make sure that the drum has stopped spinning before you set it down. Also, make sure that each sanding pass overlaps the adjacent pass. Doing so ensures that you don't miss any spots, plus it reduces the chance of gouging or leaving a ridge.

A floor sander can get only so close to the walls and into the corners. For these areas, we recommend an *edge sander*. These units use the same grades of sandpaper as floor units, but the sandpaper is disk shaped. Again, keep the unit off the floor and then start the sander. Gently lower the unit onto the floor and remove the finish. Sand with the grain and be sure to overlap the adjacent sanded area.

Corners can be especially tough to sand, and you may have to use a sanding block or paint scraper. A paint scraper works well for removing the finish in a corner. Follow that step by using a sanding block, again with the same succession of sandpaper grades. This way, you achieve a smooth, sanded surface from power-sanded to hand-sanded areas.

Filling nicks and gouges

Now is also the time to fill any nicks or gouges in the floor. Use wood putty and a broad knife to fill any spots. Let the wood putty dry according to package directions and then lightly sand the areas smooth by hand with medium or fine sandpaper.

Sucking it up

After you've completed all the sanding, you must remove all the dust from the floor, trim, and walls. Yes, dust will settle on the walls. A lot of dust. Wipe down the walls and trim once to get the dust onto the floor, and then use a damp rag on the trim to remove any residue. You don't want any dust falling onto the floor later, when the new finish is drying. Let the dust settle, and then vacuum.

A standard shop vacuum with a dust filter will do the trick. You can also hire a heavy-duty vacuum from where you rented the sanders. Use the vacuum's brush attachment to pick up all the dust and reduce the chance of blowing it around the room.

After you vacuum, wipe the entire floor surface with a *tack cloth*, a wax-impregnated piece of cheesecloth designed to pick up and hold dust residue.

Selecting a finish

The type of finish you choose depends on the look you want for your floor. Durability is also an issue. Your choices are:

- ✓ **Polyurethane,** either oil or water based, comes in various degrees of lustre. Polyurethane, or poly, has a sort of plastic look, which some people don't like at all. Both poly finish types darken or even yellow the wood's appearance, although some newer water-based products don't darken as much and leave the floor as close to natural as possible. Poly finishes are excellent for high-traffic and high-moisture areas, such as a kitchen or bathroom, because they resist water staining and abrasion.

On the downside, if the finish gets nicked or gouged, it's extremely difficult to spot-repair. You'll need to resurface the entire floor to get an even appearance.

✔ **Varnish** comes in a variety of lustres, from matte to glossy. Varnish is very durable but is slightly softer than polyurethane. The higher the gloss, the more durable the surface. Varnish often darkens with age, so keep this fact in mind. On the up side, you can make spot-repairs to varnish.

✔ **Penetrating sealer** offers the most natural-looking finish. It brings out the grain in wood; however, it may darken over time. This sealer is also available in various wood colours. Penetrating sealer offers good protection, especially when waxed. However, it's less durable than polyurethane or varnish. It's the easiest of the three to spot-repair, though, and you can usually buff out scratches. You should wax floors treated with penetrating sealer once a year.

Putting on a new face

Ideally, you want to seal the floor on the same day you finish sanding to prevent the open wood surface from absorbing moisture. For best results, apply the stain (if desired) and sealer with a sheepskin applicator. Be sure to apply the sealer evenly, and use enough to cover the surface. But be careful not to apply too much. Excess sealer doesn't soak into the wood – it pools on the surface. If you fail to remove it, the sealer leaves an ugly spot.

After the sealer has dried, follow these steps:

1. **Buff the floor with No. 2 (fine) steel wool.**

2. **Vacuum and wipe the floor again with a tack cloth.**

   Removing all the dust between finish coats is critical, or you'll have a rough and ugly floor.

3. **Apply the first of two coats of finish wax or other floor finish, such as polyurethane or varnish.**

   Follow the directions on the finish container for drying time between coats.

4. **Apply the final coat.**

   Wait at least 24 hours after the final coat dries before moving furniture back into the room.

Repairing damaged hardwood flooring

Your floor may be in generally fine shape, with a damaged spot or two. If you find damage or stains, it may be easier and more effective to make small repairs than to refinish the entire floor. This section explains how to repair small areas of damage to hardwood flooring.

Book III

Renovating a Property

Replacing a strip or plank of flooring

If a strip or plank of flooring is damaged and is beyond being saved by sanding and filling, you have to replace it. Some floors use a tongue-and-groove design for connecting adjacent strips. This design makes replacing a single strip or plank challenging, but not impossible.

First, look for any nails in the damaged board and drive as far through the board as possible by using a hammer and *nail set*, a pointed tool that you place on the head of the nail and then strike with a hammer, driving the nail into the wood. Carpenters use nail sets to drive nails flush with trim without damaging the trim with a hammer. After you've cleared the nails, it's time to remove the damaged board and install a new one. Follow these steps:

1. **Use a carpenter's square to mark a perpendicular line across the section of the board to be removed.**

   If you're removing the entire strip, skip this step.

2. **Use a 12 mm- or 10 mm-diameter drill bit and power drill to drill holes along the line.**

3. **Use a wood chisel to split the damaged board into two pieces.**

   Doing so makes removal easier.

4. **Pry out the damaged board.**

   If you take a strip out of the middle you can pry the remaining pieces away from the adjacent boards before prying them up. Remove any additional boards the same way but cut them so the end joints are staggered.

5. **Square up the drilled ends with a very sharp wood chisel, and remove any exposed nails or drive them in out of the way with a nail set.**

   You want the ends of the good sections smooth and square for easier installation.

6. **Cut a replacement strip to the same length as the one you removed. As needed, cut off the bottom side of the groove on the board.**

   Removing the bottom groove enables you to install a board between two others by inserting its tongue side first and then lowering its groove side into place. If you don't remove the bottom groove, you won't be able to get the board past the tongue of the adjacent board.

7. **Test-fit the strip to make sure that it fits.**

   If it doesn't fit, recut the board.

8. **Remove the replacement strip and apply construction adhesive to the back of the strip. Install the strip and gently tap it into place.**

   Use a scrap piece of wood to protect the strip's surface while tapping it into place. Nail the board with 50 mm-long ring-shank flooring nails and drive the heads just below the surface with a nail set.

Matching the finish of the new strip to the existing flooring may be difficult, but give it a shot before you refinish the entire floor.

Repairing a buckled board

To fix a buckled floorboard, you need to be able to access the floor from below. The way to tackle this problem is to put weight on the buckled area from above – a cement block works well. Then install a 30 mm screw in the buckled flooring from below. Allow the screw to penetrate only halfway into the flooring, or it may come up through the finished surface. Driving the screw through the subfloor and into the flooring pulls the flooring down against the subfloor and gets rid of the buckled spot.

Dealing with stains

Most stains on hardwood floors are very dark, even black. You don't need to try to get rid of the entire stain in one attempt. Getting rid of the blemish may take several tries.

Follow these steps to remove a stain:

1. **Sand off the old finish.**

2. **Mix oxalic acid crystals (sold at DIY centres and paint and hardware shops) in water, following the package directions.**

   Wear eye protection and acid-resistant rubber gloves.

3. **Soak a clean white cloth in the acid mixture. Then press the cloth on the stained area and let it set for about an hour.**

4. **Lift the cloth and check to see whether the stain has been bleached away. If it hasn't, repeat the process.**

   This process may take several applications, but eventually the stain will be bleached away.

5. **After the stain is gone, rinse the area with household vinegar to neutralise the acid. Wipe away any excess moisture and allow the area to dry completely.**

6. **Apply a matching oil-based stain lightly to the bleached area.**

   Use several coats, if necessary, to match. Don't try to match the colour with only one application. You can always darken the area with additional coats, but you can't lighten it after it becomes too dark. If you think the stain is too dark, wipe the area immediately with a cloth dampened with white spirit. Doing so will remove some of the stain and lighten the area.

   After you've achieved the desired colour, allow the area to dry overnight.

7. **Apply the topcoat finish and blend into the adjacent areas.**

Book III

Renovating a Property

Getting rid of nicks and scratches

You can usually cover up these little eyesores with colour putty sticks. Simply clean the nicked or scratched area thoroughly and rub the putty stick over the damaged spot. Let the colour dry for a few minutes and then wipe it with a clean cloth. Most of the time, getting colour into a nicked or scratched area is all you need to do to make the damage disappear – at least to those who don't know that the area was damaged before. Use the same stuff to fill nail holes in a patched floor after the topcoat is applied.

If a nick or scratch is really a dig or gouge, use wood filler and stain and try to match the existing floor colour.

Replacing a Wooden Floor

This section walks you through a typical hardwood floor installation.

Choosing the right flooring type for your project

Wood flooring is just that – all wood, either solid wood or laminated, like plywood. Most wood floors today are made of oak, which is strong and has an obvious grain. Other types of wood, such as ash and maple, are becoming popular. Softer woods, such as pine, fir, and cherry, aren't as common because they don't stand up to much wear.

- ✔ **Wood flooring** comes in strips with a variety of widths. If the flooring is 75 mm or wider, it's called *plank* or *board* flooring. *Parquet* flooring, which is made up of 225 mm to 450 mm squares of pre-made 'tiles' or wood strips, is also quite popular.

- ✔ **Laminate or synthetic wood flooring** is a combination of layers of material laminated together. The top layer is made of cellulose paper impregnated with clear melamine resins for durability. The second layer is a paper layer called the *design layer*, which has a pattern printed on it to give the appearance of wood. This layer is strengthened with resins. The third layer, the *core*, is made of chipboard or fibreboard. The bottom layer is made of paper or *melamine* (a plastic-like sheet material).

In a high-traffic area, laminate is a good choice because of its durability. But if you want the colour, richness, and warmth of wood, a real wood floor is the right choice for you.

Installing a prefinished hardwood floor – the way the pros do it!

A popular type of wood flooring uses a tongue-and-groove system to connect adjacent boards. Many systems are nailed down too, and others use glue to secure strips together. The glue method is called a *floating floor* because the flooring literally lies or floats on a thin cushioned underfelt. You can find complete installation instructions for a floating floor at DIY and flooring shops. This section shows you the general steps for installing a nailed-down wood floor on a wood subfloor and underlay.

Begin the installation at the longest wall and follow these steps:

1. **Place 12 mm temporary spacers between the first board and the wall to allow for seasonal expansion of the flooring.**

2. **Nail the first board to the underlay at the wall.**

3. **Continue installing boards, applying wood glue to the grooved edge of each piece of flooring just before installing it onto the adjacent piece.**

4. **To mark the first course for cutting, turn it so that the tongue along the edge of the board is against the wall.**

    You'll turn the plank to match the others after you cut it to length.

5. **Mark the turned board and cut it to length.**

    If you're cutting with a circular saw, turn the decorative face of the board down to avoid splintering.

6. **Turn the cut board into the correct installation position and install it at the end of the row.**

7. **Secure the tongue side of this row to the underlayment.**

    Drive the nails at a 45-degree angle through the tongue. Be careful not to split the tongue.

8. **Begin the next row with the leftover piece of the cut board.**

    Make sure that the piece is at least 200 mm long. If it isn't, use another board, but make sure that the first joints of each row of boards are staggered for a good-looking appearance and to keep a minimum of 200 mm of plank length between the joints.

9. **Place a scrap piece of flooring against the tongue of the board to act as a buffer board and tap the boards together with a hammer before nailing.**

    The block keeps the hammer from damaging the tongue.

Book III

Renovating a Property

The easiest and fastest way to nail wood flooring is with a *power flooring nailer*, an angled nailer that drives the nail through the tongue at the correct angle and depth. Use one as soon as you are far enough away from the wall to fit it against the course being installed.

10. **Continue this process to complete the job.**

    You may need to cut the final row of boards lengthwise because not every room's width exactly accommodates the various widths of flooring. Remember to leave a 12 mm expansion gap on this side of the room, too. The best technique is to cut a long board with a table saw, but you can use a circular saw. If you do use a circular saw, use a saw guide to keep your cut line straight. A length of 25 x 100 board clamped to the flooring works well as a cutting guide.

11. **Install the skirting board.**

    When you fit a board around a corner or an irregular shape, such as a doorway, measure the length and depth of the obstruction that will protrude into the board. Use a combination square for accurate measurements. Then remove the marked area with a hand-powered coping saw or jigsaw.

Doorways can be a problem because the door's jamb and architrave extend to the underlay. The best-looking and easiest approach is to cut off the bottom of the jamb and trim by using a flush-cut saw or hand-saw. Place the saw on top of a scrap piece of flooring as you complete the cut – this ensures a straight cut and one that removes just the right amount.

Ceramic Tile

Ceramic tile is one tough flooring product. In fact, tile is the toughest of the bunch – it withstands stains, liquids, and high traffic. Ceramic tile is easy to take care of and comes in a variety of sizes, colours, and patterns. On the downside, drop a large pan and you could easily be faced with a cracked or broken tile that you need to replace.

Replacing a damaged tile

Replace a cracked tile as soon as possible – not only for the appearance, but also to maintain the floor's integrity. Even one cracked or missing tile weakens the strength of the grout between the tiles, which can lead to adjacent tiles and grout becoming loose.

Follow these steps:

1. **Wearing eye protection and heavy-duty work gloves, remove the damaged tile with a hammer and cold chisel.**

   Starting at the edge of the tile and grout, break the tile into smaller pieces rather than trying to take out the tile in one big chunk. After all, the tile's a goner anyway. Just be careful not to chip the surrounding tiles.

2. **Use the cold chisel to scrape the old adhesive off the floor.**

   Remove as much adhesive as possible so that the new tile adheres properly.

3. **Apply thinset mortar to the back of the new tile by using a wide-blade putty knife.**

   Spread the adhesive right out to the edges.

4. **Set the tile firmly in position and level it with the surrounding tiles, and then tap it into place with a hammer and wood block.**

   You may need to apply more mortar if the tile isn't level. Use a short block of scrap wood to protect the tile when tapping with the hammer.

5. **After the mortar has set (usually a couple of hours), use a rubber grout float to spread the grout and fill the gaps between the tiles.**

   Hold the float at a 30-degree angle to the tile and work the grout into the gaps from all directions, and strike off the excess with the float nearly perpendicular.

6. **Wipe off any excess grout with a damp grout sponge.**

   Use as little water as possible and a light circular motion. Try not to rub or disturb the grout lines at this point. Just remove the grout on the face of the tile.

7. **After the grout has set slightly (about 15–20 minutes), go back with the grout sponge and clean up the grout lines.**

   This time, wipe parallel to the grout lines. Rinse the sponge often and wring it out well for best results.

8. **Buff off any light grout haze left with cheesecloth or a soft cloth when the grout is set.**

Book III

Renovating a Property

Replacing cracked or missing grout

Cracked or missing grout looks bad, and it's a good way for otherwise solid tiles to become loose.

Whether the grout is cracked or missing, you need to remove enough grout so that the new grout has solid grout to bond to. Follow these steps:

1. **Use a grout saw to scrape out the old grout.**

   A grout saw is a short-bladed hand tool that does a great job, although you will work up a sweat! Work the saw back and forth to loosen and cut out the old grout. The grout may come out in pieces, or it could turn into powder. Either way is fine – just get it all out.

2. **After the old grout is completely out or is back to solid material, vacuum out the joints.**

3. **Spread new grout into the joints by using a rubber grout float, as described in Steps 5 to 7 in the preceding section.**

Regrouting a tile floor with a different-coloured grout also gives an old floor a new look.

Installing a ceramic tile floor

This project may appear to be beyond the abilities of most homeowners, but most DIYers can handle it. Just don't rush it – have a little patience! The materials are relatively easy to work with, and you can rent the tools, even the big ones.

Install ceramic tiles over a subfloor that's no less than 30 mm thick. A thinner subfloor causes the floor to flex due to the weight of the tile. A flexing subfloor results in cracked tiles and grout – and a lot of headaches. Most tile manufacturers recommend installing a cement backerboard instead of any other type of underlay, such as plywood. The boards come in 900 x 1200 mm sheets and are available where tiles and grout are sold.

Getting down to business

Ever wonder how a tile layer always seems to get those tiles at a perfect 90- or 45-degree angle to the wall? They cheat! Not really, but they do use a pair of perpendicular reference lines for establishing a layout instead of relying on measurements from walls, which are neither straight nor square to each other. To ensure the reference lines are square, they use a 3-4-5 triangle rule as follows:

1. **Establish your first reference line by measuring across opposite sides of the room. Mark the centre of each side and then snap a chalk line between the two marks.**

2. **Measure and mark the centre of that line. Then use a pencil, a framing square, and a straightedge held against its shorter leg to mark a second line perpendicular to the first line.**

   Before snapping a second line across the room, make sure that the angle you formed is truly 90 degrees.

3. **Measure out 300 mm from the intersection and mark the pencilled line. Then measure out 400 mm from the intersection and mark the spot on the chalk line. Measure the distance between the 300 mm and 400 mm marks.**

   The distance should be 500 mm – the 3-4-5 rule. If it isn't, make an adjustment and pencil a new line. Now snap a chalk line across the room that falls directly over the pencilled line.

After you have reference lines, use them to establish layout lines, which guide tile placement. Dry-set two rows of tiles to extend from the centre to adjacent walls. If the last tile in a row would be less than half a tile, plan to shift the first course to be centred on the reference line rather than next to it. Snap your layout line a half tile away from the reference line. Repeat the procedure for the other row.

Laying out your tiles at 45-degree angles instead of 90 isn't that difficult. You just need a couple more layout lines. Mark the two layout lines as you would for a 90-degree job and then follow these steps:

1. **Measure out the same distance (for example, 1 metre) on the perpendicular lines.**

2. **From these points, make marks 1 metre out at right angles to the original lines.**

3. **Snap a chalk line through these new marks and through the intersection of the two original layout lines.**

   The two lines are now your layout lines for a 45-degree pattern.

After you establish your guidelines or layout lines, it's time to install the tiles. Follow these steps and check out Figure 7-1:

1. **Before you think about setting the tiles in place with mortar, make sure that the layout is even from side to side in both directions. To do so, dry-fit the tiles along the layout lines in both directions and make sure that the finished layout looks good to you.**

   One important measurement to note is the width of the tiles that meet the wall. Make sure that you never have less than half of a tile's width at the wall. If you do, adjust the layout until you get an adequate end tile size. After you establish this, snap a new layout line to follow.

Figure 7-1:
Laying border tiles around a room requires careful measuring and cutting.

2. **Pick up the loose tiles and set them aside.**

3. **Use a notched trowel to spread thinset mortar (used to secure floor tile) over a 1 metre-square section at the intersection of the layout lines.**

   Trowels come with different-sized notches, so check the tile manufacturer's recommendation for the correct size.

   Work in small, square sections – say, 1 metre x 1 metre. If you work with a larger section, the mortar may harden before you put the tiles in place. Be careful not to cover the layout lines.

4. **Begin laying tiles at the centre point of the two layout lines, setting each tile into the mortar by tapping it gently with a rubber mallet.**

   Use plastic spacers at each tile corner to maintain even grout lines between the tiles. Spacers are available where tiles are sold.

5. **Continue laying tiles until you've covered the mortared area.**

6. **Continue the process by applying mortar to another section and then laying tiles.**

7. **Fit the last tile in the row at the wall.**

   This step usually requires that you measure and cut the tile. First, set a scrap tile against the wall – it allows space for grout. Next, place a loose tile directly over the last full tile you laid (this is the tile you'll cut to size). Then place another tile on the loose one and up against the tile on the wall. Mark the loose tile and cut it to fit along the edge. (We discuss cutting in just a bit.)

8. **After all the tiles are set in the mortar, mix the grout according to the manufacturer's instructions and install it by using the rubber grout float.**

   Use a sweeping motion, pressing the grout into the gaps.

9. **Wipe away the excess grout with a grout sponge. Let the grout dry slightly and then wipe off the haze that appears.**

Cutting tiles

For most ceramic floor installations, you need a tile cutter, which you can buy or hire. To make a straight cut with a tile cutter, simply place the tile face up in the cutter, adjust the cutter to the proper width, and score the tile by pulling the cutting wheel across the tile's face. Then snap the tile along the scored line. Chapter 5 has more on cutting tiles.

If you need to make a cut-out, say to go around a corner, mark the area you plan to cut out. Secure the tile in a vice or clamps – cushion the vice jaws to protect the tile from scratches. Cut along the marks with a *tile saw*, which is a hand-saw that's similar to a coping saw, except that it has a carbide saw blade designed for cutting ceramic tile.

If you need to make a round or circular cut, mark the area and then use a tile nipper to nip out small pieces of tile until you reach the line. A tile nipper is similar to a pair of pliers, but it has hardened cutting edges for cutting through ceramic tile.

Sheet Vinyl Flooring

Sheet vinyl is a popular flooring choice for bathrooms, kitchens, and hallways. Sold in 2- and 4-metre widths, sheet vinyl's pretty durable, easy to maintain, and not too expensive.

Book III

Renovating a Property

Using a template to cut your piece

Most manufacturers sell an inexpensive template kit for laying and cutting vinyl flooring. Follow these steps to use the template:

1. **Cover the entire floor with overlapping paper template sheets, large or small. Tape every piece together with masking tape.**

   The resulting template is the shape of the area you plan to cover.

2. **Carefully lift up the template, place it on the unrolled vinyl flooring, and trace the outline onto the flooring with a felt-tip pen.**

3. **Remove the template and cut the flooring with a utility knife with a new blade.**

   Change the blade often for smooth, even cuts.

4. **Place the vinyl flooring in position and slide the edges under the door casings.**

   Be careful when positioning the vinyl – you don't want to nick or tear it.

You may find it helpful to cut off the door casings at the bottom by using the method described in the wood flooring section, earlier in this chapter.

Cutting a seam

Try to install your sheet flooring in one large piece. However, many areas are wider than 4 metres, which is the width that sheet flooring comes in. If you need to make a seam, plan to place it along a pattern line and not in a high-traffic area of the room. Follow these steps to cut a seam:

1. **Overlap the sheets by about 50 mm.**

2. **Match the pattern and tape the sheets together with masking tape.**

3. **Hold a straightedge tightly and make several passes with a utility knife to cut through both layers of flooring.**

Gluing it down

You need to glue down the flooring in an efficient yet unhurried manner. The adhesive begins to set after a while, but you have plenty of time to do it right as long as you work in a logical order. Follow these steps:

1. **Pull up half of the sheet and roll it loosely.**

2. **Use a V-notched trowel to spread the recommended adhesive around the edge of the room and wherever a seam will lie.**

3. **Let the adhesive set for about 10 to 15 minutes until it gets tacky.**

4. **Unroll the flooring over the adhesive.**

5. **Press the flooring against the underlay with a rolling pin.**

   You can also hire a floor roller. Work around the entire area, including the edges and seams.

6. **Use a seam roller on each seam to ensure a solid bond of adhesive under both pieces of flooring.**

   A seam roller is slightly smaller than a floor roller. Roll it slowly along each seam to ensure that each seam is completely flat.

Repairing a damaged spot

To repair a damaged spot of sheet vinyl flooring, you need to have a scrap piece of the flooring available.

Try to make a patch repair along a pattern line, which does the best job of hiding the cut lines. Here's what to do:

1. **Determine the size and shape of the cut-out you want to make.**

   For regular, straight patterns, size the patch so cuts are made along the 'grout lines'. For overall patterns, make a diamond-shape patch.

2. **Cut the patch material slightly larger, lay it over the damaged floor, align the pattern, and tape it in place with masking tape on all sides.**

3. **Make a guided double cut through the patch and the flooring and remove the damaged flooring.**

   If the floor is adhered in this location scrape all adhesive off the underlayment, being careful not to damage or lift the surrounding flooring.

4. **Brush adhesive on the back of the new piece and, if the surrounding flooring is not adhered, on the underlay about 25 mm under the flooring edges.**

5. **Position the patch in the same orientation it had when it was cut and roll it with a rolling pin. Clean off any adhesive on the surface.**

6. **Press the seams together and hold them in place with masking tape.**

7. **Wait half an hour before removing tape and applying the recommended seam sealer according to directions.**

Carpet

Ah, the pleasure of digging your toes into rich, plush carpet. Carpet is still the most widely used floor covering in most properties. The best carpets are made of wool or a mixture of wool and manmade fibres. Wool carpet is very expensive. However, blends of nylon, polypropylene, acrylic, rayon, and polyester help keep carpet prices reasonable. Plus, these blends are more durable and stain resistant.

Book III

Renovating a Property

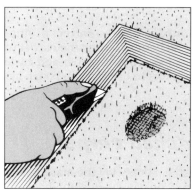 

Figure 7-2:
Replacing a patch of carpet.

A. Use a framing square to guide the utility knife as you cut an area around the damaged carpeting and a patch from a matching piece of scrap carpet.

B. Outline the bare spot with double-stick cloth tape to hold the replacement patch securely in place.

Installing carpet isn't difficult, technically. The process is challenging, however, because of the size of the rolls and the often-limited workspace. Carpet typically comes in 4 metre widths, which makes a roll of carpet heavy and hard to handle, even for an average-sized room of 4 metres x 4 metres.

If your carpet needs a seam, or you want your stairs carpeted, call a pro to install it. You'll be much happier in the long run. A competent installer plans for seams to occur in low-traffic and low-visibility areas. All seams are cut using the double-cut method described in the previous section and the pieces are joined with seaming tape. The installer places the tape under the seam and then lifts the carpet to melt the adhesive on the tape with a seaming iron. Then he presses the carpet down onto the tape and pinches the pieces together before the adhesive cools.

Laying carpet with underfelt

This type of installation requires no glue or adhesive to hold the carpet and underfelt (underlay) to the floor. You do, however, need to secure it to the floor at the perimeter to prevent the carpet from moving and forming lumps or bumps.

Install the wooden tack strip, which runs around the perimeter of the room. Nail the tack strip to the subfloor with its points angled towards the wall. The small points sticking up out of the wooden tack strip grab the carpet and hold it down once you stretch it over the tack strip. Space the tack strips away from the wall at a distance equal to the thickness of the carpet.

Next, place the carpet underfelt within the tack strip layout and then staple it to the subfloor. The underfelt is easy to trim with a utility knife. You can seal the joints that form where two pieces meet with duct tape.

Loosely lay out the carpet in approximately the correct position. The less moving this monster of a piece, the better. Getting the carpet over the spikes of the tack strip requires the use of a carpet stretcher and carpet kicker. These tools are easy for a professional to use but can be tricky for a novice to use correctly.

Laying cushion-backed carpet

This type of carpet is easy to install. Simply lay the material out in the room, cut it to fit, and then glue it down. You can cut cushion-backed carpet easily with a utility knife. The adhesive is easy to spread with a trowel. This carpet is also somewhat forgiving because you have a little time to reposition the carpet if it moves while you're laying it.

Patching a hole in carpeting

Cigarette burns and tough stains can cause permanent damage to carpet. If the blemish is on the surface fibre only, use a nail clipper or small manicure scissors to clip away the damaged fibre a small bit at a time.

If the damage is deep or the carpet is torn, replace a section of the carpet as shown in Figure 7-2. Cut a replacement patch by using a straightedge and a utility knife to make a straight cut-out around a damaged area. Then install a replacement patch cut to the same size, using double-stick cloth carpet tape to hold the patch in place.

The tape, sold in widths of 40 mm and 50 mm, is available at DIY centres and hardware stores. Cut the tape to size to outline the perimeter of the patch area. Peel the protective paper from the face of the peel-and-stick tape and press the patch of carpeting into the repair area to ensure full contact between the carpet patch and the adhesive tape. Carefully separate the carpet fibres between the patch and the surrounding fibres. Give the adhesive time to set and then use a comb or brush to blend the carpet pile between the carpet and the patch.

Rather than cutting your own patch, take out the guesswork by using a *doughnut*. A doughnut is a circular cutting tool with a razor blade cutter fixed to the perimeter, and a centre rotating pin to anchor the cutter in place. The tool cuts shapes that are 75 mm in diameter and it costs about £10.

Book III

Renovating a Property

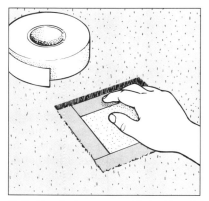

Figure 7-2: Replacing a patch of carpet.

A. Use a framing square to guide the utility knife as you cut an area around the damaged carpeting and a patch from a matching piece of scrap carpet.

B. Outline the bare spot with double-stick cloth tape to hold the replacement patch securely in place.

Silencing Squeaks

Whenever possible, fix annoying floor or stair squeaks from below. If, however, the bottom of the floor area or staircase is covered, you have to fix it from above.

Fixing a squeak from below

You have a few ways to eliminate squeaks from below. Which method you use depends on what the problem is. Take a look at each method (and see Figure 7-3):

- ✔ **Strutting:** Squeaking over a large area may indicate that the floor joists are shifting slightly and are not providing enough support to the subfloor. To solve or moderate this problem you can install strutting between the joists, which stabilises them and stiffens the floor system. Typically, you use one centred row when joists span between 3 and 5 metres, and two equally spaced rows for longer spans.

  Before a subfloor is installed, you can install either metal or steel herringbone strutting, which is installed at a diagonal between two adjacent joists and holds them in place when weight is put on the floor. You nail steel strutting from the top of one joist diagonally to the bottom of the adjacent joist. You wedge wood strutting between the two joists and then nail it to each joist.

  For existing floor systems, horizontal strutting or blocking is more feasible.

- ✔ **Blocking:** Cut and nail short lengths of wood the same dimension as the floor joist (such as 50 x 200 or 50 x 250) to fit snugly between the joists in a perpendicular row. You nail through the joist into the ends of the block with 100 mm nails and stagger block positions so that you have nailing access from both ends.

- ✔ **Shims:** Use shims (small pieces of wedge-shaped wood) to fill a small gap between the top of a joist and the subfloor. If the floor joist isn't tight against the subfloor, simply apply glue and tap tapered shims between the joist and subfloor until it is just snug. Do not overdrive the shims, which actually lifts the subfloor, causing more squeaking.

Fixing a squeak from above

If you can't access a squeak from below, you don't have much choice but to tackle it from above. Check out Figure 7-4 to see how these tricks work.

To stop a squeak, apply glue to a wood shim or shingle and drive it between the floor joist and subfloor.

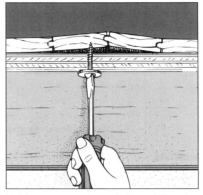

Driving a screw through the subfloor into the finished flooring can pull the boards together, stopping a squeak.

If the underside of the floor is inaccessible, drive finish nails through the flooring at an angle to silence a squeak.

Figure 7-3: Three ways to stop squeaks.

Book III

Renovating a Property

✔ **Squeaks in floor joists:** First, locate the floor joist so that you have something to nail into. Doing so involves drilling a small-diameter hole through the floor and then probing with a bent coat hanger. It's best to drill the probing hole near a wall or in another inconspicuous area. After you've located a joist, you can measure every 400 mm and you should find the next joist, then the next, and so on. After you've located the offending joist area, drill an angled hole from both sides through the flooring and subfloor and into the joist. This is a 'by feel' type of job, but it should work. Drive screws into the joists in the pilot holes to silence the squeak.

Figure 7-4:
Methods for fixing squeaky stairs.

Stop squeaking stairs by gluing and then screwing wood blocks between the risers and treads.

If you can't get to the underside of the staircase, drive lost head nails into risers at an angle to help silence squeaks.

✔ **Squeaks on stairs:** The most common squeaks on stairs occur where the front of the upper tread rests on the top of the riser just below the tread. The best way to silence this type of squeak and anchor the tread to the riser is to drive flooring nails at opposite angles through the tread and into the riser. If the treads are hardwood, drill pilot holes first, and then drive finish nails into the risers and use a nail set to recess the nails. Use wood putty to fill the nail heads.

Chapter 8

Painting and Finishing

. . . .

In This Chapter

▶ Making safety a priority

▶ Timing your painting projects appropriately

▶ Figuring out what to paint first

▶ Applying paint to various surfaces

. . . .

*P*ainting and finishing go fast, and with every brushstroke, your projects get closer and closer to completion, and hopefully look better and better. This chapter walks you through the process of actually applying paint: On the outside, from cladding to windows and doors; on the inside, from floor to ceiling and everything in between.

Preparing to Paint the Exterior of Your Property

You did your homework and chose just the right finish and colour for your house's exterior. You worked hard to repair and prepare the surfaces. But now you're having a hard time keeping up your enthusiasm. Your house, which didn't look all that bad to start, now looks terrible, scraped and sanded everywhere.

Cheer up! Now comes the relatively easy part – applying the paint. The work goes quickly, and seeing the house transformed before your eyes is very satisfying.

Safety precautions

✔ Use extreme caution around electrical power cables, especially if you're using an aluminium ladder. Don't forget to look for them when moving a ladder. Also, get help moving a heavy extension ladder so that you're in full control of it, and not the other way around.

✔ Expect bees, wasps, or bats to fly out of cracks in the fascia boards. Hopefully they won't of course, but always be prepared! Keep one hand on the ladder so that you're less likely to fall when you're startled. You can't run, so protect yourself with a long-sleeved shirt, long trousers, and a hat or painter's hood. Tap suspicious areas with a broom handle before you get too close, and use wasp spray that you can aim from a safe distance.

✔ Don't assume that you have good ventilation just because you're outdoors. There may be little or no air movement. If you're working with products that suggest application in a well-ventilated area, wear a respirator.

✔ Don't overdo it on a hot day. Drink plenty of water (or a sports drink) and take breaks to avoid heat exhaustion.

Using ladders safely outdoors

As tedious as it is to stop repeatedly to move the ladder, never overreach. When using a stepladder, the trunk of your body must remain entirely within the ladder's rails. If you use an extension ladder, a good practice is to crook the elbow of your free arm around the rail of the ladder (for example, your left arm around the left rail) and reach out with your free arm only as far as this grip allows.

Always open a stepladder fully and lock it in place before climbing on it. Don't lean an unopened stepladder against a wall to climb on it. Never lean a ladder against guttering.

Set up your extension ladder so that the bottom is the proper distance away from the house wall – approximately a quarter of the working length of the ladder. Ladder rungs are spaced 250 mm or 300 mm apart, so just count the number of rungs from the bottom to the point where the ladder rests against the house to determine its working length. Divide that number by four to determine how far from the wall you should position the bottom.

Always tie ladders at the top to stop them slipping sideways. If you are working on or near a window then you may be able to pass a rope around the central stile of the window and tie it to one of the rungs. Otherwise, pass the rope in through the window and tie it to a bed leg or other piece of heavy furniture.

Several ladder accessories make your work easier and safer. Although an accessory from one manufacturer may work for a ladder made by another, your best bet is to buy ladders and accessories from the same manufacturer. You may find the following accessories helpful:

✔ A **stand-off**, shown in Figure 8-1, gives the ladder more lateral stability and allows you to centre a ladder over a window so that you can paint the entire window without moving the ladder. In addition, if your house has roof overhangs, it stands the ladder off the wall so that you can safely paint the overhang without bending backward. We recommend the Laddermax stand-off, available from www.laddersareus.co.uk, which also doubles as a tray for holding paint tins and tools while you're working off a ladder.

✔ A **stabiliser** is a bracket or pair of legs that bolts to the bottom of the ladder to stop it slipping or sinking into soft ground.

If you use a ladder without any of these attachments, always make sure that the feet are level, and on a firm base. Try to set the feet on a concrete path or paved area, and stop them from slipping by resting a sack of sand or a couple of concrete blocks against them. If the feet of the ladder have to be on lawn or earth, place a board underneath them, and stabilise the feet by driving a stake into the ground and lashing the ladder to it.

Scooting safely up scaffolding

Scaffolding allows you access to a wider area. You can use two ladders to support a scaffold plank (see Figure 8-1). The equipment is available at tool hire shops. A wood or aluminium plank sits on a pair of ladder jacks, which hook onto the rungs of each ladder. Although this setup is relatively safe at low to moderate heights, we don't recommend it for first-storey work (above two metres). Without guardrails or fall-arrest protection, such as a safety harness, you could fall. These protections just aren't feasible for do-it-yourselfers.

For work above two metres in height, we recommend you hire or buy a scaffold tower. This is an arrangement of alloy sections and platforms that slot together to provide a safe working platform at whatever height you build it to, up to about eight metres. Because it's composed of sections, you can easily put up a scaffold tower and take it down, carry it around in the back of an estate car (or on a roof rack), and store it in a garage or shed. Any serious DIY homeowner should think about buying one – or for occasional big outside building jobs, you can hire a scaffold tower cheaply for a week or weekend from a tool hire shop.

Book III

Renovating a Property

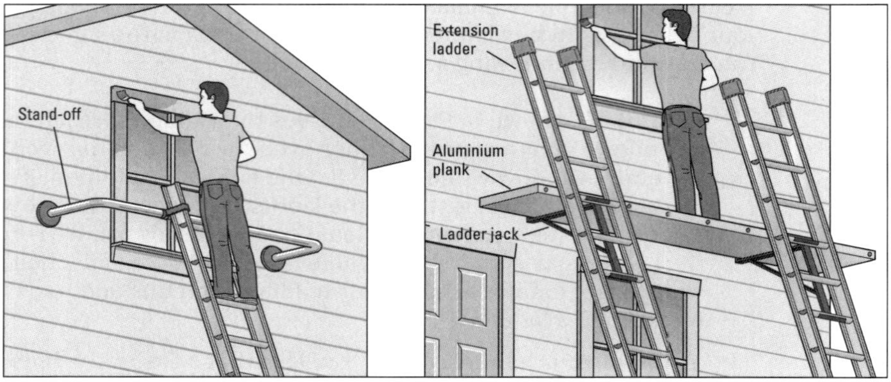

Figure 8-1:
A ladder jack scaffold enables you to paint a large area.

(Labels in figure: Stand-off, Extension ladder, Aluminium plank, Ladder jack)

Consulting the weather forecast

Coordinating an exterior paint job with the weather and your schedule can be quite difficult. First, you must wait for warm weather to allow a house to dry out after winter and early spring. Most paints and other finishes require that the temperature be at least 50 degrees and preferably above 60 degrees Fahrenheit (10C to 15C). Next, you need at least a couple of days of sunny weather to dry the house after rain or pressure-washing. You need another good day if you're priming. Finally, you need a nice day to apply the topcoat; an ideal day sees temperatures between 60 and 85 degrees Fahrenheit (15C to 30C) with no wind.

Differences between water-based and oil-based finishes may affect your decision of when to paint. Although you can apply most oil-based finishes even if you expect rain within a few hours, don't try it with water-based finishes. On the contrary, you can apply water-based on a slightly damp surface, but you're asking for paint blisters if you try it with an oil-based.

Whatever type of paint you use, allow the specified drying time between coats – or more if the weather is cool or humid. If you apply the topcoat over a primer too soon, paint failures such as surface crazing and blistering occur.

The best time to paint a surface is after the sun has warmed it but when it's no longer in direct sunlight. If you paint a hot surface, the paint dries too quickly. Then, as you go back to adjacent areas, you end up brushing over paint that has begun to dry. The result is distinct brush marks. Painting in the direct sun also may cause a variety of more serious failures, including cracking, flaking, blistering, and wrinkling – and that's just on the back of your neck.

Avoid painting or applying any surface coating outdoors on a breezy day. Windborne pollen, dirt, insects, and other debris lodge in the wet paint. The wind may also dry water-based paint too fast, causing the finish to crack or flake.

Planning your painting sequence

In most cases, you should paint the body of the house first and then paint the trim, windows, and doors. (As you paint the trim, you automatically cover any areas on the trim that were inadvertently painted with cladding paint.) Use a large brush, roller, or sprayer on the body of the house. For the trim, use a smaller brush, such as an angled sash brush, which helps you paint with more precision. Paint from the top down to minimise touch-ups for those inevitable drips.

Time is money to the pros, so they plan their ladder moves carefully. Professionals plan their work by painting everything within reach at one time: Cladding, trim, gutters, and all, even if they're using different colours or types of paint. The harder the setup, the more advisable this approach may be. This technique is the obvious one if you're using scaffolds or trying to manoeuvre around shrubs and have to level the ground to set up a 10-metre extension ladder. But at lower heights with less setup, follow the cladding-first rule.

Book III

Renovating a Property

Making last-minute preparations

After you get the brush out, you don't want to stop to remove outdoor light fittings or take time to tie back a bush that's in the way. Before you start to paint, make sure that your path is clear and that you've removed everything in the way.

Always place dust sheets below the area you're painting. This step takes only a moment and saves a great deal of clean-up time later. Use linen dust sheets or buy heavy paper dust sheets to cover under the area where you're working. Plastic dust sheets are slippery to walk on, especially when they're wet, so only use them under your painting tools.

Mix paint well before you use it. Mixing is difficult in a full container, even if you use a paint-mixing drill accessory. There may also be slight differences in colour between the paint in one tin and another, which won't be noticeable until it's too late. To overcome this problem, use a mixing process called *boxing*. Mix at least 10 litres together in a large container; then, when you've used about half, add a new 5 litres, and so on.

Before you carry that large tin of paint up a ladder, think about the mess it will make if it falls. You're better off pouring about a litre of paint – or just enough to cover the area within reach of the ladder – into a smaller tin or paint kettle.

Tooling up for the job

Which applicator you need often depends on what you're painting and the type of finish you're using. A paint pad, for example, is especially appropriate for painting cladding because the top edge of the pad paints the bottom edges of the cladding while the face of the pad paints the face of the cladding. A stain brush holds watery stain better than a paintbrush. If a roller cover is sized to suit the cladding, laying on the paint will go much faster. If you use a roller, go back with a brush to get the undersides and to remove the stippled texture left by the roller.

Have to hand sandpaper, a scraper, a wire brush, wood putty, a putty knife, and caulk so that you can clean and patch any defects you missed during preparation. Don't forget some rags to wipe off spatters.

Priming the surface

On most unpainted exterior surfaces, you need a primer coat followed by two topcoats of paint. We also recommend this procedure for any painted surface that requires significant scraping and repairs. However, if you're painting over existing paint that's still sound, a single coat of 'one-coat' acrylic water-based paint applied properly offers adequate protection and coverage.

You can apply quality water-based acrylic paint over any oil- or water-based-painted surface that's in good shape. If the paint is sound. you generally need to prime only scraped or repaired areas. You can also use a stain-blocking primer in lieu of regular primer to seal knots in board cladding or trim and to cover stains that you can't remove, such as rust.

Make sure that your primer is appropriate for the surface you're painting and that the primer and topcoat are compatible. How do you know? By telling your supplier what you're painting, reading the label, and (though not always necessary) using the same brand of primer and topcoat.

If you already have three or more coats of oil-based paint on the house, use oil-based house paint. Using water-based may cause the old paint to lift off the substrate.

Dealing with rust stains

You may have stains from rusty nails on the original paintwork. Use a bradawl or other pick to remove any caulk or glazing compound wherever rust stains are visible and hammer in any nails that are exposed. Then use a stiff-bristled brush to coat nailheads with stain-blocking, rust-inhibiting metal primer before covering them with caulk or exterior filler.

Painting the Exterior of Your Property

It's finally time to dive in and start to paint. Now comes the really satisfying bit.

Cladding

Although cladding is certainly the largest area to paint, the work goes surprisingly fast, even if you're using a brush. And if you use a sprayer, you move so fast that you have to be careful not to bump into yourself! This is your reward for doing such a good prep job.

Painting wood cladding

Consider a few tips for painting wood cladding:

- ✔ **New or untreated wood cladding:** Coat new wood cladding as soon after installation as possible. Untreated wood requires a primer and two topcoats, if painting, or two coats of stain. Previously untreated or bare cedar may bleed tannin through a paint finish unless you seal the surface with an oil-based primer-sealer (preferably two coats) before applying a 100 per cent water-based topcoat. Knots should be treated with a special knotting compound.

- ✔ **Rough lumber:** Airless spraying works best for painting or staining rough surfaces, but brush the finish as you apply it. *Backbrushing*, as this technique is called, gets paint into areas that the roller or sprayer misses and works the finish into the surface. Brushing also results in a more uniformly stained surface and gives you the chance to brush out drips and runs. If the wood is already painted, use a roller followed by a brush.

- ✔ **New, smooth wood:** Some new cladding that's installed with the smooth side out doesn't accept stain well and sometimes is even too shiny for paint or solid-colour stain, which is like thin paint. Sand the wood with 100-grit paper and then stain or paint. If you plan to use a penetrating stain, you can let the cladding weather for six months to a year and save yourself the sanding work.

Choosing finishes for decking

Unfinished decking usually requires annual applications of a protective coating. A clear water repellent (also called a water sealer) prevents the problems associated with the constant wetting and drying of wood by helping it maintain a more even moisture content. Some water repellents contain mildewcides; none blocks damaging ultraviolet (UV) rays that cause wood to fade and crack. Semitransparent stains with UV protection limit the effects of UV radiation to a small degree. Some clear wood finishes also contain UV-blocking particles. Solid-colour stains and paints offer the greatest UV protection, but solid-colour stain wears on walking surfaces, and paint is likely to peel.

Decking needs abrasion-resistant stain; don't paint it. Even railings are easier to maintain if you stain rather than paint them. Renew stained decking every two to three years. You can apply clear water repellent or, even better, a water repellent with UV blockers over a semitransparent stain as a maintenance coating between stain applications.

You can treat the largest decking in a matter of minutes using a low-pressure garden sprayer or similar tool. For best results, follow up with a bristle-type pad on a long handle.

Painting PVC-U cladding

PVC-U cladding doesn't have a surface coating of paint. The colour is continuous through the material. Painting eliminates one of the primary advantages of this cladding material, namely that it's maintenance free. Nevertheless, if you can't stand the colour or it has become dull with age, painting is an option.

Use a light colour when painting PVC-U cladding. Dark colours cause excessive expansion and contraction because they soak up the heat, resulting in paint failure and buckled cladding. Use special PVC-U paint (sold in all good decorators' merchants) and follow the manufacturer's instructions.

Painting concrete, brick, or render

You can paint brick, render, concrete, or concrete block with exterior water-based paint after you clean the surface to remove accumulated grime. Use a finish with a satin sheen to make cleaning easier the next time.

Think twice before you tamper with unpainted brick, because removing paint from brick is nearly impossible. Instead, use a water-repellent sealer or stain, both of which offer some weather protection but don't peel.

You can paint stucco or render with an acrylic water-based product. You need to seal some masonry, especially highly alkaline surfaces such as stucco, with an alkali-resistant masonry primer. Moisture from the ground and from the house's interior rises to the exposed portion of the masonry and escapes harmlessly when the masonry is unpainted. If you paint the masonry, make sure that you use a water-based product that allows moisture vapour to pass through. Use a sprayer, long-nap roller, or rough-surface painting pad/brush to paint a masonry surface.

Windows and doors

Pay special attention to windows and doors. These elements attract the most attention and are the most vulnerable to paint failure because of all the joints where water can enter if the seal fails.

Windows

The outer surface of a window is painted with gloss paint to provide weather protection.

Here's the sequence to follow:

1. **Begin painting the wood next to the glass, using an angled sash brush (also called a cutting-in brush).**
2. **Paint the stiles and rails of the sash.**
3. **Paint the window frame and architraves.**
4. **Open the lower sash to paint the exterior windowsill.**

Don't paint the edges of the sliding sash. When these surfaces are painted, they tend to stick to the frame. This advice is especially important when you're painting a window with a sash that slides in PVC-U channels. Even a little paint on the edge of the sash can make it stick shut. Instead, seal these areas with a clear penetrating wood sealer to prevent moisture from entering the sash.

If you're painting a window sash while it's in the frame, use a brush that has very little paint on it to coat the outside edge of the sash. The dry-brush method prevents paint from running into the crack between the sash and the exterior stops, where it may cause the window to stick. Also, move the window sash frequently as it dries to prevent the window from sticking. If the window does stick, try using a craft knife or thin-bladed scraper to cut through the paint that glues the sash to the exterior stop.

To form a moisture shield between the glass and the sash, overlap the paint by about 1.5 mm onto the glass. If you have a steady hand and a quality angled sash brush, apply the paint freehand and wrap a clean cloth over the tip of a putty knife to clean off any mistakes. For the mere mortals, mask the glass before you paint, or use reasonable care and plan to use a razor scraper after the paint has dried. If you decide not to mask, you can use a trim guard to protect the glass, but don't push too tightly against the glass or you won't get the desired overlap.

If you leave masking tape in place and it gets wet or the sun bakes it on, it's nearly impossible to remove. Apply painter's tape when you're ready to paint, not before, and remove the tape before you move on to the next window.

Entry doors

Choose a semi-gloss or high-gloss oil-based paint for exterior doors, which get a lot of use and abuse. Water-based enamel also holds up well. If the door was previously painted with a high-gloss paint, use a deglosser to dull the finish and clean the surface. If a wood or metal door has never been painted, or if you expose bare wood or metal by sanding, apply the appropriate primer.

You're much less likely to have drips and runs if you take a few moments to remove the door and lay it flat on sawhorses. Use a shoebox to keep all the hinges and screws together.

Make sure that you paint the bottom and top of a wooden door. If you don't, moisture can enter the door and cause it to swell or warp. A convenient mini-pad paint applicator lets you paint the bottom edge without removing the door.

If the door has a flat surface, paint it with a 50 or 75 mm-wide brush, pad, or roller. A roller typically leaves a stippled finish that may not be acceptable on surfaces when viewed up close. If you use a roller for speed, plan to back-brush with a brush or pad.

If the door is panelled, use a brush and paint the panels first. Then paint the horizontal cross pieces (the *rails*), and finally paint the vertical pieces (the *stiles*). Paint with the grain as you do when sanding. To avoid applying too much paint in a corner, brush out of the corner rather than towards it. As you paint, check often for drips and excess paint in inside corners and brush out the excess paint before moving on.

Finishing things off

Before you store painting tools and equipment, make one final inspection, making sure that you didn't miss spots or overlook drips. Make sure you remove all masking or painter's tape. If it bakes on or gets wet and dries, it can be nearly impossible to get off.

Cleaning up the garden

Your outdoor clean-up is minimal if you're careful to use dust sheets during preparation and painting. Be careful not to contaminate the ground with paint chips, especially if they contain lead.

We've found it helpful to use a wet/dry vacuum cleaner to pick up paint chips that escaped our dust sheets. If you're careful and hold the nozzle just above the ground, you can pick up paint chips and sanding dust without sucking up too much soil or an occasional squirrel.

Removing drips and spills

While drips and spills are fresh, wipe them up with water (for water-based emulsion) or white spirit (for oil-based gloss paints). Use denatured alcohol (methylated spirit) to clean up alcohol-based coatings, such as some fast-drying primers. If the paint has dried but not fully cured, use methylated spirit on water-based emulsion or white spirit on oil-based gloss paints.

On glass and other relatively nonporous surfaces, you're often better off letting the spatter dry and scraping it off with a razor scraping tool. Use caution to avoid scratching the surface. A little paint spatter is much better than a ruined pane of glass.

For fresh spatters and spills on masonry and other porous surfaces, flood the surface with water or thinner and scrub, scrub, scrub. Repeat the process as needed, using clean thinner each time. If the paint has dried, try a paint-and-varnish remover.

Painting the Interior of Your Property

When painting a room, the usual top-down sequence works best: Ceiling, walls, woodwork (including windows and doors), and then the floor. Of course, it's common to paint only the walls and the ceiling and just give the trim a good wash, thanks to the durability and scrubability of gloss paint.

The argument for painting walls before trim is that you're likely to spatter wall paint onto the trim while rolling paint on the walls. But if you want to paint the trim first, go for it! If you get wall paint on the trim it's relatively easy to wipe off, and gloss trim paint covers flat wall paint much better than the other way around. You may also find that cutting in around already painted trim by using a brush or edging pad on the wide wall surface is easier than brushing the narrow edge of the trim – we do.

If you're planning to put two coats on the trim, you may want to paint the first coat before you paint the walls so that it's dry by the time you apply the second coat. If you have a lot of trim to paint, you may want to paint the windows straight after you roll the ceiling. Then break from that meticulous work for some big moves with a roller on the walls before going back to finish the doors and skirting boards.

Ceilings and walls

Interior ceiling and wall painting is a project that's best divided into two: Cutting in and rolling. (Having two people do the work is nice – especially if you're not one of them!) One person uses a brush to cut in, or outline, all the areas that a paint roller can't cover without getting paint on an adjacent surface. The other member of the team spreads paint on the ceiling and walls with a roller. If the ceiling and walls are the same colour, you can cut in both at the same time. Otherwise, work on the ceiling first.

If you're painting with a partner, have the person with the brush, who we'll call the outliner, start by spreading a 50 mm band of paint on the ceiling, all around its perimeter. Overlap marks result if the cut-in paint dries before you blend in the rolled area with the cut-in area, so don't let the outliner get too far ahead of the roller. You also want the roller to roll over as much of the cut-in band of paint as possible. The textures that a brush and a roller leave are quite different.

To apply paint to broad, flat surfaces, such as walls and ceilings, use a 225 mm roller and either a shallow roller pan or the bucket-and-grid setup.

Before you use a new roller, wrap it in masking tape and then peel off the tape to get rid of any loose bits that might stick in the fresh paint.

Attach a pole extension or broomstick to your roller. This device enables you to do the work with less neck strain, with less bending, and without the need for ladders, staging, stilts, or platform shoes.

When rolling walls, keep these tips in mind:

- **Begin in a corner.** For ceilings, paint a big 'W' pattern about 1 metre wide. For walls, paint a roller-width coat of paint from top to bottom. Then smooth out your work by rolling lightly a 1 metre-square area on the ceiling or from ceiling to floor on walls. Continue to work your way across the ceiling or along the wall in this fashion.

- **Don't skimp on paint.** By applying a single ceiling-to-floor vertical stripe or 'W' pattern of paint per roller of paint and then smoothing only that area, you will assure adequate coverage.

- **Frequently step back and observe your work from several angles, checking for overlap marks and missed spots.** Adequate lighting is important here. As long as the paint is wet, you can go back over an area without creating noticeable overlap marks.

Decorative paint effects

Get your creative juices going by transforming walls with different paint effects. We start off by practising on a scrap of wallpaper or board, and then graduate on to a corner of the spare room that'll be hidden by the wardrobe. Don't try sponging or stencilling the lounge walls until you're absolutely confident of your ability, and are sure that you and your family will be happy with the effect!

Colourwashing

Colourwashing gives a soft, dappled, watery colour to a wall, and is popular with people who want an old-fashioned rustic appearance. Apply a basecoat of light-coloured distemper, and then brush a much thinner topcoat of colourwash (usually a darker colour) on top of it. You can buy distemper from some specialist decorating and artists' suppliers, or make it yourself in the traditional way from chalk ('whiting'), water, and rabbit-skin glue.

Dragging, stippling, and sponging

Use these quick and easy effects to make a dramatic difference to your walls.

- **Dragging** is a technique using a stiff brush to produce an effect similar to the grain of wood. Apply an eggshell base coat, then cover it with a tinted translucent oil glaze (sometimes called *scumble*). Make vertical and horizontal brush marks in this glaze.

- **Stippling** uses similar materials and technique to dragging, but instead of using a stiff brush to leave brush marks, use a softer brush to dab the wet glaze surface, leaving a dappled effect (which is actually lots of tiny pinpricks of colour).

- **Sponging** uses ordinary water-based emulsion paint as a basecoat. Dab a topcoat of oil-based scumble onto it in a rough pattern using a sponge. After the topcoat is dry, you can sponge on a second colour, giving a marbled effect.

Stencilling

Stencilling uses cut-out patterns in card or plastic to produce more uniform patterns on a wall. Start with a basecoat in either water-based emulsion (for walls) or oil-based gloss (for woodwork), and then apply a different-coloured paint on top, using the stencils to provide the pattern.

Book III

Renovating a Property

Woodwork

When painting wooden windows, doors, and interior trim, make sure that you keep your work area clean and free of draughts and airborne dirt to prevent dust and lint from settling on the wet paint. Getting professional results depends on good prep work. If the wood is bare, apply a primer.

If you're painting over already painted or varnished woodwork, prepare the surface and apply one or two coats of paint, always sanding between coats. If the finish has a glossy sheen you're not keen on, sand it or use a deglosser.

Working on windows

Paint the operational part of the window, the sash, first. Then paint the frame and the casing. (*Casing* is the top and sides of a window frame.) Paint the interior windowsill (called the *stool*) last. While you're working on the sash, paint any interior horizontal and vertical dividers (called *muntins*) before you paint the stiles and rails that make up the frame of the sash.

Don't paint previously unpainted surfaces. Instead, coat these surfaces with a clear, penetrating wood sealer to prevent moisture from entering the sash.

Taking an orderly approach to double-hung windows

Paint older double-hung sash windows in place. If someone's painted the upper sash shut or the pulley/counterweight system needs repair, correct the problem before you start painting. When you're ready to paint, follow these steps:

1. **Reverse the positions of the lower, inner sash and the upper sash, leaving both slightly open, as shown in Figure 8-2.**

2. **Using an angled 40 mm sash brush, paint the lower exposed portion of the outer sash.**

3. **After the paint dries, return the upper and lower sashes to their normal positions, but don't close them completely.**

4. **Paint the remaining portion of the outer sash and the entire inner sash.**

   Don't paint the outside-sloped portion of the window (the sill). This area is an exterior surface, and you must paint it with an exterior paint.

5. **Switch to a wider 60 mm angled sash brush to paint the casing.**

6. **Cut in the architrave where it meets the wall. Then do the stops, which form the inner edge of the channel for the inner sash, finishing with the face of the architrave.**

7. **Paint the window board (the internal sill).**

8. **After the sash has dried, paint the channels.**

Slide the sash all the way up to paint the bottom half of the channels and, when the paint dries, slide the sash all the way down to paint the upper half. If unpainted metal weather-stripping lines the channels, don't paint the stripping.

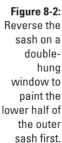

Figure 8-2:
Reverse the sash on a double-hung window to paint the lower half of the outer sash first.

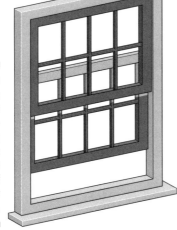

Book III

Renovating a Property

To save all the waiting, paint the lower half of the window channels before you start painting the walls and ceilings so that it can dry while you cut and roll. As soon as the channels are dry, stop rolling and do the upper half of the channels.

As you're painting around the glass, lay the paint on in the middle of the area you're painting rather than starting in a corner. Then, with less paint on the brush, work from the corners out, dipping your brush into the paint you initially laid down as necessary.

As with painting the exterior window trim, use a brush with very little paint on it to coat the vertical, outside edges of the sash to prevent the window sticking.

Working on casements from the inside out

Follow the same procedure for a casement window, with one exception – paint the outer edges of the sash first so that they start drying ASAP. Don't close the window until it's completely dry.

Pausing for breath

If you want to take a break, wrap your brushes, rollers, or pads in cling film and stick them in the fridge until an hour or so before you're ready to paint again.

You can also leave a brush in solvent. If you do so, keep the bristles off the bottom by attaching a paint stick to the handle with a rubber band so that the stick extends below the bristles.

Start by partially opening the window so that you can remove the operating mechanism from the sash. After you paint the outer edges of the sash, cut in the glass perimeter and then paint the face of the sash. Next, crank the window wide open to access and paint the frame. Finish by cutting in the casing and painting the frame and the face of the casing.

You need to overlap paint onto the glass slightly, especially on the lower third of each pane, to prevent water that condenses on cold glass from soaking into the wood behind the paint. This process causes the paint to peel and eventually leads to wood rot.

Doors

Doors take a lot of use and abuse, so for best results, choose a durable finish that has a semi-gloss or gloss sheen. Semi-gloss or gloss makes cleaning easier and holds up to frequent cleaning. You need to lay down at least two topcoats to get a uniform appearance. If the current finish on the door is a glossy paint, use a deglosser to dull the finish.

Leave doors hanging on their hinges while you paint them so that you can paint both sides at the same time. You can remove most modern lock sets in less than a minute (and replace them in under two), so removing them for painting is easier than masking. Make sure that you do one or the other.

You must seal all surfaces of new doors to prevent moisture from entering the door and causing it to warp. This step is critical for a solid-wood door or a solid-core veneered door. We even recommend sealing for hollow-core doors, which aren't as prone to warping. Slip a mirror under the door to see if the bottom edge has been painted. If it has not, either use a mini-painting pad that enables you to paint the bottom edge or remove the door from its hinges, apply a sealer to the bottom edge, and rehang the door to paint the rest of it.

Paint a raised-panel door, shown in Figure 8-3, with a brush, and paint with the natural grain of the wood.

Figure 8-3:
Paint the top pair of door panels first, then the wood around them.

First paint the top pair of panels and the wood (stiles, muntins, and rails) around them. Then move to the next lower pair of panels, and so on.

Putting on the finishing touches

Before you pack away the paint and equipment, remove any masking tape and check carefully for spots that need a touch-up. Look for paint drips, too. Drips and runs take time to form, and despite your best efforts to keep checking just-painted surfaces, you may find some. You must wait until drips and runs dry completely before you scrape, sand, and retouch the area with paint.

If you find paint on the glass in windows or doors (and you probably will), use a single-edge razor or a razor scraping tool to scrape it off. Before you scrape the paint off the glass, score the paint with the point of a utility knife and then scrape up to the scored line. Doing so prevents you from accidentally peeling paint off the wood. If you're trying to maintain a 1.5 mm overlap on the glass (see the 'Windows' section, earlier in this chapter), hold a wide filler knife against the wood as you score, as shown in Figure 8-4.

Book III

Renovating a Property

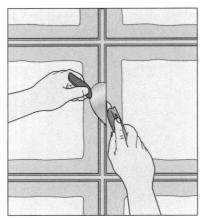

Figure 8-4:
Score a paint line before you scrape paint off glass. The wide filler knife protects a 1.5 mm border of paint.

Be careful while scraping glass. Hold the razor at a low angle with its entire edge on the glass and work slowly to avoid scratching the glass.

Next, reinstall hardware, fixtures, and socket covers that you removed when preparing the room. Finally, move the furnishings back in, and please, don't chip that fresh paint!

Book IV
Becoming a Buy-to-Let Landlord

'The salesman who sold me the porch light said it was the absolute ultimate in security lighting.'

In this book . . .

As they say in the scouts, be prepared! Knowing how to prepare for renting out your property is the name of the game in this book. Here we help you to get clued up on rents and deposits, staying on the right side of the legal line, and give you lots of tips on how to show off your property to best effect.

Here are the contents of Book IV at a glance:

Chapter 1

Decision Time: Managing Yourself or Hiring an Agent?

In This Chapter

▶ Deciding whether to manage your own property

▶ Assessing the benefits of working with an agent

▶ Knowing what to look for in a letting agent

*T*he TV property experts can make a buy-to-let investment sound so simple. But just as important as buying the right property for the right price, the key to success is a well-managed property. Although you may lack experience of being a landlord in the beginning, this is often the easiest time to manage your property portfolio because you have just one lot of tenants to deal with and one buy-to-let mortgage to pay. To help you decide, this chapter takes a look at the pros and cons of managing your own property (as opposed to hiring an agent to do it for you).

Even if you don't hire a letting agent to manage the property for you in the beginning, once you build up the number of properties on your books, you may eventually decide to pass the job onto someone else. So this chapter also looks at tools for evaluating letting agents, from the services they offer to the fees they charge. It also explains the importance of experience, qualifications, and credentials. Also, we reveal some of the common tricks that letting agents use to generate additional income that are not in your best interest.

Managing Your Rental Yourself

When you first start out, you'll probably do all the work yourself – painting, cleaning, doing repairs, collecting the rent, paying the bills, and showing the property to potential tenants. After looking at some of the advantages and disadvantages of doing this yourself, you can decide whether you want to go it alone or whether hiring an agent is for you. If you decide on the latter, check out the information later in this chapter about working with a professional letting agent. This is one of the most important decisions you'll make as a buy-to-let landlord, so take the time to look at all your options.

Even if you ultimately decide that *you* are the best manager for your rental property, the more you discover about how the professionals manage property, the better you will be at management yourself.

The Web site www.landlordzone.co.uk is a useful resource to turn to for up-to-date information as you master the ways of rental property management.

Recognising the advantages of self-management

If you have the right traits for managing property, and if you have the time and live close to your property, you should definitely do it yourself. Managing your own rental property has some definite advantages. For example, by managing your own property, you don't have to pay a monthly fee to a letting agent, which can be as much as 15 per cent of the rent for a full management service.

If you purchase a small flat as an investment property, you might not be able to generate enough money to pay for a letting agent and make a profit – at least not right away.

By keeping direct control of the management of your rental property, you also may save on maintenance costs, because *you* decide who does the repair work or mows the lawn. Doing your own maintenance is usually a good idea; if you hire someone else to do it for you the cost can eat into your profits.

Develop a list of reliable handymen and gardeners who do good work and charge low rates. Even if you hire someone to let your property for you, you're better off choosing the maintenance contractors yourself, if possible, rather than turning over the decision – and your money – to a letting agent.

Paying attention to the drawbacks

If you're just starting in the world of property management you may be thinking of it as a part-time venture – something you'll do in addition to your day job. And if you want, you can keep it that way by keeping the number of properties you own to a minimum. But you may find yourself spending far more time on managing your properties than you anticipated – either because you've bought more of them, or because you just didn't anticipate the time requirements.

If you earn your living regularly from something other than managing your rental property, managing that property may not be worth your valuable time. If you're a high-income, full-time professional, rushing off on weekdays to handle some minor crisis at your property is not only impractical, it could be downright damaging to your career. Most employers have little tolerance for a second job, particularly one that often has unpredictable and unscheduled demands.

As a jobholder, look at your annual income and work out approximately what you earn per hour. Do the same for the cash you're saving by managing your own property. Unless your management efforts produce significant cash savings compared to your job, you may be better off hiring a letting agent to manage your properties. The same guideline holds true even if you are self-employed. Your schedule may be more flexible than the fixed workday of a 9-to-5 employee. But if you're earning £50 an hour as a consultant, devoting hours of your productive work time to managing property, which may only amount to savings of £100 a month, may not make sense.

Managing your property from a distance

If you own rental property at the other end of the country, you may initially consider managing it from afar. As long as your tenants pay their rent and make only a few maintenance demands, this arrangement can work – but it's a fragile one. One major problem can turn the job of managing the rental property into a nightmare.

We know someone who had a very bad experience when he rented his own house to tenants after being transferred by his company to a job overseas. He found a nice family to rent to, and everything was fine for the first six months. Then one day he got an urgent call from his tenants, complaining that torrential rain had caused the roof to leak, making the house uninhabitable. As he was still abroad, he asked his tenants to assist him in hiring someone to repair the roof. The work was botched, and he wound up flying back and forth twice to straighten out the mess before he finally managed to get the roof fixed properly. This negative experience ended up costing thousands of pounds, easily wiping out whatever small profit he could have made.

Think twice about handling your own rental property maintenance from hundreds of miles away. You need to be in the immediate area to routinely inspect and maintain a buy-to-let property, especially when a roof leak or broken pipe demands immediate attention.

Book IV

Becoming a
Buy-to-Let
Landlord

Exploring Professional Management

Many first-time buy-to-let landlords frequently drift blindly into self-management by default, because they assume they can't afford to use a letting agent. 'Why pay someone to manage my rental property when I can keep the money myself?' is a common refrain.

Other owners would really prefer to hire a professional to manage their properties, but they've heard so many horror stories that they don't know whom to trust. Many of their concerns are real – some letting agents mismanage properties and have a total lack of ethics. Luckily, there is a detectable pattern that can help you avoid hiring the wrong letting agent.

If you think that hiring a letting agent may be the right choice for you, take the time to study this option. Here are some advantages to using a management firm:

- They have the expertise and experience to manage rental property, plus knowledge about relevant legislation and safety regulations.
- They're able to remain fair, firm, and friendly with tenants.
- They have screening procedures and can typically screen tenants more objectively than you can yourself.
- They handle property management issues throughout the day and have staffing for after-hour emergencies.
- They have contacts and preferential pricing with many suppliers and contractors who can quickly and efficiently get work done.
- They handle all bookkeeping, including rent collection.
- They have well-established rent collection policies and procedures to follow when tenants' rental payments are late.
- They can be excellent sources for purchasing additional properties because they are often the first to know when their current clients want to sell.

Of course there are some disadvantages to using a letting agent as well:

- Using a management company for small rental properties that you've recently acquired may not be cost-effective.
- They often won't have the same care, consideration, and concern you have for the rental property.
- They may take longer to find tenants for your property if the letting agent has several other vacancies they're dealing with at the same time.

> ✔ Letting agents may not be as diligent in collecting late rent as you would be.
>
> ✔ Some letting agents may try to falsely impress you by not spending enough on repairs and maintenance needed to properly maintain the property.

Be sure to consider the pros and cons to determine whether working with a letting agent is right for you.

Knowing what to look for in a letting agent

Size isn't the determining factor in whether a professional letting agent can deliver quality service. Some letting agents specialise in large rental projects, whereas small operations may focus on managing small family homes and one-bedroom flats. Don't assume that a big letting agency will do the best job for your property or that the small company has the credentials, experience, and knowledge that you need. Try to find letting agents familiar with your kind of buy-to-let property. With a little research, you can find the right fit for your property.

Professional letting agents normally handle a wide range of duties. If you opt for full management, you'll typically get the following services:

✔ Preparing, advertising, and showing the property

✔ Introducing, vetting, and selecting the tenants

✔ Preparing the tenancy agreement

✔ Advising on inventories for furnished properties, changes in legislation, and Council Tax

✔ Collecting the rent and paying the balance to the landlord's account

✔ Providing regular accounting reports

✔ Regularly inspecting the property and overseeing repairs

✔ Enforcing the property's rules and regulations

✔ Dealing with complaints from the tenants

Book IV

Becoming a Buy-to-Let Landlord

TIP More limited management services are also available from some letting agents. Maybe you just need help with finding tenants in the first place and are willing to pay a basic fee for this. Or you may want help finding tenants and collecting the rent as well. Each letting agent has his or her own scale of charges and terms and conditions.

A good letting agent may be able to operate your rental properties better and more efficiently than you can on your own. Their superior knowledge and experience can result in lower costs, higher rents, better tenants, and a property that is well maintained. Using such companies more than pays for the costs, and you have more time to pursue additional properties or other pursuits. Of course, a poor letting agent cuts into your profits, not only with their fees, but also with improper maintenance and poor quality tenants who will run your property into the ground. A bad letting agent can leave you in worse shape than if you'd never hired one in the first place.

Telling the good from the bad and the ugly

Management companies accept the responsibility for all operations of the property, including advertising, tenant selection, rent collection, maintenance, and accounting. The right letting agent can make a big difference in the cash flow your property generates, because he finds good replacement tenants quickly and makes sure that maintenance is done in a timely manner without breaking your budget. You need a letting agent who is committed to helping you get the optimum results from your properties. As the heading suggests, cowboys do exist.

Be sure to visit the office of the letting agent and spend time interviewing the specific person who will have control of the hands-on management of your property. Make a few extra phone calls to check references and don't sign a management contract until you feel confident that the company you hire has a sound track record. Checking with the letting agency's chosen referrals is not enough. Ask for a list of all their clients and contact the ones with rental properties similar in size and type to your own. Make sure the landlords you contact have been with the letting agent long enough to have a meaningful opinion on the quality of the service.

The following sections tell you specifically what to look for.

Do they manage property exclusively?

Make sure that the firm you hire manages property exclusively. This is particularly important when selecting a letting agent for a single-family home, flat, or very small rental property. Many traditional estate agents (as opposed to letting agents) offer property management services; however, property management is often a *loss leader* (meaning that it costs more for the estate agent to manage your property than they're charging you for that service, because they're hoping to get your business later on when you're ready to sell). Many letting agents who work in estate agents do not have the same credentials, experience, and expertise that an employee of a company which focuses entirely on managing properties would have. The skills required to represent clients in *selling* property are entirely different than the skills required to *manage* property.

What are their professional affiliations?

Letting agents do not have to be affiliated to a national body, but it makes sense for you to opt for one that is. Not only does this give you peace of mind, but you'll also know that they are of a certain standard. In addition, if a dispute arises, you have the right to appeal to a third party.

Examine the letting agent's credentials. Are they a member of the Association of Residential Letting Agents (Arla), the professional and regulatory body solely concerned with residential lettings? Members are kept up-to-date with changes in legislation and are governed by Arla's Principles of Professional Conduct, providing a framework of professional and ethical standards. To gain membership, agents must, among other things, demonstrate that their client accounts are professionally managed. They must also offer a full management service to landlords on top of basic letting and rent collection. Other accreditation to look out for is membership of the government-backed National Approved Letting Scheme (NALS), membership of the Royal Institution of Chartered Surveyors (RICS), or membership of the National Association of Estate Agents (NAEA).

Are they properly insured?

Verify that the letting agency is properly insured. The company should be a member of the Client Money Protection scheme, which provides professional indemnity insurance. This safeguards both the landlord's rent and tenants' deposits should the management company run into difficulties or even go bust. The management company is your agent and will be collecting your rents and deposits, so they should also have fidelity insurance to protect you in case an employee embezzles or mishandles your money. Most property managers use a single master trust bank account for all properties on their books but controls on client accounts are very strict for Arla members so this shouldn't be a problem. Every penny must be allocated to the right client at any given moment.

Book IV

Becoming a Buy-to-Let Landlord

What's their policy on handling emergency repairs?

In most management contracts, letting agents have the ability and right to perform emergency repairs without advance approval from the owner. This allows the letting agent to take care of problems that occur unexpectedly. Most management contracts contain clauses that allow letting agents to undertake day-to-day repairs, such as replacing a faulty boiler, without the owner's advance approval. When you're in the early stages of working with a new letting agent, make sure you closely monitor their expenses. Even though they may have the legal right to use funds up to a certain amount, they should always keep you informed as the owner.

Important questions to ask

The quality of your letting agent directly affects the success of your property investments and your peace of mind. Here are some important questions to ask as you interview letting agents:

- ✔ Can you provide a list of exactly what management services are provided, including dates I will receive reports, and a breakdown of management costs?

- ✔ Can I contact several of your current and former client references with rental properties that are similar in size and location to mine?

- ✔ Is your firm a member of the Association of Residential Letting Agents (Arla)?

- ✔ Who will actually manage the day-to-day activities at my property? What are his qualifications and does he exclusively manage properties?

- ✔ Do you provide 24-hour on-call maintenance services with e-mail capability?

- ✔ Given that maintenance is usually provided in-house or by an affiliated firm, do you only charge the actual cost of labour and materials without any surcharges, markups, administrative fees, or other such add-ons?

- ✔ Do all funds collected for applicant screening fees, tenant late charges, and other administrative charges go directly to the landlord and not the letting agent?

- ✔ Do you have fidelity insurance for all employees?

- ✔ Are all individual clients' monies accounted for at all times within your single master trust bank account?

When you hire letting agents, treat them well – but be sure they know that you're paying their wages. They should ask before spending significant amounts of your money, and they should keep you informed on a regular basis.

Paying your letting agent

Letting agents are paid in a variety of ways, and the type – and amount – of fees varies widely throughout the country. Make sure that you understand how your letting agent earns his money, but never evaluate the management company based on the management fee alone because, more often than not, you get what you pay for. Don't be afraid to negotiate the fee either, especially if you have several rental properties.

Letting agents essentially charge for services based on the amount of time that is required of different staff members to manage your property. An experienced property management company owner will know the average number of hours that the property manager, the accounting staff, and other support personnel will spend each month on managing your property. The owner will then calculate a management charge that should generate the fees necessary to provide the proper management company resources to effectively manage your rental properties.

Most management companies operate on a 'no let, no fee' basis, receiving a percentage of the collected income for managing a rental property. However, a few companies also charge a flat fee per month. Try to find a company that has a management fee that is a percentage of the collected income; this kind of fee is a strong motivator to the management company to ensure that the rents are kept at market rate and actually collected on time. Never pay a management fee that is based solely on the potential income of a property.

Management fees are typically tied to the size and the expected rental collections of the property. However, for properties that may be more difficult to manage, the letting agent may have higher management fees or additional charges for certain types of services or for a certain period of time. Management companies may also propose charging a minimum monthly management fee or a percentage fee (opting for whichever of the two is greater). For example, a property that is in very poor physical condition and requires extensive repairs and renovations will require a significant increase in the time spent by the property manager in supervising the improvements. This additional time is worthy of separate compensation to the property manager.

Traditionally, agents charge 15 per cent of the monthly rent for a full management service, 12.5 per cent for rental collection or 10 per cent for simply finding tenants. But there are no hard-and-fast rules as charges vary across the country and from agency to agency. In addition, comparing fees charged by different firms can be hard because they are calculated in different ways. Some charge a set-up fee for preparing the initial contract. Others charge for preparing the inventory. You can also be charged fees if the tenant renews the tenancy. The best way to compare prices is to ask several agents for a written quote of exactly what is covered.

Book IV

Becoming a Buy-to-Let Landlord

Additional fees for the leasing of buy-to-let properties are often justified, because the most time-intensive portion of property management is tenant turnover. When one tenant leaves, the property must be made ready for the next; then the managing agent must show the property and screen the tenants. Charges for this can vary, but are usually either a flat fee of a few hundred pounds or a percentage of the rent.

Generally, the larger the rental property, the lower the management fee as a percentage of collected income. Fees also vary by the income potential of the rental property with the higher end commanding a lower percentage management fee than the lower end of the market.

A friend was moving to Manchester for work and wanted to retain his beautiful home in West Sussex in case he was ever transferred back to the area. He inquired into the cost of hiring a professional management firm and was shocked by the wide variation in management fees quoted. So he began asking more questions of one prospective letting agent and learned that this particular property manager was already overseeing over 170 other rental properties and would be glad to add another client to his books. My friend quickly calculated that this property manager would only be able to spend an average of one hour a month on the management of his rental home, including rent collection, accounting, fielding tenant calls, property inspections, and all the other property management duties. For this, he was quoted a management fee of 15 per cent, or over £140 per month. Be sure that you know how many other rental properties will have a claim on your property manager's time before you sign up!

Making sense of management agreements

The management agreement is a pivotal document; it spells out the obligations of the letting agent to you, their client. Be sure to study the fine print – it's tedious but necessary in order to avoid unpleasant surprises. Be wary of clauses that are clearly one-sided in favour of the letting agent. Ensure that the management agreement does not call for the property manager to collect and keep all the income from late payments or from following up a bouncing cheque. Of course, property managers justify their entitlement to this money on the basis that they incur additional time and costs. But these fees should belong to you, because you want to give the letting agent a financial incentive to fill your property with a tenant who pays rent on time and cares for the property. A management fee based on actual rents collected is a better arrangement.

Some property management agreements indicate that there is no management fee charged when the property is vacant between tenants. Although this seems like an arrangement that saves you money, especially when rental revenues are not coming in, the property manager could rush to fill the property without properly screening tenants – and a destructive tenant can be worse than no tenant in the long run.

It is worth including a 'reasonable care' provision so the property manager is motivated to be diligent in the management of the property and avoid employing tradesmen to carry out repairs at your property if there has been a problem with them in the past. Your agreement should also mention such obvious requirements as informing you of what is happening with your rental property.

Some property management companies request long-term management contracts that cannot be cancelled or can only be cancelled with good reason. Avoid signing any property management contract that cannot be cancelled by either party with or without good reason upon a 30-day written notice. A property management company that knows they are only as good as their most recent month's performance will stay motivated to treat your property with the time and attention needed to get top results.

Make sure all your concerns are addressed in the management agreement. You need to know exactly what weekly or monthly reporting they provide, when your property expenses will be paid, and who is responsible for payment of critical items like mortgages, insurance, and property taxes. Leave nothing to chance.

If the property manager won't agree to reasonable clarification of the contract language or a complete list of the services provided for the fee, he may not go out of his way to help you later. Consider it a warning sign, and find a property management company willing to accept your reasonable terms.

Many property managers use their own proprietary agreements written strictly in the best interests of the property management company. So be sure to have your solicitor review this agreement very early in the discussions with your potential property manager.

Knowing the tax consequences of using a management company

As a buy-to-let landlord, you're running a business and must file a Land and Property form with your basic self-assessment tax return each year. Landlords are only taxed on their profit after allowable expenses, including the interest payments on any buy-to-let mortgage, cost of advertising, travel expenses incurred when checking the property, essential repairs, insurance, and management fees (whether paid to yourself or a property management firm).

Book IV

Becoming a Buy-to-Let Landlord

But although your expenses are deductible, they erode your net income from your property. If your annual expenses are greater than the rent revenues, you may find that you can use those losses to help ease the tax burden from other sources of income related to your other rental properties. But a loss is a loss, and trying to keep your rental property in the black is still a good idea, even if you have to pay some taxes on the income.

The advantage of using a management company is that they should be able to make life easier for you. Before employing a letting agent, find out whether they can provide you with a statement of account that is in a format acceptable to HMRC. This should include your income and outgoings, as the letting agent should have all the receipts to back these figures up. This saves you a lot of time, effort, and hassle when it comes to filing your tax return at the end of the year.

Chapter 2

Preparing a Property for Tenants

You may think of preparing your rental property as one of the most basic skills, but it is critical to your overall success. Because vacant rental properties don't generate rental income, you need to fill them with good, reliable tenants who pay their rent on time, and you need to do this as quickly as possible. One of the best ways to attract responsible tenants is to make sure that your vacant rental properties are clean and ready to rent when you show them.

You may think you're saving time and money by allowing a new tenant to rent a property that hasn't been properly prepared. After all, if they don't mind that the property isn't ready to rent, why should you? Unfortunately, this strategy isn't as problem-free as it seems on the surface. In fact, it's a big mistake. Why? Because the kind of tenants you attract with a rental property that hasn't been properly prepared is someone who has lower standards and may even be desperate. New tenants who accept a dirty and poorly maintained property are surely not going to make any effort to leave it in good condition when they leave.

This chapter helps you to figure out whether you need to upgrade your rental property before a new tenant moves in. It also fills you in on the proper methods of preparing the rental property so that you can get the kind of tenant you want in as little time as possible.

Coming Up with a Plan to Handle Vacancies

Because a poor first impression of your rental property's exterior is hard to reverse – regardless of how great the inside may look – the first step in getting good tenants is to develop a plan to get each vacant property in top condition. Ideally, your vacating tenant will be cooperative and allow you access to the property so that you can determine what items need to be cleaned, repaired, replaced, or even upgraded. As you walk through the property, take lots of notes on its condition and what needs attention in order to get it ready to rent again. These notes serve as the foundation for a detailed plan for getting the property ready to rent. That plan in turn helps you attract several suitable prospective tenants who want to lease the property at the rent you're asking.

Not everyone appreciates or values the same features in a rental property as you do. Although you may prefer curtains and carpets in your own home, for example, you may find that tenants prefer Venetian blinds and wooden floors. Although cleanliness has universal appeal, some features such as fitted wardrobes and microwave ovens will appeal more to some prospective tenants than others.

Considering renovations and upgrades

Almost every rental property has potential for renovation or upgrades. Often these upgrades are where you can create the real value in buy-to-let properties: When you have a rental property that is dated, you can renovate it and increase the rent.

If you have an older rental property, renovating may be more difficult due to some of the hazardous materials used in your property's original construction. Although asbestos is banned by law (breathing it in can cause cancer), it was commonly used in construction of many older properties. Removing asbestos can be quite costly because a contractor specialising in asbestos removal must perform this work to ensure that the material is disposed of safely. Your local council may have a specialist department dealing with the removal of asbestos so consult them first.

When you're considering renovations, keep these points in mind:

✔ **Before you start renovating, be sure to evaluate the cost of renovations or upgrades versus the rent increase that you'll be able to get because of the improvement.** You need to be sure of getting your money back from your investment. But remember that there's no way you can come up with an exact answer to what amount of increased rent a particular improvement will generate; some tenants value certain improvements more than others. A separate walk-in power-shower in the bathroom, for example, will have a different impact on each prospective tenant; some are willing to pay more for such amenities, and others won't. When you think about what to upgrade, pay particular attention to those items that would be quick, easy, and inexpensive to replace but that can really improve the overall look of your rental property.

✔ **Think about what features and strengths your prospective tenants will find in other rental properties.** Look for outmoded or outdated features in your own property. For example, if most rival landlords offer dishwashers but you don't have one, you may want to install a dishwasher so that you remain competitive. Your property may have a very old light fitting in the dining room that you can easily replace with a modern light fixture. Another simple upgrade is to replace your old electrical switches and sockets for a more modern look.

✔ **When upgrading or replacing electrical appliances, try to standardise the brand and model and buy white versions wherever possible to give a uniform, tidy impression.** It is often worth buying a well-known brand as well even though little-known brands tend to be cheaper. While buying the cheaper version may save you money up front, it can cost you much more in the long run when you're unable to find replacement parts. Many oven and cooker parts are easily replaceable, but this fact will be worthless if you bought an obscure brand that doesn't have replacement parts available either from the manufacturer or from a third party.

✔ **When you are considering renovations or upgrades to your rental properties, make sure that you obtain the appropriate planning permission as required.** Check with your local council's planning department to see whether any restrictions apply to renovation plans. Taking this step is important even if you're just replacing the windows or building a garden wall. Also get any permission you need in writing so that you don't have to remove your improvements at a later date – at your own expense. You definitely need permission if your property is a listed building or situated in a conservation area.

Even if your renovations are fairly straightforward and not extensive, it is worth checking with the council to avoid having to undo all your good work at a later date.

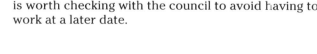

Paying attention to the exterior or common areas

You want to make sure that your prospective tenants' first impression of your rental property is a positive one. If the property exterior and garden isn't up to scratch, your potential tenant won't even bother to see the interior – where you may have just installed new appliances and expensive carpets. Start at

Book IV

Becoming a Buy-to-Let Landlord

the street and carefully evaluate your property as if you were entering a contest for the best-looking property in your area.

If you own a rental property that is leased to a Housing Association, the responsibility for the maintenance and repair of the common areas during the lease period may fall to the Association. If this is the case, contact the Association to advise them of any common area concerns that you have. The Association has a vested interest in ensuring the proper maintenance of the premises as well as maintaining a sense of desirability for owners and tenants.

To attract tenants who treat your property properly and stay for a long time, pay special attention to these things as you spruce up the exterior of your property:

- **Be sure that your garden and exterior areas are sparkling clean and well maintained.** Renovating the grounds by making sure that no rubbish, junk, or weeds are present is often a very inexpensive task. A nice green lawn, pretty flowerbeds, and neat hedge enhance any rental property.

- **Make sure that the structure of your building is presentable and inviting.** Although major architectural changes are often cost-prohibitive, you can do a lot with a little paint, landscaping, and a good clean. The good news is that such attention to detail generally doesn't cost much compared to the positive benefits you gain. Some specific exterior improvements to consider are hanging baskets, brass house numbers, or freshly painted fence or window frames.

- **First impressions are critical, and one of the key areas seen by all potential tenants is the front path and doorway of a house.** Make sure these are clean, well kept, and well lit. The front door should be cleaned or freshly painted or stained. Buying a new welcome mat also sends the right vibes out to potential tenants.

Making sure the interior of the property is up-to-scratch

The most suitable, reliable tenants will always have choices, no matter how good or bad the rental market is. You are in competition for these excellent tenants, and you need to make sure that your rental property stands out from the rest. The positive first impression of the exterior of your rental property will soon disappear if the interior is not just as sharp, well aired, and well maintained.

Don't show your rental property until it is completely ready for the tenants to move in. Prospective tenants understandably have little imagination, and if you show them a dirty rental property, that's the way they will always think of it. Although you may lose a couple of potential showing days by taking the time to get the property ready to rent, you benefit in the long run with a more conscientious tenant.

When preparing a rental property for a new tenant, make sure that you don't overlook or forget a single item. We recommend using an inspection checklist to guide you through the process and as a final inspection tool. Here's a list of things to check:

- ✔ **When you have legal possession, check to make sure that the prior tenant didn't leave anything behind.** Remove all of the prior tenant's personal possessions and rubbish.

- ✔ **Check all plumbing (toilets, taps, and pipes) for proper operation.** Make sure that there are no leaks, that the stopcock is on, and that the drainage is adequate.

- ✔ **Check all appliances for proper operation.** Run the dishwasher through a full cycle. Be sure that all the shelves are in the oven.

- ✔ **Check all hardware.** Be sure the locks have been changed and are operational. Pay attention to all latches and catches, doorknobs, and any sliding doors.

- ✔ **Check all windows.** They should be clean, unbroken, secure, and operate properly. All window locks should work as well.

- ✔ **Check all walls, ceilings, and skirting boards.** The paint and/or wall coverings should be clean, without holes, cuts, scratches, nails, or bad seams.

- ✔ **Check all floor coverings.** They should be clean and in good condition. The flooring should be properly installed, with no bad seams.

- ✔ **Check bathrooms.** Thoroughly clean the toilet, bath, shower, sink, mirrors, and cabinets. Check the toilet roll holder and towel rail to be sure they're clean. Put a new toilet roll in each bathroom.

- ✔ **Check all wardrobes, cupboards, and storage areas.** Hooks, shelves, lights, floors, and walls should be clean.

- ✔ **Check all work surfaces, cabinets, and doors.** They should be clean and fully operational, presenting no hazards.

- ✔ **Check smoke detectors, all lighting and electrical sockets, and circuit-breakers for proper operation.** Fix or replace any that don't work.

Book IV

Becoming a Buy-to-Let Landlord

✔ **Check all patios, balconies, and hallways.** They should be clean and any railings should be secure.

✔ **Check the heating to make sure it's working properly.** Be sure the thermostat, boiler, and radiators are in working order.

✔ **Check the property's external appearance, including the garden, drive, and paths.** Keep them as neat and tidy as possible.

✔ **Perform a final check of the entire property for appearance and cleanliness.** Be sure to recheck the property every few days while it is empty.

To furnish or not to furnish, that is the question

If your property is unfurnished, you may want to think about furnishing it. Unfurnished properties can look rather bleak when bare; with the right furnishings, however, you can make your rental property look cosy and inviting to prospective tenants. Done properly, furnishing your property can generate extra rent and may well make your rental property more desirable to tenants in the first place. In letting agents' experience, furnished properties are quicker to let than unfurnished, so ask yourself whether you will recoup the money you lay out for the furniture by having the property vacant for shorter periods of time.

Most prospective tenants have little imagination when shown an empty property. They can't envision what it would look like with furniture or how nice it could be. The whole idea of the show home in a new development of flats is to show potential buyers just what they could do with their properties. If you furnish your rental property, you are doing the work for the prospective tenants, demonstrating how great the place is.

 Pay attention to your windows. The right curtains or blinds can really make your rental property look great. Not only will your prospective tenant want attractive and functional window coverings, you will also want to control the appearance of your rental property from the street. Appropriate window coverings vary; some tenants prefer curtains, whereas others may appreciate blinds or shutters. You want window coverings that appeal to your prospective tenants and are easy to maintain. We recommend blinds or curtains, because they are easy to maintain and clean.

If you decide to furnish your property, keep these tips in mind:

✔ Don't think of your rental property as home for all the old, worn-out furniture you don't want or need any more. If you don't have any use for worn-out items, chances are your tenants won't either. The furniture doesn't have to be new, but it does have to be smart and clean.

✔ Buy hard-wearing, reasonable quality sofas and beds, tables, and chairs. Don't forget table and bedside lamps, chests of drawers, and bedside cabinets. Remember also that there should be ample wardrobe space in the bedroom.

✔ Keep patterns and colours fairly neutral and plain. Sofas should have washable covers, and the upholstery fabric shouldn't be a light colour. Light fabrics are very hard to keep clean and will probably need replacing after a short period of time.

✔ Bear in mind certain safety regulations when furnishing your rental property. It is an offence to let a property that contains furniture that doesn't comply with the 1988 Fire and Safety Regulations. If found guilty of breaking these regulations, you can be fined up to £5,000 or, worse still, imprisoned for up to six months. Sofas manufactured before 1988 are considered a fire hazard and should not be used. Check for the relevant safety label and, if in any doubt about the age of your sofa, throw it out and buy a new one. It's not worth taking the risk.

Whether you furnish your rental property or not, every property should have a fully-fitted kitchen with fridge, freezer, cooker, and perhaps washing-machine. A dishwasher is another useful addition that appeals to many prospective tenants. Cupboards should ideally be matching and of a neutral colour, preferably white.

Preparing Your Rental Property the Right Way

One of the best ways to maximise your rental income is to develop a system to improve your efficiency by making sure your property is ready to let again in the minimum amount of time. But you may be so overwhelmed by the amount of work you need to get done in the amount of time you have that you don't stop to consider which order you should do it in. Here's the order we recommend to make the most of your time and be as efficient as possible:

1. **Do the general cleaning.**

2. **Perform the required maintenance, including making repairs and necessary improvements.**

3. **Paint anything that needs it.**

4. **Do a final cleaning, to clean the mess you made painting and repairing things and to catch anything you missed before.**

5. **Clean the carpets or floor coverings.**

The following sections explain in more detail what each of these steps involves. Keeping handy a copy of Gill Chilton's *Cleaning and Stain Removal For Dummies* (Wiley) is also a good idea.

Book IV

Becoming a Buy-to-Let Landlord

Keeping up appearances

As soon the old tenants move out, clean the vacant rental property. This initial cleaning should include the following:

- ✔ **Remove all rubbish left behind by the former tenant.** Remember to check drawers, cabinets, and wardrobes.
- ✔ **Wipe down all surfaces.**
- ✔ **Sweep or vacuum the floors.**
- ✔ **Wash the windows and doors.**
- ✔ **Clean out the storage areas or garage as well.**

If you were unable to gain access before the tenant vacated, this is when you should walk through the property and come up with your plan for getting it ready to rent again. See the earlier section 'Coming Up with a Plan to Handle Vacancies' for details.

Keeping everything ticking over

The majority of the items requiring maintenance in your vacant property will be minor items such as cupboard doors that have come off their tracks, door knobs and towel rails that are loose, and burned-out light bulbs. But be sure to carefully evaluate the current condition of all systems and equipment, including plumbing, electrical appliances, heating, and ventilation:

- ✔ **Carefully inspect all plumbing fixtures.** Look for leaky taps, blocked extractor fans, or leaky toilets. Test the stopcock under each sink and look for signs of leaks.
- ✔ **Inspect and test the electrical components of the rental property.** Make sure that fuses are all operating properly. Replace burned-out light bulbs and check light switches. If possible, verify that the cable television and telephone lines are working, too.
- ✔ **Inspect each of the appliances and make sure that they are operating properly.** Cookers and ovens contain modular parts and you can replace the grill pans and control knobs very easily because replacement parts for most major-brand appliances are readily available. Run the dishwasher through a cycle and look carefully for any signs of leaks underneath near the pump housing.

✔ **Conserve energy by turning off the water heater and setting the refrigerator to a low setting.** Tenants are becoming increasingly aware of the importance of conservation and energy-efficiency when selecting their homes. If you install energy-saving features such as insulated windows and doors, loft insulation, weatherproofing, pilot-less ignition gas cookers and water heaters, water-saving fixtures, and other energy-efficient appliances, you'll have a competitive advantage in the rental marketplace.

✔ **Take steps to minimise the likelihood of pests.** Seal all cracks around the windows, foundations, drains, and pipes that might afford entry into the rental property. Almost every rental property will have the need for pest control at some point in time. An occasional mouse or ants in search of water or food are commonplace, and there are consumer products available to handle these limited situations. However, use professional exterminators to treat more significant problems, and talk to your exterminator about establishing a regular schedule of follow-up treatments to be sure your rental property is free of pests.

✔ **Perform regular checks as necessary on other areas.** If your rental property has a fireplace, for example, be sure to clean out the ashes and debris as well as have the chimney flue inspected periodically based on the amount of usage. If your property has a pool or spa, have a professional company evaluate the condition and provide a written report documenting its condition, including the equipment and water quality. This evaluation establishes a baseline and often can head off any tenant complaints later on.

Brush strokes

The next step in getting your vacant rental property ready is painting. Painted walls are much easier to maintain than those covered with wallpaper. And the key to success in painting is preparation and having the proper tools.

To prepare your walls, follow these guidelines:

✔ Make sure that all nails, screws, picture hooks, and other similar items are removed and that any holes in the wall have been filled in with filler.

✔ Remove all doorknobs and electrical socket covers before you start.

Book IV

Becoming a Buy-to-Let Landlord

✔ Make sure the walls have been cleaned of any dirt. Treat grease, water stains, and other blemishes with special products designed for this purpose.

✔ You may also need to do some scraping and sanding to ensure that the new coat of paint will adhere properly.

One coat of a high-quality white or off-white matt emulsion is usually sufficient, unless the colour of the walls is currently of a much darker colour. If so, you may need another couple of coats. Use silk emulsion in kitchens and bathrooms for easy cleanup and resistance to moisture. Unless you have recently painted the rental property in its entirety and only need to touch up one or two walls, you should paint throughout, including the walls, doors and doorframes, skirting boards, windows and frames, and cupboards and wardrobes, where appropriate.

Don't forget to paint the ceiling! Sparkling white walls will only make it look dirty and in real need of a lick of paint.

When you finish painting, be sure to replace any light switches and sockets that are damaged or covered with paint. Remove any paint that has strayed or splattered onto the floor, windows, work surfaces, cabinets, appliances, and woodwork, and be sure to clean out sinks or baths if you used them to clean paintbrushes or hands.

You can find more on doing a professional paint job yourself in Book III, Chapter 8.

Keep it clean, vicar

Cleanliness sells. And the only people you want as tenants are ones who will only accept dirt in their home as a temporary condition.

Pay particular attention to the kitchens and bathrooms. A dirty or grimy kitchen and bathroom can be a real turnoff to a potential tenant. Be sure that you clean and re-grout the tiles, and scrub the shower, bath, toilet, and sinks. Another final touch is to install a new toilet seat, if required.

For many landlords, the thought of cleaning up after someone else is too much to bear. Luckily, many local cleaning services do a great job for a very reasonable price. Remember, you don't have to do everything yourself.

If a rental property doesn't smell clean, it won't matter how diligently you've cleaned it. Use a pine or lemon disinfectant and cleanser to neutralise any bad odours from the previous tenants. Buy an air freshener specifically designed for the fridge and pour bleach down the drains to remove any bad odours. Some great air-freshener products are available, but you need to be careful because certain fragrances may be offensive to your prospective tenant. We recommend placing a cinnamon stick in a shallow pan of water and placing it in the oven on low heat. In a short time, the rental property will be filled with a smell that will remind your prospective tenants of homemade apple pie.

The floor's no walkover

Cleaning the carpet or floor is the last step you take in preparing your rental property for new tenants. You can clean wooden and tiled floors during the final cleaning stage; however, if carpets are particularly dirty, you may have to get in an outside contractor to do the job with professional steam-cleaning equipment. If carpets aren't too dirty, you can clean them yourself with the hand-held equipment that is available for rent.

If the carpets are too old, severely worn, or badly stained and damaged, replace them. Be sure to select colours and styles of carpet that are designed for use in rental properties. We recommend selecting a standard carpet for all your rental properties, in a neutral colour. Avoid loud prints or colours that might be to your taste but not necessarily to everyone else's. If you own a lot of rental properties and have proper storage space available, purchasing your standard carpet by the roll can offer significant savings. You can use the extra carpeting to patch or even replace a full room if needed; however, be aware that each roll of even the same carpet style and colour can be different, because the manufacturer's dye may vary slightly each time the carpet is produced.

Many rental property owners make the mistake of purchasing a more expensive carpet than is necessary and try to save money on the underlay. But the underlay can make all the difference in the world. Consider using a higher-grade of underlay with a medium-grade carpet for competitively priced, excellent results.

Unless they're damaged, thoroughly clean your wooden, tiled, or lino floors before deciding to make replacements. Lino is very competitively priced, and the range of materials available is impressive. The most common problem with a roll of lino is that any damage requires complete replacement. Some landlords prefer individual floor tiles that can be replaced as needed; however, these tiles quickly trap dirt at the seams and can look unsightly. The best choice in floor covering material will be determined by your tenant

Book IV

Becoming a Buy-to-Let Landlord

profile and the expectations of your prospective tenant and your competition in the area. Be sure to select neutral colours and basic patterns.

Inspecting Safety Items

Although tenants need to take an active role in, and have the ultimate responsibility for, their own safety you need to check all safety items every time you let the property to a new tenant. The most basic items found in virtually every rental property include door locks, window locks, and smoke detectors. Be sure that these items are in place and working before the new tenant takes occupancy.

Every door should have adequate locking mechanisms. Many insurance companies have specific requirements concerning the type and specifications of door locks. All windows that open and are accessible from the ground should have proper window locks.

London's burning . . . pour on water

Providing each tenant with a small fire extinguisher and fire blankets for the kitchen is a good idea. Although there is always the possibility that the tenant will not use the fire extinguisher properly, using a fire extinguisher quickly can keep a fire from spreading. Of course, the tenant should first ensure that someone is immediately dialling 999 before attempting to put out the fire single-handed.

Smoke detectors are inexpensive and extremely important to the safety of the tenants. Any building constructed after June 1992 is required by law to have smoke detectors on each floor. But it is good practice, and important for the safety of your tenants, that your property has working battery-operated smoke detectors dotted around. Make sure that your records clearly indicate that you tested the smoke detectors and that they were operating properly before your new tenant moved in. Then the tenant needs to take an active role in regularly testing the smoke detector and must not disconnect or disable the smoke detector in any way. The best way to do this is to have your tenant sign a Smoke Detector Agreement whereby the tenant agrees to check the smoke detector on a regular basis, usually at least once a month.

Bad things happen in threes

Here are three more points for you to ponder when you're considering safety in and around your property:

✔ Carbon monoxide poisoning through faulty gas appliances is an all-too-common feature of rented accommodation, unfortunately, and all landlords must maintain gas appliances in their properties via annual inspections and safety checks. A registered CORGI (the Council for Registered Gas Installers) engineer must carry out these checks. You can find one of these in the Yellow Pages. Keep a record of when the checks are performed and give a copy of the certificate to your tenant. Failure to do this could result in a fine or imprisonment.

✔ If you have a flat roof, your tenants may be tempted to use portions of it for their personal use, such as for sunbathing (if the weather is nice), hanging out washing, watching fireworks, or hosting parties. This is never a good idea, because roofs are only designed to shelter the rental property from the natural elements, not to hold people. In addition to potential premature damage to your roof, you could be liable if someone gets injured.

✔ Be sure that the house number or address is clearly marked on the exterior of your property so that it is easy to locate it from the street. This simple measure can be a huge help to fire or ambulance crews in an emergency.

Using Outside Contractors

Determining how to handle the work required to get the property up to scratch so that it's ready to rent to tenants again is one of the toughest decisions that landlords have to make. Most landlords of small properties are typically on their own to either handle the work personally or find contractors to do the necessary work to prepare their vacant properties as quickly as possible.

Even if you're inclined to do all the work on the property yourself, certain maintenance jobs are best handled by outside contractors. Use outside contractors for those trades that require specialised licensing or training. For example, it would be unwise for you to act as an exterminator or a contractor dealing with an environmental hazard. Specific regulations are in place, and unique knowledge is required in these areas.

Your skill level and time constraints may help determine whether you do some chores yourself or hire a professional. For example, cleaning, painting, and light maintenance may be items that you feel qualified to handle, can complete promptly, and will not cause you to forgo significant income in other areas. The ultimate answer is to let others do what they do best while you focus on what *you* do best.

Book IV

Becoming a Buy-to-Let Landlord

Every day your rental property sits empty costs you rental income you can never recover. If painting your own rental property takes you six days, working in the evenings and weekends, for example, you may actually lose money doing it. How? Well, if the rental market is strong and the daily rental rate is £50 per day, you're actually spending £300 (£50 a day for six days) for a job that you may have been able to hire a professional painter to do in one day for £200.

Chapter 3

The Big Three: Rent, Deposits, and Tenancy Agreements

In This Chapter

▶ Determining the appropriate rent for your rental property

▶ Using deposits wisely

▶ Deciding on what to include in your tenancy agreement

*B*efore advertising and showing your rental property, you need to set the rent, determine the appropriate deposit, and have a tenancy agreement ready to go. All of these decisions are important ones. Setting an appropriate rent is important because your net income from your rental property is determined by the amount of rent you charge. Determining an appropriate deposit is important because you need to make sure that the deposit adequately protects you from tenant damage or default. And a tenancy agreement is important because it outlines the terms and conditions of the agreement you have with your tenant.

In this chapter, we give you some tips on setting the asking rent and determining the appropriate deposit. We also guide you through the tenancy agreement so you know what to look out for.

Even if you buy a property with tenants already in place, you need to determine market rents so that you can calculate the appropriate rent when the time comes to renew the tenancy agreement or consider increasing rents to market level.

In addition to setting the rent, you need to make sure that the deposit on hand adequately protects you from tenant damage or default. Deposits serve as the lifeline or protection you need before you turn over your significant property asset to a tenant. The deposit needs to be large enough to motivate the tenant to return the rental property in good condition, plus serve as an accessible resource to cover the tenant's unpaid rent or reimburse the costs to repair any damage. But if your deposit is set too high, many suitable prospective tenants may not be able to afford it, and you'll have fewer rental applicants.

You will also need to draw up a tenancy agreement so that it's ready to go as soon as you find a tenant for your rental property. Most tenancy agreements are for six months in duration although you may want to draw up a shorter or longer one.

Setting the Rent

For most landlords, setting the rent is one of the most important yet difficult tasks. Although you may be tempted to pull numbers out of the air, resist that urge. If you set your rent too high, you'll have a vacant rental property. And if you set your rent too low, you'll have plenty of prospective tenants but not enough money to cover your costs and generate a return on your investment. Your profits will suffer, or, worse, you won't have enough money to even cover your expenses. Finding the optimum price takes time and effort.

If you currently own a rental property, you probably already know how much rental income is necessary to cover your mortgage and other basic running costs. And if you're looking to buy a rental property, you want to determine your minimum income needs *before* the deal is final. Having this information is essential because buy-to-let mortgage lenders can require that your rental income covers at least 130 per cent of the mortgage repayments: any less, and they won't lend you the money to buy the rental property in the first place.

You can use two common methods for determining how much rent you should charge for your rental property – return on investment and market analysis.

Examining the return on your investment

The first step in determining your rent based on the return on your investment is to calculate the costs of owning and operating your rental property. You need to estimate the costs for your mortgage, managing agent fees (where applicable), insurance, maintenance, and how much of a profit you want to make on your invested funds.

If, for example, your annual expenses per rental property are £6,000 for your mortgage and another £2,500 for other annual operating expenses (which include things like managing fees, insurance, and so on) and you want a 10 per cent (or £2,500) annual return on your original cash deposit of £25,000 in this rental property, you need to generate a total rent of £11,000 per year. That's £917 per month. (Of course, this simple calculation doesn't account for the increase in the capital value of the property, but it gives some indication of the costs involved.)

Knowing how much money you need to break even is important for evaluating the potential return on your property investment. But the reality is that the amount you need or want to collect in rent is subject to market conditions and your abilities as a landlord. Although you may have calculated that you need £917 a month for your rental property to achieve your estimated breakeven point (including your 10 per cent profit), if the rental market has determined that comparable properties are available for £850, you may not be able to make the profit you want. With most property investments, the initial returns may not match your original projections; however, in the long run, rents often increase at a greater rate than your expenses, and your return on your investment is likely to improve.

Many new landlords make a major mistake by overestimating the potential income from their rental property. They develop unrealistic operating budgets or projections, using above-market rents and anticipating virtually no void periods or bad debt. When reality strikes, they're faced with negative cash flow, and ultimately they may even lose their rental property. Don't fall into this trap yourself.

Setting the rent is particularly critical if you own just one or two small properties because the rent loss from an extended vacancy or one bad tenant can seriously jeopardise your entire investment. A landlord who owns 20 rental properties and has one tenant who absconds without paying the rent he owes can use a little of the surplus from each of the profitable properties to cover that month's rent on the vacant property. But if you only have two rental properties, you don't have that luxury. If you are a small-time landlord, follow these suggestions:

✔ **Be conservative in setting your rents.** To avoid surprises, use a conservative budget for your rental property that anticipates rental income at 95 per cent of the market rent for a comparable rental property plus provides for a void period of one to two full months each year.

✔ **Be very cautious in tenant screening.** To find out how to screen for the tenant you want, head to Book V, Chapter 1.

✔ **Be aggressive in maintaining your rental properties.** To attract good, long-term tenants who pay on time, keep your rental properties in excellent condition.

Book IV

Becoming a Buy-to-Let Landlord

Conducting a market analysis of the rent in your area

Although you can determine the amount of rent to charge by calculating a desired return on your investment and setting the rent accordingly, as explained in the preceding section, typically the best way to set your rent is to conduct a market survey of comparable rental properties in your area.

Evaluating how much rent is being charged for similar rental properties in comparable locations is a great way to gather information before setting your own rent. Make minor adjustments in your rent because of variations in the location, age, size, and features of the properties you're comparing. If, for example, one of your competitors has an available house to rent that is nearly identical to yours, your rent should be slightly higher if you also have off-road parking. Of course, be honest and make downward adjustments for aspects of your rental property that aren't as competitive or as desirable as well.

The rental value of a particular property is subjective and can vary dramatically from one person to another. When estimating the proper market rent for your rental property, be careful not to make adjustments based strictly on your own personal preferences. You may prefer a first-floor flat and believe that such flats should be priced higher than comparable ground-floor flats. But although many prospective tenants may, like you, prefer living on the first floor, just as many prospective tenants would similarly value the ground-floor flat because they may not want to climb stairs or use a lift.

In order to determine the going rent in your area, do your homework and locate comparable rental properties. *Comparable properties* are those properties that your tenants are most likely to have also considered when looking for a rental property. They may be located in the next road to your property or across town. For example, many of your prospective tenants may work at the local hospital, two miles away from your rental property. But these prospective tenants are just as likely to choose a property that is within two miles of the hospital in another direction. So your comparable properties could be four miles away. Don't assume that your comparable properties are only in your street.

After you determine which rental properties are comparable, finding out the current market rent is easy. Begin by checking the To Let signs in your area and ring to ask how much the rent is and other details. Your local or regional newspaper generally has ads listing the properties for rent in the area, along with some details and a phone number to call for more information. Although looking at ads gives you some good general information, you need to go and see the properties in person to truly determine whether the rental properties are comparable to yours.

There are two schools of thought when performing a rent survey to determine the proper asking rent for your rental properties:

- ✔ **You can be honest and tell the landlord that you're also a landlord and you're doing market analysis.** While you may find that some landlords might co-operate and share the information you need, the majority are likely to be more cagey about sharing such information with a rival.

- ✔ **You can pose as a prospective tenant and ask all the typical questions that a tenant might ask.** The landlord or managing agent will give you only the information that a prospective tenant would need about the rental property. Although this strategy may seem a bit sneaky, you're more likely to get the information you require if you pose as a prospective tenant.

If you're competing against a large management company in your area, the company isn't likely to provide you with any information about its current occupancy rates. Its actual occupancy rate is important, however, because this information can provide a good indication of overall demand for rental properties. Over the years, we have discovered some creative ways to determine the actual vacancy levels, such as talking with the postman who delivers to the block of flats run by the management company. The postman won't have exact numbers, but he can tell you whether the block is completely full or whether there are a good number of vacancies. You can also drive past the property at night and see how many parking spaces are being used.

Rental rates can vary greatly from town to town and even from street to street because many factors affect rents. Determining the proper asking rent is not scientific; views, landscaping, and traffic noise are just a few examples of the issues tenants take into account. So be realistic in setting your asking rent. Starting a little too high is better than starting too low, because you can always reduce your asking rent slightly if you encounter too much resistance. But you can't very easily raise your asking rent if you get a large response to your ads.

Setting your rents properly is an independent decision based on current market conditions. Unfortunately, the realities of the rental market may put limits on the rent you can reasonably charge for your rental property, regardless of your costs of owning and maintaining that property.

Book IV

Becoming a Buy-to-Let Landlord

Coming Up with a Fair Deposit

You should collect a deposit from your tenant when she moves into your property, and under the Tenancy Deposit Protection legislation (Housing Act 2004; see the sidebar 'Depositing the deposit' for more on this) which came into force on 6 April 2007, you need to decide how you hold the deposit until the tenant leaves. The general purpose of the deposit is to give the landlord a degree of protection against damage and rent arrears during the course of the tenancy. If you collect the first month's rent upon move-in in advance, this amount is *not* considered part of the deposit.

Most landlords ask for the equivalent of one month's rent as a deposit, although some ask for two months. Legal dangers exist in asking for too much deposit money. Some landlords opt for a compromise of six weeks, which discourages tenants from cancelling the last month's rent and asking the landlord to use the deposit in its place.

Deposits are more than just money that you hold for protection against unpaid rent or damage caused by your tenant. Although the actual cash amount may be relatively small compared to the overall value of your rental property, the deposit is a psychological tool that is often your best insurance policy for getting your rental property back in decent condition.

Depositing the deposit

The Tenancy Deposit Scheme came into effect on 6 April 2007 to protect deposits taken for Assured Shorthold Tenancies. Under the rules, landlords must provide tenants with information about the chosen scheme within 14 days of letting, and can choose between three places to lodge deposits:

✔ The Deposit Protection Service (www. depositprotection.com): This government-appointed agency runs a *custodial scheme* in which landlords can lodge deposits for free.

✔ Tenancy Deposit Solutions Ltd (www.my deposits.co.uk): An *insurance scheme*, run by the National Landlords Association and Hamilton Fraser Insurance.

✔ The Tenancy Deposit Scheme (www.tds. com): Another *insurance scheme*, run by the Dispute Service.

Landlords pay an annual premium to belong to the insurance schemes. In both insurance schemes, landlords retain the deposit in client accounts, but in the event of a dispute, lodge the disputed amount with the scheme. Any future disputes will be dealt with by a process known as Alternative Dispute Resolution set up within the schemes, or by the courts if those involved prefer.

This legislation doesn't affect existing tenancies (commenced before 6 April 2007) or periodic tenancies running on after that date. However, tenancies commenced before the scheme started but renewed after this are included.

Don't lower or waive the deposit. If the required funds to move in are too high for your tenant to manage, consider not taking that tenant, or as a very last resort collect a reasonable portion of the deposit prior to move-in and allow the tenant to pay the balance of the deposit in instalments. If you don't collect the deposit in full, you lose your bargaining tool. Your tenant could well abscond further down the line without paying the rent he owes you if he doesn't have the incentive of the return of his deposit. Or he might think nothing of making cigarette burns on the sofa or wine stains on the carpet if he knows he won't be penalised for it by losing some of his deposit.

Keeping deposits separate from your other funds

Deposits are a liability, because they are funds that legally belong to the tenant. If you are in one of the insurance schemes (see the sidebar 'Depositing the deposit') you hold these funds in trust as protection in the event that the tenant defaults in the payment of rent or damages the property. Where landlords opt for the custodial scheme, the deposit monies are held within the scheme which is funded with the interest earned on the money, and so is free to both landlord and tenant.

Because the funds don't belong to you, you may want to hold the deposits in a separate bank account rather than mix them in with the other funds from your rental properties or personal resources. Keeping the deposits separate from the rest of your funds ensures that whenever a tenant moves out and is potentially entitled to the return of some or all of that money, the deposit is available. Besides, it's a nice gesture to pay the tenant the interest earned on the deposit when you return it at the end of the tenancy (see the later section 'Paying interest on deposits' for information on this option). However, you're not legally required to do this.

Setting a reasonable deposit

Most landlords opt for the equivalent of one month's rent as a deposit. One problem with this approach is that tenants may misconstrue that the deposit is to be used as the last month's rent (because it's equal to a monthly rent payment).

The deposit is absolutely not for this purpose. If any damage has occurred to the property or professional cleaning is required, such as having the carpets steam-cleaned, you don't have any recourse but to subtract these costs from the deposit. If the deposit is used as the last month's rent, you're out of luck entirely.

Book IV

Becoming a
Buy-to-Let
Landlord

We recommend that you collect slightly more than a month's rent as a deposit. To avoid tenants using the deposit as the last month's rent, we suggest that you ask for five or six weeks' rent as a deposit and explain your policy to minimise any confusion.

Avoiding non-refundable deposits

Some landlords charge non-refundable fees, for cleaning or keeping a pet. But we recommend avoiding such non-refundable fees and just incorporating these charges into your rent. This way, you avoid potentially time-consuming disputes with your tenants.

If you have a specific concern, such as a tenant's pet, increase the amount of your refundable deposit to protect yourself from any damage. You could also ask the tenant to sign a supplemental pets agreement whereby they agree to accept any additional costs for cleaning or damage at the termination of the tenancy as a result of keeping the pet.

Many letting agreements have an absolute ban on keeping pets, but this type of clause has in fact been deemed to be unfair by the Office of Fair Trading's Guidance on Unfair Terms in Tenancy Agreements. However, landlords do have the right to be asked to approve a pet as being suitable for the accommodation, and to have the tenant acknowledge the possibility of additional costs if damage occurs or extra cleaning is needed.

Having the deposit fully refundable is an incentive to the tenant to return the premises in good condition. A non-refundable deposit is not now acceptable under the Tenancy Deposit Scheme rules, and in any case would actually deter the tenants from making any effort to return the premises in good condition, because they figure that they're forfeiting the deposit anyway.

Paying interest on deposits

No law requires that landlords pay interest on the tenant's deposit. However, if you hold the deposit yourself through one of the insurance schemes you may want to offer to pay the interest generated by the deposit to the tenant at the end of the tenancy agreement – this policy is likely to act in your favour and make your rental property more attractive to prospective tenants.

If you're going to pay interest, put the deposit in the savings account paying the highest rate of interest that you can find. The best savings rates are available via Internet-based accounts rather than high-street banks, so shop around online for a reasonable rate. The tenant is unlikely to receive back a lot of interest, but it's a nice gesture, which is likely to be appreciated.

No law prevents you from voluntarily paying interest on deposits, and some owners offer to pay interest as a competitive advantage or as an inducement to collect a larger deposit. If you are able to get a much larger deposit, we recommend paying interest on that deposit. The additional peace of mind is worth the relatively small amount you will lose by not receiving the interest yourself.

Increasing deposits

If you have a long-term tenant and your rents have increased significantly over time, you may want to consider increasing your deposit. Doing so is legal as long as you comply with the normal requirements for the Tenancy Deposit Scheme and any change in the terms of the agreement.

If you have a six-month tenancy agreement, for example, you must wait until that agreement expires before you request an increase in the deposit. If you have a shorter tenancy agreement, then you can increase the deposit the same way that you raise the rent, typically by giving the tenant a written 30-day notice in advance.

Using a Tenancy Agreement

The tenancy agreement is the primary document that specifies the terms and conditions of the agreement binding the landlord and the tenant. It is a contract between the owner of the rental property and the tenant for the possession and use of the rental property in exchange for the payment of rent.

Most landlords use the Assured Shorthold Tenancy agreement. When this tenancy agreement was introduced in 1988 and later amended under the 1996 Housing Act, it revolutionised the residential letting market. For the first time, it granted the landlord a series of guarantees that made it easier for the landlord to let property at a market rent and to recover possession of the rental property if needed. The tenant has no security of tenure after the end of the term agreed between landlord and tenant; the landlord is certain to obtain possession of the property and doesn't have to give a reason as to why he wants possession. You will still have to follow the correct procedure, however, and give two months' notice in writing.

An Assured Shorthold Tenancy tends to start with an initial fixed period. No upper limit is specified, but six months to a year is normal. If you opt for six months, for example, you can't repossess the property during this length of time unless the tenant breaks the terms of the agreement. After the fixed term, you can renew the agreement for another fixed period or allow it to continue indefinitely on a periodic basis, such as month to month.

Book IV

Becoming a Buy-to-Let Landlord

If you're renewing for a fixed period, you need to draw up a fresh tenancy agreement. If you're continuing indefinitely on a periodic basis, you don't need to take action to continue the letting.

You don't have to employ a solicitor to draw up a complicated tenancy agreement because the Assured Shorthold Tenancy is a fairly standard form. All letting agencies have them, and you can obtain them from legal stationers and the Internet, or you can use the tenancy agreement printed later in this chapter (see Form 3-1). An Assured Shorthold Tenancy is legally binding between landlord and tenant; however, it can be difficult to enforce if one of the parties decides not to abide by it.

Before you can offer an Assured Shorthold Tenancy agreement on your rental property, certain conditions must be met:

- The tenant (or each of the joint tenants) must be an individual, not a company.
- The tenant must occupy the dwelling as his only or principal home.
- The annual rent must not be greater than £25,000.
- The landlord must not live at the rental property. However, if the landlord has converted the basement in his house into a self-contained flat with separate entrance and lets this to tenants, an Assured Shorthold Tenancy can be created as normal.

The tenancy agreement must also include certain definitions as to what you mean by the terms *landlord* and *tenant* and on what grounds the tenancy can be terminated. You should also clearly state the notice period to be served by either party – one month by the tenant; two months by the landlord – and the agreement should state that the tenancy must run for at least six months.

You and your tenant have to sign the tenancy agreement, preferably in the presence of witnesses, though this isn't vital. It then becomes legally binding.

With an Assured Shorthold Tenancy, you cannot increase the rent or change other terms of the tenancy until the current agreement expires. Also, you cannot terminate or end the tenancy before the agreement expires, unless the tenant does not pay his rent or violates another term of the tenancy agreement. (The majority of tenants move only because of a job transfer or another significant reason, or because the landlord does not properly maintain the property.)

Although the tenancy agreement legally binds both you and the tenant, it's not difficult for a tenant to walk away from a tenancy agreement. The tenant is responsible for paying the rent for the whole of the initial period even if he leaves early. If you find a replacement tenant during that time, you should let your former tenant off the hook and only charge him for the rent up until the new tenant moves in and begins paying rent. However, you are not obliged to do this, and you're entitled to charge your reasonable reletting expenses to your tenant in this situation.

Although oral rental agreements are binding, make sure all your tenancy agreements are in writing, because so many issues surrounding those agreements involve monetary considerations. Memories fade, and disputes can arise that could well be resolved in the favour of the tenant should legal action be required. Oral agreements also create the potential for charges of discriminatory treatment. Always put all terms and conditions in writing, even if you know the tenant personally or you only intend to let the property for a short period of time. Oral agreements are only as good as the paper they are not written on because they can't be substantiated and they're not always enforceable.

Rent Assessment Committee

Under an Assured Shorthold Tenancy agreement, if the tenant feels the rent you're charging is too high – and if it's higher than rents on comparable properties in the area – the tenant can apply to a Rent Assessment Committee for the rent to be reduced. (Keep in mind, however, that few tenants actually apply to the Rent Assessment Committee because they feel they are being charged too much rent.)

The tenant can take this action only within the first six months of a tenancy. And the committee can make a decision only if enough similar properties in the area are let on Assured Shorthold Tenancies. The committee compares the rents charged on similar rental properties in your area with what you charge and decides what the rent for your property should be. You don't have to panic, though, because this amount will never be lower than the market rent.

You are only at risk of being forced to accept a lower rent if you charge significantly higher than the going rate for a similar property in your area.

A standard tenancy agreement

Form 3-1 shows a standard tenancy agreement. For peace of mind, it is worth asking your solicitor to review these documents and all other forms in this book before using them, particularly as you may well want to add your own terms and conditions.

TENANCY AGREEMENT

THIS AGREEMENT is made on the date specified between the Landlord and the Tenant. It is intended that the tenancy created by this Agreement is and shall be an assured shorthold tenancy within the meaning of the Housing Act 1988 as amended by the Housing Act 1996.

DATE: _____

LANDLORD: _____

LANDLORD'S ADDRESS: _____

_____

LANDLORD'S AGENT (if applicable): _____

TENANT(S): _____

_____

_____

PROPERTY: _____

_____

CONTENTS: The Landlord's fixtures, fittings and furniture listed in the attached Inventory, and signed by the Landlord and Tenant.

TERM: For the term of _____ months
Starting from: _____

RENT: £_____ (_____ pounds) per calendar month, in advance. Tenant is to make the first payment on the signing of this Agreement, and subsequent payments on the same day of the month as the start date.

DEPOSIT: A deposit of £ _____ (_____ pounds) to be paid to the Landlord on the signing of this Agreement.

1. **The Landlord agrees:**

1.1 To let the Property and its Contents to the Tenant for the Term at the Rent payable as above. As long as the Tenant complies with the Tenant's obligations (see below), the Landlord agrees not to interfere with the Tenant's use and enjoyment of the Property.

1.2 To pay the balance of the Deposit to the Tenant as soon as possible after the conclusion of the tenancy, minus any reasonable costs incurred for the breach of any obligation. Where applicable, the Landlord may retain the Deposit until the Local Authority confirms that no Housing Benefit paid to the Landlord is repayable.

1

Form 3-1: Tenancy Agreement (Page 1 of 6).

1.3 To keep the structure and exterior of the Property in good repair.

1.4 To keep the installations of the Property in good repair and proper working order for water, gas, electricity, sanitation and heating.

1.5 To ensure that the Property has an up-to-date gas safety certificate under the Gas Safety (Installations and Use) Regulations Act 1998. All gas appliances, f ues and other fittings to be checked annually to ensure they are safe and working properly.

1.6 To comply with the obligations under the Fire and Safety Regulations 1988. All of the Landlord's furniture and furnishings, including sofas, beds, cushions and pillows, must meet these fire safety standards.

2. The Tenant agrees:

2.1 To pay the Rent on the days and in the manner stated in the Agreement without any deduction, and by direct debit to the Landlord's bank account.

2.2 To pay the Deposit as security for the performance of the Tenant's obligations and to pay and compensate the Landlord for the reasonable costs of breach of these obligations. It is agreed that this sum shall not be transferable by the Tenant in any way, and at any time against payment of the Rent and that no interest shall be payable on the Deposit.

2.3 That if the Landlord has recourse to the Deposit during the tenancy, the Landlord may immediately demand from the Tenant whatever amount is required to restore the amount of the Deposit to the original sum.

2.4 To arrange immediately with the relevant supply company for all accounts for water, gas, electricity and telephone (where applicable), and television licence, at the Property to be addressed to the Tenant in their own name and pay all standing charges for these.

2.5 To pay the council tax, water, gas, electric, telephone bills and television licence for the Property. The Tenant shall also pay for the total cost of any re-connection fees relating to the supply of water, gas, electricity and telephone, if disconnected. The Tenant also agrees to notify the Landlord before changing supplier for any of the utility services.

2.6 Not to damage the Property and Contents or make any alterations or additions. Before embarking on any redecoration the written consent of the Landlord or Landlord's Agent must be obtained first.

2.7 Not to leave the Property vacant for more than 28 consecutive days without notifying the Landlord in writing beforehand, and to properly secure all locks and bolts to the doors, windows and other openings when leaving the Property unattended.

2.8 To keep the interior of the Property and its Contents clean and tidy and in good decorative condition up to the standard existing when the Tenant moves in (reasonable wear and tear excepted). To remove rubbish from the property on a daily basis, to clean the windows regularly both inside and out, and to keep all rooms well ventilated.

2.9 To immediately pay the Landlord or Landlord's Agent the value of replacement of any furniture or effects lost, damaged or destroyed, and not to remove or permit to be removed any furniture or effects belonging to the Landlord from the Property.

2

Form 3-1: Tenancy Agreement (Page 2 of 6).

2.10 To pay for any cleaning that may be required to reinstate the Property to the same order that it was provided at the beginning of the Tenancy, including the washing or cleaning of all carpets and curtains which have been soiled during the Tenancy.

2.11 To ensure the drains, drainage system and gutters are free from obstruction.

2.12 To replace all broken glass in doors and windows damaged during the Tenancy.

2.13 To promptly notify the Landlord of any defect, damage or disrepair in the Property, especially if it compromises health and safety or may give rise to a claim under the Landlord's insurance policy.

2.14 To permit the Landlord or any person authorised by the Landlord or Landlord's Agent to enter the Property on giving 24 hours' notice (except in case of emergency) to inspect its condition and Contents; repair or replace the Contents; replace locks; carry out gas and electrical safety checks or repairs, or show prospective tenants or buyers round the Property.

2.15 To use the Property as a private residence for occupation by the named Tenant(s) and, if the Landlord has given his consent, by the named Tenant's children under the age of 18.

2.16 Not to assign, sublet, or part with, possession of the Property, or let any other person live at the Property.

2.17 To use the Property as a single private dwelling and not to use it or any part of it for any other purpose nor to allow anyone else to do so.

2.18 Not to receive paying guests or carry on or permit to be carried on any business, trade or profession on or from the Property.

2.19 Not to do anything that gives the insurers of the Property and its Contents any reason to refuse payment or increase the premiums.

2.20 Not to keep any animals, birds, or other living creature at the Property without the Landlord's written consent. Such consent, if granted, to be revocable at any time by the Landlord.

2.21 Not to keep any dangerous or inflammable materials at the Property or in any outbuildings.

2.22 To keep gardens (if any) including all driveways, paths, lawns, hedges and flower beds neat and tidy and properly tended at all times. The Tenant is not to cut down or remove any trees or shrubs without the Landlord's prior consent.

2.23 Not to alter or change or install any locks on any doors or windows in or about the Property or have any additional keys made for any locks without the prior written consent of the Landlord.

2.24 Not to use the Property for any illegal or immoral purposes.

2.25 Within seven days of receipt thereof to send to the Landlord all correspondence addressed to the Landlord and any notice order or proposal relating to the Property (or any building of which the Property forms part), given, made or issued under or by virtue of any statute, regulation, order, direction or by-law by any authority.

3

Form 3-1: Tenancy Agreement (Page 3 of 6).

2.26 To pay and compensate the Landlord fully for any reasonable costs, expense, loss or damage incurred or suffered by the Landlord as a consequence of any breach of the agreements on the part of the Tenant in this Agreement and to indemnify the Landlord from, and against, all actions, claims and liabilities in that respect.

2.27 Not to deface or damage the Property by fixing anything whatsoever to the interior or exterior using glue, Sellotape, pins, nails, hooks or screws, without the Landlord's written consent.

2.28 To take all reasonable precautions to prevent damage to the Property by frost.

2.29 To comply (where the Property is a leasehold dwelling) with the rules regulating the use of the Property and the conduct of its occupiers.

2.30 In order to comply with Gas Safety Regulations, it is necessary:

2.30.1 that the ventilators provided for this purpose in the Property should not be blocked.

2.30.2 that a build up of soot on any gas appliances should immediately be reported to the Landlord or the Landlord's Agent.

2.31 To ensure the chimneys (where applicable) are swept when necessary.

2.32 Not to use any portable gas or electric heaters in the Property without the Landlord's prior written consent.

2.33 To be responsible for testing all smoke detectors fitted in the Property once a month and replace the batteries as necessary.

2.34 Within the last two months of the Tenancy to allow the Landlord or any person authorised by the Landlord or Landlord's Agent to enter and view the Property with prospective tenants at reasonable hours.

2.35 That where the Property is left unoccupied, without prior notice in writing to the Landlord or Landlord's Agent, for more than 28 days and the Rent for this period is unpaid, the Tenant is deemed to have surrendered the Tenancy. This means that the Landlord may take over the Property and take steps to find another tenant.

2.36 To return the keys to the Property to the Landlord or Landlord's Agent at the end of the tenancy. The Tenant also agrees to pay for any reasonable charges incurred by the Landlord or the Landlord's Agent in securing the Property against re-entry where keys are not returned.

2.37 That Housing Benefit, where applicable, is paid direct to the Landlord.

2.38 Not to be a nuisance to the neighbours. The Tenant will not make any noise that is audible outside the Property from 11pm to 8am daily, or be guilty of harassment or abuse on grounds of sex, sexual orientation, disability or race.

3, The Landlord can terminate the Tenancy on the last day of the Term, or after the Term, by service of the Landlord's notice of intention to seek possession.

3.1 The Tenant can terminate the Tenancy by vacating the Property on the last day of the Term, or after that by giving the Landlord one month's notice in writing.

4

Book IV

Becoming a Buy-to-Let Landlord

Form 3-1: Tenancy Agreement (Page 4 of 6).

4. If the Tenant does not pay the rent due to the Landlord under this agreement within 14 days of the due date, the Tenant will be issued with a reminder from the Landlord, in writing, for which there is a charge of £20. Interest will also be charged at the rate of 5 percent per annum, calculated on a daily basis from the due date until the rent is paid.

5. By obtaining a court order, the Landlord may re-enter the Property and immediately thereupon the Tenancy shall absolutely determine without prejudice to other rights and remedies of the Landlord if the Tenant has not complied with any obligation in this Agreement or should the Rent be in arrears by more than 14 days.

6. The parties agree:

6.1 Notice is hereby given that possession might be recovered under Ground 1, Section 2 of the Housing Act 1988 if applicable. That is, that the Landlord used to live in the Property as his or her main home; or intends to occupy the Property as his or her only or main home.

6.2 Before the Landlord can end this tenancy, he shall serve any notice(s) on the Tenant in accordance with the provisions of the Housing Acts. Such notice(s) shall be sufficiently served if served in accordance with section 196 of the Law of Property Act 1925. Under this, a notice shall be sufficiently served if sent by registered or recorded delivery post (if the letter is not returned undelivered) to the Tenant at the Property or the last known address of the Tenant or left addressed to the Tenant at the Property.

7. The Tenant irrevocably authorises the Local Authority, Benefit Office, Post Office and the relevant utility companies (including electricity, gas, water and telephone) to discuss and disclose to the Landlord or Agent all financial and other information relating to the Property or any housing benefit claim. This authority shall extend to disclosure of the Tenant's whereabouts if the Tenant has left the Property with rent or other money owing.

8. This Agreement, which includes all the attachments referred to below, constitutes the entire Agreement between Landlord and Tenant and cannot be modified except in writing and signed by all parties.

9. Addenda. By initialling as provided, Tenant acknowledges receipt of the following optional addenda, as indicated, copies of which are attached hereto and are incorporated as part of this Agreement:

_____ A.   Policies and Rules
_____ B.   Inventory
_____ C.   Animal Agreement
_____ D.   Other _____

SIGNED by the LANDLORD: **In the presence of:**

5

Form 3-1: Tenancy Agreement (Page 5 of 6).

SIGNED by the LANDLORD: In the presence of:
(or the Landlord's Agent)

_____   Name _____

                                           Address _____

                                           _____

                                           Witness Signature _____

SIGNED by the TENANT(S):   In the presence of:

_____   Name _____

_____   Address _____

_____   _____

                                           Witness Signature _____

6

Form 3-1: Tenancy Agreement (Page 6 of 6).

Standard tenancy agreements are great because they save you the expense of getting your solicitor to draft an agreement for you. But they don't allow you to add your own clauses. However, you can modify the terms of your tenancy agreement fairly easily with the Addendum to Tenancy Agreement, shown in Form 3-2.

Be careful about adding additional clauses or language to your tenancy agreement unless you seek the advice of a solicitor.

The number one reason for tenants to insist on a tenancy agreement is that the rent is fixed for a minimum period of time. The landlord cannot unilaterally vary the terms of a tenancy after it has been granted. So you cannot increase the amount of rent without the consent of the tenant, unless the terms of the tenancy allow you to do so. Therefore, be sure to include a term in the tenancy agreement allowing you to increase the rent.

Book IV

Becoming a Buy-to-Let Landlord

Addendum to Tenancy Agreement

This Addendum to the Tenancy Agreement entered into on _____ (date), between
_____ (Tenant) and _____(Landlord) for the
property located at: _____

This Addendum shall be and is incorporated into the Tenancy Agreement dated _____
between Tenant and Landlord.

Tenant and Landlord agree to the following changes and/or additions to the Tenancy Agreement:_____
_____
_____
_____
_____
_____
_____
_____
_____
_____
_____

This Addendum is to be effective as of _____ (date).

Signed: _____   _____
                                                    _____
                                                    _____
        LANDLORD/MANAGING AGENT   **TENANT(S)**

Date: _____   Date: _____

Form 3-2: Addendum to Tenancy Agreement.

Chapter 4

Advertising and Showing Your Property

*M*ore than almost any other single factor, good quality tenants make your experience as a landlord enjoyable and profitable. But finding a good tenant can be a long and arduous process if you don't know how to do it well. So in this chapter, you can see the process from beginning to end – from creating a marketing plan (which helps you narrow your focus and set goals) to writing good copy for your ads, to showing your property effectively. This is the place to start if you've just found out one of your properties will be vacant in a month, and it's the place to turn to if your property has already been empty for twice that long. It's never too late to start advertising effectively, and this chapter gives you all the tools you need to do exactly that.

Developing a Marketing Plan

The key to success in owning and managing rental properties is to keep your rental properties full with long-term paying tenants who treat your rental property and their neighbours with respect. But first you need to determine the best way to attract and retain these highly desirable tenants. A marketing plan can help you do just that.

A *marketing plan* can be anything from a formal written outline of your marketing strategies to some general marketing ideas you keep in mind as you try to find tenants for your property. If you only own one or two properties, or even if you own 20 or 30 rental properties in several towns, you may not think that you need a marketing plan. Developing a marketing plan may seem like an unnecessary use of your time and energy. But the basic concepts of a marketing plan are important for *all* owners of rental property, regardless of the number of flats or houses they may own.

If you don't attract and retain tenants, you can rest assured that your competition will. And you are in competition with other owners and property managers for the best tenants, even if you only have a few rental properties. In most rental markets, prospective tenants have many options, and the most responsible tenants are very selective, because the rental property they select will be their home.

The likelihood of finding responsible tenants is often a numbers game. The more prospective tenants you are able to attract, the greater your opportunity to carefully evaluate their qualifications and the higher the probability that you will be able to select the most qualified applicant.

Determining your target market

One of the first steps in developing a basic marketing plan is to determine the *target market* for your rental property. The target market consists of prospective tenants who are the most likely to find that your property meets their needs. The target market can be relatively broad or it can be fairly narrow, depending on the location, size, and features of your property. If you have several properties, you may find that each one has a different target market or you may find that the target markets overlap.

To determine your target market, first carefully evaluate your property by looking at the location, size, and the specific features that make it unique.

- ✔ **Location:** What are some of the benefits of your property's location? Is your property located near transport links, factories or offices, a hospital or doctor's surgery, shops, or other important facilities, such as a sports centre? Paying attention to your property's location may provide you with a target market that includes employees of certain companies or people who have a need to live in close proximity to certain facilities, such as a mainline train station.

- ✔ **Size:** Larger properties tend to be more attractive to families or several tenants who wish to share accommodation (such as students), whereas studio flats are more suitable to a single tenant or a couple on a budget.

- ✔ **Amenities:** A property that allows pets and has a large garden typically appeals to pet owners and/or tenants with children. If your property has storage space or a garage, this is often an additional attraction to prospective tenants.

When you consider your property's features, you will probably discover that it meets the needs and requirements of certain tenants more than others. You can use this knowledge to target specific audiences, but your rental efforts must never discourage, limit, or exclude *any* prospective tenants from having an equal opportunity to rent from you.

Knowing what your tenants stand to gain from your property

When you have established who your most likely tenants are, you need to shift your focus to incorporating and implementing the concept of a target market into the marketing plans for your rental property. This is when we usually think of the WIFM approach. *WIFM* stands for 'What's In It For Me?' (yes, we know that it's technically 'WIIFM', but that just doesn't look right!), and it represents the thought process of virtually all consumers (including your potential tenants) when evaluating a purchase decision. The WIFM concept can be used in all business and reminds us that, in general, people are most interested in the benefits that they personally will receive in any given relationship or business transaction.

When it comes to marketing and advertising your rental property, the important concept of WIFM can help you see the rental decision process through the eyes of your prospective tenants and makes your goal of finding long-term, stable tenants more attainable. Unfortunately, owners and managers of rental properties are human and, just like most people, although they are very good at seeing the world from their own perspective, they often fail to critically evaluate the advantages and disadvantages of the product that they are selling – their rental property. As a landlord or manager, you have a competitive advantage if you understand the opportunities and challenges presented by your particular property. You can also have a competitive advantage if you find ways to enhance the deficits or narrow your marketing focus to those specific types of tenants who will be attracted to your property.

Understanding the Importance of Good Advertising

Tenants rarely come looking for you. Your local newspaper may have a column for 'Properties Wanted to Rent' or one of your current tenants may contact you enquiring on behalf of a friend who is looking for a rental property. But this is the exception, not the rule. The majority of your tenants will come from the efforts you make to find suitable tenants for your property.

Book IV

Becoming a Buy-to-Let Landlord

Advertising is how you let people know that you have a vacant property available to rent. When it's done well, the money you spend on advertising is money extremely well spent, but when it's done poorly, advertising can be another black hole for your precious resources. Advertising is more of an art than a science at times, because what works for one particular property may not work for another.

Advertising rental properties is no different in many ways than all other types of advertising. The key to success in rental property advertising is determining how you can reach that very small, select group of suitable tenants who will be interested in your rental property when it's available to rent. In your ads, you want to show that your property offers what your target market is looking for.

The best way to determine the most desirable features of your rental property for your target market is to use the WIFM approach and ask your current tenants what they like about where they live. You may also figure out from talking with the *rental traffic* (all the people who look at your property, whether or not they agree to rent) what they found of interest in your rental property. The key is to remember that your rental property has different features that appeal to different prospective tenants, but over a period of time you will be able to determine certain common factors that most prospective tenants desire. Incorporate these selling points into your marketing and advertising efforts.

Review the information from your marketing plan about the most marketable features and attributes of your property and present it to prospective tenants in your advertising.

Rifle versus Blunderbuss: Picking an advertising approach

Creating interest in your rental property used to be as simple as putting up a sign or placing an ad in the local newspaper. Although these tried-and-tested methods of notifying potential tenants that you have a property to rent are still very successful, many other excellent options are available for you to consider. The target market for your property has a lot to do with which method of advertising works best for your particular rental property. Here are your options:

- ✔ **The rifle approach:** Advertising that is very specific and targets a narrow group of prospective tenants is often described as a *rifle approach*.

- ✔ **The blunderbuss approach:** Advertising that blankets the market with information to tenants and non-tenants, suitable and unsuitable alike, is commonly called a *blunderbuss approach.*

Many methods of advertising your rental property fall into the blunderbuss category and very few fall into the rifle category. Big regional newspapers (blunderbuss approach) often have impressive circulations. However, they can't tell you how many of those readers actually read the rental property ads or are actually looking for a flat on the specific day your ad will run. Advertising is, for the most part, a numbers game. Reach enough readers and you are bound to find a few that will be looking for a rental property like yours on a given day. Two good rifle approaches to advertising are word-of-mouth referrals and postcards on student noticeboards under 'Accommodation'. But if you rely solely on these approaches to find tenants, you may end up with an empty property for much longer than you'd like.

One size rarely fits all. When it comes to advertising a rental property, you need to employ a combination of both the blunderbuss and the rifle approach to be successful. Clearly, both methods have advantages. Referrals and student noticeboards often give you good exposure to prospective tenants in your local area, whereas newspaper and Internet ads let people moving to your area know about your rental property as well. Check out Table 4-1 for a comparison of the pros and cons of various approaches to advertising.

Table 4-1   Pros and Cons of Different Advertising Approaches

Approach	Pros	Cons
Flyers	Allows more details	Limited distribution
Internet	Ease of use	Uncertain effectiveness
Local employers	Suitable tenants	Narrow market
Newspaper	Widely used by prospective tenants, broad reach	Potentially expensive
noticeboards in supermarkets and sports centres	Inexpensive	Narrow market
Property signs	Very effective, inexpensive	Narrow market
Specialist rental publications	Widely used by prospective tenants	Expensive for small properties
Word of mouth	High credibility, inexpensive	Narrow market

Kerb appeal: Getting your property to rent itself

The best advertisement for your property is its exterior appearance. The *kerb appeal* is the impression created when the building is first seen from the street. Properties that have well-kept grounds with green grass, trimmed hedges, beautiful flowers, and fresh paint are much more appealing to prospective tenants than a property that looks as though it has seen better days. For help completing a professional exterior paint job yourself, see Chapter 8 in Book III.

Kerb appeal can be positive or negative. Positive kerb appeal can be generated by having a rubbish-free garden, well-manicured landscaping, well-maintained walls and fences, a clearly identifiable address, and clean windows. All extras (such as the driveway) should also be clean and well maintained.

Properties with negative kerb appeal can be rented, but finding a tenant often takes much longer. You may have fewer suitable tenants to choose from or you may have to lower the rent. Because time is money in the rental housing business, the lost revenue caused by poor or negative kerb appeal is often much greater than the cost to repair or replace the deficient items. Besides, a well-maintained and sharp-looking property often attracts the type of tenant who will treat your property with care and respect and pay a higher rent.

Kerb appeal is also important to retaining your current tenants. One of the most common complaints of tenants and a major reason for tenants to move is the failure of the owner or property manager to properly maintain the rental property. If the tenants are frustrated with the property's appearance or if they get the runaround when they need things repaired, the tenants have little reason to remain unless the rent is significantly below market value. Poor kerb appeal is the direct result of poor management. There is no excuse for poor kerb appeal, and there are no benefits to anyone involved, because the lost revenue is never regained, and the property value ultimately declines.

Even the best advertising campaign in the world cannot overcome a poor physical appearance. Making sure your property looks good on the outside as well as the inside significantly improves your chances of finding just the right tenants.

Before you spend money on advertising, take another look at your property with a critical eye or ask someone you know to do this for you. You probably have a relative or friend who has a sharp eye for finding those little details that aren't quite right. So put those people to work helping you identify and then correct those niggling aspects that detract from your rental property.

Looking at Your Advertising Options

When it comes to advertising, you need to think like a tenant. Many landlords have been a tenant at some point in time. You may have personal experience yourself as a tenant looking for the right place to live. You may have found the experience very frustrating, or maybe you developed a successful system for finding quality properties at a fair price in your area. Your experience as a tenant can be helpful as you place your current ads as a landlord.

Many landlords may remember that, when they began looking for their own buy-to-let property years ago, they either drove around the area or looked for advertising that was specific to a particular geographic location. That strategy still holds true, because tenants typically look for a property in a specific location and try to find ads on supermarket noticeboards; in gyms, health clubs and colleges; or in the local newspaper that cover just their area of interest.

Most tenants dislike moving. Although moving is enough of a disruption in your daily routine, adapting to a completely different neighbourhood is even worse. Thus, the majority of tenants move to another address within the same geographic area, unless they are forced to move for work, for their children to attend another school, or for another significant factor that requires relocation to another part of the country.

The following sections outline the different ways you have to reach your prospective tenants; everything from word-of-mouth to the Internet. Use more than one form of advertising and you'll find a new tenant more quickly.

Word-of-mouth

Often the best source of new tenants is a referral from one of the neighbours near your rental property, one of your other tenants, or possibly even the tenant who has just vacated your property. Many times, referrals also come from work colleagues or friends. Word-of-mouth is often your most effective and least expensive method of finding new tenants, especially if people like your property or like where it's located. In the long run, your best source for new tenant leads is other satisfied tenants.

Many of your tenants or other people who own or rent in the area may have a family member or friend who is looking to move into the area as well. Creating a sense of community in which your tenants have friends in the immediate area can persuade tenants to stay longer. This means less hassle and better cash flow for you.

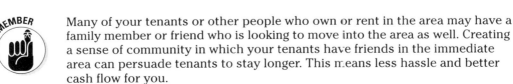

Book IV

Becoming a Buy-to-Let Landlord

Suitable tenants are the name of the game

Unsuitable applicants can be a major waste of time. You only want suitable potential tenants to apply. There are always going to be some prospective tenants who do not pass your financial checks or who have a poor rental history. But if you receive applications from several unsuitable prospective tenants from a certain source of advertising, re-evaluate either the method of advertising or the message in your ad.

Answering phone calls and showing your rental property are two of the most time-consuming areas of property management. These areas are also two of the most critical for determining your success in the long run. The last thing you need is for unsuitable prospective tenants to call and ask numerous questions or even arrange to view the property, only to find out that they do not meet your requirements to rent your property.

You need to put all applicants referred by word-of-mouth through the same tenant application and thorough background check as any other applicant. Always screen every referral carefully, but be particularly careful if the referring tenant has a poor payment history or has created other problems in the past. Just as a referral from an excellent tenant often leads to another excellent tenant, a referral from a problem tenant often leads to another problem tenant.

Property signs

A property sign is the first step in renting most properties because it is one of the most economical ways to promote a vacant flat or house. The use of a simple 'For Rent' or 'To Let' sign can be very effective and generate great results for only a minimal cost. In certain areas with only limited availability of rental properties, a sign on the property is all that you need to generate several queries from suitable potential tenants.

Unless your property's kerb appeal is poor or signs are not allowed in your flat's lease, you should immediately put up a property sign when you find out that you're going to have an upcoming vacancy.

An advantage of the property sign is that applicants already know the area and have seen the exterior of the building. The attractiveness and aesthetic qualities or kerb appeal of a rental property are essential. The rental property must look good from the street, or prospective tenants won't even bother to stop and see the interior of the property.

When putting up a sign, keep these things in mind:

- ✓ **Use signs that are in perfect condition, with large, crisp easy to read lettering.** The condition of the sign reflects the image of your rental property – whether good or bad. A well-maintained sign provides a good first impression. A faded, worn out, or tacky sign is worse than no sign at all.

- ✓ **Make sure that the sign is clearly visible from the street and that the lettering is large enough to read.** The two-sided sign should ideally be placed perpendicular to the street so that it is easier for passing vehicles to view the sign.

- ✓ **The sign does not need to include too many details about the property, but the phone number and the date of availability should be very clear.** You can also add the number of bedrooms and bathrooms, as well as any special features. Don't get carried away or put so much information on the sign that it cannot easily be read from the street. If you have the expertise, or you know someone who has, it's not a bad idea to add a Web address, where you can post more details about the property including photographs of internals.

- ✓ **Drive by your property from both directions at the usual speed of traffic and make sure that the sign can be seen and understood easily.** The main objective is to get the driver's attention with the words 'For Rent' or a similar basic message. The driver should pull over and stop to write down the details and the phone number.

- ✓ **When the exterior of the property does not do justice to the actual rental property itself, you're better off *not* including the amount of rent on your property sign.** The value of some rental properties cannot be appreciated until the prospective tenant has seen the interior of the property. Because you will typically not be there to actually show the property at the time the prospective tenant sees the sign, the prospective tenant may think that the rent is either too high or too low and immediately decide not to call.

Generally, we don't recommend indicating the amount of rent on the property sign. You've got a better chance of convincing a potential tenant who didn't want to pay quite as much money that your property is worth the extra if you get a chance to speak to them on the phone. If the prospective tenant doesn't even bother calling because the stated rent is more than they wanted to pay so your property seems out of reach, you could be missing out on someone

Book IV

Becoming a Buy-to-Let Landlord

who would have made a good tenant. The other problem with advertising the rent is that you lose any competitive advantage you have as other landlords in the area will find out how much you are charging your tenants.

Property signs don't work as well if your rental property is not on a busy street or your property sign is not clearly visible from a main road. Property signs on dead-end streets or cul-de-sacs are still worthwhile, but don't expect the kind of response you would get if your property were on a main road.

A disadvantage of signs is that they announce to the world that you have a vacant property, which, in some cases, can lead to vandalism or squatting. To avoid this happening, many landlords use a rental sign while the property is still occupied by the outgoing tenant and then remove the sign once the property has been vacated. Depending on your tenants and their level of co-operation, you may also want to indicate on the sign that the current tenant should not be disturbed.

To minimise the chances of vandalism when the property is vacant, you can indicate on the property sign that the property is occupied and include a statement such as, 'Please do not disturb the occupant'. Although not a guarantee, this simple statement may deter the amateur criminal elements who don't want to take the chance of running into any residents.

Newspapers

The most commonly used medium for advertising rental properties is the newspaper classified ads. These ads can be very effective if you follow some basic rules of advertising:

- ✔ Attract the reader's attention.
- ✔ Keep the reader's interest.
- ✔ Generate a desire to learn more about your property.
- ✔ Convince the reader to contact you for more information.

Important considerations when using newspaper advertising include selecting which newspaper to advertise in, the size of your newspaper ad, what to include in the newspaper ad, and how often or on which days the newspaper ad should run. We cover each of these issues in the following sections.

Which newspaper should you advertise in?

Most towns have at least one local newspaper to advertise your rental property in. Those living in a city have more choice with one major regional morning or evening newspaper covering the whole area to choose from, plus several weekly or fortnightly local newspapers as well. Such papers are usually reasonably priced and can reach prospective tenants already living in the area. Some local papers even offer free ads.

Another source of ads for properties to rent is the dedicated property sections of national newspapers. The burgeoning interest in buy-to-let means several pages are often dedicated to rental ads. Of course, such ads cost much more than those that run in local papers, so you need to weigh up whether you'll reach more suitable tenants by advertising in the nationals.

If your rental property is located near a big company, be sure to run an ad in the in-house newspaper. Advertising in magazines such as *The Lady* or *The Spectator* will also reach more upmarket tenants. See the later section 'Local employers' for details on tapping into in-house publications.

Should you advertise in the local weekly throwaway, the regional major daily, or the property section of a national? Unfortunately, there is no right answer to this question. You need to try each newspaper and see which one works best for a particular rental property.

Often the local newspapers offer cheap or even free ads. You may think you can't go wrong with a free ad. But when your phone begins ringing every few minutes and none of the callers are suitable, you pay for that ad again and again with your most precious resource – your time. Dealing with unsuitable prospective tenants can be very time-consuming and frustrating.

Although many newspaper sales representatives proudly speak of their total circulation or readership, the only number that matters to you is the number of suitable prospective tenants that see your ad for your property. For example, the *Daily Telegraph's* circulation is just under 1 million readers. Although the potential of that many people reading your ad may sound enticing and the cost per reader is miniscule, the actual number of suitable prospective tenants nationwide for your 3-bedroom rental property in Scunthorpe will be measured in dozens.

Book IV

Becoming a Buy-to-Let Landlord

Evaluate the cost-efficiency of regional papers such as London's *Evening Standard* by comparing the cost of the ad with the best estimate of the actual number of readers of your specific ad. If the cost per suitable prospective tenant is reasonable, then you may be wise to use this resource.

Keep your advertising costs under control, but don't overlook the fact that each day that your property sits empty is another day of lost income that you will never see. Just as airlines lose money for every empty seat on a plane, you can end up being penny-wise and pound foolish with your advertising, particularly if your best advertising source is *The Sunday Times'* property section and you need to wait until the following week to place another ad. In that week, you may have lost a couple of hundred pounds (or many times the cost of the ad).

The key to effective advertising is not the overall number of calls that you receive but the number of suitable prospective tenants per pound you spend on advertising. Typically, advertising that costs £10 to £30 per suitable prospective tenant is an effective ad in most major regional newspapers. So if your ad in the *Evening Standard* costs £55, you should expect to receive inquiries from two to three suitable potential tenants every time the ad runs. Of course, you'll receive additional inquiries from people who aren't suitable, but you can also measure the effectiveness of your ad by noting how *few* unsuitable prospective tenants call in response to your ad.

How big should your newspaper ad be?

Newspapers typically offer two different types of rental ads: display and classified. Display ads can be (but aren't always) more effective and eye-catching. However, they are significantly more expensive and beyond the needs and budgets of most small-time landlords. Typically, only the owners or property managers of large blocks of flats in your area use display ads on a regular basis. And most of these advertisers also use classified ads to augment or supplement the display ads, particularly on the days when their display ad is not running.

Newspapers are in the business of selling space, and large classified ads cost more than smaller ads. The good news is that the larger ads are not always more effective. A large classified ad that fails to attract readers' attention and keep their interest is a complete waste of money.

Owners or property management companies with several properties in a certain geographic area often use display ads because they can combine more than one rental property into one large display ad, making the ad more cost-effective. If you are a small-time landlord, unless you have several properties with vacancies in the same general geographic area, use the classified 'Property to Let' advertising section of your newspaper.

The trick is to develop a classified rental ad that does its job of promoting your property but doesn't place a higher priority on low cost while sacrificing the ability to attract and keep the attention of the prospective tenant. Your potential tenant needs to be able to easily read your rental ad. One of the best ways to make your ad readable is through the use of white space in the ad. *White space* is the blank space that makes your ad stand out from the others, many of which are so crammed with information that readers instinctively skip them. You can easily add more detail without cluttering advertisement space if you have a Web address on your advertisement. This will refer your enquiries to a Web page with full details of the property complete with colour photographs.

You'll be lucky if a prospective tenant spends more than just a few seconds looking at your rental ad. If you cannot attract and keep the attention of prospective tenants in those brief seconds, they'll move on to the next ad. So when it comes to writing your ad, you want to provide as much information as possible, while also keeping the ad readable. But the overall size of the ad also needs to be kept to a minimum, or you risk a major shock to your advertising budget.

Most tenants actually prefer to rent from small-time landlords rather than big agencies, which is why classified ads can be very effective. Classified ads need to be directed to a specific target market and should stress the particular advantages of a property from the tenant's point of view, as explained in the following section.

What should you include in your newspaper ad?

An effective newspaper ad (like the ones shown in Figure 4-1) provides the basic facts, plus a *hook,* which is a call-to-action that helps your rental ad stand out from the rest:

The basics

Every ad should include the following basic information:

✔ **General geographic location of the property:** The most important aspect of promoting your rental property is to identify the location. Most newspapers sort their rental ads by location, and if your ad isn't listed properly, then all the prospective tenants who want to live in your area will miss your ad. Some newspapers automatically put your ad in a certain geographical area based on the property's address. In many cities, the property's postcode makes an immediate impression on potential tenants. This impression can be very positive or very negative, depending upon the reputation of the particular area. So if the address would give a negative impression, leave it out. (The sidebar 'Considering whether to include the address in your ad' outlines the advantages and disadvantages of including the property address in your ad.)

✔ **Number of bedrooms and bathrooms:** After the location, this is the second most important aspect of the rental property that the tenant is interested in. If four friends want to share a house, for example, a two-bedroom flat is unlikely to be big enough. A three-bedroom house might

Book IV

Becoming a Buy-to-Let Landlord

be okay, as long as they are prepared to use the lounge as a fourth bedroom. But one bathroom for four tenants may not be enough so they will be looking for a rental property with more than one bathroom.

✔ **Major features or amenities:** This should include anything that makes the property stand out and would be considered desirable by tenants. If you have a swimming pool, for example, you are onto a winner and should obviously mention it in your ad. Likewise, if the property boasts original fireplaces or there is a garage or off-road parking, it is worth mentioning these as they could persuade a prospective tenant to opt for your property over another.

✔ **Monthly rent:** Include the amount of rent you charge per month. This info lets prospective tenants know what you're expecting upfront. Most prospective tenants are scanning through the newspaper rental ads just trying to eliminate the ads that are not worthy of their time to call. Generally, any ad that does not give the prospective tenant enough information to determine their level of interest will be immediately dismissed.

✔ **Telephone number where you can be reached**.

✔ **The date when the property becomes available:** This lets the tenant know whether the property is right for them: if you want to let it immediately but they have only just given a month's notice on their current rental property, you would clearly prefer someone who could move in straightaway.

✔ **Who pays the bills – landlord or tenant?** This is a major factor when the tenant is working out whether he can afford the rent on the property. If the rent is a bit higher than he was hoping to pay but the landlord pays the utility bills, he may well find that it is affordable after all.

✔ **Whether the property is furnished:** Some tenants have their own furniture, others don't. And if a tenant doesn't have her own furniture, there is a strong likelihood that she won't want to fork out hundreds of pounds buying furniture until she buys her own property. If you state in the ad whether your property is furnished, you won't waste time fielding calls from tenants looking for an unfurnished property.

The hook

The hook can be monetary or it can be an improvement to the rental property – anything that makes your ad grab the prospective tenant's attention. For example, offering the tenant the opportunity to select new tiles for the kitchen floor or hallway is an excellent hook.

If you are in a soft rental market with many of your competitors offering good deals, such as lower rent, you may need to match or even outdo them. This is when using the upgrades to your rental property as an incentive comes in handy. Besides providing new floor tiles, common upgrades landlords can offer include a new kitchen or walk-in power-shower. You can also offer new appliances, double glazing, or a burglar alarm. For rental properties in which the tenants are responsible for garden maintenance, a new lawnmower might be handy for both the new tenant and for the landlord concerned about absent-minded tenants who may forget to mow the lawn.

Figure 4-1:
Good newspaper ads like these can help you find the right tenant quickly.

> First Class Schools
>
> Impressive and beautifully presented 1920s house close to excellent primary and secondary schools in Guildford. Entrance hall, 2 receptions, kitchen/breakfast room, utility room, 4 bedrooms, 2 bathrooms, triple garage, gardens of approx 1 acre, pets welcome. Unfurnished. £3,600 pcm. Available immediately. Call 01234 567 890.
>
> Farnham: Close to Everything
>
> Large 1 & 2 bedroom townhouse apartments, on bus route. Within walking distance of schools, shops and main railway station. No pets. Furnished or unfurnished. From £600 pcm, bills included. Call 01987 654 321.

Although prospective tenants who are looking for the absolute lowest rent won't be interested in rental property upgrades, the tenant who is aware of the competitiveness of the rental market and wants to be treated fairly will often appreciate the upgrades more than the cash in their pockets. Plus, you are making improvements to your own rental property, and these upgrades make your property more desirable now and for future tenants as well.

Other stuff

In addition to the basic information and the hook, be sure to include in your ad every detail that your prospective tenant wants to know. Remember the concept of WIFM (what's in it for me; see the earlier section 'Knowing what your tenants stand to gain from your property' for details) and be sure to include the features of your rental property from the point of view of the prospective tenant.

Although leaving out some information saves you money in the cost of the classified ad, don't forget that incomplete information either leads to suitable prospective tenants skipping over your ad or may lead to many unsuitable prospective tenants calling to ask you every question under the sun.

Book IV

Becoming a Buy-to-Let Landlord

> # Considering whether to include the address in your ad
>
> Although there are differences of opinion regarding including a property's address in a newspaper ad, we generally recommend including the name of the road or street where the rental property is situated. This informs prospective tenants of the exact location of your property and enables them to independently determine whether the property is one they're interested in renting.

Abbreviations: Should you or shouldn't you?

Be careful with abbreviations in newspaper ads. Although abbreviating some words can stretch your advertising budget without cutting into your message, the use of abbreviations often discourages tenants from reading your ad. An ad that's hard to understand won't generate the phone calls you want. And if your ad doesn't generate phone calls, you've wasted your time and money.

We recommend using only basic abbreviations – and then only if most landlords advertising in your area commonly use them. Although you can ask your newspaper classified advertising representative, we strongly recommend that you determine which abbreviations are commonly used by reading through other rental ads in the section yourself. When in doubt, don't use abbreviations. Table 4-2 lists some common abbreviations used in newspaper ads.

Table 4-2	Common Newspaper Ad Abbreviations
Abbreviation	**Translation**
bath/WC	bathroom/toilet
bed	bedroom
dbl	double
furn	furnished
GCH	gas central heating
gdn	garden
hse	house
incl	included

Abbreviation	Translation
lge	large
mth	month
nr	near
pkg	parking
pw	per week
refurb	refurbished
unfurn	unfurnished

Some newspapers even provide a key of the common abbreviations and print this index in the 'Property to Let' section. This key can be very helpful to prospective tenants. But remember that you want to attract and keep the attention of the prospective tenant. And one of the best ways to do this is to make your ad one that is the easiest to read and provides the most information. Prospective tenants who are looking to solve puzzles are typically more interested in the newspaper crossword than trying to decipher the abbreviations commonly found in many 'Property to Let' classified ads.

How often or on which days should your newspaper ad run?

Many local and national newspapers have dedicated property sections that run on certain days of the week. Find out which days these appear and ensure that your ad is submitted in time to meet the deadline; otherwise, you'll have to wait another seven days to have it published. Following are some tips that may make your ad more cost effective:

✔ Check with your local newspaper to see whether they offer any discounted rates for running consecutive days or weeks.

✔ If you have many rental properties, look into advertising contracts where you agree to run a minimum number of ad lines over a given period of time at often greatly reduced rates compared to the single insertion ad rate.

✔ Some newspapers even offer special ads that offer guaranteed results. For example, if you haven't found a tenant for your property after the ad has run for a certain period of time, the newspaper will give you up to an additional week for free.

✔ Check with your newspaper sales representative for special sections that are run featuring editorials on rented housing and news features. These special sections are written with the tenants in mind and can increase the likelihood of your ad being seen by prospective tenants.

When your ad first appears, be sure to check the newspaper personally to see that it is listed in the proper section of the classifieds and is worded exactly the way you wrote it. The newspaper ad representatives are very skilled at taking down complicated ads with abbreviations, but mistakes can and do occur. Nothing is worse than not receiving any phone calls because your ad was placed in the wrong section or because the phone number was listed incorrectly. If you find a mistake, be sure to notify the paper at once, and, if the paper made the mistake, they should run the corrected ad at no charge.

Checking your ad for accuracy may be relatively simple if you regularly buy the newspaper. However, if you don't, be sure to have your newspaper ad sales representative send you a copy of your ad.

Be sure to change your ad regularly. Tenants often look for several weeks when they are just beginning to search for a new rental property. If they see the same ad for more than a week, they could assume that your rental property is undesirable.

Flyers

Distributing and posting flyers informs the neighbours that you have a property available to rent, which can be helpful to them because they may know someone who would like to live close by. You can also pin flyers onto noticeboards in local hospitals, colleges and universities, supermarkets, and personnel departments of large companies.

The cost to reproduce flyers is nominal. If you have access to a computer you can produce a very simple flyer yourself for just the cost of the electricity and paper. Alternatively, plenty of printing shops will do the job for you, which can result in a more professional end product.

If you decide to use a printing shop, remember that prices vary considerably, so shop around and get a couple of quotes. The Internet is a good source of competitive quotes. For example, we found a print company offering 500 flyers for £121, using one colour. Prices increase the more colours you use, so two colours will cost £151 for 500 flyers, or £191 for three colours. All come with a good quality matt finish. The extra money is well worth it – anything that can make your flyer stand out from the others is worth considering. Although keeping your costs low is always important for landlords, remember that you may be losing £20 to £50 each day your property is vacant – and that is money you will never get back again! So if you have a property that looks great with a three-colour flyer, spend the extra money and generate those important rental leads today!

An advantage of flyers is that they allow you a lot more space in which to describe your rental property. You can go into detail and list many of the features that you couldn't afford to list in a newspaper ad.

You can also use flyers to direct people to more information (including maps and additional photographs) on a Web site. See the later section 'Internet' for more information on using the Internet to advertise your rental property.

High-tech flyers

With the wide availability of word-processing programs, making great-looking rental flyers that contain all of the pertinent information, plus even a photo and a map, is very easy. Although the widely used word-processing programs have everything you would need to make basic flyers, we highly recommend that you invest in a basic desktop publishing software package. Several great desktop publishing programs are available, but two of the easiest to use are Quark XPress and Adobe PageMaker. These programs have templates that simplify the process and can provide you with the graphics and additional features to make your flyer really look sharp.

Another invaluable tool for all rental property owners is a digital camera. A digital camera helps you prepare advertising that works! There is nothing like a photo to separate your rental property flyer from the others that may be circulating at any given time. Check out Figure 4-2 for a great example of a flyer that effectively uses photographs to draw attention to the property.

Some people think that a handwritten flyer actually has greater appeal and implies that the owner is a non-professional who has a rental property at a below-market rental rate. Although this may be true, we believe that the benefits of having a sharp, easy-to-read, typeset flyer with a high-quality photo and detailed map provide superior results.

Although your goal is to rent your property quickly, the reality is that you are likely to be marketing your rental property over a couple of weeks. This is particularly true if you are able to start your marketing during the current tenant's notice period. One of the problems with flyers is that knowing which ones are current and which ones are out of date is difficult. We recommend that you put a date on your flyers and keep them fresh. You should also consider having a series of flyers with a different look. Include the monthly rent on your flyers so prospective tenants can immediately determine if your rental property is in their price range.

Flyer distribution

The key to success when it comes to flyers is distribution. Either distribute the flyers personally or consider hiring a reliable individual to distribute flyers door-to-door in the area where your rental property is located. You can also have the flyers distributed to locations that current and prospective tenants are likely to visit.

Figure 4-2:
Flyers are a great way to attract attention to your property, giving you the space to highlight the extra details you may not have room for in a small newspaper ad.

Converted Barn For Rent

Situated in the charming village of Windlesham, Surrey, this two-bedroom converted barn has plenty of character. Boasting many original features, the unfurnished property comprises a large drawing room and open-plan kitchen. The master bedroom comes with en suite bathroom, and there is a second bathroom and shower room. There is parking for two cars and a private orchard. Windlesham itself has a lot to offer, with a variety of shops and good restaurants a short drive away and easy access to the M4, M25 and M3. The nearest mainline station is Sunningdale, which is two miles away from the property, with an approximate journey time of one hour to London Waterloo. Available immediately for £2,500 per calendar month.

Call 01344 873081.

Reproduced by permission of Hamptons International.

Flyers can be targeted to a specific geographic area and can be very effective in reaching good prospective tenants. Because they are most often distributed in the area near the rental property, the flyers are effective; tenants looking to relocate already live in the local area and want to stay close by or know someone who would also be interested in living in the area. Flyers, like all forms of advertising, are only as good as their distribution, so be sure to distribute the flyers to the places where potential tenants are most likely to see them.

Although some people suggest that tenants look for a new property in the last two weeks of the month, we find that, in most rental markets, there are always tenants on the look out throughout the entire month. Begin distributing your flyers as soon as you can. Each week, distribute the latest version with the current information and dates so that they are fresh.

Rental publications

A number of publications carry classified and display 'Property to Rent' ads. *Loot*, the daily free ads paper, has a number of South East editions, covering London, Bedfordshire, Buckinghamshire and Hertfordshire, Kent, Croydon and Surrey, and Essex. There are also a number of North West editions covering Manchester, Cheshire, Lancashire and North Staffordshire, Liverpool, Chester, Wirral, and North Wales. *Loot* also has a major presence on the Internet, as outlined in the next section.

Hot Property is an alternative weekly rental publication offering advertising for London and the South East. It also has an accompanying Internet site where prospective tenants can search for suitable properties to rent. Landlords can choose between text-only ads or add a picture to illustrate their property. The rental publications are a good source of potential tenants and often allow your ad to run for a number of consecutive issues, without you having to give instructions to run the ad again.

If you're thinking about using a rental publication, take the time to determine which one has the best distribution in your area for your target market.

Internet

As more and more people have access to the Internet, it is becoming more useful as a source of prospective tenants, even for owners of small rental properties. However, if you are a small-time landlord, you probably shouldn't rely solely on the Internet to find prospective tenants. More conventional advertising methods, discussed throughout this chapter, should be used alongside the Internet. The problem with relying solely on the Internet is that prospective tenants are unlikely to find your specific ad on the Internet, because the Internet is so vast and contains so much information that it can be difficult to search for rental ads in specific locations.

One of the reasons for the difficulty in sifting through the numerous ads is the minimal barriers of entry and low cost of placing information about your rental property on the Internet. Although the likelihood of someone actually finding your specific rental property on the Internet may be minimal, unless you utilise the services of a major rental property marketing firm, rental publication or regional newspaper, the Internet still has tremendous potential to assist the small-time rental property owner.

Although online advertising is primarily for major property managers with lots of properties on their books, there is one way that the Internet can be invaluable to owners and managers of small-to-medium rental properties or even a single-family rental home. If you have developed flyers or brochures, you can easily post these marketing pieces online. You can then put the Web page address (or URL) in your newspaper ad and allow prospective tenants to gain additional information at their convenience. When a prospective tenant calls, you also have the option of referring them to the Web page, if they have access to the Internet, for more information.

The online rental information you can offer is virtually unlimited. With a digital camera, you can place photos of the rental property online. If you have a wide-angle digital camera, you can even put interior photos online, which is very helpful if the property is currently occupied and you cannot or do not want to bother the current tenant by showing the place. You can also show floor plans and provide detailed directions. If you are really computer-savvy, or know someone who is, you can add a narrative soundtrack or some music. (Keep in mind that music can be annoying to Web site viewers, however. The last thing you want to do is frighten potential tenants off with a medley of your favourite punk songs.)

Of course, be careful that the graphics do not slow down the loading of the Web page so significantly that it takes too long to load the page. Just like the short attention span of your prospective tenant when scanning through the newspaper ads, you want to make sure that your Web site loads very quickly with all of the basic information. Use a simple text file format that loads quickly. If you get the attention and interest of the prospective tenant, you can offer links to the graphics of floor plans and property photos.

Local noticeboards

As with posting flyers, noticeboards can also be very effective in small villages or towns. Often the local newsagents, pharmacies, hospitals, or corner shops have noticeboards or window space that is available at no cost or for a small charge. You may find that you are limited to a postcard, but you can tailor it to the people who will be most interested in and attracted to your rental property.

If your rental property has unique features like a garage or large garden, you may have some additional promotional opportunities. Carefully evaluate your rental property and determine the unique aspects of the property and the specific target market that will be most interested in these specific elements. For example, a rental property with a large garden appeals to tenants with pets, so a listing on a noticeboard at a local pet shop may reach that specific target market. Likewise, a rental property with a garage appeals to customers of a hardware store.

As with any ad in which the property address is clearly stated, a disadvantage of local noticeboards is that you may be promoting the fact that your rental property may be vacant to squatters or burglars. One way to minimise this problem is to use this method only when the property is still occupied and clearly state that it will be available at a future date. You should also consider indicating that the current tenant should not be disturbed.

Local employers

Another great source for prospective tenants are the local employers in your area. Employees of these companies will, most likely, have stable employment and will be looking for long-term rental properties.

Many firms offer employees assistance or have ads in in-house magazines to help workers find reasonably priced housing. Most rental properties located in cities or towns are located near at least one major employer. As a sharp rental property owner, you may already have determined that the employees of certain major firms are part of your target rental market.

Likewise, the major firms in your area have a vested interest in their employees being able to find good quality and affordable rental housing in close proximity to their location. Progressive employers are always looking for inexpensive ways to assist their employees and improve morale. You can even offer all employees of companies an incentive to rent your property, such as offering a discount on the rent.

Letting agencies

One of the recent trends in the property market are firms that assist tenants in finding suitable rental properties. These services are available in virtually every major city. Some offer their services for no charge to the tenant and are paid by the property manager when the tenant signs a rental agreement. Other firms charge tenants for their service and are only paid when they find a rental property that meets the tenant's needs.

Although most owners of small-to-medium size rental properties don't need the services of a letting agency, there are some definite advantages to consider.

Book IV

Becoming a Buy-to-Let Landlord

Letting agencies often have close working relationships with major companies and relocation services and have excellent tenants looking for rental properties at the top-end of the market. These tenants relocating into an area typically don't have the time to search for a rental property and want the letting agency to handle matters for them. Also they are not usually candidates for purchasing a home because they'll only be staying for a specific period of time or because they want to rent in the area before deciding if, and where, they are going to purchase a property. There is often a trade-off with these tenants: They are usually very suitable with good references, but they are not as likely to rent long-term. But the reality is that not all tenants will stay for a long period of time anyway, and if you know that the tenant will only be with you for a set period (such as a 1-year lease), you can adjust the rental rate to reflect this rental term.

Agent referrals

Besides selling properties, many estate agents are also in the business of referring tenants to property managers. Many of the calls that estate agents receive are from individuals moving from other areas who contact an estate agent to enquire about the future purchase of a home. Although they may have long-term plans to purchase, they often rent while they become familiar with the area.

Estate agents don't mind referring tenants to an owner or property manager, because they know that today's tenant may likely be a homebuyer further down the road. Estate agents are also very interested in referral fees from owners or property managers. Although the referral fee may be a small amount of money compared to the potential commission the estate agent would earn on a sales transaction, agents are willing to be patient and accept a small reward in the short run knowing the big money will be earned down the road.

Advertising without Discriminating

Whether you are the owner of a one-bedroom flat or several small-to-medium size family homes for rent, when you advertise you are subject to the law. All landlords are required to comply with anti-discrimination laws and human rights legislation. For instance, you will need to know what the legal situation is regarding the Sex Discrimination Act, the Race Relations Act, and the Disability Discrimination Act to ensure you don't violate any of them, even inadvertently. For example, the Race Relations Act makes it illegal for a land-lord to discriminate between tenants because of their race – and this applies to advertising for new tenants too. Likewise, you cannot discriminate against people on the basis of religion, sexuality, or disability.

Any discrimination when advertising a property to rent is illegal and can result in very severe penalties.

While it's understandable that you want to rent your property to the tenants of your choice, as a landlord you must not discriminate or show any prefer-ence, limitation, or discrimination based upon race, colour, ethnic origin, reli-gion, sex, or physical disability. You are only allowed to discriminate on critical factors such as whether your prospective tenant has the ability to pay her rent or has references that back up her good character.

Compliance with the law is critical for all owners of rental property. This begins with advertising to all suitable prospective tenants, continues throughout the screening and tenant selection process, and remains a key issue throughout the entire tenancy. If you plan to be in the letting business, you need to make sure that all of your advertising, tenant screening, and selection and management policies reflect the intent as well as the letter of the law. Also, be aware that these laws are constantly being redefined and expanded. Ignorance is not an acceptable excuse if you are challenged for your policies.

Showing Your Rental Property

When your potential tenants arrive, be sure to greet them and introduce yourself. Ask for their names and shake their hands. Refer to any notes you took during your initial phone conversation and let them know that you remember speaking with them. This will give the prospective tenants a good feeling that you are not just going through the standard rental spiel.

Listen to any questions or concerns that may have come up since you spoke on the phone or while travelling to your property. Ask them whether they found your directions accurate and easy-to-use. Also ask them if they have any other needs that they are looking for in a property that haven't already been discussed.

Don't just let the prospective tenants wander around the property by them-selves. (Of course, this is particularly true if you are showing an occupied property.) Listen carefully to your prospective tenant and anyone they

Book IV

Becoming a Buy-to-Let Landlord

brought with them as you informally guide them through the property. Pay close attention to the features that your tenants have indicated are of particular interest or comments made during the viewing.

Showing a vacant property

If you're showing a vacant property, begin the tour of the flat or house and act as a tour guide. Don't be too controlling; instead, let the prospective tenants view the property in the manner that suits them. Some go right to a certain room, which gives you a clue about the importance they place on that aspect of your property. Of course, if they hesitate, or are reluctant to tour on their own, you can casually guide them round the property yourself.

Encourage your potential tenant to see the entire property, including any garage or storage areas and the exterior grounds or garden, if there are any. You want to be sure that they have the opportunity to observe the condition of all aspects of the property and ask any questions.

There are as many different ways to show a property as there are landlords. Keep in mind the information provided by the prospective tenant and customise the tour by beginning with the feature or room that you feel has the most interest to that person. This is not the time to head straight to *your* favourite feature. When in doubt, start with the kitchen, then move on to the living areas and the bedrooms.

As you begin to show the interior of your property, avoid making obvious statements such as 'This is the living room' or 'Here's the bathroom!' Instead, listen and observe the body language and facial expressions of your interested viewers as they walk through the property. You don't need to oversell if they seem pleased, but you should feel free to point out the benefits of your property (for example, 'It sounds like this neutral coloured carpet will go great with your living room furniture' or, 'The view from the kitchen of the sunsets is so relaxing').

During an open house you might quickly find yourself dealing with several people at once, all of whom seem to have better timing than a synchronised swimming team. Do your best to courteously greet and speak with each potential tenant individually. At least cover the basic information and get them started on the property tour before beginning to work with the next interested party. Be sure to communicate clearly that you will answer all of their questions, and be sure to treat all potential tenants openly and fairly to avoid any allegations of favouritism or discrimination.

Showing an occupied property

If your current tenants are at the end of their lease or have given notice of their intention to leave, you, as the landlord (or your managing agent) are usually allowed access to the property, by arrangement, in order to show it to a prospective tenant, during the last 28 days of the tenancy. (To avoid problems or confusion, the tenancy agreement might include a clause expressly allowing such access.)

Showing a vacant property is generally much easier, but guiding your prospective tenant through an occupied flat or house does have some distinct advantages. Your current tenants can actually be a real asset if they are friendly and co-operative and take care of the property. The prospective tenants may want to ask the current tenant questions about their experience of living at your property.

If you're showing an occupied property, try your best to co-operate with the current tenants and schedule mutually convenient times to show the property. Be sure to respect their privacy and avoid excessive intrusions into their lives.

Still, showing an occupied rental property can have some disadvantages: Although the current tenant may legally be required to allow you and your prospective tenants to enter the property for a viewing by virtue of your agreement, you can't make them do it if they don't want to and they don't have to make any efforts to ensure that the property is clean and neat. They also are not required to help you in your efforts to impress the potential tenant. Keep this fact in mind when deciding whether you want to show your property while it is still occupied.

If your current tenant is being evicted, is not leaving on good terms, or has an antagonistic attitude for any reason, don't show the property until she has vacated it. Be sure to complete your rent-ready preparation work and any upgrades to the property. This strategy is also more suitable if your current tenants have not taken good care of the property or if their lifestyle or furnishings could prove to be objectionable to some potential tenants.

If you can, get copies of recent utility bills from your current tenant, in case your prospective tenants have any questions about utility costs. Utility costs for electricity, gas, and water are becoming significant items in the budgets of many tenants. You don't want your tenant to be unable to financially handle the typical monthly utility costs, because that may affect their ability to pay your rent. You may also be able to use low utility costs as a marketing tool.

Book IV

Becoming a Buy-to-Let Landlord

Checking if the prospective tenant is suitable during the property viewing

While you're touring the property, you can verify any information that the prospective tenant provided during your initial phone conversation. Refer to your notes and verify his desired move-in date, the number of occupants, the rent, his employment, and other important information. Also make sure the tenant is aware of your rental policies and any limitations on pets or other important issues.

You don't want to be abrupt or refuse to let the prospective tenant and the other rental applicants begin looking at the property until they answer numerous questions, but verifying the basic information upfront can save a lot of time if there was a misunderstanding or if the prospective tenant's needs have changed.

Convincing the prospective tenant

After you have confirmed the suitability of the prospective tenant, you need to convince her that you have the best property available. Remember that people

- ✔ want more than just a place to live
- ✔ want to feel they can communicate with you if a problem arises
- ✔ appreciate it when someone shows an interest in their lives

And by showing an interest, you are clearly setting yourself apart from other landlords. We believe that tenants will even accept a property that is not exactly what they're looking for if they have a positive feeling about the landlord.

We have never seen a property that can rent itself. So *you* need to make the difference. No matter how close your property meets the stated needs and wants of your potential tenants, they'll often hesitate and doubt their own judgment. You don't need to be pushy, but you should be prepared to actively convince them that your property is right for them.

Inviting the prospective tenant to rent your property

When you've convinced your prospective tenants that your property is the right one for them, it's time to close the deal. This is one area where many landlords and managers suddenly get cold feet. They can do a great job handling the initial telephone rental enquiry, the preparation and showing of the property, and even objections, but when it comes to shaking hands on the deal – they become shy and freeze.

Your goal is to receive a commitment from the prospective tenant to rent by getting him to complete your rental application and pay his first month's rent, and a month's rent as a deposit on the spot. Of course, you still need to thoroughly screen the prospective tenant and confirm that he meets your rental criteria before signing a rental agreement.

If, despite your best efforts, the prospective tenant is still undecided, you should make sure that he gives you a holding deposit. Remind him that you may make a deal with the very next applicant and he'll be out of luck. Of course, if you have a lot of demand for your properties, you should develop a priority waiting list.

Persuading the prospective tenant to complete a rental application

You need to offer every interested tenant the opportunity to complete a written rental application (like the one shown in Form 4-1). There are two important reasons for this policy:

- ✔ **You want to have all of the information so that you can begin the screening process and select the best tenant for your property using objective criteria and your rental requirements.** The rental application is the key document you use to verify information and conduct your entire tenant-screening procedures.

- ✔ **You want to avoid the situation where prospective tenants accuse you of discriminating against them by not permitting them to fill out the rental application.** It is important not to prejudge an applicant. The prospective tenant may have already volunteered enough information about his financial situation and tenant history to make you believe having him complete an application would be a waste of time and effort. But even in these situations, always be sure to offer your rental application form to every prospective tenant old enough to legally rent the property.

Have several rental applications and pens available at the property. Although you want to make sure that you offer a rental application form to every prospective tenant, you don't just want to hand them out and let them leave without making a commitment.

Here are some important guidelines to remember when accepting rental applications:

- ✔ **Every prospective tenant who is currently 18 years of age or older should complete a written application.** This applies whether the applicants are married, related in some other way, or unrelated housemates.

- ✔ **Before accepting the rental application, carefully review the entire form to make sure that each prospective tenant has clearly and legibly provided all requested information.** Pay particular attention to all names and addresses, employment information, national insurance numbers, driver's licence numbers, and emergency contacts. Any blanks should be marked with a 'N/A' if not applicable so that you can tell that they were not inadvertently overlooked.

- ✔ **Each prospective tenant must sign the rental application authorising you to verify the provided information and to run a credit check.**

- ✔ **Ask each prospective tenant to show you his current photo-ID driver's licence or other similar photo identification so that you can confirm that the applicants are providing you with their correct names and current addresses.**

You may be asked by the prospective tenant – or you may determine on your own – to go over the rental application with him and assist in providing the information. If you do so, be very careful to ask only questions that are part of the rental application. Avoid asking questions that may directly or indirectly discriminate. Do not ask the rental applicant about his birthplace, religion, marital status or children, or a physical or mental condition. You can ask him if he has ever been convicted of a crime and whether he is at least 18 years of age, however.

Holding a deposit

Some prospective tenants are willing to make a firm commitment, but they will not or cannot give you the full deposit and first month's rent. Maybe they just don't have the funds at the time or maybe they want to keep your property as a standby while they continue looking for a better one. In these situations, you may want to ask for a holding deposit to allow you to take the property off the market for a limited period of time while you obtain a credit check or verify other information on the rental application.

RENTAL APPLICATION

SURNAME_____ FIRST NAME _____

CO-APPLICANT SURNAME _____ FIRST NAME _____

TELEPHONE _____ DATE OF BIRTH _____

CO-APP DATE OF BIRTH _____

NATIONAL INSURANCE NUMBER _____ DRIVER'S LICENCE _____

CO-APP'S NI NUMBER _____ DRIVER'S LICENCE _____

NAME AND AGES OF ALL PERSONS TO RESIDE IN PROPERTY

_____

EMPLOYMENT HISTORY LAST 5 YEARS (USE REVERSE IF NECESSARY)

PRESENT EMPLOYER _____ TELEPHONE _____

ADDRESS _____

GROSS SALARY ____ JOB TITLE _____ DATE EMPLOYED ____

FORMER EMPLOYER _____ TEL_____

ADDRESS _____

GROSS SALARY _____ PERIOD EMPLOYED FROM _____ TO _____

CO-APPLICANT'S EMPLOYER _____ TEL _____

ADDRESS _____

GROSS SALARY _____ JOB TITLE _____ DATE EMPLOYED ____

OTHER INCOME

_____

CAR Year ____ Make _____ Colour _____

HOW MANY PETS DO YOU HAVE? _____ WHAT TYPE? _____

Have you or any proposed occupant listed above ever:

Received a County Court Judgement against you? _____

Been evicted or asked to vacate a property? _____

Broken a lease or rental agreement? _____ Been declared bankrupt? _____

Been sued for damage to rental property? _____

If yes to any of the above, please indicate year, location and details _____

_____

IN CASE OF EMERGENCY NOTIFY _____ Relationship _____

ADDRESS _____

TELEPHONE _____

LAST THREE PLACES OF RESIDENCE (MANDATORY)

1. Date from /to _____ Address _____

Landlord's name _____ Telephone _____

2. Date from /to _____ Address _____

Landlord's name _____ Telephone _____

3. Date from /to _____ Address _____

Landlord's name _____ Telephone _____

1

Form 4-1: Rental Application (Page 1 of 2).

CREDIT REFERENCES
Bank name _____ Branch _____
Account name _____ Account no _____
Sort code _____ How long have you been with this bank? _____

Co-applicants bank _____ Branch _____
Account name _____ Account no _____
Sort code _____ How long have you been with this bank? _____

PERSONAL REFERENCE (this should be someone who is not related to you but knows you well and can vouch for your character)
NAME _____ JOB TITLE _____
TELEPHONE _____

Falsification or unverifiable information will be grounds for denial of rental application, Applicant states that all of the above information is true and correct and hereby authorises verification of the above items including, but not limited to, the obtaining of a credit report, and agrees to furnish additional credit references on request.
Applicant agrees that the Landlord shall not be liable for any delay in the date said property is ready for occupancy. The first month's rent and deposit, equal to a month's rent, must be paid by BACS transfer to Landlord's account prior to moving in.

SIGNED:

LANDLORD
NAME _____
SIGNED _____
DATE _____

APPLICANT ONE Name _____
SIGNED _____
DATE _____

APPLICANT TWO Name _____
SIGNED _____
DATE _____

2

Form 4-1: Rental Application (Page 2 of 2).

Don't allow the prospective tenant to reserve your rental property with a small deposit for more than a couple of days. A couple of days gives you more than enough time to screen him, and any additional time the property is off the market often translates into rent that you will never see. After you approve the prospective tenant, you should ask him to sign the tenancy agreement. If he still insists that he needs more time, he should agree to pay the daily rental rate, or you should refund his holding deposit and continue your leasing efforts.

By taking the property off the market, you're losing the ability to rent it to someone else. If the prospective tenant fails to go on and rent your property for any reason, you will have potentially lost revenue while the property has been vacant and reserved. On the other hand, prospective tenants don't want to pay rent while you're running them through your tenant-screening process. The solution is to use a written holding deposit agreement and receipt, like the one shown in Form 4-2, which outlines the understanding between you and the prospective tenant.

If you use a holding deposit you must have a written agreement or you are very likely to encounter a misunderstanding or even legal action.

Book IV

Becoming a Buy-to-Let Landlord

Holding Deposit Agreement and Receipt

On the date below _____ (Owner) received £_____ from _____ (Applicant) as a Holding Deposit for the premises located at _____ (Property address) on the terms and conditions set forth herein.

1. Rent of £____ per month shall be payable in advance on the first of each month. The tenancy will begin on the ____ day of _____, 20__, but subject to any present tenant vacating or the unavailability of the property.

2. Of the total funds hereby received by Owner, the sum of £,,,,. is an Application Fee that the Applicant understands and agrees is non-refundable. The Application Fee represents the estimated costs incurred by the Owner in obtaining and verifying the credit information, employment and references of the Applicant and similar tenant screening functions.

3. Of the total funds hereby received by the Owner, the sum of £____ represents a Holding Deposit.

4. The Applicant has paid the Application Fee and Holding Deposit to the Owner in the form of cash, cheque, or banker's draft. Owner is free to deposit all funds received herein and shall maintain this Holding Deposit in liquid funds subject to review by Owner or its agents of the Applicant's rental application.

5. Applicant shall be entitled to a full refund of the Holding Deposit within ____ days if the Owner determines that:
   a)   The Owner does not approve the Applicant's rental application; and/or
   b)   The premises are not available on the agreed date

6. Upon notification by the Owner to the Applicant that their rental application has been accepted, the Applicant agrees to execute all lease or rental agreement and related documents and pay any balance still due for the first month's rent and full deposit. Applicant understands that once their rental application has been approved, the rental property is taken off the market and reserved for the Applicant and any or all other potential Applicants will be turned away.

7. If after acceptance of the Applicant's rental application, the Applicant fails to comply, the Owner may immediately deduct from the amount received the sum of £___ per day (daily rate) for each day the rental property is vacant from the date the Applicant's tenancy was to begin through to the date the rental property is let to another tenant, but not in any event to exceed 30 days. It is agreed that the daily rate is calculated as an amount equal to 1/30th of the above monthly rental rate. In addition, the Owner shall be entitled to retain reasonable administrative fees and advertising expenses associated with remarketing the rental property. The Applicant agrees that the daily rate plus the actual incurred administrative expenses and advertising costs are reasonable and liquidated damages since the actual damages would be difficult or impossible to ascertain.

1

Form 4-2: Holding Deposit Agreement (Page 1 of 2).

8. The Owner, within _____ days after the rental property is re-let, shall return to the Applicant, to the Applicant's address shown below, any remaining balance of the Holding Deposit and shall include an itemisation of the Owner's losses.

9. If any legal action or proceeding is brought by either party to enforce any part of this agreement, the prevailing party shall recover, in addition to all other relief, reasonable solicitor's fees and costs. By signing below, both the Owner and Applicant acknowledge and accept all terms contained herein.

_____   _____
Applicant's Signature   Applicant's Signature

_____   _____
Applicant's Name (print)   Applicant's Name (Print)

_____   _____

_____   _____
Applicant's Address   Applicant's Address

_____   _____
Date   Owner/Agent

2

Form 4-2: Holding Deposit Agreement (Page 2 of 2).

Chapter 5

Safety, Security, and Insurance

- -

In This Chapter

▶ Taking precautions to keep your tenants and your property safe

▶ Addressing environmental issues

▶ Insuring yourself against loss and liability

- -

*A*s a landlord, you need to take an active role in implementing policies and security measures for the safety of your tenants and their guests. Even if your property is located next door to the local police station, you still need to implement proper building security measures. Crime can strike anywhere, even in seemingly respectable neighbourhoods. And even if crime is not a problem in your area, you may face potential safety challenges from Mother Nature. Take the lead in working with local experts and the Environment Agency if your rental property is in an area at risk from flooding.

Insurance is one of the major financial responsibilities you face as a landlord – from protecting your investment to ensuring you are covered if your tenants don't pay the rent or damage your property. Landlord insurance, which is very different from normal householder insurance, also covers you for general and public liabilities. Claims from injuries can run into hundreds of thousands of pounds, and this is perhaps the biggest risk you take as a landlord. This chapter makes sure you are prepared for all eventualities.

Taking Security Precautions

One of the best ways to prevent crime from occurring at your rental property is to make security a top priority. In this section, we cover some important security issues worth considering, not only for the safety of your property but for your tenants' well-being, too.

You can't guarantee your tenants that their property will be safe. But you can and should do what you can to increase the likelihood that they'll be free of problems.

Keys

Rental property locks are useless as security devices when you don't have effective control over keys. Some properties have a master key system where one single key works on all locks. Although such a system is convenient, we strongly recommend against using a master key system, because one lost key can require you to change all the locks in the entire property. Instead, use a duplicate key system with different keys for each lock.

Rather than giving tradesmen and contractors a key, always arrange to have someone you know and trust let them into the rental property.

Keep all landlord or agent keys in a metal locking key cabinet or key safe. So that the keys can't be used easily if they're lost or stolen, don't label the keys with the tenant's address; instead code the keys so that you know which property they belong to. If a tenant reports a lost or missing key, change the lock instead of giving him a duplicate key, unless he is sure the key is irretrievably lost. Charge the tenant a reasonable fee to cover your costs of getting a new key cut or a new lock fitted.

Although you must always change all entry locks when a tenant moves out, some tenants want to change or install additional locks. This is fine as long as they give you a duplicate key so that you can enter the rental property during emergencies and to make previously agreed repairs. If you become aware that a lock has been added or changed, verbally explain your policy and request a copy of the key. If the tenant doesn't want to give you a copy of the new key, send a polite but firm letter informing him of your policy. Ultimately, you may need to consider eviction if you aren't able to get a copy of the key.

Use standard rental property security devices such as the following: A five-lever mortice deadlock (make sure it conforms to British Standard BS 3621). All wooden entry doors should be solid core and have wide-angle peepholes or door viewers. They should also be fitted with a safety chain. Key-operated window locks are also a must and are valuable security devices.

Make sure that any security devices you install are easy to operate and difficult to disable. A determined criminal can clearly break in to any rental property, but you want to make your flat or house a more difficult target. Also avoid installing security devices that create an illusion of security, because they can actually lower a tenant's guard and make him more vulnerable to crimes. For example, don't install fake closed-circuit television cameras (CCTV) in an attempt to deter criminal activity.

If your rental properties are large, expensive houses, regularly occupied by wealthy tenants with valuable belongings, you may want to consider installing an alarm, linked to your local police station. When activated, the police turn up at the property. A number of installation companies offer this service; ensure the one you pick is accredited in accordance with the provisions of the Association of Chief Police Officers Requirements for Security Services. This service is expensive, but the cost can be passed onto the tenants and reflected in the rent. If your tenants do have a lot of valuables, they're likely to welcome such a service and may even demand it.

 Make sure that your tenant initials that all these security devices are operative on her inventory when she moves into the property and knows that she must contact you immediately if any locks or security devices are inoperative. Repair any broken locks or security devices immediately upon being notified.

Lighting

Outdoor lighting has many benefits. Proper lighting is an extremely cost-effective way to protect your property and your tenants. It can serve as a deterrent to vandalism while illuminating your building's paths and gardens to help prevent injuries to tenants and guests. The right lighting plan can also improve the appearance of your building and hence its kerb appeal.

 Lighting is only effective if it is in good working order, properly located, and has the right type of fixture and light bulb for the intended purpose.

 To keep your property well lit, opt for lights with built-in sensors so that they automatically detect movement. These types of lights reduce electricity costs because they don't need to be on during daylight hours and energy isn't wasted as they are only illuminated when you really need them. Such lights are also a good deterrent to burglars or other people up to no good because they're visible to people who approach the property.

Establish a regular schedule for inspecting exterior lighting and immediately repair broken fixtures and dead bulbs. The best time for inspecting and testing your lights is at night, when you can see that all fixtures are working properly and providing sufficient illumination in the correct locations. Be sure to log your lighting inspections and repairs or bulb replacement in your maintenance records.

Book IV

Becoming a Buy-to-Let Landlord

Addressing Environmental Issues

Although crime is usually the first safety concern that comes to mind for landlords, important tenant safety topics also include fire protection, environmental challenges, and the potential for flooding or strong gales.

Fire safety

Fire safety is a critical issue for landlords. Every year, hundreds of people die in fires and many thousands more are injured. Fires can spread quickly and fully engulf a room or even an entire rental property in a matter of minutes. Fires also produce poisonous gases and smoke that are disorienting and can be deadly.

Unless your rental property is a House in Multiple Occupation (HMO), there are no specific fire regulations for residential properties in the UK. However, regulations do apply to furniture and smoke alarms and you should make yourself familiar with these. Your Fire Prevention Officer, located at your local fire station, can help you with these.

Work with your local Fire Prevention Officer to develop an evacuation plan for your property. Think about means of emergency escape for tenants, particularly where sleeping accommodation is on second or third floors. You should also consider fire doors and emergency exits, along with other escape routes.

If you are really worried or just want to be on the safe side, ask for a fire inspection of your property; when your property is inspected you receive written notification of any deficiencies. You must address these noted items immediately and contact your local Fire Prevention Officer in writing to acknowledge that the items have been corrected and to request a re-inspection. Be sure to get written confirmation that all items have been satisfactorily corrected.

Fire extinguishers and blankets

No compulsory requirement exists to provide your tenants with a fire extinguisher or fire blanket, but doing so may be wise, particularly in the kitchen. If you do provide a fire extinguisher make sure to have it serviced every 12 months to ensure it's in good working order. These checks should be carried out by a company registered by the British Approvals for Fire Equipment (BAFE). Your fire extinguisher should also conform to the appropriate British Standard; look for the kitemark or special BAFE mark. Fire blankets should conform to British Standard BS 6575.

Evaluate your potential liability in the event of the fire extinguisher being defective, used improperly, or even improperly maintained by your tenant. If your tenant gets hurt because the fire extinguisher you provided wasn't working properly when she needed it, you could be held liable and sued. Your local Fire Prevention Officer can offer your tenants instruction on the proper use of extinguishers, and this could be a valuable lesson.

Smoke detectors

Fires are always serious, but the most dangerous fires are the ones that start while the tenants are asleep. That is one reason why landlords are legally obliged to install smoke detectors in all rental properties built after June 1992. The Smoke Detectors Act, 1991 requires that all properties built after this date must have at least one hard-wired smoke detector installed on every floor level. Even if your rental property was built before this date, we strongly recommend that you install smoke alarms in all hallways and near or preferably just inside all sleeping areas, in compliance with the manufacturer's specifications.

Always inspect and test smoke alarms according to the manufacturer's instructions when a tenant moves out and before a new one moves in. If a fire hurts a tenant because the smoke alarm wasn't working properly when he moved in, you could be sued and held responsible. So be sure to keep written records of your inspection and testing of the smoke detector and get your tenant to initial his tenancy agreement indicating that the smoke detector was tested in his presence and that he can perform his own tests and renew batteries when necessary. Remind him that the alarm should be tested on a regular basis to ensure that the battery is working – if he aims to do this on the first day of every month, it should be easy for him to remember.

Also, be sure to immediately address all tenant requests for smoke alarm inspections and repairs. Note these requests in your maintenance log along with the date that the smoke detector was repaired or replaced. If the tenant is present, get him to sign acknowledging that the smoke alarm now works properly. Smoke alarm complaints are always a top priority requiring immediate attention, so keep new smoke alarms on hand for this reason.

Carbon monoxide

Carbon monoxide is a colourless, odourless, and poisonous gas produced when fuel burns incompletely. It can build up in a rental property in just a few hours. If a leak occurs when the tenants are asleep, they could easily lose consciousness and suffer a serious injury before noticing anything was wrong, or even die.

Book IV

Becoming a Buy-to-Let Landlord

Appliances such as Calor gas fires and oil-fired boilers, gas water-heaters, and wood-burning stoves and fireplaces can all emit carbon monoxide. When these appliances are working properly, the carbon monoxide is directed to the chimney or other air vent, and there's no danger. However, if the appliances or fireplace are not properly serviced and there is a blockage or malfunction, then carbon monoxide can build up.

Naturally, carbon monoxide poisoning is a particular concern for landlords with properties with a gas supply, particularly where tenants rely on Calor gas fires to heat their rental property. Carbon monoxide detectors are a good idea, and we strongly advise installing a carbon monoxide detector if your rental property has a fireplace or uses carbon monoxide-producing heating appliances.

Gas appliances in rented accommodation must abide by very strict legal requirements. The Gas Safety (Installation and Use) Regulations, 1994, require all landlords to maintain the gas appliances in their rental properties through annual inspections and safety checks. You cannot perform this check yourself; instead you must have a CORGI-registered engineer carry it out annually or before any tenancy starts. Your tenant must receive a copy of this gas safety certificate each year. Failure to ensure that these annual checks are carried out could result in a fine or imprisonment.

If you have fireplaces, you need to employ a chimney cleaning company to periodically inspect your chimney, chimney connections, and insulation for cracks, blockages, or leaks. Have the recommended work done as soon as possible and quickly respond to any complaints from tenants about possible carbon monoxide poisoning.

Electromagnetic fields

Electromagnetic fields (EMFs) are a relatively new environmental hazard with varying scientific opinions regarding the potential danger to humans. Electric power-lines, electrical wiring, and even appliances all create some level of EMFs. Although the forces created by these sources are minimal when compared to even the normal electrical activity found within the human body, scientists cannot agree definitively as to whether exposure to EMFs can, or does, increase a person's chance of developing certain types of cancer, particularly childhood leukaemia.

This potential problem is well beyond your control, but although little conclusive scientific evidence that EMFs cause cancer exists, you should be aware of this issue in case you receive a tenant complaint. The bottom line is that, because you cannot insist that the electric utility remove its power lines and transmitters, the only viable solution for a tenant with legitimate concerns about EMFs is to move. Evaluate the legitimacy of your tenant's concerns to determine whether it's in your mutual best interest to release a tenant from his tenancy agreement.

The Health Protection Agency offers advice and information as to the risk of radiation around the country. If they are at all concerned, direct your tenants to its Web site at `www.hpa.org.uk/radiation` for more information.

Natural disasters

Although the UK is different to many other countries in that earthquakes and tornadoes are thankfully rare, we do have our own set of challenges from Mother Nature. Make sure that both you and your tenants are prepared for floods, if the property is situated on or near a flood plain, or severe gales. The Environment Agency offers advice and tips on ways in which you and your tenants can minimise flood risk, before any damage is done and an emergency occurs. For more information, log onto its Web site at `www.environment-agency.gov.uk`.

In winter, snow and ice accumulation can create dangerous conditions on paths and driveways. Landlords aren't responsible if a tenant slips and falls on natural accumulations of snow and ice. However, it may be worth supplying a shovel in the garden shed or garage, if your rental property has one of these, so that the tenant can remove any ice and snow if they want to before it builds up and becomes treacherous.

Handling Hazardous Materials

One of the major challenges to being a successful landlord is keeping abreast of the constantly evolving health and safety requirements that affect rental properties. In addition to providing your tenants with a clean and habitable property, you need to take precautions to ensure that it is a safe and healthy environment.

Although legal implications and substantial liability occur for failing to meet required laws, most landlords would not want to see their tenants get sick or injured anyway. In the following sections, we cover some of the most common issues facing rental property owners today.

Book IV

Becoming a Buy-to-Let Landlord

New legislation is constantly under consideration, and rental property owners must stay up-to-date with all requirements or face serious consequences. Ignorance is not an adequate legal defence.

Lead-based paint

Although lead-based paint is not a hazard when in good condition, it can be a serious problem (particularly for young children) when it cracks, peels, or turns to dust due to age. The UK banned the use of white lead in paint in the 1960s so older rental properties, such as period houses, may still contain lead paint underneath more recent decoration unless it has previously been stripped down to the bare wood and repainted with modern paint which is lead-free. You cannot tell whether paint contains lead just by looking at it; a special lead test of each different painted surface in your property by a professional is the only way to verify the existence of lead.

DIY lead-testing kits are available but studies have shown that they can be inaccurate and unreliable in detecting lead paint. Laboratory analysis is the most accurate way to test for lead paint.

In older properties, lead is usually found on:

- Exterior painted surfaces
- Interior trim
- Windows, windowsills, and horizontal painted surfaces
- Doors and frames, railings, and banisters

If you are buying a property built before the 1960s which has paint in thick layers, a chance exists that it contains a lead-based paint. Left to deteriorate, it is dangerous because lead dust can be created by activities such as opening a window, removing wallpaper, or repainting. Nearly all cases of acute lead poisoning in adults and children are attributed to unsafe home renovations and maintenance.

Lead-based paint is not easy to remove and must be done very carefully. Lead dust and fumes are particularly dangerous, and we recommend you hire an expert to remove the paint for you. Your local Yellow Pages lists licensed contractors who specialise in paint-stripping services and will be able to address your concerns about lead. Unfortunately, the removal of lead can be quite expensive, but it is well worth making sure you do it right to avoid problems later on.

Asbestos

Asbestos has received a lot of media coverage over the past 20 years and is now banned by law in the UK because breathing it in can cause cancer. However, asbestos was frequently used in the construction of many older properties – so you may find that you have some in your property. Because asbestos was not banned in the UK until 1999, an awful lot of it is around. Products containing asbestos are quite often not labelled either. It has been used extensively in over 3,000 commercially manufactured products. Hence many areas of a rental property could potentially include asbestos, such as pipe and boiler insulation, fire door insulation, roof and wall cladding, vinyl flooring, paints and sealants, and textiles.

Left alone asbestos is safe. But the concern in most rental properties is that asbestos-containing materials will be disturbed. If disturbed or damaged, asbestos-containing material may release asbestos fibres, which can be inhaled into the lungs. The fibres can remain there for a long time, increasing the risk of disease.

If you have asbestos-containing substances in your rental property and the material is in good condition, leave it alone. If the material is damaged, you may want to have the material repaired or removed. Always seek the advice of a professional contractor to evaluate and recommend the best course of action concerning asbestos.

Repair usually involves either sealing or covering asbestos material:

- ✔ Sealing is also commonly referred to as *encapsulation* and involves coating materials so that the asbestos is sealed in. Encapsulation is only effective for undamaged asbestos-containing material. If materials are soft, crumbly, or otherwise damaged, sealing is not appropriate.

- ✔ Covering involves placing something over or around the material that contains asbestos to prevent the release of fibres.

If sealing or covering isn't an option, you have to have the asbestos removed. The removal of asbestos-containing materials is an expensive and hazardous process and should be a last resort. Removal is complex and requires special training, tools, and techniques. A licensed contractor who specialises in asbestos-containing materials should be used, because improper removal could very easily increase the health risks to the workers, yourself, and your future tenants.

All about asbestos

Asbestos is a mineral fibre that historically was added to a variety of products to strengthen them and to provide heat insulation and fire resistance. In most products, asbestos is combined with a binding material so that it isn't released into the air. As long as the material remains bonded so that fibres aren't released, asbestos doesn't pose a health risk. Several types of asbestos exist, including white, blue, and brown asbestos, and the type can be positively identified only by using a special type of microscope.

The risk of lung cancer and *mesothelioma,* a cancer of the lining of the chest and the abdominal cavity, increases when a high amount of asbestos is inhaled. The risk of lung cancer from inhaling asbestos fibres is also greater if you smoke. People who get asbestosis have usually been exposed to high levels of asbestos for a long time. The symptoms of these diseases do not usually appear until about 20 to 30 years after the first exposure to asbestos.

Recent legislation affecting the management of asbestos in building mainly affects commercial landlords but also has implications for residential landlords. You can find out more information at `www.hse.gov.uk/pubns/indg223.pdf`.

Asbestos is a very dangerous material if disturbed. Do not attempt to test for asbestos on your own. Hire a professional environmental testing firm because the act of breaking open potentially asbestos-containing material to obtain test samples could release asbestos into the air and create a very dangerous situation.

Radon

Radon is a radioactive gas, known to cause cancer and found in soil and rock. It is formed as a by-product of the natural decay of the radioactive materials radium and uranium. Radon gas is invisible; it has no odour or taste. However, most radon found in buildings poses no direct threat to human life because its concentration is generally low.

As a landlord, you should be aware of radon levels in your rental properties, and check with your local authority for more information about the prevalence and appropriate precautions that should be taken to avoid radon exposure.

Although radon may be found in all types of homes and buildings, it is more likely to occur in the lower levels of tightly-sealed, energy-efficient buildings where ventilation is poor. According to the Building Research Establishment (BRE), the UK authority on radon in buildings, the principal areas of the country in which radon is a problem are the granite areas of Cornwall and Devon, and the limestone areas of Derbyshire, Northamptonshire, North Oxfordshire, Lincolnshire, and Somerset.

The Radiation Protection Division of the Health Protection Agency (HPA) recommends that radon levels should be reduced in properties where the average is more than 200 Becquerels per cubic metre. The Government endorses this recommendation. For more information about radon, go to www.hpa.org.uk/radiation.

The only reliable guide to monitoring the level of radon in a building is a simple process taking three months to complete. For a fee of around £40 payable to the HPA you get a radon detector pack, subsequent analysis and their report of the result. If your tests reveal dangerous levels of radon the cost of rectifying the problem will depend on the work carried out. The most effective way to reduce high levels is by using a radon sump, which can cost several hundred pounds.

If you want to find out whether the rental property you are interested in buying is in a radon-affected area, you can get hold of a report from the HPA on a building's radon potential. The service covers the whole of England and is based on published data.

Cover Me, I'm Going In! Making Sure You Have the Insurance You Need

The thought of your property burning down or a tenant absconding owing you six months' rent are big enough fears to keep you awake at night. But if you have sound ownership and management policies combined with insurance cover that has been customised for your specific needs, you're probably okay.

Insurance buys you peace of mind. No law says that your property must be insured – although mortgage lenders insist that you have buildings insurance – and you'd be very foolish not to consider other forms of insurance as well.

Book IV

Becoming a Buy-to-Let Landlord

The following sections explain what to think about when you're shopping for an insurance company and the types of coverage you'll need.

Choosing a company and getting the coverage you need

Some insurers cover you against any possible danger or loss in the world. And a sharp insurance salesperson is a master at describing all sorts of horrible problems that could befall your rental property. If you want to make sure you're covered at a reasonable cost, you need to sift through the sales pitch and decide which cover is right for you. Cover can be extended as required to include almost any conceivable eventuality when letting a property, but make sure the cover you get is essential. Your goal is to pay only for cover for events and losses that are most likely to occur at your property. The right insurance cover is worth a lot, but buying hurricane insurance in Chester doesn't make much sense.

Here are some tips to getting the cover you need at a competitive price:

✔ Be sure to shop around and use an insurance broker when sourcing the best insurance cover for your needs. The cover you can get as a landlord varies from insurer to insurer. The insurance broker can provide you with information on the kinds of policies worth considering. The Internet is also a good source of broker sites; most allow you to input your insurance requirements and then find you the best deal in a matter of seconds.

✔ When selecting an insurer, always use a reputable company. It is only when you come to make a claim that you are likely to find out how good your insurer is, so think very carefully before making a selection.

✔ To ensure that you're receiving the cover you need at a competitive price, consult an insurance broker and contact a couple of insurance providers directly. But bear in mind that the lowest premium shouldn't be the determining factor in your decision. Going for the lowest premium may not always be the best policy for your needs. Ask a lot of questions.

✔ After you've chosen a policy and paid your premium, insist on evidence that the insurance company is actually providing you with cover. Your best proof of cover is a formal certificate of insurance, which should be carefully stored along with all policy documents.

You must notify your mortgage lender and insurer that you're letting the property. Not obtaining written consent from these parties beforehand may render your cover void in the event of a claim. If you decide to rent out your own home, immediately contact your insurance company and ask for your homeowner's policy to be converted to a landlord's policy. A landlord's policy covers the higher risk of having another person living in your home. Because of the increased liability risk for rental properties, your current insurance company may decline to offer you this cover. Certain insurance companies specialise in this business, however. Either way, make sure that you have proper landlord's cover for your rental property, or you could face the possibility of having your claim denied.

If you own several rental properties, you may be able to negotiate a discount with your insurance company in return for covering all of them. Using one insurance company for all your properties makes it easier to keep track of your insurance cover and know when the policies are up for renewal.

Understanding the types of insurance cover available

One of the first steps in getting the right insurance is understanding the different types of cover available. Insurance is broken down into two main types, outlined in the following sections:

- ✔ Buildings insurance
- ✔ Contents insurance

Good insurance cover protects you from losses caused by many perils, including fire, storms, burglary, and vandalism. A comprehensive policy also includes property owner's liability cover in case of injury, death, or damage to individuals (such as a postman or meter reader) on, or adjacent to, your property. You could also opt for legal expenses insurance covering all of your legal costs, solicitor's fees, and costs that arise from ending up in court with your tenants. Such policies usually cost around £100 per annum – and given that the average cost of a possession hearing in 2001 was £785, according to the Association of Residential Letting Agents (Arla), that's money well spent.

Buildings insurance

Buildings insurance covers you in case anything happens to the building itself – if it burns to the ground, for example – and all mortgage lenders require that you have it. Landlords' buildings insurance should cover your property in the event of fire, lightning, explosion, smoke, impact, burst pipes, storm or flood damage, malicious damage, subsidence, and theft.

The property is covered for the cost of rebuilding the property – not the market value. Therefore, you must make sure you are adequately covered. Arla believes that 40 per cent of UK properties are under-insured, so if those property owners make a claim, their insurers will not pay the full amount of that claim.

Although most insurance companies supply quotes on the basis of information provided by you as to the size and age of the property, employ a qualified surveyor to calculate the rebuild cost of your rental property. Buildings insurance is index-linked to reflect the fact that building costs increase on an annual basis.

Some insurers won't offer you buildings cover if you are letting to tenants that they deem to be high risk. Such tenants include students, a group of single people living in a property together, or tenants receiving Housing Benefit. If your tenants fall into these categories, you may have to shop around a bit to find cover, and you'll probably end up paying more than you would for tenants who are considered to present a lower risk.

Contents insurance

Contents insurance covers a rental property's contents (as the name implies) rather than the property's structure. Two types of contents cover are available: a *full* policy or *limited* cover.

If you let your rental property either unfurnished or part-furnished, you may want to choose limited cover. *Limited* contents cover insures items such as carpets, curtains, light fixtures, and fittings in your rental property. The total you can claim on such a policy tends to be limited to around £5,000. These policies often include Employer's liability and Landlord's liability cover in relation to the rental property's contents. Such cover is vital in case, for example, your tenants or their guests are injured by tripping over a loose carpet or burn themselves on a faulty light fitting. Such accidents often result in expensive compensation claims. Upwards of £100,000 in compensation for modest injuries is not uncommon.

If your property is fully furnished, you should have full contents cover. With this type of cover, your insurer will ask you how much you want to insure the contents for. Specify a large enough sum to replace all the items on a new for old basis.

Even if you have hardly any furniture in your rental property, basic contents insurance and liability cover are well worth considering. Seriously consider how much replacing your rental property's furnishings would cost. Walk through the rental property, room by room, noting down all its contents. This is the best way of ensuring that you don't miss anything, which could happen if you rely solely on your memory.

Rent guarantee insurance

Some landlords who take out a buy-to-let mortgage to purchase a rental property think it makes a lot of sense to get a policy that guarantees the rent in case the tenant doesn't pay up. Not only are you guaranteed to receive the rent you expect from your property, enabling you to make your mortgage payments regardless of the tenant's ability to pay, but the premiums you pay for this type of insurance are also tax deductible.

Some landlord insurance policies include cover for loss of rent and alternative accommodation for your tenants, should the property become wholly or partly uninhabitable due to fire or flood. Checking policies for this, and if necessary paying a little extra for the cover, is a good idea, especially if it is available for a property in a flood risk area.

If you rely on the rent to make the monthly payments to the mortgage lender, having rent guarantee insurance means you don't have to worry about finding the cash to make your payment if your tenant defaults on the rental payments.

Policies tend to guarantee rent for a fixed period, usually 6 or 12 months. Premiums are calculated in different ways, from a fixed cost policy to a percentage of the annual rent. The latter tends to be more common – usually 3 to 4 per cent.

Determining the right excess

Excess is the amount of money that you must pay out when you make an insurance claim. The higher the excess, the lower your premiums, so calculate what you can realistically afford to pay upfront when making a claim. Some insurers set the excess quite high – at around £300 or so, but for many landlords £100 is a more manageable amount. The amount you decide upon should depend on what you are personally comfortable with.

Evaluate the possibility of having a higher excess and using your savings on the premiums to purchase other important insurance cover.

Book IV

Becoming a Buy-to-Let Landlord

Home contents insurance: Cover your tenants should buy

Home contents insurance is something your tenants should get and pay for themselves; it covers losses to the tenant's personal property as a result of fire, theft, water damage, or other loss. (Any item a tenant brings into the rental property is her responsibility to insure.)

A basic home contents insurance policy offers some protection for tenants' belongings against damage and theft. But specific tenants' contents insurance goes a lot further. Most policies cover tenants for accidental damage caused to the landlord's fixtures and fittings, the building itself, and your furniture. Your tenancy agreement should make the tenant liable for damage such as red wine stains, and the cost of cleaning or replacing the carpet is usually deducted from their deposit at the end of the tenancy. If the damages are excessive, tenants are often not in a financial position to replace or pay for the cost of repair to items themselves, and such a loss could be devastating. If they take out tenants' contents insurance, they would be able to claim for such accidents on their policy.

Tenants often think they do not need home contents insurance because they have few valuables and because they have already shelled out a deposit, a month's rent, and administration fees when they first move into your rental property. When money is tight, insurance is often the last thing on tenants' minds. In addition, many tenants wrongly believe that the landlord has insured their personal possessions.

As a landlord, you benefit from tenants' contents insurance because it covers any claims in the event that the tenant starts a fire or flood. (As an added bonus, the tenant's premiums go up instead of yours). So be sure to have a clause in your tenancy agreement that clearly points out that every tenant must have his or her own home contents insurance policy.

Handling potential claims

Immediately document all facts if an incident occurs at your rental property, particularly if it involves injury. Use the Incident Report Form (like the one shown in Form 5-1) to record all the facts. Be sure to immediately contact your insurance company or your insurance broker. Follow up with a written letter to ensure they were notified and have the information on file.

Incident Report

Date _____ Time _____ Name of Reporting Person _____
Date of Incident _____ Time of Incident _____ Property _____
Specific Location of Incident _____

Type of Incident: Accident _____ Crime _____ Fire _____ Police _____ Ambulance _____
Mechanical _____ Theft _____ Flood _____ Other _____

Details of what happened: _____
_____
_____
_____

Details of injury/damage: _____
_____
_____
_____

Names, addresses, phone numbers of people involved: _____
_____
_____

Names, addresses, phone numbers of witnesses: _____
_____
_____

Specific conditions at time of incident: _____
_____
_____
_____

Name of insurance company _____ Policy no _____
Name, address and phone number of insurance broker: _____
_____
Date and time insurance company notified _____ By phone _____ By mail _____

Request from/permission granted by insurance company to document incident: Yes or No
If yes, how: Photos _____ Video _____ Audio _____ Written statements _____

Date and time police/ambulance notified: _____
Time of police/ambulance arrival: _____ Report number _____

Follow-up required/taken: _____

Form 5-1: Incident Report Form.

Book V
Managing a Tenancy

'To make rent paying more pleasurable, I'm
employing a singing rent collector.'

In this book . . .

This book takes you through the nuts and bolts of having tenants in a rental property – finding them, dealing with them, and moving them out. We look at ways of finding the best tenants . . . and how to keep them once they've moved in! We also look at collecting rent, and help you to know what to do when things don't quite go to plan.

Here are the contents of Book V at a glance:

Chapter 1: Selecting and Screening Your Tenants

Chapter 2: Moving In Your Tenant

Chapter 3: Collecting and Increasing Rent

Chapter 4: Sweet and Sour: Keeping Good Tenants and Dealing with Problem Ones

Chapter 5: Moving Out Tenants

Chapter 1

Selecting and Screening Your Tenants

....

In This Chapter

▶ Setting up written criteria for your tenant-screening process

▶ Verifying your applicants' information

▶ Knowing the anti-discrimination laws

....

*M*ost landlords are paranoid about whether their tenants are going to be able to pay the rent. Bad tenants who don't pay their rent or pay it late every month and trash your property are the type of tenants you don't want. So ensuring you pick the tenants most likely to pay the rent and treat your property with respect is fundamental to your success as a landlord. This means that one of your most important tasks is screening and selecting tenants: You can't prevent your tenant defaulting on the rent, but you can reduce the risk of this happening as much as possible.

Because the process of screening tenants is time-consuming, you need to have a system in place for doing it efficiently, so this chapter is here to help you navigate these unfamiliar waters with ease.

Actually tenant selection and screening can be summed up very simply:

✔ Develop and use objective, written tenant selection criteria.

✔ Consistently screen all prospective tenants against these minimum criteria.

✔ Select the most suitable tenant based on your review.

With a good system in place, tenant screening really isn't that difficult; it just requires assertiveness, diligence, and patience.

Another critical part of choosing your tenants is making sure you handle the selection process without bias or discrimination. This can be a murky issue, but it's an important one, and one you need to pay attention to no matter what your situation, to ensure that you don't end up with an embarrassing and costly court judgment against you. This chapter also tells you how to avoid these problems.

Establishing Tenant Selection Criteria

Tenant selection criteria are written standards that you use to evaluate each prospective tenant's qualifications to live in your property. You should determine your exact minimum qualifications and adhere to them. Of course, your written criteria cannot be discriminatory or violate any anti-discrimination laws (see the section 'Avoiding Complaints of Discrimination' for details).

To establish your tenant selection criteria, review what you're looking for in a tenant. Your ideal tenant may be different from someone else's, but here are five important traits to look for:

- ✔ Someone who will be financially responsible and always pay his rent on time
- ✔ Someone who will respect and treat the property as if it were her own
- ✔ Someone who will be a good neighbour and not cause problems
- ✔ Someone who will be stable and likely to renew his lease
- ✔ Someone who will leave the premises in a condition the same as or better than she found it

To have the best results in selecting your tenants and make sure that prospective tenants understand your tenant-selection criteria, develop a *statement of rental policy,* which is a formal, written statement explaining your screening criteria.

Giving all prospective tenants an overview of your rental screening procedure and requirements up front lets them know exactly what you're looking for in a suitable tenant. Because these are the minimum standards you'll accept, prospective tenants will know why their rental application may be rejected.

If you make an exception for one applicant and not another, you could find yourself accused of discrimination in your tenant selection process.

Form 1-1 shows a sample statement of rental policy that you can develop for your rental property and provide to each and every prospective tenant over the age of 18. Your policy standards may be more or less stringent depending on the current rental market and experience. But no matter what, be sure that they comply with the law.

Statement of Rental Policy

We are glad that you are interested in our rental property. For your convenience, we have prepared this overview of our guidelines used in processing all rental applications. Please feel free to ask any questions.

We are an equal opportunities housing provider: It is our policy to rent our properties in full compliance with anti-discrimination laws. We do not discriminate against any person because of their race, colour, ethnic origin, religion, sex, age, marital or family status, physical disability, or sexual orientation.

Rental property availability: Rental properties only become available when they are completely ready to rent, including cleaning, painting, and the completion of all maintenance work and planned improvements. Rental property availability can change as properties become available during the day or are removed from the rental market based on finding tenants, cancellations, or maintenance issues.

Valid photo identification and written authorisation: You must be able to present current photo identification such as a driver's licence or passport so that we can verify your identity. If your rental application is approved, we will require a photocopy of your ID when you move into the property to be kept in your tenant file. You must authorise us to verify all information provided in your rental application from credit sources, credit agencies, current and previous landlords and employers, and character references.

Occupancy guidelines: In compliance with local authority guidelines there are restrictions on the total number of persons that may occupy a given rental property. Our guidelines allow two people per bedroom as long as that room is at least 10.2m square. Bedrooms of 6.5m square are suitable for one person. These guidelines are to prevent overcrowding and are in keeping with the limitations of the property. Occupancy will be limited to the persons indicated on the original rental application and lease only unless otherwise agreed in writing. Any proposed additional tenants must complete a rental application and be processed and approved through this same tenant-screening process prior to occupying the rental property.

Application process: All rental applications are evaluated in the same manner, and each adult applicant must voluntarily provide his or her national insurance number and other details which will enable us to conduct a consumer credit report. Every adult applicant must complete a separate rental application form and pay the non-refundable application fee in advance. Any false or incomplete information will result in the denial of your application. If discovered after you are approved and have moved in, we reserve the right to terminate your tenancy. We will verify the information provided on each rental application through our own screening efforts and/or with the assistance of an independent tenant-screening firm. A credit report, along with references from your employer and current landlord for each and every applicant in a given rental property will determine whether our rental criteria has been met. Unless we need to verify information by regular mail, we are usually able to process a rental application in a couple of days.

1

Form 1-1: Statement of Rental Policy (Page 1 of 2).

Rental Criteria

Income: The total combined monthly gross income of all rental applicants in a given rental property must be at least three times the monthly rental rate. Only income that can be verified will count. We expect rental applicants with income to prove at least one year of continuous employment. Full-time students are welcome if the total income of all applicants combined is sufficient or they have a guarantor. You must provide proof of a source of income if you are unemployed. Remember: all adult tenants are joint and severally liable, which means that each one can be held responsible for the payment of all funds due regardless of ability to pay.

Credit history: You must be able to demonstrate fiscal responsibility. If you have any unpaid debts or a pattern of late payments or county court judgements (CCJs) against you, your application may be denied.

Rental history: Each rental applicant must be able to demonstrate a pattern of meeting their rental obligations, leaving prior rental properties in good condition and not causing a barrage of complaints from neighbours. We will require satisfactory rental references from at least two previous landlords. If you have ever been evicted for violating a lease, your application may be denied.

Guarantors: If you do not meet one or more of the above criteria, you may be able to qualify to rent a property if you have a third party living in the UK who will guarantee your lease. The guarantor must pass the same application and screening process except that we will deduct the guarantor's own housing costs before comparing his or her income to our income criteria.

2

Form 1-1: Statement of Rental Policy (Page 2 of 2).

Developing your own statement of rental policy has several benefits:

- ✔ You have explained to the applicant that you're aware of and comply with anti-discrimination laws.
- ✔ You have outlined that your policy and your maintenance of good records can minimise accusations of discrimination.
- ✔ You have explained your process of evaluating prospective tenants so the applicant knows what to expect.
- ✔ Your objective tenant-screening criteria show that all applicants are evaluated consistently and fairly.

Your statement of rental policy should be given to each and every applicant with the rental application. Insert the policy in a see-through, waterproof folder and place it in clear view on a worktop in the kitchen in the rental property or another surface where all prospective tenants can see it as they view the property.

Although you must offer all prospective tenants a rental application and process each one received, you aren't required to provide your prospective tenants with a copy of your written tenant-selection criteria. You may want to, however, because there is a benefit to prospective tenants making their own decision not to apply to rent your property based on the criteria you've set up. The key is to follow the criteria without exception and have the information available if you're challenged.

Some landlords feel more comfortable discussing the tenant-selection criteria right from the first rental enquiry call; others wait and distribute copies only to those who actually apply. You need to decide which policy works best for you and then apply it consistently.

Always be very thorough when you perform tenant screening, and use the same process with all prospective tenants. You run the risk of a charge of discrimination if you deviate from your written standards for certain applicants. There are many legally acceptable reasons to deny a rental application. Be sure that your requirements are clearly understood and followed.

The fact that you carefully pre-screen all prospective tenants is a positive factor not only for you, but also for your rental applicants, your current tenants, and even the neighbours. In fact, you have a responsibility to your current tenants to weed out the unsuitable tenants with a track record of disrupting the neighbours everywhere they go, particularly if you rent out a couple of properties that are situated next door to each other. The good prospective tenants will appreciate the fact that their neighbours had to meet your high standards, too.

Over 90 per cent of your rental applicants will be good tenants, pay their rent on time, take good care of their homes, and treat you and their neighbours with respect. You just need to carefully guard against those few bad apples, and don't hesitate to deny applicants who cannot meet your standards.

Verifying Rental Applications

Bad tenants don't walk around with a helpful sign on their foreheads declaring that this is the case. The tenant-screening process requires you to be a detective, and all good detectives verify each fact and take thorough notes. You want to ensure that the prospective tenant meets the minimum standards outlined in your statement of rental policy (see the preceding section for information on these criteria).

We recommend that you use a rental application verification form, like the one shown in Form 1-2, to collect and review the necessary information that allows you to properly evaluate the suitability of your prospective tenant. This document is very important because it enables you to collate all the information necessary in helping you decide whether you want this applicant as your tenant.

Ensure that your rental application form clearly informs the prospective tenant that credit checks and references will be made in accordance with the Data Protection Act. If you intend to charge a fee for the credit check, this should also be stated on the application form.

Keep copies of all rental applications, the corresponding rental application verification forms, credit reports, and all other documentation for both accepted *and* rejected applicants for at least three years. That way, if anyone ever makes a claim that you discriminated against him, your best defence will be your own records, which will clearly indicate that you had legal rental criteria and you applied it consistently.

Verifying the identity of all adults

The very first step to take in verifying a rental application is to personally meet each prospective adult tenant. You should require each prospective adult tenant to show you his or her current driver's licence or other similar (and official) photo ID such as a passport so that you can confirm that the applicant is providing you with the correct name and current address. Advise the prospective tenants that if their application is approved, you will need a photocopy of their ID to be kept in their tenant file. Initial the rental application to record that you did indeed verify this information.

Enquire about any discrepancies between the application and the ID provided. Even if the explanation seems reasonable, be sure to write down the new information so that it's there to check if any need should arise in the future. Maybe an old address appears on the photo ID; if so, making further checks through a credit reference agency is worth considering.

Having a photocopy of the ID for each adult tenant can be very important if a dispute concerning the tenant's identity arises in the future. In these situations, you want to be able to clearly show that you positively identified the tenant before he or she moved in.

Rental Application Verification Form

Name of Applicant _____

Address of Property _____

Rental History (*Note:* Use separate sheets to verify at least two previous landlords.)

Name and Phone Number of Prior Landlord _____

Prior Address _____

_____

How much rent does the applicant pay each month? _____

Are you related to the applicant? _____

Is the applicant a lodger or guest? _____

How long has the applicant been your tenant? _____

Did the applicant pay their rent on time? _____

If late, please provide details

_____

Did you ever begin legal proceedings against the applicant or other occupants?

_____

If yes, what was the outcome of these proceedings? _____

Why is the applicant moving out? _____

If the applicant is leaving voluntarily, have they given you proper notice? _____

How many days? _____

Did the applicant or other occupants damage the property (beyond normal wear and tear)

or damage the common areas? _____

If yes, please describe_____

_____

Did the applicant pay for any damage? _____

Has the applicant maintained the property in a clean and sanitary condition? ____

_____

What type of pets does the applicant have? _____

1

Form 1-2: Rental Application Verification Form (Page 1 of 3).

Were there any problems with the pets? _____

Would you rent to this applicant again? _____ Why or why not? _____

Other Comments _____

_____

Employment Verification

Contact Name _____

Company _____

Contact's Job Title _____

Contact Telephone Number _____

Date contacted _____

Date joined Company _____

Applicant's Job Title _____

Salary _____

Staff position/fixed term contract? _____

Comments _____

Credit History

Credit report obtained from _____

Date of credit report _____

Information consistent with rental application? _____

Summary of results _____

_____

Character reference

Contact Name _____

Contact Telephone Number _____ Date contacted _____

Relationship to Applicant _____

How long have you known applicant? _____

Comments _____

2

Form 1-2: Rental Application Verification Form (Page 2 of 3).

Additional Information

_____

_____

Reason for Rejecting Applicant (if applicable)

_____

_____

3

Form 1-2: Rental Application Verification Form (Page 3 of 3).

Reviewing occupancy guidelines

Take a look at the rental application information provided by the tenant concerning the number of people that plan to occupy your rental property to ensure that the anticipated use is within your established occupancy guidelines.

One of the major concerns of landlords is excessive wear and tear of the rental property. Clearly, the greater the number of occupants packed into a rental property, and the longer they live in the property, the more possibility for wear and tear. Local authorities provide guidelines for houses in multiple occupation (HMOs), which are defined as those occupied by people who make up more than one household. This could be a house converted into bedsits, flats, or private rooms with common areas such as entrances, exits, bathrooms, and kitchen. It could apply to 20 people living in separate flats or as few as three people sharing a house.

The exact number of occupants needed for a house to be classed as an HMO varies from one local authority to another, so unfortunately universal guidelines as to how many people can occupy the property don't exist. You can contact the housing or environmental health department of your local council for information on the regulations concerning occupancy in your area and advice on the legal requirements.

A much stricter system exists in Scotland. If you let properties in Scotland, make sure you are well aware of the legal requirements.

Landlords need to ensure that layouts and facilities meet minimum standards and that the property is maintained in a safe and habitable condition. Occupancy must also be at an acceptable level.

Checking rental history

Contact the prospective tenant's current landlord and go through the questions on the rental history portion of the rental application verification form. When you first contact the previous landlord, you may want to listen to his initial reaction and let him tell you about the applicant. Some landlords welcome the opportunity to tell you all about your prospective tenant. Listen carefully.

Some prospective tenants provide you with letters of reference from their landlord or even a copy of their credit report. This is particularly true in many competitive rental markets where only the prepared tenants have a chance to get a good quality rental property. Although the more information you have, the better decision you can usually make, be very careful to evaluate the authenticity of any documents that the prospective tenant provides. Accept any documents that the prospective tenant provides, but always perform your complete tenant-screening process to independently verify all information.

We've heard of instances where a prospective tenant provided a glowing written reference from a previous landlord when in fact it was written by her boyfriend. Make sure you double check all references.

If the information you receive about your applicant from the current landlord is primarily negative, you may decide that you've heard enough and not bother to check with any other former landlords before turning the applicant down. However, be wary that the current landlord may not be entirely honest; he could be upset with the tenant for leaving his property. Or he may not want to say anything bad about a problem tenant so that he can get the tenant out of his property and into yours. Not all landlords are going to be as honest as you!

Current or previous landlords may not be entirely forthcoming with answers to many of your questions. It is likely that they will be concerned that they may be liable if they provide any negative or subjective information. Of course, it is unlikely that a tenant would actually follow up a bad reference and pursue the landlord for compensation, but many landlords simply don't want to take this risk.

When a current or previous landlord is not overly cooperative, try to gain his confidence by providing him with some information about yourself and your rental property. If you are still unable to build up a rapport, try to get him to at least answer the most important question of all – 'Would you rent to this applicant again?' He can simply give you a 'yes' or a 'no' without any details. Of course, silence can also tell you everything that you need to know.

Verifying employment and income

Although credit reference agencies may provide information on your prospective tenant's employment and income, they typically won't have all the information you need to properly evaluate this extremely important rental qualification criteria.

Independently verify the employer information and phone number the applicant puts on her application. You may have reason for concern if the employer is a major company and the telephone is not answered in a typical and customary business manner, for example. You also need to be careful that you confirm the sensitive questions of how much the prospective tenant earns and the stability of their employment only with an appropriate representative of the employer.

Occasionally, you may find that an employer, or the current or previous landlord, will not verify any information over the phone. So be prepared to send letters requesting the pertinent information and include a stamped, self-addressed envelope. Be sure to tell your prospective tenant that you may have a delay in providing her with the results of your tenant-screening process.

In addition to your credit reference information and the results of your verification calls, your prospective tenant should provide you with proof of her employment and income with pay slips for the past three months. No matter how compelling the information is, you must still verify it directly with the employer or source of the income.

Always require written verification of all other sources of income that a prospective tenant is using to meet your income qualification requirements. If you cannot verify the income, you do not have to include it in your calculations to determine whether the applicant meets your minimum income requirements.

When you have a prospective tenant whose income relies on commission or bonuses, make sure you review at least six consecutive months of her most recent pay slips. Of course, the best policy is to require all applicants with any income other than a monthly salary to provide a copy of their signed self-assessment tax return for the last two years. Although you must be careful to ensure that it is an authentic document, we have yet to find a prospective tenant who overstates her annual income on her tax return.

As a detective, you need to pay close attention to applicants who seem to be overqualified or anxious to be approved and take possession of your rental property. Remember the old saying, 'If it sounds too good to be true, it probably is'? That definitely applies in the world of rental property, so keep it in mind at all times.

Be particularly careful of prospective tenants who seem to have plenty of cash to pay your deposit and first month's rent, but who do not have verifiable sources of income that seem consistent with their spending patterns. The applicant may be involved in an illegal activity, and you may need to evict her later at considerable expense and loss of income.

Reviewing the applicant's credit history

You can and should check out an applicant's credit history by making a credit check. Information is held on all of us; this can include where we have lived, how we use our credit cards, and what our loan repayments are. You can also find out whether a tenant has been declared bankrupt or has county court judgments (CCJs) against him.

So what are you looking for with a credit check? You want someone with a pattern of financial responsibility and prudent or conservative spending. You want to avoid prospective tenants who seem to use excessive credit and live beyond their means. If they move into your rental property and have even a temporary loss of income due to illness or because they lose their job, you may be the one with an unexpected loss of income because of it!

What's in a name?

Identity theft is a growing problem in the UK. It occurs when someone's identity is stolen and used to apply for credit cards, loans, mortgages, and passports. It can also be used by someone trying to rent a property – in other words, the applicant interested in living in your 3-bedroom family home.

The case of Derek Bond, the 72-year-old British pensioner who was arrested on holiday with his wife in Durban, South Africa because the FBI thought he was Derek Sykes, a conman wanted for allegedly fleecing hundreds of Americans in an investment scam in the mid-1990s, shows how widespread identity theft is. Mr Sykes had been using Mr Bond's identity for years, but it wasn't until the FBI caught up with him that Mr Bond knew anything about it. And so hard was it to clear his name that Mr Bond spent nearly three weeks in jail until his innocence could be proved.

Unfortunately, identity theft on this scale is growing more common. Landlords also need to look out for cases of mistaken identity where several people share a name and subsequently get muddled up. When checking out applicants,

make sure they are who they say they are. Photo identification in the form of a driving licence or passport should be your first port of call. But you must run checks to ensure as far as possible that everything the applicant tells you adds up. Ensure you check their employer, landlord, and character references.

In some cases, perfectly good prospective tenants are turned down because their information is not carefully screened and verified and in some cases, is not information on the actual prospective tenant. In the US, you can find instances of some very responsible and qualified applicants being turned down when they submitted rental applications, because they have the same name as an individual with a very poor credit report. This problem occurred when certain tenant-screening companies didn't cross check their information sufficiently to prevent such a mix up.

So what's the upshot of all this? It's to be sure to verify the applicant's name, National Insurance number, and several former addresses to ensure that you are using the correct information in your screening efforts.

Carefully compare the addresses contained on the credit check to the information provided on the rental application. If you find an inconsistency, ask the prospective tenant for an explanation. Maybe they were temporarily staying with a family member or they simply forgot about one of their residences. Of course, be sure to contact previous landlords and ask all the questions on the rental application verification form just to make sure that the applicant didn't tell you about that residence for a reason.

Information obtained through credit checks must be kept strictly confidential and cannot be given to any third parties. The prospective tenant is entitled to a copy of his own credit check upon request.

Credit checks can have their limitations. So make sure that you are reviewing the credit report of your actual applicant. People with poor credit or tenant histories have been known to steal the identity of others, particularly their own children if they are 16 or over, by using the child's national insurance number.

A number of credit-reporting agencies offer a credit-checking service and prices can vary significantly. Credit checks usually take a couple of days, and the tenant tends to bear the cost. Experian and Equifax, the two main credit reference agencies, offer a tenant-verifier service – a credit-checking service for landlords – but this tends to be cost-prohibitive for most small-time landlords. However, large managing agencies who have to check the references of hundreds of tenants tend to use it.If you receive a large number of rental applications, review them first and then only run the credit check on the most suitable applicants. Be sure to return any unused credit check fees to those for whom you don't run the credit check.

The Internet is quickly changing the tenant-screening procedures for many landlords. Credit reports and tenant history information are now available from your computer in a matter of hours, and often this capability enables you to approve your prospective tenant in a single day, which can be a strong competitive advantage. Many firms are entering this market, and all offer very impressive services designed to save you time and help you fill your vacancies faster (check out the Web site www.tenantverify.co.uk for a cost-effective credit referencing service aimed specifically at landlords). Using technology can improve the efficiency of the information collection for tenant screening and provide you with more information to make a better decision. However, don't rely just on what you find out online. You still need to personally contact past landlords, verify the applicant's income and employment, and consider your own dealings with your prospective tenant. Rental property ownership and management is still, and always will be, a people business.

Many types of applicant-screening products are available to landlords. With the wide choice of tenant-screening services, you may have a hard time deciding exactly what you need. So we recommend that you use a tenant selection service that offers a retail or consumer credit report, an eviction search or tenant history, an automated crosscheck of addresses, and an employment or reference verification.

Talking with all character references

Although you could expect that character references only give you glowing comments about how lucky you are to have the applicant as your new tenant, investing the time and making the calls is important for several reasons.

You will occasionally find someone who tells you that the prospective tenant is her best friend but she would never loan the applicant money or let him borrow her car. Plus, if you call the references given and find that the information is bogus, you can use this information as part of your overall screening of the applicant.

Dealing with guarantors

Just as parents often act as *guarantors* when their children are trying to get on the property ladder for the first time because they couldn't afford to do it otherwise, your prospective tenant might not meet the criteria outlined in your statement of rental policy but he is ready to offer a guarantor. The guarantor needs to read and understand the tenancy agreement before signing a Guarantee of Tenancy Agreement form (shown in Form 1-3); however, you still need to screen the guarantor and make sure he or she is financially qualified, or the guarantee is worthless.

Make sure the guarantor completes a rental application, pays the application fee, and goes through the same tenant-screening process as the applicant. Keep in mind that the guarantor will not actually be living at the rental property and thus will have his own housing costs. So in order to ensure that the guarantor can meet all of his own obligations and cover your tenant's rent in case of a default, you need to deduct the guarantor's cost of housing from his income before comparing it to your income requirements. For example, if the proposed guarantor has a gross monthly income of £4,000 with a £1,000 mortgage payment, he has an adjusted gross income of £3,000. So assuming you have an income standard that requires the tenant to earn three times the monthly rent (and assuming the guarantor meets all of your other screening criteria), the person could be the guarantor for your prospective tenant as long as the rent does not exceed £1,000 per month.

Although a guarantor can be very important and can give you the extra resources in the event of a rent default by your tenant, overseas guarantors are not as valuable as those living in the UK. Enforcing the guarantee against an overseas party can be very difficult or even financially unfeasible.

Guarantee of Tenancy Agreement

On the date below, in consideration of the execution of the Tenancy Agreement, dated

_____, 20__, for the premises located at:_____

_____ (Rental property) by and between

_____ (Tenant)

_____ (Owner) and

_____ (Guarantor);
for valuable consideration, receipt of which is hereby acknowledged, the Guarantor does hereby guarantee unconditionally to Owner, Owner's agent, and/or including Owner's successor and assigns, the prompt payment by Tenant of any unpaid rent, property damage and cleaning and repair costs or any other sums which become due pursuant to said lease or rental agreement, a copy of which is attached hereto, including any and all court costs or solicitor's fees incurred in enforcing the Tenancy Agreement.

If Tenant assigns or sublets the Rental property, Guarantor shall remain liable under the terms of this Agreement for the performance of the assignee or sublessee, unless Owner relieves Guarantor by express written termination of the Agreement.

In the event of the breach of any terms of the Tenancy Agreement by the Tenant, Guarantor shall be liable for any damages, financial or physical, caused by the Tenant, including any and all legal fees incurred in enforcing the Tenancy Agreement. Owner or Owner's agent may immediately enforce this Guarantee upon any default by Tenant and an action against the Guarantor may be brought at any time without first seeking recourse against the Tenant.

The insolvency of Tenant or non-payment of any sums due from Tenant may be deemed a default, giving rise to action by Owner against Guarantor. This Guarantee does not confer a right to possession of the Rental property by Guarantor, and Owner is not required to serve Guarantor with any legal notices, including any demand for payment of rent, prior to Owner proceeding against Guarantor for Guarantor's obligation under this Guarantee.

Unless released in writing by the Owner, Guarantor shall remain obligated by the terms of this Guarantee for the entire period of the tenancy as provided by the Tenancy Agreement and for any extensions pursuant thereto. In the event Tenant and Owner modify the terms of said Tenancy Agreement, with or without the knowledge or consent of the Guarantor, Guarantor waives any and all rights to be released from the provisions of this Guarantee and Guarantor shall remain obligated by said additional modifications and terms of the Tenancy Agreement. Guarantor hereby consents and agrees in advance to any changes, modifications, additions, or deletions of the Tenancy Agreement made and agreed to by Owner and Tenant during the entire period of the tenancy.

1

Form 1-3: Guarantee of Tenancy Agreement (Page 1 of 2).

If any legal action or proceeding is brought by either party to enforce any part of this Agreement, the prevailing party shall recover, in addition to all other relief, reasonable solicitor's fees and legal costs. By signing below, Owner, Tenant and Guarantor acknowledge and accept all terms contained herein.

_____	_____	_____
Tenant's Signature	Guarantor's Signature	Owner's Signature
_____	_____	_____
Tenant's Name (print)	Guarantor's Name (print)	Owner's Name (print)
_____	_____	_____
_____	_____	_____
Tenant's Address	Guarantor's Address	Owner's Address
_____	_____	_____
Daytime phone no	Daytime phone no	Daytime phone no
_____	_____	_____
Date	Date	Date

2

Form 1-3: Guarantee of Tenancy Agreement (Page 2 of 2).

Notifying the Applicant of Your Decision

Landlords are legally allowed to choose which tenant they want to live in their property as long as their decisions comply with anti-discrimination laws and are based on legitimate business criteria.

One of the most difficult tasks for the landlord is informing a prospective tenant that you have rejected his application. You obviously want to avoid an argument over the rejection, but even more importantly, you want to avoid being accused of discrimination based on the applicant's misunderstanding about the reasons for being turned down.

Regardless of whether you accept or reject the prospective tenant, be sure to notify the applicant promptly when the decision is made. If you have approved the applicant, contact him and arrange for a meeting and a viewing of the rental property prior to the move-in date. Do not notify the other qualified applicants that you have already rented the property until all legal documents have been signed and you've collected in full all funds due upon move-in.

If you reject an applicant, be prepared to account for the reasons why you have done so because they are bound to ask you. In fact, we recommend that you notify your rejected prospective tenant in writing, using the notice of denial to rent form (shown in Form 1-4). In addition to notifying the applicant of the denial, this form also helps you to document the various reasons for your rejection of the applicant.

If you notify the applicant only by phone, you may have difficulty giving all of the details and required disclosures. The written notice of denial to rent avoids a situation in which the applicant may unintentionally (or sometimes intentionally) form the opinion that you are denying his application in a discriminatory manner and make a complaint.

Although you need to carefully follow the law, never compromise your tenant-screening criteria or allow yourself to be intimidated into accepting an unsuitable prospective tenant. Rejecting an applicant who doesn't meet your tenant screening criteria isn't discrimination.

NOTICE OF DENIAL TO RENT

To: _____

_____

(Full Names of All Applicants Listed on Application)

Thank you for applying to rent at: _____

We have carefully and thoroughly reviewed your rental application. We are hereby informing you of certain information as to why your application was unsuccessful. Based on the information currently in our files, your application has been denied for the following reason(s):

I. Rental History

_____ Could not be verified __ Unpaid or missed payments __ Property damage reported
_____ Disruptive behaviour reported ___ Prior eviction reported __ Other _____

II. Employment and Income

_____ Employment could not be verified   _____ Insufficient income

_____ Irregular or temporary employment   _____ Income could not be verified
_____ Other _____

III. Credit History

_____ Could not be verified   _____ Unsatisfactory payment history

_____ Declared bankrupt   _____ County court judgements (CCJs)

_____ Other _____

IV. Character References

_____ Could not be verified   _____ Lack of non-related references

_____ Negative reference __ Other _____

1

Form 1-4: Notice of Denial to Rent Form (Page 1 of 2).

V. Application

_____ Application unsigned   _____ Application incomplete

_____ False information provided   _____ Rental property let to prior qualified tenant   _____ Other _____

The credit reporting agency (if used) that provided information to us was:

Name _____

Address _____

Telephone _____.
This agency only provided information about you and your credit history and was not involved in any way in making the decision to reject your rental application, nor can they explain why the decision was made. If you believe the information they provided is inaccurate or incomplete, you may call the credit reporting agency at the number listed above or communicate by post.

_____
Signature of Owner or Agent for Owner

_____
Name of Owner or Agent of Owner (print)

_____
Date

2

Form 1-4: Notice of Denial to Rent Form (Page 2 of 2).

Avoiding Complaints of Discrimination

In the UK, suing landlords for discrimination is not a common occurrence but that doesn't mean you don't have to worry about being anti-discriminatory. It is all too easy to slip up, with problems arising when landlords are unaware that their policies or practices are discriminatory. For example, you may think that you are just being a courteous and caring landlord by only showing elderly prospective tenants your empty flat located on the ground floor because you think they wouldn't be able to cope with the flight of stairs at another property. But not giving all applicants the same treatment is a form of discrimination – even if that wasn't your intention.

What it is and what it isn't

Discrimination is a major issue for landlords and has serious legal conse-quences for the uninformed. If you don't know the law, you may be guilty of various forms of discrimination and not even realise it until you've been charged with discrimination. That's why knowing the law is so important, and it's up to you to make yourself familiar with the relevant aspects of it.

There are two types of discrimination:

- **Treating people differently.** For example, if you had two applicants with similar financial histories, tenant histories, and other screening criteria, but charged one applicant a larger deposit, you could be found guilty of discrimination or a complaint on the basis of different treatment.

- **Treating all prospective tenants equally, but having a different impact because of an individual's particular situation.** If your occupancy stan-dard policy is two persons per bedroom, you may be accused of discrim-inating against applicants with children. Although you have set an occupancy standard policy that is applied equally to all tenants, your restrictive policy will discourage applicants with children. This policy has a *disparate impact* – the policy is the same for all applicants, but the policy has a much different effect on certain applicants and essentially creates an additional barrier to rental housing for families.

You are not allowed to discriminate on the basis of race, colour, religion, national origin, sex, age, familial status, or disability.

Here are some other practices that may result in discrimination and that you need to keep in mind:

- **Gender stereotypes:** Be careful that you don't inadvertently favour one sex as tenants. For example, some rental property owners may have the perception that male tenants aren't as clean or quiet as female tenants. Conversely, some owners with a rental property in a rough area may believe that male tenants are less susceptible to being victims of crime. Don't allow any stereotypes or assumptions to enter into your tenant selection criteria. Men and women make equally good tenants and should all be judged on their own merits.

  You cannot refuse to rent on the basis of gender, nor can you have special rules for tenants based on gender, such as limiting female tenants to upper-level flats only.

- **Ageism:** Be careful with the whole issue of age. Typically, you will be able to deny renting a property to applicants who are under 18 years of age. Applicants over the age of 18 cannot be turned down on an issue of age, however, as this would be discriminatory.

- **Other issues:** There are other issues that are not specifically protected under the law. Examples include marital status, sexual orientation, and source of income. But common sense should prevail: For example, you can't refuse to rent to a couple on the basis that they are not married but are cohabiting. This would be seen as being discriminatory.

Steering

Steering means to guide, or attempt to guide, a prospective tenant towards living where you think he should live based on his race, colour, religion, national origin, sex, age, familial status, or disability. Steering is not advisable because it deprives people of their right to choose to rent a property where they want. Not showing or renting certain properties to minorities is one form of steering; however, so is the assigning of any person to a particular section or floor of a building, because of race, colour, religion, sex, handicap, familial status, or national origin.

Rental property owners often have only good intentions when they suggest that a prospective tenant with children see only rental properties on the ground floor or near a playground. However, the failure to offer such an applicant an opportunity to see *all* the available rental properties on your books is steering – and breaking the law.

Be very careful not to make suggestions or comments that could be misinterpreted as steering a prospective tenant. All prospective tenants should receive information on the full range of rental properties available and be able to decide which they want to see, making the choice themselves.

Children

No law says you must rent your property to adults with kids, but be very careful about discriminating against children. Rental property owners cannot cite moral reasons or concerns about additional wear and tear that children might cause, because it effectively discriminates against them.

Some rental property owners are concerned about renting to adults with children because there are hazards that may be dangerous to them. For example, the property may not have any safe areas for the children to play, particularly if it is a flat on the third-floor of an apartment building located next to a busy main road. Although you may truly only have the children's best interests in mind, it is up to the parents to decide whether the property is safe for their children. Of course, you do need to take steps to make your property as safe as possible by reminding parents to not let their children play in unsafe areas or to play while unattended.

Charging prospective tenants with children higher rents or higher deposits than applicants without children is also illegal, as is offering different rental terms, such as a shorter lease, fewer amenities, or different payment options because they have children. The property facilities must also be fully available for all tenants, regardless of age, unless there is a clear safety issue involved.

We always recommend that landlords openly accept tenants with children. Families tend to be more stable, and they are looking for a safe, crime-free, and drug-free environment in which to raise their children. They are unlikely to move around from property to property as much as single tenants because, in many cases, they have schooling needs to consider. Along with responsible pet-owners, who also have difficulty finding suitable rental properties, families with children can be excellent, long-term tenants. And typically, the longer your tenants stay, the better your cash flow and the easier life is for you.

Disabled tenants

Letting property to disabled people is governed by the Disability Discrimination Act. It makes it unlawful for landlords to discriminate against disabled people. Discrimination occurs when a disabled person is treated less favourably than someone else and the reason for this is related to the person's disability. Most rental premises, including houses and flats, are covered by the Act.

With residential housing, unlawful discrimination occurs when a landlord:

- ✔ Offers less favourable terms to a disabled person
- ✔ Refuses to let to a disabled person
- ✔ Offers different facilities to a disabled person
- ✔ Refuses a disabled person access
- ✔ Evicts a disabled person
- ✔ Refuses to give tenants consent to sub-let to a disabled person

However, certain circumstances are exempt under the Disability Discrimination Act. The Act says that it may sometimes be justifiable to treat disabled people differently from other people. It may be justifiable:

- ✔ To refuse a disabled person on health and safety grounds, for example, to refuse to rent to a disabled person
- ✔ To refuse a disabled person access to a facility, such as a shared kitchen or lounge, if allowing them access stops others from using it
- ✔ To give a disabled person different access to a facility, if this was necessary to allow others to gain access
- ✔ To refuse to rent to a disabled person who is not capable of entering into a legally enforceable agreement, or of giving informed consent

Landlords must not charge a disabled tenant a higher rent for the property or a higher deposit against damages. Both count as discrimination.

Don't forget your managing agent, if you use one. A landlord who lets their agents or other representatives discriminate against disabled people is acting unlawfully under the Disability Discrimination Act. But if you can show that you have taken reasonable steps to prevent your agent from acting unlawfully you won't be considered to have broken the law, even though your agent has.

Any landlord who discriminates against a disabled person can be taken to court. The disabled person may take action to seek damages to help make up for the loss or for injury to their feelings. Falling foul of the law can be costly, in terms of time and money, so take steps to ensure you don't make that mistake.

Reasonable accommodations

Landlords do not have to alter their premises in order to make them more accessible for disabled tenants. However, as a landlord, you should act in such a way as to make life easier for the disabled tenant and make accommodations where possible. Reasonable adjustments to your rules, procedures, or services should be considered upon request. Examples of reasonable accommodations that the landlord may be asked to offer might include:

- ✔ Providing a parking space that is wider and closer to the rental property of a wheelchair-bound tenant, in instances where the property has a parking space

- ✔ Arranging to read all management communications to a tenant with poor vision

- ✔ Adjusting the date when the rent is due to take into account when the tenant receives his or her disability benefit

Reasonable modifications

Landlords should think about allowing the disabled tenant the right to modify her living space at the tenant's own expense. The modifications can only be to the extent necessary to make the environment safe and comfortable, only as long as the modifications don't make the property unacceptable to the next tenant, or only if the tenant agrees to return the rental property to its original condition when she moves out. Alternatively, the tenant can pay the landlord to restore the property to its original condition at the end of the tenancy.

Reasonable modifications that tenants may request to make at their expense include:

- ✔ Ramps at the entry to the property where there are stairs that are difficult for the tenant to negotiate

- ✔ Lower light switches and removal of doors or widening of doorways to allow for wheelchair access

- ✔ Grab bars or call buttons in bathrooms

The modifications must be reasonable. You can ask the tenant to obtain your prior approval and ensure that the work will be done in a workmanlike manner, in line with any government or local authority guidelines. You can also ask the tenant to provide proof for the need for the modification from their GP. But you cannot ask about the specific handicap of the tenant that necessitates these changes.

Guide dogs

Many landlords include in the lease a clause preventing tenants from keeping pets in their rental property. But guide dogs for the blind or hard-of-hearing that assist tenants with daily life activities are exempt and must be allowed in all rental properties, regardless of any no-pet policies.

Sexual harassment

Sexual harassment, in the world of property management, occurs when you refuse to rent to a person who refuses your sexual advances or when you make life difficult for, or harass, a tenant who resists your unwanted advances. Most landlords understand this concern and find such behaviour unconscionable; however, the problem often arises when rental property owners hire someone to assist them with the leasing, rent collection, or maintenance requirements at their properties. The rental property owner is accountable, because these individuals are the employees or agents of the owner.

Make sure that you have a clear written policy against sexual harassment, provide an open-minded procedure for investigating complaints, and conduct thorough and unbiased investigations that lead to quick corrective action, if necessary.

Chapter 2

Moving in Your Tenant

- -

- -

*A*fter you select your new tenants, you still have to complete one very important step to ensure that you establish a good tenant/landlord relationship: moving them in. In order to ensure that this goes smoothly, you need to hold a tenant orientation and rental property inspection meeting, which gives you the opportunity to present the rental property and your ownership and management skills in the best possible light. You also need to ensure that your new tenants understand and agree to the policies and rules you have established for the rental property.

Tenants are very excited and motivated to begin moving in to their new home, but moving is very stressful for most people. New tenants can remember a bad move-in experience for months; the memory may stay in their minds throughout their entire tenancy. Although you can't guarantee your new tenant a simple and painless move (many aspects of the tenant's move are beyond your control), you can take steps to ensure that you are organised and ready to handle any complaints or concerns about their new home. By being organised and prepared, you'll be able to quickly and efficiently handle the administrative steps to get the tenants into their new rental property, thus making this process smooth and pleasant for everyone.

In this chapter, we outline the important steps to ensure that your tenant/ landlord relationship gets off to a good start, including scheduling the move-in date and the tenant orientation meeting; performing the pre-occupancy inspection and the inventory; and sharing important policies in the tenant information letter.

Establishing the Move-In Date

When you have informed your prospective tenant that his rental application has been approved, you need to determine a mutually agreeable move-in date. You and the tenant may have discussed this during your initial telephone conversation or when you showed the rental property, but be sure to raise the issue again to make sure that you agree on the date.

After new tenants have been approved, some tenants suddenly stall on setting the move-in date. They may stall because they are still obligated under another tenancy agreement or 30-day notice at another rental property and they don't want to pay two lots of rent. Unless you're willing to suffer additional rent loss that you can never recover, insist that the tenant starts paying you rent on the originally scheduled move-in date. The time for your new tenant to negotiate the move-in date was *before* you approved him.

In some situations, your rental property may not be available at your mutually agreed move-in date. Perhaps the prior tenants didn't vacate as they said they would, maybe the property was in much worse condition than you anticipated, or maybe you just weren't able to complete the work required in time. If it becomes apparent that there will be a delay in getting the rental property ready as promised, you need to tell your new tenant immediately. Often, new tenants can adjust their move-in date as long as you give them reasonable notice. If they can't adjust their move-in date, communicate with them and try to work out other possible arrangements.

Sometimes new tenants ask if they can begin moving just a few items into the rental property before your pre-occupancy conference. Don't allow it! You will create a tenant/landlord relationship simply by letting the new tenants have access to the rental property without being there or by allowing them to store even a few items in the flat or house. If you need to cancel the tenancy agreement for any reason, you would then need to go through a formal legal eviction that could take several weeks.

Although the rental property should be in rent-ready condition before being shown to prospective tenants, the property can quickly get dirty or dusty if there is any delay between showing the property and the date when the new tenant actually moves in. So before meeting with your tenant prior to move-in (covered in the following section), make one last visit to the rental property and go through your rent-ready inspection checklist again just to make sure that you won't encounter any surprises when move-in day arrives.

If at all possible, arrange to be on the premises while they are moving in so that you can answer any questions they may have.

Meeting with Your Tenant Prior to Move-In

After you and your tenant have decided on a move-in date, you need to get together to deal with some of the technicalities, like inspecting the property, signing some paperwork, and giving the tenant the keys. Getting together to do this is a very important step, and you need to do it before your new tenant actually moves in and takes possession of the rental property.

Schedule a meeting with the tenant either for the day that they move in or within just a few days before they move in.

At this meeting, you review your property policies and rules, review, and sign all the paperwork, collect the move-in funds, and conduct a thorough property inspection with your new tenant, including the completion of the inventory (covered later in this chapter), and take the meter readings. Having a checklist to make sure you don't forget anything at this meeting is a good idea.

Going over the rules with your new tenant

When you meet with your new tenant, start by giving him a copy of your house rules (see Form 2-1 for an example of this kind of document). Give him a chance to read over the rules and ask any questions, and provide clarification as necessary. Then ask for his signature, indicating that he has received and understands the rules and agrees to abide by them.

Policies and Rules

We are proud of this Property and we hope that you enjoy living here. The support and cooperation of you, as our Tenant, is necessary for us to maintain our high standards.

This is your personal copy of our Policies and Rules. Please read it carefully as it is an integral part of your Tenancy Agreement. When you sign your Tenancy Agreement, you agree to abide by the policies and rules for this rental property, and they are considered legally binding provisions of your Tenancy Agreement. If you have any questions, please contact us and we will be glad to help.

This document is an addendum and is part of the Tenancy Agreement, dated _____, by and between _____, (Owner), and _____ (Tenant), for the Property located at:_____
_____

New policies and rules or amendments to this document may be adopted by Owner upon giving 30 days written notice to Tenant.

Guests: Tenant is responsible for their own proper conduct and that of all guests, including the responsibility for understanding and observing all policies and rules.

Noise: Although the Property is well constructed, it is not completely soundproof and reasonable consideration for neighbours is important. Either inside or outside of the Property, no Tenant or their guest shall use, or allow to be used, any sound-emitting device at sound level that may annoy, disturb, or otherwise interfere with the rights, comforts or conveniences of the neighbours. Particular care must be taken between the hours of 9:00 pm and 9:00 am.

Parking: No vehicle belonging to a Tenant shall be parked in such a manner as to impede passage in the street or prevent access to the Property. Tenant shall only use assigned and designated parking spaces, for their own use and not sub-let them. Tenant shall ensure that all posted disabled or other no parking areas remain clear of vehicles at all times. Vehicles parked in unauthorised areas or in another tenant's designated parking space may be towed away at the vehicle owner's expense. No trucks, commercial vehicles, boats, caravans, or trailers are allowed anywhere on the Property without advance written approval of the Owner. Tenants shall ensure that their guests abide by all of these parking policies and rules.

Balconies, Patios, and Hallways: Balconies and patios are restricted to patio-type furniture and are to be kept clean and orderly. No barbecues or similar cooking devices are to be used at the Property without advance written approval. No items, such as washing or flags, may be hung from the Property's walls, windows, or balconies at any time, and all hallways and paths must be kept free from items that

1

Form 2-1: Policies and Rules (Page 1 of 3).

could be a hazard. Owner reserves the right that items that detract from the appearance of the Property be removed immediately upon request. No unauthorised storage is allowed at any time.

Wall Hangings: Pictures may be hung on a thin nail. Adhesives which mark the walls, such as Blu Tack, sellotape, and drawing pins should not be used for attaching posters to the walls. Mirrors, wall units, shelves, and hanging wall or light fixtures need special attention and professional installation. Please contact the Owner for approval in advance as damage to the Property will be the responsibility of the Tenant.

Rubbish: Tenant is responsible for keeping the inside and outside of the Property clean, sanitary, and free from objectional odours at all times. Tenant shall ensure that all rubbish is sealed in rubbish bags and placed in the wheelie bin or dustbin. No rubbish or other materials shall be allowed to accumulate so as to cause a hazard or be in violation of any health, fire, or safety regulation. Tenant shall refrain from disposing of any combustible or hazardous material and all rubbish shall be disposed of routinely per the local rubbish collection procedures.

Animals or Pets: No animals or pets may be kept or are allowed at the Property by the Tenant or their guests unless the Tenant and Owner have approved an Animal Agreement in advance.

Maintenance: Tenant agrees to promptly notify Owner of any items requiring repair at the Property. Requests for repairs or maintenances should be made by contacting the Owner or their agent during normal business hours, where possible. Emergencies involving any immediate health and safety matter should be handled by the appropriate agency (police, fire, ambulance) and the Owner shall be contacted as soon as practical thereafter. Costs for any repairs, including repair or clearance of blockages in waste pipes or drains, water pipes, or plumbing fixtures caused by the negligence of the Tenant or their guests are the responsibility of the Tenant.

Inclement Weather: Tenant shall close all windows, doors and other building openings tightly when leaving the Property to prevent damage from the elements to the Property. When the Tenant will be away from the Property during the winter, the thermostat will be placed at a minimum of 50 degrees to avoid freezing of pipes and other damage.

Keys: If you lose your key and need a new one, there will be a minimum replacement charge during normal business hours for the first request. Subsequent requests or after-hours lockout service will be handled at an additional charge of £20.

Key Release: Owner will not give a key to the Property to anyone unless their name is on the Tenancy Agreement. This is for the Tenant's protection. If you are expecting guests or relatives, please be sure they will have access to the Property.

2

Form 2-1: Policies and Rules (Page 2 of 3).

Insurance: The Owner's insurance cover offers no protection for the Tenant's personal property or any liability claims against the Tenant. The Tenant should obtain home contents insurance to cover damage against your personal belongings.

Right to Enter: Owner reserves the right to enter the Property with 24 hours' notice with or without the Tenant's permission at any reasonable hour for any lawful reason or without notice in the event of an emergency.

Safety/Security: Safety and security is the sole responsibility of each Tenant and their guests. Owner or their agent assumes no responsibility or liability, unless otherwise provided by law, for the safety or security of the Tenant or their guests, or for injury caused by the criminal acts of other persons. Tenant should ensure that all windows and doors are locked at all times, and Tenant must immediately notify Owner when leaving property unattended for an extended period. Tenant shall not smoke in bed or use or store any combustible materials at the Property.

3

Form 2-1: Policies and Rules (Page 3 of 3).

Many owners and managers with just one rental property or a small studio or flat to rent do not worry about detailed rules and regulations because they think the tenancy agreement covers it all. But setting up some basic rules that can easily be changed as necessary upon proper written notice to the tenants is a good idea. Doing so ensures that you and your tenants are on the same page and gives you flexibility as you manage your property.

The term *rules and regulations* can sound rather imposing to most tenants. So we recommend using the term *policies and rules* or simply *house rules* whenever possible. Your policies and rules are separate from the tenancy agreement, which is drafted by a solicitor using lots of formal and hard-to-understand terminology. The rules you draft should be more informal and conversational in tone than your tenancy agreement. Be sure to use language that is clear, but not harsh or demeaning. Here are some tips regarding house rules:

> ✔ **Be clear, direct, and firm – but not condescending.** Review your rules with several of your friends and colleagues and see if there is a better way to say the same thing.

✔ **Try not to use too many negative expressions.** It is easy to be too blunt or negative when you are stating rules, such as 'No cash will be accepted for rent payments', 'No smoking in the bedrooms', 'No washing on your balcony', or 'Don't chain bikes to the front of the property'. Although each of these rules may be reasonable and important to the safe and efficient operation of your rental property, you can say the same thing in a much more positive way. For example, instead of saying, 'Don't chain bikes to the front of the property', you could say, 'Please put your bikes in the garage'. Or instead of saying, 'No cash will be accepted for rent payments', you can say, 'We gladly accept direct debits'. Phrasing the rules in a more positive tone and minimising the negative statements makes the rules – and you – seem friendlier to your tenants.

✔ **Make sure your policies and rules are reasonable and enforceable.** They must not discriminate against anyone because of their race, gender, ethnic origin, religion, and so on.

Be particularly careful to review your house rules to avoid any reference to children unless the reference is related to health and safety issues. For example, if your rental property has a swimming pool, you can have a rule that states, 'Persons under 14 must be accompanied by an adult while using the pool', because unattended children in swimming pools pose legitimate safety concerns. But a rule that says, 'Children are not allowed to leave bicycles chained to the railings outside the property' is inappropriate, because it singles out children (implying that adults can leave bikes there if they want). A better way to handle this issue would be to use wording that isn't age specific, such as 'No one is allowed to leave bicycles chained to the railings at the front of the property.' Stated that way, the rule applies to everyone and doesn't discriminate based on age.

✔ **Regularly review and make improvements in your policies and rules based on situations that you've encountered.** But remember that you're not running a prison camp, and you don't want to alienate your tenants by harassing them with rules or controlling their day-to-day life. (Remember, you want your tenants to actually read and follow your rules, so try not to be too overbearing.)

As you revise your policies and rules, indicate the latest revision date in the lower left-hand corner of the document so that your tenants know which rules are the most recent. When you distribute the revised rules, be sure to remind your tenants that these policies and rules supersede any earlier versions. Get signatures from all of your tenants, indicating that they have received and will comply with the new rules.

And then there was light!

Tenants are usually not very anxious to begin paying for utilities, so you need to be sure that your procedures verify that your new tenants immediately contact the utility companies and put the utilities that are their responsibility in their name. These utilities could include electricity, gas, water, and telephone, depending on what's included in the rent. Most landlords let the utilities revert to their name when the rental property becomes vacant for the duration of rental showings. So if your new tenants don't change the utility billing information, you may end up paying for some of their electricity, gas, and water bills. Confirm that the tenants have dealt with the utilities soon after they have moved into the property.

Reviewing and signing documents

Tenants and landlords alike are usually aware of all the legal paperwork involved in renting a home. And although sifting through all those documents isn't fun for anyone, it is important. Landlords and tenants each have specific legal rights and responsibilities that are outlined in these documents, and being aware of what you're agreeing to – and being sure that your tenants know what they're agreeing to – is crucial.

In this section, we outline the documents you need to go over with your new tenant and which need his signature.

The tenancy agreement

Be sure that your tenant understands that, when he signs your tenancy agreement, he is entering into a business contract that has significant rights and responsibilities for both parties. Before your tenant signs the document, carefully and methodically review each clause of the tenancy agreement.

Certain clauses in the tenancy agreement are so important that you should have the tenant specifically initial them to indicate that he has read these points and understands his rights and responsibilities in relation to them. For example, the clause concerning the need for the tenant to obtain his own home contents insurance policy to protect his belongings should be initialled by the tenant.

Also get your new tenant to initial that he has received the keys for the rental property and acknowledge that you had the locks changed since the last tenant moved out.

Be sure to get the tenant to review and sign any other amendments to the tenancy agreement before taking possession of the rental property.

After the tenant has been given the keys and taken possession of the rental property, getting him to sign your required legal documents can be very difficult. Even if the tenant failed to sign the tenancy agreement, a verbal tenant/landlord relationship is established when you give the tenant the keys to the property – and when you're relying on verbal agreements, you and the tenant are likely to disagree on the terms. Regaining possession of your rental property can be a long and expensive process, so be sure that every adult occupant signs all documents prior to giving your new tenant the keys.

Gas safety certificate

All landlords have a duty to maintain gas appliances in their property through annual inspections and safety checks under the Gas Safety (Installation and Use) Regulations, 1994. A gas safety certificate, which you will have to pay for, must be obtained every 12 months from a fully qualified CORGI engineer (you can find an engineer registered with CORGI – the Council for Registered Gas Installers – in the phone book). The certification should cost in the region of about £60, although it varies from plumber to plumber. Keep a record of these inspections, and any remedial work, in a safe place and make this information available to the tenant on request.

Failure to comply with the regulations can result in a fine or imprisonment. The landlord must produce this record to the tenant when he moves in and within 28 days of each annual inspection. The record must be kept for a minimum of two years from the date of the inspection.

Smoke detector agreement

Inform your new tenant of the importance of smoke alarms. The Smoke Detectors Act 1991 states that any property built after June 1992 must have smoke detectors installed on each floor. You may even want to create a separate smoke detector agreement, like the one shown in Form 2-2, to be sure your tenants fully understand the importance of this vital safety equipment and realise that they must take an active role in ensuring that the smoke alarms remain in place, operate properly, and have electrical or battery power in order to protect them in case of smoke or fire.

Many tragic instances have occurred in which fires broke out and tenants had completely removed or disabled the smoke alarms because they were annoyed when they repeatedly went off, triggered by smoking or cooking. Some tenants fail to regularly test the smoke alarms or replace the batteries as needed. Your tenants need to understand that you can only address conditions brought to your attention, so the tenants must be actively involved in ongoing inspections of the rental property to ensure their own safety.

It can be easy for the tenant to forget to check their smoke alarms, so suggest that they test the alarms on the first day of every month. That way they are less likely to forget.

Smoke Detector Agreement

This document is part of the Tenancy Agreement, dated_____ by and between

_____ (Owner/Agent), and _____ (Tenant), for the Property

located at: _____

In consideration of their mutual promises, Owner/Agent and Tenant agree as follows:

1. The Property is equipped with a smoke alarm/s.

2. Each Tenant acknowledges the smoke alarm/s have been tested and their operation

explained by management in the presence of the Tenant at the time of initial occupancy and

the alarm/s in the property was working properly at that time.

3. Please be aware that the Tenancy Agreement requires that you as Tenant/s ensure that the

smoke alarm/s are operable at all times, to test for correct operation of the smoke alarm/s on a

regular basis (perhaps weekly). Also Tenant must replace the batteries with new ones as and

when required.

4. If after replacing the battery the smoke alarm does not work, inform the Owner or

authorised Agent immediately in writing. Tenant(s) must inform the Owner or authorised

Agent immediately in writing of any defect, malfunction or failure of a smoke alarm.

5. In accordance with the law, Tenant shall allow Owner or Agent access to the Property for

the purpose of verifying that the required smoke alarm/s are in place and operating properly

or to conduct maintenance service, repair, or replacement as needed.

_____   _____   _____   _____
Date   Owner/Agent   Date   Tenant

Form 2-2: Smoke Detector Agreement.

Animal agreement

Marketing your rental property to tenants with pets can be very profitable, because you usually have lower turnover and higher rents. If your new tenant has pets, you need to get him to complete and sign an animal agreement, like the one shown in Form 2-3. The animal agreement outlines the policies and rules at your rental property for your tenant's animals or pets.

Dogs, cats, birds, and fish are not the only pets that people keep in their homes. With the broad variety of animals that tenants are known to keep, we have broadened the concept from merely pets to animals in general. A good pet or animal policy clearly outlines exactly which animals are acceptable. It may just be semantics, but you don't want to get to court only to hear your tenants argue that the large pot-bellied pig that trashed your rental property is not subject to your rules because it is not their 'pet'.

Keep current photos of each animal living on your property in the individual files of their owners. This may seem ridiculous, but no matter how large your deposit or how strict your rules, animals have the potential to cause significant damage. Determining the source of the problem can be difficult if you cannot accurately identify the guilty animal.

After they have moved in, tenants may be tempted to take advantage of your policy and bring in additional animals or pets. We have seen the goldfish in the small glass bowl be replaced by a 200-gallon aquarium. Your tenant may decide that the small poodle you agreed to is lonely and needs the company of a Great Dane in your studio flat! Often tenants have very good and heart-warming stories about how they've ended up adding new animals to the mix, but you need to retain control over the number, type, and size of the animals on your property. One way to do this is to actually meet and photograph the animal so there is no doubt as to what you have approved. Also, remember that small puppies can grow into large dogs. Make sure that your policies anticipate the animal at its *adult* size.

Animal Agreement

This document is an addendum and is part of the Tenancy Agreement, dated
_____ by and between _____, (Owner/Agent) and
_____ (Tenant), for the Property located at:
_____

In consideration of their mutual promises, Owner/Agent and Tenant agree as follows:

1. The Tenancy Agreement provides that without Owner/Agent prior written consent, no animals whatsoever shall be allowed in or about the Property. Tenant shall not keep or feed stray animals in their rental Property or anywhere in the grounds. Tenant may not allow an animal to be in their rental Property even temporarily. Tenant must advise their guests of this policy prohibiting animals or secure advance approval of the Owner/Agent.

2. Tenant desires to keep the following described animal (see attached photo), herein after referred to as Pet, and represents it as a domesticated dog, cat, bird, fish, or _____
Said Pet is: Breed: _____; Size (Current and Adult Height//Weight):
_____; Colour: _____
Tenant represents to Owner/Agent that said Pet is not vicious and has not bitten, attacked, harmed or menaced anyone in the past.

3. Tenant agrees to comply with all applicable regulations and laws governing pets. If Pet is a cat, it must be spayed or neutered and Veterinary proof is required. Tenant must provide and maintain an appropriate litter tray, where required, placed in a safe location in the Property. Pet shall not be fed directly on the carpet or any floor covering in the Property. Tenant shall prevent any fleas or other infestation of the Property.

4. Tenant acknowledges and agrees that Owner/Agent may, at any time and in Owner/Agent's sole and absolute discretion, revoke its consent by giving Tenant thirty (30) days' written notice, if Owner/Agent receives complaints from neighbours about Pet, or if Owner/Agent, in their sole discretion, determines that Pet has disturbed the rights, comfort, convenience, or safety of neighbours. Tenant shall permanently remove Pet from Owner's Property upon Owner/Agent's written notice that consent is revoked.

5. If any rule or provision of this Animal Agreement is violated, Owner/Agent shall have the right to demand removal of Pet from the Property upon three (3) days' written notice. Any refusal by Tenant to comply with such a demand shall be deemed to be a material breach of the Tenancy Agreement, in which Owner/Agent shall be entitled to all the rights and remedies set forth in the Tenancy Agreement for violations thereof, including but not limited to, eviction, damages, and solicitor's fees.

6. Tenant agrees that Pet will not be permitted outside Property unless restrained by a lead, cage, or other appropriate animal restraint. Tenant shall not tie Pet to any object outside the Property. Use of the grounds or garden for any sanitary purposes is prohibited and Tenant agrees to promptly clean up after Pet, if necessary.

_____ _____   _____ _____
Date   Owner/Agent   Date   Tenant

Form 2-3: Animal Agreement.

Collecting the money

In your meeting with the tenant just before he or she moves in, be sure to get the first month's rent and the deposit, equal to at least one month's rent. You need to collect this money *before* you give the tenants the keys to the rental property. Be sure to give your tenants a receipt for their payments.

Before giving the keys to your new tenant and allowing him to take possession of your property, you need to insist on having the cash in hand through *good funds* (as opposed to *insufficient funds,* where a person writes a cheque and doesn't have the money to cover it in his account). Most owners do this by requiring cash, a banker's draft, or building society cheque. The banker's draft or building society cheque are superior to personal cheques because they represent good funds and, at the very least, won't be returned to you because there was no money to cover them. Consider these bits of advice:

- ✔ **Although cash is legal tender, have a firm policy *against* accepting cash, and only accept cash when the tenant moves in or for the monthly rent payment when absolutely necessary.** Regularly collecting cash for your rent can make you a target for crime. Because you will often have tenants moving in on the weekends and in the evenings, you don't want to have cash on you or at your home until you can get to the bank. Cash is also harder to keep track of.

- ✔ **Payment of the deposit and first month's rent should be in the form of a banker's draft or building society cheque.** Don't accept a personal cheque because you have no way of knowing whether the cheque will clear. (You also may prefer to insist on a direct debit paid directly to your bank account each month because then the tenant is less likely to forget to pay his rent on time and – unlike cheques – direct debits don't bounce. Either way, be sure to let your tenant know whether your rent collection policy allows him to pay his future monthly rent payments with a personal cheque.)

- ✔ **If, despite our advice, your tenant persuades you to accept a personal cheque, then at least don't give him access to the property until you have called and verified with his bank that the cheque will be honoured.** Your best bet is to take the cheque to the tenant's bank and cash it or at least have it certified. If the bank certifies the cheque, it is guaranteeing that sufficient funds are available. In addition, the bank will also put a hold on the funds. Of course, cashing the cheque is the only way you can be certain of collecting your funds, because a devious tenant can always stop payment even on a certified personal cheque.

Inspecting the property with your tenant before the move-in

The number one source of tenant/landlord disputes is the deposit. Many of these potential problems can be resolved with proper procedures even before the tenant takes possession of the rental property by using an inventory, like the one shown in Form 2-4. This form is an excellent tool to protect you and your tenant when the tenant moves out and wants the deposit returned.

The first column of the inventory is where you can note the condition of the property before the tenant actually moves in. The last two columns are for use when the tenant moves out and you inspect the property with the tenant again. Often, you won't immediately know the estimated cost of repair or replacement, so you can complete that portion of the inventory later and then include a copy when you send your tenant the remainder of his deposit.

When properly completed, the inventory clearly documents the condition of the rental property upon acceptance and move-in by the tenants and serves as a standard for the entire tenancy. If the tenant withholds rent or tries to break the lease claiming the property needs substantial repairs, you may need to be able to prove the condition of the rental property when they moved in. When the tenants move out, you'll be able to clearly note the items that were damaged or were not left clean by the vacating tenants so you can deduct the necessary money from their deposit.

The inventory is just as important as your tenancy agreement. The purpose of the inspection is not to find all the items that you forgot to check, because you should have already been through the rental property looking carefully to ensure that it met your high standards. The purpose of the inspection is to clearly demonstrate to the tenant's satisfaction that the rental property is in good condition except for any noted items.

The inventory is unique in that you will use the form throughout the entire tenancy – upon initial move-in, during the tenancy (if there are any repairs or upgrades to the rental property), and when the tenant finally vacates the rental property. Be sure to give your tenants a copy of the completed and signed form for their records.

Inventory

Tenant Name(s) _____
Property Address
_____
Move-In Date _____   Move-Out Date _____

Tenants have inspected the entire premises both inside and outside, including but not limited to, each item listed on this form. The condition of each item is clean, undamaged, in good working order and adequate for usual and customary residential use unless otherwise noted. Tenants understand and agree that the Condition on Arrival versus the Condition on Departure comments will be compared and that all Tenants will be joint and severally liable for all discrepancies in an item's condition. Tenants also understand that when they move out of the property, the Owner/Manager may make deductions from the deposit for cleaning, repairing, or restoring said items to their move-in condition except for damage caused by ordinary wear and tear. Tenants note that the property must be returned completely clean and that cleaning is not subject to allowance for normal wear and tear. Cross out items that are not applicable. Use additional sheets for bedrooms and bathrooms as necessary.

Condition on Arrival	Condition on Departure	Estimated Cost Of Repair/Replacement

Kitchen
Floor covering
Walls & ceiling
Windows/locks/blind
Door
Light fixtures/bulbs
Cupboards
Drawers/worktops
Sink/taps
Shelves/drawers
Stove/oven
Fridge freezer
Dishwasher
Washing machine
Electric kettle
Toaster
Iron
Ironing board
4 glass tumblers
4 mugs
4 soup bowls
4 side plates
4 dinner plates
4 knives, forks, and spoons
4 teaspoons
Wooden spoon

Form 2-4: Inventory (Page 1 of 5).

Spatula
Sieve
Tin opener
3 saucepans with lids
Frying pan

Living Room
Floors/floor covering
Walls & ceiling
Windows/locks
Curtains
Doors
Light fixtures/bulbs
Cupboards/shelves
Fireplace
Coffee table
Two-seater sofa
Armchair

Dining room
Floor/floor covering
Walls & ceiling
Windows/locks
Curtains/blinds
Light fixtures/bulbs
Cupboards/shelves
Table and chairs
Other

Hallway/Stairs
Floors/floor covering
Walls & ceiling
Windows/locks
Curtains/blinds
Light fixtures/bulbs
Mirror
Rug
Cupboard/shelves
Other

Front entry/Porch
Light fixtures/bulbs
Doorbell
Other

Garage
Floor type/condition
Doors/locks
Light fixtures/bulbs

Form 2-4: Inventory (Page 2 of 5).

Cupboards/shelves
Other

Storage
Exterior
Interior
Loft/basement
Other

Garden
Lawn/trees
Flower beds
Sprinklers/hose
Path
Driveway
Patio
Swimming pool
Spa
Other

Bedroom 1
Floors/floor covering
Walls & ceiling
Windows/locks
Curtains
Cupboards/shelves
Double bed
Bedside table
Chest of drawers
Light fixtures

Bedroom 2
Floors/floor covering
Walls & ceiling
Windows/locks
Curtains
Cupboards/shelves
Wardrobe
Double bed
Bedside table
Chest of drawers
Light fixtures

Bathroom
Floors/floor covering
Walls/tiles/ceiling
Blind
Doors/locks
Light fixtures

Form 2-4: Inventory (Page 3 of 5).

Extractor fan
Cupboards/shelves
Mirrors/cabinets
Power shower
Bath
Sink/toilet
Toilet paper holder
Lavatory brush
Shower curtain
Towel rail
Other

Other items
Boiler
Heating thermostat
Cable TV/TV aerial
Telephone/intercom
Fire extinguishers
Other

Keys/Alarms	**Received**	**Returned**	**Charge for missing key**
Door			
Garage			

Additional items/comments

_____

_____

_____

Move-in comments

_____

_____

_____

Move-out comments

_____

_____

_____

Smoke Alarm(s)

_____ By initialling here, Tenants acknowledge that all smoke alarms were tested in their presence and found to be in proper working order. Tenants have been advised as to the proper testing procedure and agree to test the smoke alarm(s) at least once a month and to immediately report any problems to the Owner in writing. Tenants agree not to remove, disable, or remove the batteries from the smoke alarm(s) for any reason and Tenants agree to immediately replace/install all smoke alarm batteries as necessary.

Form 2-4: Inventory (Page 4 of 5).

Burglar Alarm

___ By initialling here, Tenants acknowledge that the alarm system was tested in their presence and found to be in proper working order. Tenants have been advised as to the proper operating instructions and testing procedure and will immediately contact the Owner if there is any malfunction of the system. Tenants have also been given an instruction manual that they have and will read.

Inventory completed upon **move-in** on _____ at _____, and approved by:

                 Date   Time

_____ and _____

Owner/Manager

                  _____

                  Tenants

Inventory completed upon **move-out** on _____ at _____ and approved by:

                 Date   Time

_____ and _____

Owner/Manager

_____ _____

Tenant's Forwarding Address(es)   Tenants

Form 2-4: Inventory (Page 5 of 5).

Noting the condition of things

You need to physically inspect all aspects of the rental property with your new tenants and guide them through the inventory. Let the tenants tell you the conditions they observe and make sure that your wording of the noted conditions and comments are detailed and that they accurately describe the conditions. As you note the condition of each item, follow these guidelines:

- ✔ **Print legibly and be as detailed and specific as possible.** This may sound obvious, but you'll want to be able to read what you wrote at a later date, and if you're scribbling down things in a hurry, your writing may be difficult to decipher several months later. Try to give as much information as possible for each item, so there is no doubt as to its condition.

- ✔ **Note any items that are dirty, scratched, broken, or in poor condition.** Be particularly careful to note any and all mildew, mould, pest, or rodent problems, because these are health issues that must be addressed immediately before the tenant takes possession of the property. If the problems persist after the tenants have moved in, consult with the appropriate licensed professional to evaluate any potential health risk to the tenants and for the necessary response and remedial action.

✔ **Be sure to indicate which items are in new, excellent, or very good condition.** If the linoleum flooring in the kitchen is new, be sure to indicate that on the form.

Many disputes can be resolved if the inventory specifically notes the condition of the item. If you only comment on dirty or damaged items, a court may conclude that you didn't inspect or forgot to record the condition of a component of the rental property that you are now claiming was damaged by the tenant. You may think that everyone knows and agrees that all items without any notation are in average or okay condition, but the tenant is likely to tell the court that the item was at the very least rather dirty or damaged and that you should not be able to charge her for that item.

✔ **Be sure to note the condition of the carpets and floor coverings.** This is one of the most common areas of dispute with tenants when they move out of the property. Although tenants should not be charged for ordinary wear and tear, if they destroy the carpet, they should pay for the damage. Indicate the age of the carpet and whether you've had it professionally cleaned as part of your rental turnover process. When a tenant leaves after only six months and has destroyed the carpet, you can be sure that their memory will be that the carpet was old, dirty, and threadbare. The tenant's selective memory will not recall that the carpet was actually brand new or at least in very good condition and professionally cleaned upon move-in!

✔ **Be specific.** Rather than generally indicate that the oven is 'broken', for example, note that the 'built-in timer doesn't work'. The oven works fine, but the tenants know that they need to use a separate timer and that they will not be held responsible for this specific item when they move out.

You and the tenant should go through the inventory *together* before they move in or as they move out of the property. If it is impossible for you to do this with your tenant, you should complete the inventory and ask all the adult tenants to review and sign the form as soon as possible once they move in.

When used properly, your inventory not only proves the existence of damage in the rental property, but it can also pinpoint when the damage occurred. Don't fall for one of the oldest tenant ploys in the book. Tenants often try to avoid inspecting the rental property with you when they move in because they want to wait and be able to avoid charges for damage that occurs while they are actually moving in. You must ensure that the tenants do check the property and agree that all items are in clean and undamaged condition *before* they start moving in their boxes and furnishings.

If you discover any problems while you are checking the inventory, note them on the form and take steps to have them corrected, unless doing so is not economically feasible. You may, for example, have a hairline crack along the edge of one of the kitchen worktops. If you have decided that refinishing or replacing the worktop would be too costly, just note the condition on the inventory so that your tenants are not charged in error when they move out.

Be sure that your inventory reflects any repairs or improvements made after the initial property inspection. For example, if you and your tenants noted on the form that the bathroom door didn't lock properly, you would have that item repaired; then you would update the inspection form and get your tenants to initial the change. Or you may install new carpeting or make other improvements to the property that should be reflected on the form.

Another excellent way to avoid disputes over deposits is for you to take photos or video the rental property before the tenant moves in. In addition to your inspection form you will have some photos to help refresh the tenant's memory or show the court if the matter ends up there. Here are some suggestions for such a video:

✔ Be sure to get the tenant on the tape stating the date and time. If your tenant is not present, bring a copy of that day's newspaper and include it in your video.

✔ With all detailed photography, it's not always easy to understand exactly what the picture is showing unless specifically stated. So be sure to include a caption or descriptions with all still photos and provide a running detailed narrative with the video. Be sure to get your tenant to initial and date the back of the landlord's copy of every photograph, giving the tenant a duplicate set to be attached to the agreement.

Explaining basic use and care of appliances and utilities

Do not assume that your tenants are familiar with the appliances and how they work. Provide your tenants with photocopies of the appliance manuals as in our experience the originals often go missing.

Part of your new tenant orientation should include showing your tenants exactly where and how to shut off the water at the mains in case of a leak. You should also point out the fuse box, in case a fuse blows. If they smell gas at any time, you should remind them to contact the gas board; they will find the emergency telephone number in the phone book.

Giving your tenant an informational letter

The key to success in managing rental properties is to develop an efficient system that reduces the time you spend managing those properties. A good way to minimise your phone calls from tenants is to provide them with a *tenant information letter* (see Form 2-5) outlining all your policies and procedures that are too detailed to include in your tenancy agreement. You can also attach information on the proper operation and care of appliances, plus other important information that they should know about the rental property.

Customise the letter to present the policies and procedures you have implemented for each rental property. Although the letter should be customised for each property, here are some of the items to include:

- ✔ Property manager's name and contact number, where relevant

- ✔ Procedures to follow and contacts in case of emergency

- ✔ Rent collection information, including when rent is due, how payment is to be made, landlord's bank account details for direct debits, and how late fees and other charges are handled

- ✔ Requirements for ending tenancy, including notice requirement

- ✔ Procedures for the return of the tenant's deposit

- ✔ Handling of new or departing flat- or housemates

- ✔ Proper procedure for requesting maintenance and repairs

- ✔ Charges for lost keys

- ✔ Tenant's home contents insurance requirements

- ✔ Guest occupancy policy

- ✔ Annual safety inspection information

- ✔ Photocopies of appliance operating instructions (keep the originals safe as these can be very difficult to replace if lost)

- ✔ Utility shut-off locations, including a separate diagram for the individual property

- ✔ Rubbish collection and recycling programme information, where applicable

- ✔ Parking policies

Tenant Information Letter

Tenant Name (s)_____
Property address:
_____

Dear _____

We are very pleased that you have selected our property to be your home. We hope that you
enjoy living here and would like to share some additional information that will explain what
you can expect from us and what we will be asking from you.

1. Owner/Manager:

2. Rent Collection:

3. Notice to End Tenancy:

4. Deposit:

5. Maintenance and Repair Requests:

6. Lockout procedure/Lost Keys

7. Home Contents Insurance:

8. Guest Occupancy Policy:

9. Animal Safety Inspection:

10. Utility shut-off locations:

11. Rubbish collection or recycling programmes:

12. Parking:

Form 2-5: Tenant Information Letter (Page 1 of 2).

Please let us know if you have any questions.
Sincerely,

_____   _____
Owner/Manager   Date

I have read and received a copy of this move-in letter.
_____   _____
Tenant   Date

_____   _____
Tenant   Date

Form 2-5: Tenant Information Letter (Page 2 of 2).

Distributing the keys

Key control is a very serious issue, with significant liability for landlords and managers. A problem in key control can allow access to a tenant's rental property, and theft or worse can occur. Keys require careful handling and should be stored only in a safe, if possible.

As the landlord, you're responsible for ensuring that the rental property can be properly secured. Include a five-lever mortice lock and a rim-mounted lock to British Standard BS3621 on the front door. Peepholes should be provided on the main or primary exterior entry door as well.

Windows should have locks, particularly if the property is a ground floor flat or a house. However, we recommend that you provide locks for all windows that can be opened. Although not legally required, we recommend installing window locks on upper level windows as a safety device and to minimise the chance that young, unsupervised children could fall from an open window.

For the convenience of your tenants, have a single key that works all entry locks for their particular property.

One of the least desirable aspects of managing rental property is handling calls from tenants who have locked themselves out of the property. When this happens, you usually have to go round to the property to rescue them. The problem is that tenants rarely seem to get locked out of their rental property during the day – for some reason, it always seems to happen at 3:00 a.m. on a Sunday morning. To minimise disputes, inform your new tenants about your policies and charges for when they are locked out or have lost their keys. Set up a policy that acknowledges the difference between being locked out during reasonable business hours and non-working hours. For example, you could charge the tenant £15 for getting locked out between Monday and Friday from 9:00 a.m. to 6:00 p.m. and £25 for all other times.

Changing the locks between tenants is extremely important. Previous tenants may have retained copies of the keys and could return to steal or commit some other crime. You can purchase and install an entirely new lock, or, if you have several rental properties, you may decide for economic reasons to substitute the existing lock set with a spare lock set. Keep several extra lock sets so that you can rotate locks between properties upon turnover. Your new tenant should sign a statement indicating that they are aware that the locks have been changed since the previous tenant vacated the property. Give them a copy of the locksmith's receipt for their records.

If you have a master key system for your rental properties, be extremely careful with it. Don't have any extra copies or loan the master key to anyone whom you don't trust implicitly. Although locksmiths are not supposed to duplicate certain keys, remember that an individual who wants a copy of your key to commit a crime is not likely to be concerned that he is illegally copying the key.

Setting Up the Tenant File

You need to be able to immediately access important written records, and one way of doing that is to have an organised filing system to ensure that you don't waste time searching aimlessly for a lost or misplaced document. The best way to accomplish this goal is to immediately set up a new tenant folder for tenants when they move into one of your properties.

Set up a file folder for each rental property with individual files for each tenant. Your tenant file should include the following:

- ✔ Rental application
- ✔ Rental application verification form
- ✔ Credit report
- ✔ Background information
- ✔ Holding deposit agreement and receipt
- ✔ Signed tenancy agreement

- ✔ Annual gas safety certificate
- ✔ Smoke alarm agreement
- ✔ Inventory
- ✔ Photos or videos of the unit, taken when the tenant moves in

You'll continue to turn to this file throughout the tenancy, adding to it all new documents such as rent increases, notices of entry, maintenance requests, and correspondence. Keep tenant files for three years after the tenant vacates the property in case of later problems.

Chapter 3

Collecting and Increasing Rent

*I*f location is the most important element when buying a property, then collecting rent in full and on time is the most important element in managing a buy-to-let investment. But how can you make sure that your tenants will pay their rent on time every month? The reality is that most people who rent do not have significant cash resources, and many live from payday to payday. So if a tenant's pay cheque is delayed or her car breaks down or she has an unexpected major expense, then her ability to pay the rent in full and on time is in jeopardy. And since the tenant's funds are likely to be so tightly budgeted, when she falls even one month behind on rent, catching up again is even more difficult.

However, you can take some steps to increase the likelihood of getting your rent money in full and on time. The key to success in rent collection is establishing policies and procedures and being firm with your enforcement of collecting your rent.

Review your rent collection procedures with each adult tenant renting your property. Make rent collection a featured topic of your meeting with the tenants prior to the move-in date, when they review and sign the tenancy agreement. Include your rent collection procedures in the informational letter you give to all new tenants as well. This way you can at least be sure the tenant is informed.

Collecting the rent is a key part of property management, as is keeping the rent competitive in your market. Raising the rent to reflect the trends in your area is a necessary part of managing rental properties. Many property owners hesitate to raise the rent for existing tenants, but it can be done well, without risking the loss of your tenants.

In this chapter, we fill you in on what you can do to ensure that you're getting paid on time and that your rent is competitive in your area.

Creating a Written Rent Collection Policy

The fundamentals of property management are very straightforward: you provide the tenants with a clean and comfortable place to live; and they pay the rent, live quietly, and keep the property clean. Problems and confusion can arise, however, if you and your tenant do not understand the rights and responsibilities that come with the tenant/landlord relationship.

Establishing a successful rent collection policy, putting it in writing, and giving it to your tenants in the tenant information letter is the best way to avoid confusion. No single rent collection policy works for *all* landlords, but every policy should cover certain key issues, which we outline in the following sections.

When rent is due

We recommend that you require your tenants to pay the full monthly rent, in advance, on or before the first day of each month. This method is the most common.

Although rent is traditionally paid in full at one time, it is perfectly legal for you and your tenant to agree that the rent is divided up and paid twice a month, every week, or in any other mutually agreed timeframe. Generally, however, try to avoid accepting more frequent payments, because your goal is efficiency, and handling the rent collection process only once each month is definitely more efficient.

You and your tenant can agree that the monthly rent is paid on any mutually agreeable date during the month; rent does not have to be paid on the first of the month. This may make sense if your tenant receives his salary, maintenance payments, or income support on certain dates. For example, you may have a tenant who gets paid on the 10th of each month, so you set the monthly rent due date for the 15th of each month.

Think about the ramifications of accepting rent based on the tenant's scheduled receipt of income rather than your usual rent due date. By accommodating the tenant, you are tacitly acknowledging that the tenant needs that
payment in order to afford the rent. But one of the most fundamental issues in
the management of buy-to-let property is to avoid tenants who cannot afford
the rent. If your tenant needs that income in order to pay your rent that month,
no safety net is in place if the tenant's cheque is lost in the post, or his car
breaks down, or he is temporarily laid off from his job. To avoid surprises and
missed rent cheques, you don't want your tenants to have their finances so
tight that they need this month's income to pay this month's rent. Your tenant-
screening process should provide you with the information so that you can
effectively select tenants with enough financial cushion that they are paying
this month's rent from cash already on hand as of the first of each month.

Some owners make the rent payable each month on the date the tenant first
moved in. If, for example, the tenant moves in on the 25th of the month, her
rent is due on the 25th of each future month. This policy is legal and may be
acceptable if you have only a few tenants and are willing to keep track of
each due date. But having all of your rents due on a single date makes life
simpler and avoids confusion or the chance of making an error on legal
notices for non-payment of rent.

If your rent due date falls on a Saturday, Sunday, or a Bank Holiday, the tenant
should be allowed to pay it by the next business day.

Pro rata rents

Life would be simpler if all your tenants moved in and out only on the first of
the month, but they won't. If your tenant's occupancy begins in the middle
of the month and you have a rent collection policy that all rents are due on
the first of each month, then you need to calculate the pro rata rent from the
date she moves in. There are two basic ways to work out the pro rata rent at
the beginning of your new tenant's occupancy.

If your tenant moves in towards the end of a month, collect a full month's
rent (for the next month), plus the rent due for the additional pro rata portion of the current month. For example, if your tenant takes occupancy on
July 25, upon move-in collect seven days' rent for the period of July 25 to
July 31 *plus* a full month's rent for the month of August. Your new tenant will
usually be glad to do this if there are only a few days pro rata.

However, if your tenant moves in early in a month, expecting him to pay a full
month's rent plus the pro rata rent upon move-in may be unreasonable. If
your tenant moves in on July 10, for example, he will most likely baulk at your
request for payment of seven weeks' rent upon move-in. In these situations,

collect a full month's rent prior to move-in and then collect the balance due for the pro rata rent on the first of the next month. For example, prior to your tenant taking occupancy, collect a full month's rent covering the period of July 10 through August 9. Then on August 1, collect the balance of the rent due for August 10 through to August 31, or 22 days. By September 1, the tenant is on track to pay his full rent on the first of each month.

Unless otherwise agreed, rent is normally uniformly apportioned from day-to-day using a 30-day month. Take your monthly rental rate and divide it by 30 to determine the daily rental rate. This formula applies to February as well.

Providing a grace period

Many landlords allow for a grace period that provides tenants with a few extra days to make the monthly rent payment in full before incurring late charges. And most tenants incorrectly believe that if they pay rent within the grace period, their payment is legally on time. However, the rent is due on or before the rent due date and is late from a legal perspective regardless of the terms of the grace period.

Make sure that the tenancy agreement and the tenant information letter are very clear and unambiguous about the fact that the rent is due on or before the first of the month and is technically late even if paid during the grace period.

Grace periods are optional and can be any number of days in length. We recommend that your grace period runs for 7 days after the rent due date, allowing time for any administrative errors with standing orders or direct debits to be corrected or for a missing rent cheque to be reissued.

You do not have to wait until the grace period expires to begin your collection efforts. Rent arrears need immediate action so that the tenant knows he cannot get away with it and you can take appropriate steps at an early stage. Contact tenants who are regularly late paying their rent.

How rent is paid

Your tenancy agreement should clearly indicate how rent is to be paid: by standing order or direct debit, cheque, or cash. Tenants who pay by cash are likely to require a receipt; those paying by cheque, standing order, or direct debit are much less likely to request one.

Standing order or direct debit

Paying rent these days is far easier than in the past when the landlord collected the cash in person or the tenant had to remember to write out a cheque and post it each month. Most tenants pay by standing order or direct debit with a pre-authorised amount deducted from their bank account on a set date each month. The money is transferred directly into your account with the minimum amount of fuss and hassle. And because cancelling a standing order requires some effort on the part of the tenant, he is less likely to try dodging out of his rent payments.

Once a direct debit or standing order is set up, payment is guaranteed (unless the tenant doesn't have money in his account). You are much more certain of getting paid than relying on the tenant to remember to put a cheque in the post.

If you opt for payment by standing order or direct debit, you must regularly monitor your bank account to ensure that rent has been paid on time because mistakes do happen. You don't have to visit your local branch to verify that a payment has been made; you can do it over the telephone or Internet. If you don't check on a regular basis, some time could pass before you realise a payment hasn't reached your account.

Cheques

Tenants can pay by cheque, but this method of payment isn't conducive to getting the rent on time because cheques can be delayed or go missing in the post. You must also go to the trouble of paying a cheque into your account and wait several working days for the funds to clear. Cheques place an additional burden on tenant and landlord when your goal is to simplify the rent collection process for everyone involved.

If you and the tenant agree that he will post the monthly rent to you, you may run into some questions about when the rent is actually considered paid. Is rent considered paid when it is postmarked or when it is received? Have a clear written agreement in your rent collection policy. We recommend that you consider the rent paid when the payment is postmarked. By posting the rent cheque on time, the tenant is acting in good faith, and you don't want to unfairly penalise your tenant if the post is delayed.

Payment by cheque is conditional. If the cheque is not honoured for any reason, it is as if the tenant never paid and late charges should apply.

Never accept second party cheques, such as a pay cheque. Have a policy that all rent payments made after the grace period must be in the form of a bank or building society cheque.

Cash

Avoid cash whenever possible. Turning down cash is always difficult, and your tenants may remind you that cash is legal tender. However, you have the legal right to refuse to accept cash. What's wrong with cash?

- ✔ **You become a target for robbery.** Even if you use a safe, you have an increased risk.

- ✔ **Accepting cash attracts tenants that may be involved in illegal businesses that deal primarily in cash.** These tenants don't want to have their activities tracked and prefer to rent properties where cash payments are allowed. Don't make your buy-to-let property more attractive to the criminally inclined.

Do not accept even small amounts of cash for rent or late charges. Clearly state in your tenancy agreement that cash is not accepted under any circumstances.

Clearly document all of your income and expenses. HMRC may become interested in auditing your tax returns if they become aware of frequent cash transactions in connection with an investment property.

Dealing with multiple rent cheques

When you have a number of tenants living in one of your properties, you may receive several cheques for portions of the total rent due. And you may not receive all the rent at the same time or for the proper amount. When you call the tenants, you may hear from one of them that he paid his share and you need to track down one of the other tenants for the money. How your tenants choose to divide the rent between them shouldn't be your problem, however.

Accommodating your tenants and accepting multiple cheques can cause administrative nightmares and lead tenants to erroneously believe that they are not responsible for the entire rent. If your tenants pay by cheque, we recommend that you have a firm policy of requiring one cheque for the entire month's rent.

Besides the administrative convenience for you, this policy has other benefits. Legally, each tenant in your rental property is 'joint and severally' liable for all lease or rental agreement obligations. This means that if one disappears, the others owe you the entire amount. If you allow them to pay separately, they may forget that they are each responsible for the entire amount.

You may also want to have your tenants assume responsibility and take the lead in getting the tardy tenant to pay their rent. Let the responsible tenant know that even if they have already paid a portion of the rent, they will be held responsible for the balance of the unpaid rent. After all, they are in a better position to track down their elusive flatmate than you are.

Dealing with Rent Collection Problems

As a landlord you're not in the banking business. So your tenants must always pay the entire rent due on or before the due date. However, you need to establish policies for the most common problems you will encounter in collecting rent.

These policies outline the specific penalties that are enforced for tenants whose cheques bounce, who fail to pay in full, or who occasionally pay after the due date and the expiration of the grace period, if any. We cover some of these key issues in the following sections.

Collecting late rent

One of the most difficult challenges for a landlord is dealing with a tenant when the rent is late. You don't want to overreact and begin serving threatening legal notices demanding rent, because that tactic will definitely create tension and hostility if a legitimate reason has caused the delay. On the other hand, late rent can be a very serious issue and demands immediate action.

If you are having trouble collecting rent on time, consider mailing your tenants a monthly payment reminder or an invoice.

You can also call your routinely slow rent payers and remind them that the rent is due on or before the first of the month. You can remind your tenants that you expect your rent to be their top priority among their various financial obligations. However, we don't recommend that you call and remind tenants indefinitely, because your time is too valuable to spend chasing your tenants. If they consistently fail to pay the full rent on or before the due date, you may have no alternative but to seek possession of the property if you want to avoid further losses.

The key to keeping your response in line with the magnitude of the problem is to communicate. You need to remain calm and businesslike and determine why the rent is late before taking any action.

The most effective way to collect rent and determine whether you should exercise a little patience is to contact your tenant directly. Simply posting a rent reminder or hanging a late notice on the front door typically doesn't get the job done. Your goal in personally contacting your tenant is not to harass them but to remind them or to work out an agreement to get your rent. Whatever agreement you reach, make sure that it is in writing and signed by the tenant.

Call your tenant at home and at his place of business. Although you may not want to bother the tenant at work, you have a right to know when to expect your rent. You can also go to the property and speak with your tenant directly. Don't be shy, or paying the rent will quickly become a low priority for your tenant.

If you're having trouble tracking down your tenant, check with the neighbours or call the emergency contact listed on their rental application. Check to see whether the utility company has been notified to cancel the utilities; maybe the tenant has done a runner and not notified you.

Charging late fees

Charging tenants late fees when they don't pay their rent on time is one of the most effective ways to encourage on-time payments. Although many landlords have late charges, they are often enforced inconsistently and therefore become ineffective. Other landlords have very long grace periods or set their fees so high that they are unenforceable if challenged in court, so they are often waived. If you institute a late fee, keep these things in mind:

- ✔ Late charges can be controversial, and most courts rule that excessive late fees are not enforceable. Implementing and enforcing a late charge policy makes sense, as long as the policy is reasonable and relates to your actual out-of-pocket costs or expenses incurred by the late payment.

- ✔ Don't allow tenants to form the impression that your late charge policy approves of late rent payments as long as the late charges are collected. Your late charges should be high enough to discourage habitual lateness, but not so high as to be unreasonable. Send a written warning to those tenants who regularly pay late (even if they pay the late charges) clearly indicating that their late payments are unacceptable and a legal violation of the terms.

Include a Non-Payment of Rent Clause in the tenancy agreement. This clause should allow for a charge if the tenant fails to pay their rent within seven days of the due date. You should also include further charges that will be incurred for subsequent reminder letters if the tenant still fails to pay the rent.

If the tenant's rent is not forthcoming, you should take action, depending on how late it is:

- ✔ **Seven days late:** If the rent is not paid within seven days of the due date, it is reasonable to charge £30 for the first letter you send, advising the tenant she will be charged £20 for any subsequent letters if she remains in arrears.

✔ **Fourteen days late:** You should send a second letter threatening legal proceedings.

✔ **Twenty-one days late:** Visit the property to persuade the tenant to pay, but be sure not to hassle her.

✔ **If the rent is still unpaid:** Send a final letter to the tenant reminding her that this is her last opportunity to pay before you begin legal proceedings. (Keep in mind, however, that a mandatory possession order is unlikely to be granted until she has been in rent arrears for at least two months.)

Take legal advice before constructing a reminder letter and deciding on charges for repeat letters.

Handling bounced cheques

Rent cheques that bounce can cause major problems for your collection efforts, so you need to charge tenants a fee when one of their cheques is returned from your bank.

Often, when you contact your tenant, he will have some excuse for the returned cheque and tell you that his cheque will now be accepted. We recommend that you don't try to redeposit the cheque, however. The best policy is to demand your tenant immediately replace a returned cheque with a bank or building society cheque.

Housing Benefit

Housing Benefit enables people on low incomes to pay their rent and is not directly linked to whether they are working or receiving Jobseekers Allowance. Many landlords prefer not to take on tenants who receive Housing Benefit. But there is an advantage to letting your property to a tenant receiving Housing Benefit because the local authority can arrange for this money to be paid directly to you, with the tenant's consent, though this practice may stop soon. The Government is running pilot schemes in selected areas where Housing Benefits are paid directly to the tenant, apart from in exceptional circumstances. The amount of Housing Benefit a tenant receives depends on his or her income and savings. A rent officer may also assess the rent you are charging to compare it with prices charged by landlords with similar properties in the area.

A rent officer from the Housing Benefit department will carry out a pre-tenancy determination if you want to find out the maximum amount of rent that will be met by Housing Benefit.

If a tenant has a second returned cheque, regardless of the tenant's excuses, require all future payments be made only with a bank or building society cheque, which are guaranteed to have sufficient funds. But tenants can still request a stop-payment on a bank or building society cheque, claiming they were lost or stolen, so be sure to deposit the money straight away.

Like late charges, bounced cheque charges should be reasonable. Try setting the fee at £10 to £20 per cheque, or slightly higher than the amount your bank charges you for the cheque bouncing.

Unless the returned cheque is replaced before the end of your grace period, your tenant is also responsible for late charges.

Serving legal notices

If you're having trouble collecting rent from one of your tenants, you may need to pursue legal action. If your tenant is on an assured shorthold tenancy agreement with a term of six months, it may be possible, depending on how long he has lived in the property, to wait until the mandatory possession notice can be served in the normal way.

Mandatory possession is possible where the tenant is a full two months in arrears both at the time of service of the notice and at the actual court hearing. In the case of a weekly tenancy, the tenant must be a full 13 weeks in arrears.

Increasing the Rent

Raising the rent is one of the most difficult challenges landlords face. If you need to raise the rent, you may be worried that the tenant will leave, or you may not even know how much to increase the rent by.

Even if you're raising the rent for the first time in several years, most tenants will naturally have a very negative reaction to the rent increase. So you need to do your homework and make sure that your rent increase is reasonable and justified. When the rental market is tight, you should adjust your rents by small amounts with greater frequency rather than a very large increase more sporadically. Most tenants won't leave over a small rent increase.

Deciding when and how much

You can review the rent as often as specified in the tenancy agreement. If the agreement is for a fixed term, say 6 or 12 months, the rent usually remains the same for the duration of the contract. But you can review the rent at regular intervals during the tenancy, as long as you have a clause in the tenancy agreement stating this.

Normally, you can raise the rent as much and as often as your good business judgment and the competitive rental market allows. Of course, don't be too aggressive, or you'll lose your best tenants. Trying to get that extra £50 a month over and above what is reasonable could frighten off your tenant, leaving you with significant turnover costs plus lost rent while you hunt for a new one.

The best policy is to regularly review and survey the rental market to determine the current market rate for comparable rental properties – ones that are of similar size and condition and that have the same features and amenities.

Many wise landlords intentionally keep their rents slightly below the maximum the competitive rental market allows as a policy to retain the best tenants. Unless planning a major upgrade of your property with more upmarket tenants and much higher rents, tenant turnover is usually bad business.

Be careful when raising the rent so that you are not accused of imposing rent increases out of spite in response to something the tenant did or because you want to encourage the tenant to leave the property. As always, your best defence is to have a sensible rent increase policy, keep good records, and be consistently fair and equitable with all of your tenants.

Informing the tenant

The tenant must receive a month's notice of any increase in rent. If the tenant agrees to the increase, she should start paying it from the date specified at the end of the notice period. If the tenant doesn't agree to the increase, she must apply to a rent assessment committee, who decide what the rent should be. This application must be made before the date on which the new level of rent is due.

Rent assessment committees are independent of central and local governments and usually comprise three people, including a chairperson, surveyor, and someone who doesn't have any specialist knowledge of the market. They decide what the maximum rent should be, using comparable properties in the area and documents provided by you and your tenant. The committee may agree that the proposed rent is fair or suggest a lower or higher rate. The rate set by the committee is the legal maximum you can charge your tenant and restricts you from increasing the rent for another year.

Although you are legally required to give only a month's notice of a rent increase (if the rent is paid on a monthly basis), we recommend a minimum rental increase notice of 45 days. If the rent increase is significant (10 per cent or more), a 60-day written notice is advisable. Some owners fear that giving their tenant notice of a rent increase also gives them plenty of time to find another property. However, if you've set your increased rent properly you want your tenant to have the opportunity to compare the new rental rate to the market conditions rather than just overreact with a notice to vacate. If possible, inform your tenant personally of the pending rent increase and be sure to follow up by legally serving a formal written notice and keeping a copy in the tenant's file. The letter doesn't have to be a literary work, but you may consider attaching any market information obtained from your market survey so that your tenant can see that you have made an informed decision.

Sweetening the pill

Before increasing the rent, be sure to determine whether you will make improvements to the property to sweeten the pill. We suggest that you set a budget equivalent to three to six months of the rent increase and plan on making an immediate upgrade to the tenant's property. Often, just painting and cleaning or replacing the carpet can help your tenant accept the rent increase. Installing new light fixtures are usually appreciated as well and needn't cost too much money.

Chapter 4

Sweet and Sour: Keeping Good Tenants and Dealing with Problem Ones

*T*he key to your success as a landlord is an occupied rental property. But this basic fact is something many landlords quickly forget.

Although advertising your vacancy, having a well-polished presentation, knowing all the latest sales-closing techniques, implementing a thorough tenant-screening programme, and moving in your prized tenant with amazing efficiency are all important parts of your job, the reality is that the day your tenant moves in is the day your most important job – keeping your good tenants satisfied and happy – begins.

Your goal is to have your tenants stay and pay. If you offer a quality rental property at a reasonable price, you'll have lower turnover than other rental properties in your area.

As a landlord you are also going to come across a problem tenant or two. Some tenants don't pay their rent, disturb the neighbours, damage the property inside and out, or keep a growing collection of old bangers on the front lawn, and you need to take immediate steps to remove them from the rental property and replace them with someone else. But other tenants – like the one who pays his rent a few days late every single month, or the one who sneaks in an animal even though pets aren't allowed – are more subtle in the problems they present, and their behaviour may not warrant eviction.

In this chapter, we let you know what most tenants are looking for when renting a property so you can make sure you're meeting those needs. We also give you tips for handling some common tenant problems and discuss valuable alternatives to evictions.

What Tenants Want

If you're trying to raise your level of tenant satisfaction (and that should always be your goal), you need to determine what your tenants want and work out how to make sure they get it. Your tenants are basically looking for the following:

- ✔ Timely and effective communication
- ✔ Professional maintenance of the interior and common areas
- ✔ Respect for their privacy
- ✔ Fair and consistent policies and rules, as well as equal enforcement of them
- ✔ Reasonable rent in relation to what they're getting for their money

These crucial demands are covered in the following sections.

Timely and effective communication

A variety of issues concern most tenants – and those issues are usually fairly obvious. Good tenants don't like loud or noisy neighbours, unkempt common areas, broken or unserviceable items in their rental property, or unsubstantiated rent increases on a regular basis. But the good news is that most of these problems can be solved if you communicate well with your tenants.

The one problem that tenants will not ignore is a landlord's apathy. If you seem uncaring or nonchalant about your tenant's concerns, he will get the message that you don't value his business. The perception of apathy is often created by an unwillingness or failure to communicate. If you give your tenants the impression that you only care about them when their rent is late, you're headed straight down that apathy path.

Keep your tenants informed. No one likes surprises, and tenants are no different. If the pest control company cancels its routine appointment to check the property, let your tenant know right away. If the handyman you have employed to fix a broken shower door can only visit the property earlier in the day than previously arranged, call, or e-mail your tenant to avoid an unwelcome and inconvenient surprise. Common courtesy goes a long way.

Quick responses to maintenance requests

One way to set *your* rental property apart from your competition is to handle tenant maintenance requests quickly and professionally. Promptly resolving your tenants' problems will keep them happy.

Speed is of the essence

After a new tenant moves in, if he notes any problems, don't view these complaints as negatives. Instead, think of them as opportunities to let your tenant know that you care. By quickly and professionally addressing the problem, you actually improve your tenant relations. Successful landlords don't have to be perfect; they just need to admit the mistake or problem, communicate openly and candidly, and take the necessary steps to resolve it.

Rental property owners often also overlook punctuality when it comes to making repairs. Undoubtedly, you're a very busy person, but it's easy to lose sight of the fact that your tenants are busy, too. If you tell your tenants that you will call or meet them at a certain time, be sure to be there when you said you would – or at the very least, call and let them know if you're running late. Ensure that your letting agent, handyman, or contractors treat your tenants with the same level of respect as well.

Treating your tenants as important customers can be the best decision you ever make. When trying to solve a tenant's concern or complaint, try to ask yourself how you would want to be treated. Treating your tenants as you want to be treated makes your tenant relations much more pleasant, and you dramatically decrease your tenant turnover and improve your net income – a win-win situation for all!

The appliance of science

One of the most common complaints about landlords is that they are unwilling to maintain, and especially upgrade, their rental properties for the current tenants. In our experience, tenants have a valid complaint. Refusing to repaint, recarpet, or upgrade the appliances for a great tenant makes no sense. Because if you don't do it for the great tenant you already have, and that tenant is frustrated with your lack of effort and moves out, you'll have to do the work anyway in order to be competitive in the rental market and attract a new unproven tenant.

Respect for your tenants' privacy

One of the biggest complaints most tenants have is a landlord who fails to respect the tenant's privacy.

You can only enter the premises with advance written notice or the tenant's permission, except in case of an emergency. Although you only need to give tenants a minimum of 24 hours notice for access to the property, that isn't enough to maintain a positive and mutually respectful relationship with your tenants. Even though you own the rental property, the last thing you want your tenant to feel is that their home isn't really theirs. If you don't respect the privacy of your tenants in their own home they will be less likely to show respect for you or your rental property during or at the end of their tenancy.

If possible, you should only enter the property during normal business hours. We recommend limiting your request for entry to Monday to Saturday from 8:00 a.m. to 7:00 p.m., unless the tenant requests or voluntarily agrees to a different time.

Enforcement of house rules

A frequent source of tenant complaints is the landlord's failure to enforce reasonable policies and rules.

Good tenants actually *want* and *appreciate* fair and reasonable policies and rules. They know that, if they are quiet and respectful of their neighbours, their neighbours are more likely to treat them the same way. Establishing standard policies and house rules for your rental properties and enforcing them fairly is all part of the job of managing rental property.

Tenants talk to one another, and if you have several properties in the same block or area, they will quickly discover if you have different rules for different tenants. Inconsistent or selective enforcement of rules has legal implications, because it can be seen as a form of discrimination. For example, you may think that waiving a late fee for a tenant you've known for years but charging the late fee to a new tenant in similar circumstances is okay. After all, you've known the first tenant longer, and you're willing to forgive that oversight once in a while, right? Wrong. You can't have different interpretations of the rules, because the legal consequences you may face are severe.

Fair rent and increases

Rent increases are always unpopular, and if you don't handle them properly, they can easily lead to increased tension and tenant dissatisfaction. No one likes to pay more, but we all know that the good things in life aren't cheap. Most tenants don't mind paying a fair and competitive rent as long as they're sure you're not plaguing them with unnecessary rent hikes. As long as the increase keeps your rent in line with that charged by landlords with similar properties in your area, your tenants probably won't object. If you are raising it by more than the rent charged on similar properties, you should think of a couple of sweeteners, such as repairs or improvements, to justify the increase.

Although they may initially be upset with the increase, your tenants may be thinking to themselves that you will now finally be able to address the peeling paint and faded curtains. And if your rental property has peeling paint and old, tatty curtains and you've just increased the rent, you'd better be sure to address those problems right away, not months down the road, if you want your tenants to be satisfied.

There is nothing wrong with increasing your price – after all, you're running a business, not a charity. But common sense and prudence dictate that you explain to your tenants the reasons for the rent increase and what benefits are in it for them.

Renewing Tenancy Agreements

Tenancy agreement renewals are a sign that you're doing a good job at keeping your tenants satisfied and meeting their needs. Of course, renewing tenancy agreements is also one of your most productive activities as a landlord.

In a competitive rental market with increasing rents, most tenants who intend to stay will be glad to renew their current tenancy agreement or even sign a new one at a higher, but still reasonable, rent. Renewing a tenancy agreement in a strong rental market may not be in your best interest, however, because it prevents you from raising the rent or changing any terms during the period covered by the new agreement. Plus, with a tenancy agreement in place, evicting a problem tenant is much more difficult.

If you want your tenant to stay, don't be afraid to approach her and ask her to sign another tenancy agreement effective from when the current one expires. Contact your tenant at least a couple of months before the tenancy agreement expires.

Another option is to do nothing at the end of the fixed term agreement and allow the tenancy to automatically become a periodic one – month to month if you collect rent monthly. This avoids putting the tenant on the spot to renew her assured shorthold tenancy for a new fixed term, but allows her the freedom to leave with one full month's notice in writing, ending on the last day of a period. Landlords must give two months' notice ending on the last day of a tenancy period to terminate a periodic tenancy.

If the tenant moves out, you'll incur extensive turnover costs for maintenance, painting, and cleaning, plus you'll lose rent for every day the rental property is empty. So why not make a few upgrades to the rental property a couple of months before the tenancy agreement expires, just as a reminder that you care about the tenant's satisfaction.

Recognising and Responding to Common Tenant Problems

The level of response you have toward a problem tenant depends on how severe the problem is and how frequently it occurs. Some issues – including non-payment of rent, additional occupants not on the tenancy agreement, noise or disturbances, and threats of violence or intimidation – are breaches of the tenancy agreement and clearly call for action. You should document non-payment of rent along with other breaches of the tenancy agreement in writing, using a Tenancy Agreement Violation Letter, like the one shown in Form 4-1.

Whenever you have a problem with a tenant, documenting the problem is critical. Even minor problems are worth documenting, because over time, they may add up or increase in severity. If you find yourself needing to evict a tenant, having written proof of how long the problem has dragged on is necessary, especially if the matter comes to court.

Late payment of rent

One of the toughest issues you'll encounter is how to deal with a tenant who is consistently late in paying her rent. In other respects, the tenant may not create any problems, but she just can't seem to get the rent in on time. You may have even had to serve a Notice of Non-payment of Rent in order to get the tenant to pay – and even then, she may have not included the late charge. In our experience, this nagging problem won't go away unless you put a stop to it; flick back to Book V, Chapter 3 for more information on dealing with rent collection problems.

Tenancy Agreement Violation Letter

_____

Date

_____

Name

_____

_____

Address

Dear _____

This is a formal reminder that your Tenancy Agreement does not allow:

_____

_____

It has come to our attention that recently or beginning _____ and continuing to the present, you have broken one or more terms of your Tenancy by:

_____

_____

_____

_____

It is our sincere desire that you will enjoy living in our rental property. To make sure this happens, we enforce the Policies and Rules and all terms and conditions of your Tenancy Agreement. So please immediately:

_____

_____

_____

_____

If you are unable to promptly resolve this matter, we will exercise our legal right to begin eviction proceedings.

Please feel free to contact us if you would like to discuss this issue.

Sincerely,

_____

Owner/Manager

Form 4-1: Tenancy Agreement Violation Letter.

When you're faced with a tenant who just can't seem to pay her rent on time, you have many factors to consider (such as whether the tenant is creating any other problems for you). But the strength of the rental market is usually the most important issue. If it's a tenant's market and you know that finding another tenant to rent the property will be difficult, you may be willing to be more flexible and tolerant.

Even if you know you'd have trouble finding another tenant, you shouldn't ignore the problem of a tenant who consistently pays late. Clearly inform the tenant in writing that she has breached the tenancy agreement – and be sure to do so each and every time she pays late. If you fail to enforce your late charges, the tenant can later argue that you've waived your rights to collect future late charges. Be sure to let the tenant know in writing that very late payments are grounds for eviction – even if you're not necessarily willing to go that route just yet.

Additional occupants

Tenants frequently abuse the guest policy by moving additional occupants into their rental property for extended periods of time. But you may have trouble determining the difference between a temporary guest and a new full-time live-in occupant.

If you suspect that your tenant has moved an additional occupant into his rental property, your first step should be to talk to your tenant to find out what's going on. Get your tenant's story before jumping to any conclusions. This policy is sound not only because it's considerate, but also because you need to be careful to avoid claims of discrimination, particularly if the additional occupants are children.

If you find that the tenant is not in compliance with your guest policy, immediately send him a Tenancy Agreement Violation Letter in which you should indicate that he must ensure the additional occupant leaves as soon as possible or be formally added to the tenancy agreement as a tenant, as long as the property has room for another tenant. If the new occupant is an adult, that person must complete a rental application, go through the tenant-screening process, and sign the tenancy agreement if approved. If the tenant fails to co-operate, you may need to take legal action.

Inappropriate noise levels

You usually hear about a noisy tenant from one of the tenant's neighbours. Some landlords we know who live near their rental properties often ask the neighbouring tenants to call them when the problem tenant is generating unacceptable noise levels and then go round themselves to investigate. The advantage of this policy is that you are witnessing first-hand the extent of the problem – information which can be useful when speaking to the noisy tenant. In such a scenario, it is also quite useful to knock on the tenant's door to have a word with them while the music is blaring because the tenant will find it harder to deny that the noise is excessive. If the problem continues, you should issue a written warning.

Most local councils have a special unit known as a *noise patrol*. You can find details of this out-of-hours service in your telephone directory. The noise patrol is responsible for coming out and checking complaints about excessive noise levels. If the tenants continue to cause problems with loud music or continual parties late into the night, the neighbouring tenants may well have to call out the noise patrol to monitor the level of noise, particularly if talking to the noisy tenants about the problem doesn't make any difference.

Encourage tenants to air any grievances they may have about their neighbours, who are also your tenants, in the first instance by writing to you. Neighbours usually don't want to go to court to testify; they just want you to quickly solve the problem and allow them to keep their anonymity. But if the noisy tenant disputes the charges, the courts are usually reluctant to accept your unsubstantiated testimony – and the neighbour's testimony becomes critical. Evidence from your local council's noise patrol, if they have to be called in, and a written complaint made at the same time by a neighbour, carry a lot of weight.

Exploring Alternatives to Eviction

Evictions are not only expensive but emotionally draining as well. They can be costly in terms of lost rent, legal fees, property damage, and turnover expenses. And they can earn a negative reputation for your rental property with good tenants in the area. So be sure to evaluate each situation carefully and only turn to eviction as a last resort.

When you're looking for an alternative to evicting a problem tenant, don't underestimate the importance of communicating with your tenant. And for your records, make a note of any conversations you have or agreements you reach.

If the most likely outcome of a problem with a tenant is an expensive and time-consuming eviction, do your best to minimise or cut your losses. A County Court Judgment (CCJ) against a tenant without any assets won't help your cash flow, but a non-paying or bad tenant is much worse than no tenant at all. Your primary goal should be to regain possession of the rental property and find a new tenant as quickly as possible.

Negotiating a voluntary move-out

You may be able to negotiate an agreement with your tenant whereby she voluntarily moves out of the rental property. Some landlords have negotiated agreements with their problem tenants, in which they (the landlords) forget about the unpaid rent if the tenant agrees to leave by a mutually agreed upon date. Other owners have agreed to refund the tenant's full deposit immediately after the tenant has vacated the property (as long as no significant damage has been done to the property). Although you may feel strongly that your tenant should keep her side of the tenancy agreement, a voluntary move-out may work to your advantage if you can avoid legal action and don't have to worry about the problem any more.

While legal action may be daunting, don't be afraid to start legal proceedings against a tenant if that's the only solution left. You may well need to threaten legal proceedings at some stage in order to get what you want – if this is the case, you must be prepared to act on your threat otherwise you'll lose face, and you won't ever get your money.

Never count on a verbal agreement. Any voluntary agreement to move out must be in writing.

Using mediation or arbitration services

If you aren't able to reach an agreement with your tenant on moving out voluntarily, consider taking your dispute to a neutral third-party mediator or arbitration. *Mediation* is an informal opportunity for both parties to resolve their disputes with the assistance of a local mediation group at little or no cost. Often confused with mediation, *arbitration* is legally binding and enforceable and can be a relatively quick and inexpensive alternative to legal action. Mediation typically involves only the parties to the dispute (you and your tenant), whereas arbitration often uses solicitors, witnesses, and experts. Many organisations offer both mediation and arbitration services, so if mediation does not resolve the issue, you can always try arbitration.

Taking your tenant to court

Your nearest county court is the place to go if you have problems with tenants caused by non-payment of rent or if you want to evict a tenant. Speak to a court official who can explain the procedure to you; remember, though, that they can't give legal advice. Many cases relating to property rental are heard in the small claims court, which is part of your local county court. You should go to the small claims court if you're claiming £5,000 or less.

Evicting a Tenant

Unfortunately, some tenants just don't pay their rent; others break the rules or are involved in criminal activities. In these situations, after you've explored your other options, you may have no other reasonable alternative but an eviction. The eviction process can be intimidating and costly, but keep in mind that allowing the tenant to stay only prolongs the problem.

Serving legal notices

The law states that non-paying or unsatisfactory tenants can be evicted after eight weeks of behaviour that directly defies their tenancy agreement. In order to evict a tenant, you have to instruct a solicitor to serve an eviction notice on your tenant, which must be handed to her in person. You have to pay for this service; be aware that you may not recover your money. If your tenant does not leave or pay up what she owes of her own accord, the next step is to take her to court, if you think doing so is worth it.

Taking a tenant to court is now a quick, simple, and straightforward process. County court actions can even be conducted online these days at www.money claim.gov.uk/csmco2/index.jsp. You don't need to be afraid: Just tell yourself that you are owed money, and tenants who don't pay their rent or damage rented property shouldn't be allowed to get away with it.

Going to court

If your tenant has fallen into rent arrears, you may feel that an accelerated possession procedure (see 'Accelerated possession' later in this chapter), is not for you if you want to recover outstanding rent, because with this procedure you can only regain possession of the property and the costs of bringing the action. If the rent is late, write to the tenant immediately, saying that the rent doesn't seem to have been paid. It may be a simple mistake; perhaps the tenant just forgot to do it or she had a mix-up with her bank account. If the tenant puts the situation right immediately, that should be the end of the problem. But if you don't get a response, write to the tenant again, giving her 14 days to pay the amount in full and stating that, if she fails to do so, court proceedings will be instigated.

Nobody wants a CCJ (County Court Judgment) against them – see 'Exploring Alternatives to Eviction' earlier in this chapter if you're not sure what this is – because it makes renting another property or getting any form of credit very hard. Any right-minded tenant will want to avoid that scenario at all costs and may well pay the money owed before it comes to court.

If they don't, you must fill out a form, available from your local county court, detailing the amount you are owed in arrears, plus any damage to the property or goods stolen. You'll be charged a court fee, calculated on a sliding scale and depending on the amount owed. If you win your case, you get this money back from the tenant.

The court then sends the completed form to the tenant. He can either pay up there and then, counterclaim, or let the judge decide the outcome of the matter at a court hearing.

If the tenant simply can't afford to pay you, the courts say that there is no point in taking legal action in the first place to get back the money he owes you in unpaid rent. A judge can order the money to be paid, but it is up to you to enforce this judgment.

If you have started legal proceedings against a tenant, never discuss the matter with them in person or on the phone. The conversation could turn nasty or the tenant could try to emotionally blackmail you into giving more time or another chance. If you can, distance yourself from the conversation and tell the tenant that the court will decide on the outcome.

Accelerated possession

It doesn't have to end up in court. An *accelerated possession procedure* enables tenants to be evicted without a court hearing, purely on the basis of a written representation. Such a procedure does not include a claim for rent owed to you however, so if your tenant owes you a lot of money this procedure may not be the best solution for you. But it is a means whereby bad tenants can be evicted – and quickly.

You can use this procedure where the tenancy is of the Assured Shorthold kind, claiming possession under Section 21 of the Housing Act 1998. If your tenant has an Assured Tenancy dating back to before 1997 you can use this procedure under Section 8 of the Housing Act. Whichever tenancy agreement you have, you must supply reasonable grounds for taking the action.

Under Section 21, reasonable grounds include:

- ✔ The tenancy was for a fixed period, which has expired.
- ✔ The existing tenancy is for an unspecified period.
- ✔ You have given your tenant at least two months' written notice under Section 21, informing him that you wanted possession of the rental property.

Claiming under Section 8 of the Housing Act 1988 is more complicated and more limited. Grounds include:

- ✔ The property is your main home and you want to reclaim it.
- ✔ You intend to live in the property as your main home.
- ✔ The tenancy was a holiday let, let to students, or is now needed as a residence by a minister of religion.

Where these grounds apply, you must give your tenants at least four months' notice before the end of the tenancy. If he still fails to vacate the property, you then need to file your application to the court, along with all the papers required, including a copy of your tenancy agreement after the four months are up. The tenant is given 14 days to reply. If an order for possession is made, the tenant is normally told to leave the property within 14 days. The court may extend this period for up to six weeks maximum if the tenant can prove that to leave within this timeframe would cause exceptional hardship.

Because an accelerated possession procedure is carried out purely on written evidence, all of your documents must be in order. The tenancy agreement must be written and can't be verbal.

Enforcing County Court Judgments

If a CCJ is made against the tenant for non-payment of rent, the judge decides how much the tenant needs to pay you back. If the tenant doesn't pay, she could be paid a visit by a bailiff with the legal authority to remove the goods to sell to pay off the debt she owes you. Alternatively, the judge may decide that the debt should be deducted in instalments from the tenant's wages or benefit.

Chapter 5

Moving Out Tenants

*A*lthough hanging on to your great tenants forever would be nice, the reality is that all tenants leave at some point. Your goal is to make the experience as straightforward and painless as possible, maintaining clear communication and having procedures in place to deal with every eventuality.

Don't assume that your tenants are familiar with the proper move-out procedures. You need to have a proactive plan that gets your tenants involved in the process of preparing the rental property for the next tenant.

This chapter covers the importance of written notice (the Move-Out Information Letter) and proper procedures for the return of the deposit. We also cover the definition of 'normal wear and tear'. And we help you handle special move-out situations.

Start preparing for your tenants' eventual move-out when they first move in. The Tenant Information Letter (covered in more detail in Book V, Chapter 2) provides the tenants with the legal requirements of move-out as well as your expectations for giving proper notice. The inventory (also covered in Chapter 2) is completed upon move-in to establish the condition of all aspects of the rental property. Use this same detailed inventory to evaluate the condition of the property when the tenant moves out and calculate the appropriate charges, if any.

Requiring Written Notice

When giving notice that they plan to move, most tenants often just call or verbally mention it when they see you – even though your tenancy agreement is likely to contain clauses that require written notice.

Some tenants put their notice in writing by sending you a simple letter. Often these written notices are only one or two sentences and can be ambiguous, leaving out critical information or important details. Although any type of written notice from the tenant is usually legal, a proper notice should provide much more information.

To be sure that you're complying with the law in all regards, ask your tenants to use a Tenant's Notice of Intent to Vacate Rental Property (like the one shown in Form 5-1). This form contains important information, including the tenant's approval of your ability to enter upon reasonable notice to show the rental property to workers, contractors, and prospective tenants.

When you receive verbal or written notice, go ahead and honour the date of the notice but still ask the tenant to complete the form. Insisting that the tenant gives you a written Notice of Intent to Vacate is a good policy. If you don't have this information in writing, opportunities for misunderstandings can arise. You may not remember the move-out date and be caught by surprise, or you may schedule a new move-in only to find that the tenant won't be out until the following week. Surprises are not a good thing for landlords!

Time really is of the essence when it comes to a tenant moving out. In most cases, they need their deposit back so that they can pass it on to their next landlord. Or they might need the deposit to put towards some of the costs of buying their own home, if that's their next move.

Tenants' deposits must now be held under the rules of one of the Tenancy Deposit Schemes, so you need to comply exactly with the scheme rules to avoid falling foul of the law. If you opt to use the *custodial scheme*, the scheme will hold the funds so the return of the deposit to the tenant is out of your hands. However, if you opt for one of the *insurance schemes* you are still responsible for repaying the deposit direct to the tenant, unless you're in dispute over deductions. For more on Tenancy Deposit Schemes, take a look at Book IV, Chapter 3.

Tenant's Notice of Intent to Vacate Rental Property

_____
Date

_____
Owner/Manager

_____
_____
Property Address

Dear _____,

This is to notify you that the undersigned Tenant,
_____
hereby give your written notice of intent to vacate the rental property at
_____
_____ on
_____

I understand that my Tenancy Agreement requires a minimum of _____ days' notice before I move. This Tenant's Notice of Intent to Vacate Rental Property actually provides _____ days' notice. I understand that I am responsible for paying rent through, the earlier of: (1) the end of the current Tenancy; (2) the end of the required notice period per the Tenancy Agreement; or (3) until another tenant approved by the Owner/Agent has moved in or begun paying rent.

(Optional Information)
We are sorry to learn that you are leaving. We would appreciate a moment of your time to tell us the reason for your move:

___ Moving to a larger property _____ Moving to a smaller property __ Buying a home

___ Moving out of area
___ Dissatisfied with rental property (explain)
_____
___ Dissatisfied with management (explain)
_____
___ Other (explain)
_____
Is there anything we can do to encourage you to continue as our tenant?
_____
_____
_____

Form 5-1: Tenant's Notice of Intent to Vacate Rental Property (Page 1 of 2).

Other comments

_____
_____
_____

In accordance with our Tenancy Agreement, I agree to allow the Owner/Agent reasonable access with advance notice in order to show our rental property to prospective tenants, workmen, or contractors.

Sincerely,

_____

Tenant

Form 5-1: Tenant's Notice of Intent to Vacate Rental Property (Page 2 of 2).

Giving Your Tenants a Move-Out Information Letter

Many tenants are afraid that you'll try to cheat them out of their deposit refund, but these fears should now be allayed by the Tenancy Deposit Scheme. Just as the Tenant Information Letter (covered in Book V, Chapter 2) helps to get the tenant/landlord relationship off to a good start, the Move-Out Information Letter (shown in Form 5-2) can help end the relationship on a positive note.

Provide your tenants with a Move-Out Information Letter as soon as they give their written notice to vacate. This letter thanks your tenants for making your rental property their home and provides them with the procedures to follow to prepare the rental property for the final move-out inspection. It also informs them of your policies and method of returning their deposits after any legal deductions. Although your tenancy agreement and the Tenancy Deposit Scheme information you gave to your tenant may contain information on the deposit refund process, most tenants appreciate receiving this information so they know what to expect without having to search for their tenancy agreement while they're trying to pack.

Move-Out Information Letter

Date _____
Tenant Name (s) _____
Rental Property Address _____

Dear _____

We are pleased that you selected our property for your home and hope that you enjoyed living here. Although we are disappointed to lose you as a tenant, we wish you good luck in the future. We want your move-out to go smoothly and end our relationship on a positive note.

Moving time is always chaotic and you are likely to have many things on your mind, including getting the maximum amount of your deposit back. Contrary to some landlords, we want to be able to return your deposit promptly and in full. Your deposit is £ _____ Note that your deposit shall not be applied to your last month's rent as the deposit is to ensure the fulfilment of tenancy conditions and is to be used only as a contingency against any damages to the rental property.

This move-out letter describes how we expect your rental property to be left and what our procedures are for returning your deposit. Basically, we expect you to leave your rental property in the same condition it was when you moved in, except for normal wear and tear that occurred during your tenancy. To refresh your memory, a copy of your signed inventory is attached reflecting the condition of the rental property at the beginning of your tenancy. We will be using this same detailed inventory when we inspect your rental property upon move-out and will deduct the cost of any necessary cleaning and the costs of repairs, not considered normal wear and tear, from your deposit.

To maximise your chances of a full and prompt refund, we suggest that you go through the inventory line by line and make sure that all items are clean and free from damage, except for normal wear and tear. All cupboards, shelves, drawers, worktops, storage, fridge freezer, and exterior items should be completely free of items. Feel free to tick off completed items on this copy of the inventory, as we will use the original for your final inspection.

Some of our tenants prefer to let professionals complete these items. You can contact your own professional or, upon request, we will be glad to refer you to our service providers so that you can focus on other issues of your move. You will work directly with the service provider on costs and payment terms, knowing that you are working with someone who can prepare the property for the final inspection. Call us if you would like contact information or for any questions as to the type of cleaning we expect.

Please make sure you remove all personal possessions, including furniture, clothes, household items, food, plants, cleaning supplies, and any bags of rubbish or loose items that belong to you. Of course, please do not remove any appliances, fixtures, or other items installed or attached to your rental property unless you have our prior written approval.

Please contact the appropriate utility companies and arrange for the disconnection of the phone and utility services in your name.

Please contact us when all the conditions have been satisfied to arrange an inspection of your rental property during daylight hours. To avoid a key replacement charge, please return all your keys at the time you vacate the property.

You have listed _____ as the move-out date in your notice. Please be reminded that you will be charged £ ____ per day for each partial or full day after the above move-out date that you remain in the rental property or have possession of the keys. If you need to extend your tenancy for any reason, you must contact us immediately. Please be prepared to provide your forwarding address where we may post your deposit cheque.

It is our policy to return all deposits to an address you provide within _____ days after you move out **and** return all keys. If any deductions are made for rent owed or other unpaid charges, for damages beyond normal wear and tear, or for failure to properly clean, an itemised explanation will be included with the deposit accounting.

If you have any questions, please contact us at _____

Thank you again for making our property your home. It has been a pleasure to have you as our tenant(s) and please accept our best wishes and thanks for your co-operation. Should you need a reference for a future landlord please don't hesitate to contact us.

Yours sincerely,

_____
Owner/Manager

Form 5-2: A Move-Out Information Letter.

The Move-Out Information Letter includes a reminder to the tenants that their deposit cannot be applied to the last month's rent and is only to be used as a contingency against any damages to the rental property or for other lawful charges. If no portion of the tenant's deposit was called 'last month's rent', you are not legally obliged to apply it in this way. Unless your tenancy agreement uses this wording don't allow your tenants to try to apply their deposit toward their final month's rent, or you may not have enough money on hand to cover any legally allowed charges.

If the tenant moving out is a good one, ask him if you can provide him with a letter of recommendation. A positive reference can be very helpful to tenants, whether they are moving to a new rental property or buying a home. This kind of offer is welcome and courteous – and one that most tenants have never received from prior landlords. If you make this kind of offer, the tenant will often work extra hard to make sure that the rental property is clean and undamaged in order to thank you for your positive comments and offer to provide that letter.

A good way to motivate your tenants to comply with your move-out procedures is to give them a simple reminder that they will have their deposit returned to them in full if they leave the rental property in clean condition, with no damage beyond normal wear and tear.

Inspecting the Property's Condition at Move-Out

Try to schedule the move-out inspection with your vacating tenants just *after* they have removed all their furnishings and personal items, handed over all their keys, and had the utilities disconnected. The only way to determine the condition of some parts of the property is to wait until the rental property is vacant. Also, you want to make sure that the tenant doesn't do additional damage after the inspection while they're removing their possessions.

Unfortunately, you can't always arrange to do the inspection with the tenant at this time. If that's the case, conduct the move-out inspection as soon as possible and preferably with a witness present. If you wait too long to inspect the property and then discover damage, the tenant may claim that someone else must have caused the damage, and you may face an uphill battle in court.

Noting damages

Tenants have been known to show up for the final inspection but deny that they know anything about the damaged items you find. Refer to your inventory in these situations. If the item is clearly indicated on the inventory as being in good condition when the tenant moved in, the tenant doesn't stand much of a chance. However, if the inventory remarks are blank or vague, you may have some problems justifying a deduction. As you are the rental housing professional, the courts hold you to a higher standard and interpret your vague documents in favour of the tenant.

Although the tenant should be present for the move-out inspection, you may not know the actual charges for certain items until later, when the work is completed and you receive the final invoice from a contractor. Plus, damages are often not discovered until the rental property preparation work is being done. So just note that the item is damaged on the inventory and advise the tenant that you reserve the right to deduct the actual repair costs. When you know the actual charges, you can fill in the column on the inventory for the estimated cost of repair or replacement and include a copy of the completed inventory with your deposit itemisation.

Under the rules of the Tenancy Deposit Scheme, landlords must justify any deductions they propose taking from the deposit. Under the insurance schemes, any disputed amount has to be placed in the custody of the scheme administrators pending arbitration, with the balance being paid back to the tenant immediately. Tenants are often counting on the return of their full deposit and will request the chance to do some more cleaning or make repairs if you indicate that deductions will be made. If they can act quickly and you feel that they are capable of the work, you may want to give them a second chance at cleaning or simple repairs. However, be wary of tenant repairs that could cost you more to correct later or that create liability issues. Even a simple touch-up to the paintwork by your tenants can become a disaster if they are sloppy decorators or mismatch the paint. When it comes to the majority of repairs, you're better off refusing the tenant's request to fix them himself.

Defining 'normal wear and tear'

Legally you are entitled to claim for damages beyond 'normal wear and tear'. But virtually all disputes over deposits revolve around this elusive definition. Your job is to be able to tell the difference between normal wear and tear and justify this if necessary to an arbitrator. More serious damage can then reasonably be claimed for deduction from your tenant's deposit.

The standard definition of *normal wear and tear* is deterioration or damage to the property expected to occur from normal usage. The problem then is what is considered to be 'normal usage'. Decisions vary from court to court. If you ask 100 small claims court judges, you are likely to get nearly 100 different interpretations of this definition.

The bottom line is that there are no hard and fast rules on what constitutes normal wear and tear and what the tenant can legally be charged. Table 5-1 gives you some room for comparison to help you determine what normal wear and tear is and what goes beyond normal into damage you can charge for.

Table 5-1	Normal Wear and Tear versus Damage
Normal Wear and Tear	*Damage beyond Normal Wear and Tear*
Smudges on the walls near light switches	Crayon marks on the walls or ceiling
Minor marks on the walls or doors	Large marks on, or holes in, the walls, or doors
A few small tack holes	Numerous nail-holes that require filling and/or painting
Faded, peeling, or cracked paint	Completely dirty or scuffed painted walls
Carpet worn thin from normal use	Carpet stained by bleach or dye
Carpet with moderate dirt or spots	Carpet that has been ripped or has pet stains
Carpet or curtains faded by the sun	Carpet or curtains with cigarette burns
Moderately dirty blinds	Damaged or missing blinds

Deducting repairs from the deposit

Before the introduction of the Tenancy Deposit Scheme, some landlords saw the tenant's deposit as a source of additional income that is theirs for the taking. However, as a business practice, the return of the full deposit is actually much better for the landlord. The only lawful deductions from the tenant's deposit are for unpaid rent, damages beyond normal wear and tear, keys, and cleaning.

If you claim deductions from the deposit, make sure that your paperwork is accurate and detailed. Because property damage deductions are only for damages beyond normal wear and tear, you need to be sure that your description of the item explains why the damage exceeds that. If you merely indicate, 'Pet damage – £100' on the Deposit Itemisation Form, you may very well be challenged. However, if you provide details like 'Steam cleaned carpeting in living room to remove extensive pet urine stains – £100', you greatly improve your chances in the arbitration process or if the matter gets to court or, better yet, of not even being challenged in the first place.

Excessive claims for deductions almost always lead to acrimonious discussions with the former tenant that result in arbitration under the Tenancy Deposit Scheme or end up in the small claims court. Spending your day in court can be very counterproductive, particularly because the courts often seek a compromise that requires at least a partial return of the deposit to the aggrieved tenant. You may feel that there are no legal bases for a judge to find in the tenant's favour, but the court may rule merely to compensate the tenant for their time and costs of going to court.

Here are some guidelines to follow when listing the charges on your Deposit Itemisation Form:

- ✔ **Indicate the specific item damaged.** List each damaged fixture, appliance, or piece of furniture separately.

- ✔ **Indicate the specific location of the damaged item.** Note the room and which wall, ceiling, or corner of the room the damaged item is located in. Use compass directions, if possible.

- ✔ **Note the type and extent of the damage.** Be sure to describe the damage in detail using appropriate adjectives, such as *substantial, excessive, minor, scratched, stained, ripped, cracked, burned,* or *chipped.*

- ✔ **Note the type and extent of repair done.** Describe the repair, using adjectives such as *patch, paint, steam-clean,* or *refinish.* Indicate if an item was so damaged that it had to be replaced and, if so, why.

- ✔ **Indicate the cost of the repair or replacement.** List exactly how much you actually spent or plan to spend based on a third-party estimate.

Some landlords give all vacating tenants a pricing chart with a list of prices that will be charged for different services or damaged items. These owners believe the pricing charts minimise disputes because the charges are predetermined and are given to the tenants in advance. Further, they argue that the tenants will see how expensive repairs are and will take care of some of the work on their own. There is some logic to this method, but it also poses some potential problems. For example, prices frequently change, and courts insist on actual, not estimated, charges. So the price chart would have to be consistently updated. Plus, many items can't possibly have preset prices for repair, and different contractors may charge different amounts. You can be assured that the arbitrator or judge won't rule in your favour if your actual charge turns out to be much higher than the preset charge indicated on your pricing chart. But if the tenant challenges your deductions and your actual invoice shows you paid less than what you claimed, you'd better have your cheque book ready.

Deposit disputes are the number one problem in tenant/landlord relationships. Although proper use of the inventory and the Tenancy Deposit Scheme should eliminate many of these disputes, the definition of 'normal wear and tear' is one of life's greatest mysteries. You can minimise arguments with former tenants and avoid arbitration or small claims courts by claiming only fair and reasonable deductions and providing the deposit accounting and any refund within reasonable time limits.

Using a Deposit Itemisation Form

After you have inspected the rental property and determined the proper charges, you need to prepare the Deposit Itemisation Form (shown in Form 5-3). You need to complete this form and give the vacating tenant a cheque for any balance due within a reasonable period of time. If you are in the custodial scheme you'll need to instruct the scheme administrator to repay the deposit accordingly.

Send the deposit accounting and refund as soon as you are sure of the final charges. Tenants need this money, and the longer they wait the more impatient and upset they get – and the more likely they are to challenge your charges. Of course, you need to make sure that you have inspected the entire rental property carefully and found any tenant damage beyond ordinary wear and tear. In theory, you can always seek reimbursement for items discovered after you refund the deposit, but your chances of collecting would be slim.

Some tenants want to personally pick up the deposit as soon as possible; others won't even tell you where they can be reached. Generally, you post the Deposit Itemisation Form to the address provided by your tenants on their Tenant's Notice to Vacate Form. If you do not have your vacating tenant's forwarding address, send the deposit itemisation to their last known address, which may be your own rental property. There's a chance they've had their post forwarded to their new address; if not, the cheque will just be returned to you.

If your Deposit Itemisation Form and refund cheque are returned undeliverable, be sure to save the returned envelope in case the former tenant claims you never sent the legally required accounting. Also send the deposit via recorded mail in order to prove that you sent it and the date you sent it on.

Deposit Itemisation Form

Deductions for unpaid rent, damages beyond normal wear and tear, and cleaning

_____
Date

_____
Name

_____
_____

_____
Forwarding address

Rental property address: _____

Move-in date _____ Date that Notice to Vacate was received _____

Actual date vacated _____

Rent _____   New tenant move-in date, if applicable _____

1. Deposit received   £ _____

2. Interest on deposit   £ _____

3. Total credit (sum of 1+2)   £ _____

4. Defaults in rent covered by any court judgement   £ _____
_____
_____
_____

5. Court judgement for rent, costs, solicitor fees   £ _____

6. Itemised property damages and repairs   £ _____
_____
_____
_____

7. Necessary cleaning of property upon vacation   £ _____

8. Other deductions   £ _____

9. Total deductions (sum of 4 – 8)   £ _____

10. Balance due

_____ Total amount Owner owes Tenant   £ _____

_____ Total amount Tenant owes Tenant   £ _____

Comments
_____
_____
_____

Form 5-3: A Deposit Itemisation Form.

Tenants, particularly housemates or married couples in the midst of a separation or divorce, may fight amongst themselves over the deposit. Legally, the deposit belongs equally to all tenants who signed the tenancy agreement, unless otherwise agreed in writing. If you arbitrarily split the cheque between the tenants, you can find yourself liable to the other party. So always make your deposit refund cheque payable jointly to all adult tenants; then post copies of your Deposit Itemisation Form to each of the tenants at their respective forwarding addresses. Include the deposit refund cheque to one of the tenants with a copy of the cheque to the others. Leave it up to the tenants to handle the endorsement of the cheque. However, if you have a court order or a written agreement or instructions signed by all tenants, you can handle the deposit as directed.

Unless the tenancy agreement states otherwise, the landlord should repay the deposit with interest, even if you do not keep it in an interest-earning account. The amount of interest is unlikely to be high, given that interest rates are so low, and although paying interest on the deposit may not be required by law, it is good practice to do so.

Handling Special Move-Out Situations

Although you may have worked very hard to make sure everything goes smoothly during your tenant's move-out, a few special situations inevitably arise. And the more you know as a landlord about how to handle these situations, the less likely they are to become significant problems.

When damage and unpaid rent exceed the deposit

As a landlord, you will probably encounter a situation in which a tenant's deposit is not sufficient to cover the unpaid rent and the damage caused by the tenant. Under Tenancy Deposit Scheme rules, you will not now be able to claim deduction of unpaid rent form the deposit. You'll have to deal with unpaid rent separately and if necessary you'll need to pursue any debt and excess damage above and beyond the deposit amount through the Small Claims Court.

The crucial thing for both damage claims and rent arrears, either through a Tenancy Deposit Scheme arbitration process or through the Small Claims Court, is having good evidence to prove your case. Having a good inventory – either one you have completed yourself with the tenant's approval or one produced by an independent inventory clerk – is very important here. You can find a really useful list of independent inventory clerks at `www.landlord zone.co.uk/Directory/inventory-services.htm`.

Photograph and video evidence is also useful, but to be admissible as evidence you must have got the tenant to sign and date the back of every photograph, and videos must be dated too.

Small claims can be expensive if you use a solicitor because you cann't claim legal costs. A solicitor's fee often outweighs any gain from winning your case. However, the system is designed for the layman, so with some careful attention to detail when processing the paperwork and reading a guide , you can work through the Small Claims Court process yourself. Liz Barclay's *UK Law and Your Rights For Dummies* (Wiley) can help you here, and you can also find more information at `www.hmcourts-service.gov.uk`.

Be sure to always keep track of the actual costs for damages even if you don't intend to pursue the tenant for the balance owed. This way you can prove your expenses in court if you ever need to.

Even if your lawful claims for deductions exceed the departing tenant's deposit charges, you must provide the tenant and the Tenancy Deposit Scheme arbitrator with a full accounting of the damages. This is true even if you file a small claims lawsuit for the balance due. So be sure to always follow the required procedures for the accounting of the deposit.

When disputes arise over the deposit

No matter how fair and reasonable you are with your deposit deductions, sooner or later you are bound to have a former tenant challenge your deductions. Even if your deductions were proper and you are sure that you're right, going to court over the deposit deduction may cost you more than the amount in dispute. Often, the actual disagreement is over a relatively small amount of money.

For example, you may have deducted £100 for touching up the paintwork, but your former tenant may believe that the charge should be only £50. So you're only arguing over a £50 difference. Explore possible negotiations to resolve the matter before going into dispute with the Tenancy Deposit Scheme arbitrator or to court. If you're sure that your charges were fair, be sure to always maintain that in your discussions with your former tenant, even if you want to see if a settlement is a possibility.

If you charge your tenants for damage to the rental property either during their tenancy or by deducting from the deposit, you need evidence to back up your claim in case your tenant disputes the damage. Videoing the damage can be an effective tool to resolve disputes with tenants or prove your position in court. Many courts now have video monitors that you can use to show your evidence. Be sure that you have possession of the property or have given proper legal notice before entering to videotape, however.

When the rental property is abandoned

Occasionally tenants will abandon your rental property without notice. This can be good news if you're taking legal action against the tenant, because you save lost rent days and you may be able to reduce your legal costs.

Determining whether the property is really abandoned

Abandonment is the voluntary surrender of a legal right, for example, an interest in land or property, such as a tenancy. Tenants sometimes leave their accommodation unoccupied for long periods of time, with the intention of coming back at some point. So the best way to know for sure whether the rental property has been abandoned or not is to contact the tenants and ask them for a statement in writing relinquishing their rights to possession of the rental property.

Have a clause in the tenancy agreement saying that your tenants must inform you if they are going to leave the property unoccupied for more than two weeks. This policy can be helpful in determining whether the property has been abandoned or the tenant is just on a long holiday. You'll also need to inform your insurance company if the property is to be left vacant for more than 14 days.

If you think that the tenant has abandoned your property, but you have no written confirmation, consider whether the rent is still being paid, if the tenant has left the keys to the property, whether the neighbours know anything about it, and if you can see the tenant's possessions through the windows. If these factors indicate abandonment and the property has been left insecure, you may have a case for entering the property and fitting a secure lock. A reliable independent witness should confirm the circumstances in writing.

If the property doesn't appear to be abandoned or there is some doubt, you need a court possession order before taking over the property or re-letting. When you have met the legal requirements, you can take possession of the rental property and begin your turnover work to put it back on the rental market.

Dealing with personal property left behind

One of a landlord's worst nightmares is discovering that one of their tenants has suddenly abandoned the rental property and left all of his furnishings and household items behind. More common, however, is finding that a tenant has moved out and returned the keys, but left behind a few items of personal property. Often these items are junk that even your favourite charity will refuse to accept.

The landlord is under a legal obligation to take care of the tenant's possessions. The law relating to this is the Torts (interference with Goods) Act 1977. Under this law, the landlord could suffer a financial loss for moving and transporting the uncollected goods, or disposing of the goods.

When you first discover that your tenant appears to have left abandoned personal property, immediately try to locate the tenant and ask her to reclaim her property. You should write to the tenant by registered post or recorded delivery, enclosing a legal notice that informs her that her goods are available for collection and will be kept for up to three months.

If the goods remain uncollected after three months, the original owner loses all rights to the goods, and you can sell them. Once you have covered your expenses for carrying out this process and any rent arrears, any remaining proceeds belong to the original owner or tenant. But this only applies if they turn up to claim them within six years.

Book VI
Selling Up at a Profit

'You'll find living here very quiet & peaceful,
the people in the flat above work nights, so
they sleep during the day.'

In this book . . .

Getting the best price you can in the shortest time possible is essential when you've bought your property as an investment. Choosing the right estate agent, preparing the property for viewings, and knowing what to do when the offers (hopefully) start coming in are vital skills to have, and this book sets you on your way to completing a successful sale.

Here are the contents of Book VI at a glance:

Chapter 1

Selling with a Pro: Getting the Most from Estate Agents

*D*espite the obvious attractions of selling your property privately – you don't have to deal with estate agents or pay their commission – most people end up using an agent. Leaving the advertising, viewings, and price negotiations to someone else is simply much easier.

But things can – and do – go wrong. Anyone can set up in business as an estate agent because you don't need any formal qualifications. And even though professional bodies exist, such as the National Association of Estate Agents (NAEA) and the Ombudsman for Estate Agents (OEA) scheme, these are entirely voluntary, and only a third of agents are members. If you have a complaint about an agent who doesn't belong to one of these bodies, little redress is available. Therefore, it is important that you protect yourself against rogue agents – in this chapter we show you how.

The Role of the Estate Agent

The estate agent may be the middleman, but when you sell your property, if you're like most people, you probably couldn't do without him. Yes, selling your property yourself may be cheaper because you avoid paying the agent's commission – a percentage of the sale price, usually between 1.5 and 4 per cent. But the question is whether you can get the right buyers through the door and negotiate the price you want, all within a reasonable amount of time. If the answer is 'no', you've no choice but to hire an agent.

Most sellers use agents because agents are experts at selling property. Every week, thousands of prospective buyers call into their local estate agents, read the ads they place in local and national newspapers, and browse their Internet sites. Most buyers make an agent their first port of call. For this reason, an estate agent is one of the first people you want to call when you sell.

The agent works for you rather than the buyer because you pay her commission. She guides you through the selling process and is responsible for several vital steps in ensuring a successful sale:

- ✔ **Giving an estimate:** The estate agent's first job is to give you an idea of how much you can sell your property for. See 'Accepting the agent's estimate and setting the price' later in this chapter.

- ✔ **Suggesting improvements/repairs:** The agent's job is to sell your property, but he needs good tools to work with. If your place is untidy, cluttered, or full of unfinished do-it-yourself work, he may suggest you address the problem in order to achieve a successful sale.

  Let the agent guide you. If you're thinking about replacing a tired old bathroom suite with a gleaming new white one, ask the agent first whether he thinks this is necessary or worth the cost.

- ✔ **Writing the property particulars:** These are a description of your property. The agent uses this, along with a photo of the property (which he also arranges), in his advertising. Some agents charge extra for this, so check beforehand. To prepare the property particulars, the agent will inspect, measure the rooms, and note down special features that might interest prospective buyers. Although the agent tries to make your property sound as desirable as possible, he can't make false or misleading statements; doing so is a criminal offence.

- ✔ **Advertising the property:** Your success in selling rests on suitable buyers knowing it's for sale. Thus the advertising is crucial. Ask the agent how he plans to do this – in the agent's window, in the local paper, via mailing lists, over the Internet, and so on. Most agents put a 'For Sale' sign up outside your property. The key is using direct advertising toward the right type of buyer.

- ✔ **Handling viewings:** Some agents rely on sellers to show their properties to prospective buyers, but you may prefer not to. Don't feel bad if you would prefer to leave this to the experts.

  If you are at the property while the agent is showing people round, stay in the background. You should be as discreet as possible. Don't stalk the agent and prospective buyers, pointing out things they may have missed.

✔ **Negotiating a deal:** If you receive lots of offers, having an emotionally uninvolved third party who can negotiate the best deal is helpful. Even if only one offer is on the table, the agent is obliged to inform you promptly in writing. Be guided by your agent: If the offer is much less than the asking price, ask him whether he thinks you should hold out for a higher offer or accept it. If you decide the offer is too low, the agent will try to negotiate a higher price with the prospective buyer. If the buyer refuses – and you're adamant that the offer is too low – you'll have to wait for another buyer to come along.

✔ **Arranging mortgages, surveys, and conveyancing:** Some agents offer these services, but you're under no obligation to take up all or any of these. Because you'll be taking out a new mortgage in order to buy a new property (unless you have enough cash to buy outright), we recommend that you refuse any home loan offered by your agent. You can find a much better deal by shopping around using an *independent* mortgage broker (see Book II, Chapter 1 for more on this). But when it comes to surveys or conveyancing, it may be cheaper to use the surveyor or solicitor your agent recommends because the agent should be able to get you a discount for putting work their way.

You should be put under no pressure to sign up for any of the services recommended by your agent. Some agents receive more commission on mortgage advice and insurance than on house sales. Be wary.

After you accept an offer, instruct your solicitor to start conveyancing (see Book I, Chapter 4 for more details). At this point, the agent's work is done but you don't pay him until completion.

Wanted: An Honest and Competent Estate Agent

If you work with a good agent, you're likely to sell your property more quickly and for the price you want. Unfortunately, there are many bad agents. A bad agent will struggle to sell your property and may be unable to negotiate effectively on your behalf. If you've already found a property you want to buy, his incompetence could hold up the chain while you hang around waiting for a buyer.

Do your research carefully and pick a good agent. The work involved in finding a good agent is well worth the time and effort and could save you heartache further down the line. Check out the following:

Book VI

Selling Up at a Profit

✔ **Membership of professional organisations:** Charges are a big consideration when you choose an agent, but price should only be part of your decision. Far more important is membership of a recognised professional body, which indicates that the agent meets certain standards and protects you against malpractice. Use agents who are members of the NAEA, the Royal Institution of Chartered Surveyors (RICS), or the OEA scheme.

Some agents claim to belong to a professional trade body and use its logo in their advertising when they aren't members at all. You can check the truthfulness of these claims on the following Web sites: www.naea.co.uk, www.rics.org.uk or www.oea.co.uk.

✔ **Personal recommendations:** As well as having a professional qualification, the best agent to use is one that a friend or relative has personally recommended to you. The likelihood is that, if your friend enjoyed success, you will too. But remember, not all agents are adept at selling all types of property. Opt for an agent who has a number of properties on his books similar to yours.

Interviewing your prospective agents

After you narrow your choice to two or three agents, invite all of them to (separately) value your property. The purpose of this is to ascertain whether you can envision working with them. To help you answer this question, ask each agent the following:

✔ What price should I ask for my property? Remember: The highest quote may not be the best one to go with. If you get three quotes, we recommend opting for the middle one.

✔ How will you market it – 'for sale' board, estate agent's window, local or national newspaper adverts, mailing lists and brochures, or on the Internet? The more outlets the better.

✔ How much do you charge? Check what is included in the price in order to compare costs between agents.

✔ Will you personally be handling the sale? If a more junior agent will be handling it, find out how closely they will be supervised.

✔ How experienced are you? If the agent seems a bit 'wet behind the ears' you may prefer someone more experienced.

✔ How do you want to conduct viewings? Do you want a key to show people around or do I have to be in? Go with what suits you best.

✔ What is the tie-in period on your contract? (See 'Making sense of the contract' later in this chapter).

Your final choice should be the agent who not only gives the most satisfactory answers to your questions but who knows a bit about the locality. It's also important that you like him. After all, he'll be your ambassador and you want to give the right impression to buyers.

Go with your gut feeling: If you don't get the right vibes from the agent, prospective buyers aren't likely to either.

Accepting the agent's estimate and setting the price

One of the agent's most important functions is helping you set the asking price. This shouldn't be too high (which dissuades buyers from arranging to view your property) or too low (you could miss out on thousands of pounds). The agent will bear in mind what similar properties in the area are fetching, the condition of your property compared with those, and the number of interested buyers. Here are a couple of things to keep in mind about the agent's estimate:

✔ The agent's estimate is just that – it's not a valuation and a lender won't accept it as proof of the value of the property. Only surveyors can make accurate valuations, but this can cost several hundred pounds and isn't necessary at this stage.

✔ Your property is only worth what someone is prepared to pay for it, so don't get too worked up over the asking price.

✔ You don't have to accept the agent's estimate, but we recommend that you be guided by it. Agents usually have a better idea than you of market conditions and, because they're not emotionally attached to your property, can be more dispassionate.

After you have the agents' estimates, you can set the asking price. Because estimates aren't an exact science and can vary a lot, we recommend that you get estimates from several estate agents (they're free) and put your property on the market at the average price.

Getting the asking price right first time is important. Although you may be tempted to pick the highest estimate, if your property is much pricier than similar properties, you'll only have to reduce the price when it doesn't sell. This doesn't send out the right signals to buyers, who may get the impression that you're desperate to sell or that something is wrong with the property. If your asking price is fair, you should stick to your guns until a buyer eventually comes along who is prepared to pay what your house is worth.

Book VI

Selling Up at a Profit

Set the price slightly too high rather than too low. Buyers usually offer below the asking price and if this is already low, they'll try to pay even less. If your property is on the market for slightly more than you hope to get, you are more likely to end up with the price you want.

Assessing the agent's market reach

It doesn't matter how hot an estate agent's negotiating skills are, if he can't find prospective buyers in the first place, he's of limited use to you. You must ensure that as many serious prospective buyers as possible get to see your property. Follow this advice:

- **Ask the agent how he plans to market your property.** Will your property be advertised in the local newspaper or nationally? National advertising is particularly effective if you own a large, expensive property.

  Some agents charge extra for advertising on top of the standard commission. Check the charges before signing the contract and don't forget that you can negotiate these.

- **If your agent has an Internet site (as many do nowadays) log on and have a look.** Can prospective buyers take a virtual tour of the property? Can buyers register their details for e-mail alerts when a property goes on sale matching their criteria? An increasing number of buyers are using the Internet so it will help if your property is featured on it.

Making Sense of the Contract

Once you instruct an agent to act on your behalf, you enter a legally binding contract. Most contracts include the following:

- **Cost:** Agents work on a no-sale, no-fee basis, with commission ranging from 1.5 to 4 per cent of the sale price. Most of the complaints received by the Ombudsman are generated by dissatisfaction over commission. The Office of Fair Trading (OFT) advises that the contract should clearly state the exact amount you will be charged. Failing this, the agent should state how the cost will be calculated and estimate what it will be.

  Make sure there are no hidden costs. Some agents charge a low commission plus additional charges to cover advertising and a 'For Sale' board. Others charge a higher percentage of the selling price but this includes all costs. Some agents charge a fixed fee rather than commission so insist on a full breakdown of the costs.

✔ **How long it will run:** Most contracts have *tie-in periods,* which stipulate how long the agent has to sell your property before you can cancel the contract. You'll probably be offered a fairly long tie-in period and should try negotiating this. We recommend that you sign up with an agent for no more than eight weeks. This gives him plenty of time to find a buyer. If your property remains unsold, take your business elsewhere. Don't be sentimental, you owe the agent literally nothing (as he doesn't get paid if he doesn't get a sale).

Find out how long the contract will run and whether you can cancel it at any time. If you don't read the small print you may find you have signed up to an agent for several months. If the agent is useless, you're stuck until the tie-in period ends. If you instruct another agent who sells your property while you are still contracted to the first one, you have to pay commission to both.

Book VI

Selling Up at a Profit

✔ **The notice period:** This is the amount of time you have to continue working with an agent after you inform him that you want to cancel the contract. To figure out how long you could be saddled with the agent, add the notice period for cancelling the contract to the tie-in period. *Note:* The best contracts are those with a notice period and no tie-in period.

✔ **When payment is due:** Most agents are paid just before completion. Check that the contract doesn't state that she gets paid on exchange of contracts otherwise you'll have to fork out thousands of pounds from your own pocket before the sale is completed – money you might struggle to come by.

Some contracts are complicated, misleading, and even unfair. If you don't understand something, ask. And if you don't like something, refuse to sign. The Citizens' Advice Bureau (see Yellow Pages for your nearest branch) offers advice on contracts, or get your solicitor to take a look.

The contract will also include a number of terms including:

✔ Sole agency

✔ Joint sole agency

✔ Multiple agency

✔ Sole-selling rights

✔ Ready, willing and able purchaser

The following sections explain these terms in more detail.

Sole agency

With sole agency, one agent has exclusive rights to sell your property. Many sellers prefer sole agency for the following reasons:

- ✔ Because the agent earns all the commission if she is successful, she is likely to work hard to sell your property.

- ✔ It is the cheapest way to sell your home, with commission from as little as 1.5 per cent. And if you find a buyer yourself (see the next item in this list), you pay no commission at all.

- ✔ You don't pay commission if you find a buyer yourself unless the agent has 'sole-selling rights' (see the later section of the same name).

- ✔ Buyers often prefer dealing with sole agents because there is less chance of being gazumped – when the seller accepts an offer after already accepting an offer from another buyer. This is more likely when two or more agents are selling a property and competing for the same commission because, even after one agent has negotiated an offer that the seller has accepted, the other may continue to market the property.

Keep in mind, however, that if you instruct a second agent to sell your property after signing a sole-agency contract that is still in force, you're asking for trouble. If the second agent sells your home, you're obliged to pay commission to both him and the original agent.

Joint sole agency

One way of increasing the chances of selling your property is by instructing two agents to work together. Your local agent may recommend a link-up with a national partner to extend the reach of the advertising. To set up a joint sole agency, contact your local agent. The agents split the commission between them if they secure a sale – this is usually around 2 per cent. If you sell your own property you don't have to pay commission (as long as the contract doesn't give the agents sole-selling rights).

Multiple agency

If you instruct two or three competing agents to sell your property it's known as multiple agency. The agent who finds a buyer gets commission, the others get nothing. Keep these points in mind:

✔ This arrangement can speed up your hunt for a buyer because several agents promote your property. But you also have to juggle a number of agents who want to arrange viewings at different times.

✔ Multiple agency increases the likelihood of your property being marketed by another agent after you've accepted an offer, and this puts off buyers because they are afraid of being gazumped. Some buyers also think that multiple agency means you are desperate to sell, which can affect the size of their offers.

✔ Competition doesn't always spur agents on. Because they get nothing if they don't find a buyer, some agents reserve their real effort for properties on which they have sole agency – and are guaranteed to earn commission if they secure a sale.

✔ Make sure the contract is clearly worded so only one agent receives commission for finding a buyer. Expect to pay more than sole agency – usually around 3 to 4 per cent of the sale price.

If you use several agents, select them in the same way you would if you were using only one.

Book VI

Selling Up at a Profit

Sole-selling rights

The term 'sole-selling rights' should set alarm bells ringing. Never, ever agree to this. It means that when you sign a contract, that agent – and nobody else – can sell your property. Even if you sell your property yourself, you still have to pay the agent commission. Some sole-agency agreements include sole-selling rights clauses so check the small print of the contract.

Ready, willing, and able purchaser

Another term to watch out for is 'ready, willing, and able purchaser'. This means that if the agent finds a buyer who is prepared and able to buy your home and exchanges unconditional contracts, you have to pay the agent, even if the sale falls through.

Checking Up on Progress

Keep an eye on your agent. He should provide feedback after a viewing, so you know how prospective buyers react to your property, but some are better than others at doing this. If you've had several viewings and no takers, you need to know why so that you can correct any problems. Build a relationship with the agent so that he keeps you informed.

Agents are obliged to pass on to you all offers for your property, in writing. If you find out that he didn't, complain to the Ombudsman, if your agent is a member of the OEA (Ombudsman for Estate Agents) scheme.

Taking Your Business Elsewhere: When to Give Up on an Agent

If your home isn't selling, the problem may not be your property or the price but the agent. Following are warning signs that your estate agent isn't up to par:

- **You haven't heard from him in weeks:** You should expect at least a call or two soon after your property goes on the market. If you don't hear anything at all for some time, that's not good enough.

- **You get no feedback after viewings:** Your estate agent should report back to you after every viewing to tell you how it went, what the prospective buyer thought, and whether he wants to make an offer. If you don't hear anything, contact the agent yourself.

Give your agent a couple of months to sell your property. If you aren't happy with his performance after this time, give him notice and switch agents (if your contract allows you to do so).

Take the same steps to find a new agent as you did to find the original one; you may just have been unlucky the first time. Discuss with the new agent whether the asking price is right and ask whether she has suggestions about the presentation of your property. Sometimes a fresh perspective is all you need.

Complaining about an Estate Agent

Dealing with an agent isn't always smooth sailing, as the 6,000 complaints the Ombudsman received last year testifies. But getting a result when you complain is far harder than you may think because agents aren't regulated. There's very little a trade body can do if an agent has messed up, so your challenge is to minimise the chances of this happening by following the tips in this chapter and choosing and monitoring your agent carefully. Sometimes though you will be dissatisfied with your estate agent.

Chapter 2

Going It Alone: Selling Your Property Privately

In This Chapter

▶ Setting the asking price

▶ Advertising your property

▶ Handling viewings with prospective buyers

▶ Accepting an offer

▶ Selling at auction

*O*ne in 20 properties is now sold without an estate agent, according to property portal HouseWeb. An increasing number of people are selling privately because it speeds the process up considerably since it cuts out the middleman. And you also save money because you knock out the estate agent's commission, which can be as much as 4 per cent of the sale price. If you're selling a property for £200,000, for example, the estate agent's commission works out to be £9,400, after VAT (value-added tax) is added on. No wonder an increasing number of people are looking at ways of avoiding this charge! Of course, going it alone isn't always easy. The reason so many people use estate agents to sell their property is because it makes life easier. Your agent handles the advertising, viewings, and price negotiations – tasks many people don't feel comfortable doing themselves. But if you're prepared to give it a go, selling your property yourself can be worth the extra effort. In this chapter we look at what's involved, as well as setting the asking price, marketing, and handling viewings. We also cover what you need to know about selling at auction.

Setting the Asking Price

Your property is worth what someone is willing to pay for it. The difference between receiving loads of offers – all at the asking price – and not hearing a dickey bird all comes down to the asking price and demand. While you can't influence demand, apart from making your property as attractive to buyers as possible, you should get the price right. Although making as much profit as possible is tempting, setting the price too high doesn't always pay. You may find that you've priced yourself out of the market.

When you sell privately, you can determine a realistic asking price by following these strategies:

- ✔ **Get quotes from three different estate agents and then work out the average.** Simply call up agents and tell them that you're considering putting your house on the market via their agency and want an idea of the price the property would fetch. Agents are called upon to come up with asking prices all the time, so they won't think this request is unusual or out of order. You don't need to tell the agent that you have no intention of actually employing their services in selling your property.

  An estate agent won't give you a valuation of you property – just an indication of what you could get for it. For a professional valuation, you have to employ a surveyor, which costs extra and there isn't much added value in doing this.

- ✔ **Compare your property with similar ones in your street.** If Number 43 down the road went for £180,000 three weeks ago, chances are that if your property is in a similar state of repair with the same sort of features, you can get the same sort of sum.

- ✔ **Be aware of things you can't see.** The owners of Number 43 may have installed a hot tub in their conservatory, put in double-glazing, or recently redecorated, and your place might not be as desirable. Or maybe when they put their property on the market, demand was greater, and that's why they got several prospective buyers so easily. Treat neighbours' experience as a general guide – there is no guarantee you'll get the same price.

- ✔ **Scan your local papers and property Web sites.** The local paper will reveal the price similar properties in your area are being advertised for. And don't forget the property Web sites on the Internet as well: several web sites now list selling prices:

    - www.landreg.gov.uk/houseprices

    - www.hometrack.co.uk

    - www.thisishouseprices.co.uk

Before putting your property on the market, don't forget to prepare it for prospective buyers to view. Clean thoroughly, repair any broken tiles, fix cupboard doors that don't shut properly, replace worn carpets and faded curtains, and clear away the clutter.

Advertising Your Property

The easiest way to sell a house privately is if you personally know someone who wants to buy it. Maybe someone has approached you and asked whether you'd consider selling, or a friend of a friend has heard that you're thinking of putting your property on the market and wants to get in ahead of the rush. If this is the case, lucky you. You can save time, money, and the hassle of advertising.

But most people aren't in this position. Instead, you have to let prospective buyers know that your property is up for sale. This is where advertising comes in. Do it correctly, and money spent on advertising is money well spent. Do it badly, and you may as well throw your cash down the drain.

The key to success in selling your property is in reaching the small number of people who are interested in buying it. To do this, you must advertise in places where these people are likely to see your ad – the local newspaper or national papers, the Internet, specialist property publications, or on a board outside your property. In the following sections, we go into more detail as to how each of these works and show you how to write a property ad.

Putting up a property board

The first step to take if you're selling your house privately is to do as the estate agents do and erect a 'For Sale' sign outside your property. The idea is to catch the attention of prospective buyers who may pass by. The property board informs them that the property is for sale and provides a telephone number if they want more details.

You don't have to pay a fortune to erect a board. As long as the wording is legible and the sign is clean, even a homemade effort can be effective. Get a large piece of wood, paint it white, and write 'For Sale' and your telephone number for enquiries. Then nail this board firmly to a post and stick it at the front of the garden where it can clearly be seen from the road. If you're selling a flat or house that doesn't have a garden, nail your sign onto the outside wall.

You can even have DIY signs prepared on the Web site www.elmleaf.co.uk and sent to you through mail order. They also place your house on the main

Book VI

Selling Up at a Profit

Web sites, with photos and a dedicated Web page, and put the Web address on the board for your property.

Your aim is to attract people who are passing by, some of whom will be driving. So keep these tips in mind:

- Make sure your writing is legible. That means neat and large enough to easily see from the road.

- Don't put too much information on the board. If you do, prospective buyers won't be able to take it in while they drive past. 'For Sale' and your phone number are enough. If they register that the property is for sale and are interested, chances are they'll pull up and take down your phone number.

Advertising in newspapers

Nearly every national and local newspaper has an extensive property section. As well as pages full of big display ads paid for by estate agents to justify their commission to clients, you can also find scores of pages of classified ads, often placed by private sellers. Because the classifieds are probably going to be your main source of advertising for your property, you have to familiarise yourself with the paper's circulation schedule and the information included in the ads. Why? Because you have to write your own.

When writing a newspaper ad, remember what you're aiming for:

- To attract the reader's attention
- To keep the reader's interest
- To generate a desire to find out more information about your property
- To convince the reader to contact you for more details
- To arrange a viewing

You need to decide what sort of ad to opt for, where you're going to advertise, and what information you want to include. We cover each of these in the sections below.

Information to include in a newspaper ad

An effective newspaper ad is short and snappy yet conveys all the vital information the reader needs. The essential points to cover are

- The property's location
- Period style

✔ Size, number, and type of rooms

✔ Any unusual features

✔ Whether it's leasehold or freehold

✔ Price

✔ A contact telephone number for interested buyers to use to get in touch with you

Make sure that the telephone number is one you can be contacted on during the day – a mobile phone or office number is best. There's not much point in giving your home number if you are at work all day.

Book VI

Selling Up at a Profit

Most papers use abbreviations of words that regularly appear so that you can fit in as much information as possible as inexpensively as possible. Familiarise yourself with these and use them, as appropriate. But remember that abbreviations can look untidy, so try not to use more than you need. Also avoid using your own abbreviations, which are likely to leave readers mystified. Table 2-1 shows common abbreviations used in newspaper ads.

Table 2-1	Common Newspaper Ad Abbreviations
Abbreviation	*Translation*
Apt	Apartment
bed	Bedroom
d/g	Double-glazing
det	Detached
dble	Double
exc	Excellent
ex l/a	Ex-local authority
ff	Fully fitted
FH	Freehold
flr	Floor
GCH	Gas central heating
gdn	Garden
immac	Immaculate

(continued)

Table 2-1 *(continued)*

Abbreviation	Translation
lge	Large
LH	Leasehold
ono	Or nearest offer
refurb	Refurbished
sq ft	Square feet
sep	Separate
ter	Terrace
WC	Water closet or toilet
yr	Year

Before you write your ad, look at other ads in the publication you're planning to advertise in. Doing so gives you a good idea of how you should word your ad.

Including a photo of your property: Yes or no?

The saying 'A picture speaks a thousand words' is certainly true with something as emotive as property: Most people have a set idea of what sort of home they can live in – and what they can't.

The trouble with including a photo with your newspaper ad is that it costs a lot of money and could blow your advertising budget out of the water. But if you're advertising on the Internet, a picture or two of the property is vital.

If you decide to include a photo, make sure it is as clear as possible, shows the front of the property, and if you arrange it, is taken on a sunny day. If you aren't a budding David Bailey, consider paying a professional to take the pictures for you. Even if you do know your shutter from your flash, forking out a bit of cash to get a more professional finish is often worth the extra expense.

Many Web sites have their own photographers who can take photos of your property for a fee. Otherwise, you could look up photographers in the Yellow Pages.

What sort of ad should you go for?

Newspapers carry two sorts of ad: *display* and *classified*. Display ads are more eye-catching, tend to be far bigger than classifieds, and usually include photos of the property. They are also much more expensive. Classified ads provide the buyer with the necessary info but are usually only a few lines long. For these reasons, they tend to be much smaller and, therefore, much less expensive.

Classified ads are likely to be your best bet because they're more reasonably priced than the huge display ads favoured by agents with big advertising budgets. Most newspapers offer bold print for an extra sum which you may be prepared to pay for because anything that makes your ad stand out from the crowd is money well spent.

A huge ad doesn't guarantee you more interest from prospective buyers. A classified ad that's worded correctly can be more effective than a badly worded display ad that takes up a lot more space.

Picking a newspaper to advertise in

All national and most local newspapers have substantial property sections. But because you probably have an advertising budget you want to stick to, you can't advertise in all of them. A local paper typically charges around £1 a word, with a minimum number of words, say 16, so an ad in a local paper would cost you a minimum of £16 plus VAT at 17.5 per cent. A national newspaper on the other hand, has much higher advertising charges. For a mono ad (black and white) stretching over a single column, you can expect to pay £53 for the ad itself, plus £10 per line. And don't forget to slap the VAT on top of that.

The trick is to be selective and choose those papers that are most likely to be read by your target market. If you're selling an end-of-terrace house in Manchester, for example, placing an ad in the London *Evening Standard*'s property section is unlikely to result in many calls from interested buyers. Spend your money wisely.

To place an ad, buy a copy of the paper you are going to advertise in. The phone number you need to call will be prominently displayed inside. Alternatively, look on the paper's Web site. You may be able to complete an ad online, or find a number to call. To help you make your mind up about which type of paper you should advertise in, consider the following:

- ✔ **Local papers:** Whether your budget stretches to an ad in a national newspaper or not, your first port of call should be your local paper. Most have reasonably sized property sections. Many local papers also have their own Web sites, which are updated more frequently than the paper – particularly because many local papers are published weekly. If your local paper has a Web site, find out whether your ad will appear online as well and if this service costs extra. Even with an extra charge, the online ad may be worth it because it means your ad will probably reach more potential buyers.

✔ **Regional papers:** You don't have to restrict yourself to one small-time local paper. There could well be some bigger regional newspapers covering your area with a bigger catchment of readers. Place an ad there too to broaden your chances of selling your property.

✔ **National papers:** If you have the spare cash, you may want to think about advertising in a national newspaper as well as your local one. The principles are the same as with a local rag. The ad should be carefully worded and include all the necessary information the prospective buyer needs. National newspaper advertising is best suited to those with expensive or unusual properties for sale.

You will have to pay a lot more to advertise in a national newspaper so consider whether it is worth it. We recommend trying the local paper first and if you have no joy after a few weeks, trying a national. Otherwise, you could be spending a lot of money unnecessarily.

Don't write off the free ads. *Loot* publishes a number of regional papers in the South East (including London, Croydon & Surrey and Essex) and the North West (including Manchester, Liverpool, and the Wirral & North Wales) and has an extensive Web site (`www.loot.com`) with details of thousands of properties for sale. If your area is covered by *Loot*, it's worth placing a free ad. You never know, you might get lucky!

Timing your ad

If you want it to appear in the next edition of the paper, make sure you find out the submission deadline. If you miss it, you've lost out on as much as a full week of advertising.

Checking your published ad

After you place an ad, make sure you buy a copy of the paper when it goes on sale. The reason? To check that the ad appears in the first place, to verify that it's worded correctly, and to make sure that your contact details are correct.

If you ad has been printed incorrectly because the salesperson who took your details down over the phone got it wrong, request that a free ad is run in the next edition.

Using specialist property publications

There are a number of specialist property publications available, many of which cover only the local area. Weekly property magazine *Hot Property*, for example, covers property for sale in London or the Home Counties. It also has a Web site (`www.hotproperty.co.uk`) you can use. Check out your local newsagent to see what specialist publications are available.

Advertising on the Internet

The Internet offers a number of Web sites you can use to sell your property. This is cheaper than advertising in your local paper, enabling you to include a lot more information in your ad. And some Web sites allow your property to appear until it is sold, unlike newspaper ads where you have to pay for the ad to be repeated over several weeks.

Selling over the Internet is by no means a foolproof process. Buyers can have a hard time locating properties for sale if the seller doesn't use one of the big Web sites, pages can be slow to download, and information can become outdated. And nothing is more frustrating for a buyer than enquiring about a property that has already been sold. (And from the seller's perspective, the last thing you want are buyers ringing you up weeks after you have agreed a sale.) But if you're aware of the potential pitfalls and know how to minimise them, the Internet can be an effective way to show off your property to buyers.

Several good sites are available that you can advertise your property on. By far the best is HouseWeb's (www.houseweb.co.uk), which boasts 100,000 visitors a month. You pay a one-off price, and your property appears on the site until it's sold. HouseWeb prices start at £47 for a standard advert with one photo, but you can pay quite a bit more depending on the number of photos you include, whether you opt for normal, bold, or red type, and whether you have a link through to your own Web site). If you want to include a panoramic virtual tour, for example, where the buyer can examine the interior of your property online through a series of pictures, you'll pay £299, which includes VAT and the cost of the filming – a process that takes a photographer about an hour.

Writing the ad is straightforward. After you register on the site and write your ad (this is likely to include details similar to those that would appear in a newspaper, although you may also include the size and a description of the rooms), and uploaded any photos you want to include, the ad is automatically created and appears on the site. In addition to the ad

- ✔ All HouseWeb ads also include a location map enabling the prospective buyer to see exactly where your property is.

- ✔ HouseWeb notifies buyers by e-mail if a property meets their requirements. An interested buyer can contact you by e-mail via HouseWeb or call you directly through a personal phone number that you can include in your ad.

- ✔ HouseWeb gives you, the seller, direct access to your ad so you can amend it at any time.

- ✔ To eliminate the problem of out-of-date information, HouseWeb insists you update your ad every 30 days in case you sell your property or it is under offer.

Here are a couple of tips to make your online ad more effective:

✔ When you advertise on the Internet, use photos. Most sellers do – if you don't, buyers will wonder why and may assume you're trying to flog a hideous-looking property. If you don't have a scanner and can't upload your own photos, many Web sites do this for you for an additional charge if you post them the hard copies. HouseWeb charges £10, for example, for this service.

✔ If you can afford it, include a visual tour. It may cost a bit extra, but it can cut back on timewasters. If you get a call from a prospective buyer following up your ad, she's already seen the interior of your property and is impressed enough to want to see it in person.

Handling Viewings

After your ad appears in whatever advertising media you select, prepare yourself for calls. With a bit of luck, they will come flooding in from serious prospective buyers, enabling you to arrange a number of viewings. Because you aren't using an agent, you have to organise a convenient time and date for yourself and the prospective buyer and guide him through the property, answering his questions. In the following sections, we look at how you can prepare for a viewing – and what to do to make sure it goes off without a hitch.

Taking the call

Your first contact with a prospective buyer is likely to be over the telephone. She may have spotted your ad in the local paper or driven past the property and seen the board you erected outside. As soon as you advertise your property, you need to be prepared to receive phone calls from interested parties and to deal with these in a professional manner.

Preparing for the call

To prepare for conversations with prospective buyers, have the following by the phone:

✔ **A copy of any ads you ran.** The prospective buyer may want confirmation of details, such as the size of the master bedroom. Even if you stated this information in the ad, you need to have it on hand just in case you need a reminder of what you said. The last thing you want to do is contradict yourself or sound flustered because you don't know the answer to a question.

> ✔ **A property knowledge sheet.** Compile a *property knowledge sheet* with details about your property. Make sure it contains all the basic information about your property, such as its size and type. Also include important information about the local area, such as transport links, local schools, childcare facilities, leisure centres, and shopping facilities.

Talking to prospective buyers

When you receive a call, answer the phone quickly and politely, taking care not to sound harassed. To sound professional and give the impression that you know what you're doing, say 'Hello' and state your name.

Keeping the caller waiting or being too casual in your approach when you do eventually pick up the phone doesn't impress, which is what you're trying to do. If you absolutely can't speak to the caller at that particular moment, politely ask him for his name, his telephone number, and a convenient time when you can return his call. Then make sure you call exactly when you said you would.

During this phone conversation, you have three goals: to answer the buyer's questions, to sell her on your property so that she'll want to come around to see it, and to actually arrange the viewing.

Be friendly and chatty and try to build up a rapport with the prospective buyer. Some would-be purchasers are wary of buying privately because they aren't dealing with a recognisable firm of agents. They may be particularly concerned about the safety aspects of the viewing. So reassure them that you aren't a psychopath by being friendly and helpful and building up a rapport over the telephone.

Answering the buyer's questions

When you're speaking to the prospective buyer, she may want some more details from you before committing herself to a viewing. Her inquiries can save you time, as well as her time, if for some reason the property isn't suitable. Maybe, for example, it isn't close enough to the local primary school or the mainline train station into London – factors which weren't clear in the ad.

Selling the prospective buyer on your property

While you don't want to waste your time arranging a viewing if the caller is only half interested, your goal is to get as many prospective buyers as possible, who have the means to purchase your property, round to look at it. The trick to turning a call into a viewing is to be as persuasive as possible, while listening to the caller's requirements at the same time. He may, for example, express concern at the fact that your property has only three bedrooms when he really wanted a fourth bedroom for guests. If you can convince him that the bedrooms are such a good size that he could easily put a sofa bed in at least one of them, you may be able to convince him to come and take a look.

Arranging a viewing

If the prospective buyer is still interested in viewing your property by the end of the telephone call, you can make the necessary arrangements:

✔ **Set a time and date convenient to both you and the prospective buyer.**
Most buyers want to come around after work or at the weekend, particularly if they want to bring a partner and/or children. Although you may initially baulk at this, be as flexible as possible and put up with the disruption. Hopefully these disruptions will last for only a relatively short period of time.

When you arrange a viewing, make sure you also arrange for a friend or relative to be there with you in case of trouble. If this isn't possible, we recommend arranging the viewing for a time when you can get somebody present. Don't take any unnecessary risks.

✔ **Provide the prospective buyer with the full address of your property, together with clear directions so that he knows how to get there.** This is particularly important if the buyer doesn't know the area very well or your property is hard to find. Make sure directions are clear and easy to follow. If giving directions isn't your forte, ask a friend or relative who knows the area well and is good at directing people to provide them for you. Also try and avoid directing people past the council rubbish tip or sewerage works if possible. A local park or attractive village pub or two create a much better impression of the local area.

Don't be late for the viewing – or cancel it. Prospective buyers tend to see several properties. If you mess them about, there will be scores of other sellers more than happy to roll out the red carpet. If something unavoidable does crop up that that will make you late or necessitate you having to cancel the viewing altogether, give the prospective buyer as much notice as possible and, if you can, arrange another viewing.

Guiding prospective buyers round your property

When the buyer arrives, switch into professional mode. Answer the door with a smile and welcome her into your property (which, by the way, should be clean, tidy, and fresh smelling). Offer to take her coat and ask whether she had a pleasant journey. If she came a long way, you may also want to offer her a cup of tea or a cold drink.

As you and the prospective buyer walk through your house, keep these suggestions in mind:

- ✔ **Allow yourself to be guided by the buyer if she seems happy to lead the way (not all buyers will feel comfortable leading).** If your buyer wanders into the lounge and starts commenting on the room before you've a chance to direct her into the kitchen, go along with it and point out any features that you think need highlighting. The key is to be flexible and see how each viewing pans out. The buyer may want to start in the garden instead: let her guide you on this if she seems happy to do so.

- ✔ **If the buyer doesn't take the lead, start the viewing at the hallway and work round the ground floor of the property before moving upstairs.** Once upstairs, you may want to start with the Master bedroom and move on from there.

- ✔ **Avoid stating the blindingly obvious, such as 'Here is the bathroom'; it sounds patronising.** Far better to highlight certain features that the buyer (probably overwhelmed by everything she has to take in) could well miss. If there are French windows in the lounge, which open out onto a patio, for example, open the doors and demonstrate how convenient they are. This might be a better time to look at the exterior of the property as well, if you haven't already.

Answering prospective buyers' questions

It is highly unlikely that you and the prospective buyer will wander around your property in complete silence. Most prospective buyers have lots of questions to ask, such as whether you've had any trouble with the neighbours, what's the nearest bus route, and whether there is gas central heating or not. Answer questions as truthfully as you can. If you aren't sure of the answer, say so but promise to find out as soon as possible and get back to them.

Bluffing your way through the answers makes you look as if you're deliberately trying to mislead the prospective buyer – especially if something doesn't turn out to be what you said it was.

Predicting every question a prospective buyer will ask is impossible, but you can prepare yourself for the most obvious ones. Anticipate the commonest: point out that since you are a property investor, there's no troublesome chain to worry about. Following are two questions you're likely to be asked and how you should reply:

✔ **What's included in the asking price?** Most properties are sold with the fixtures and fittings, such as the kitchen and bathroom suite, light fittings, and tiles, all as part of the asking price. If you plan to leave the carpets and/or curtains behind as well, mention this to the prospective buyer.

✔ **What are the neighbours like?** If the neighbours play loud music at all hours, and the noise reverberates around your semi, saying that you never get a peep out of them is deliberately misleading and could get you in trouble later. As much as you may wish otherwise, you have to be honest. While you must tell the truth, don't spend ages slagging off the neighbours and going into great detail of the feud you've got running with the family across the road. If you do, you'll send your prospective buyer running a mile. Indicate that you've had a problem and stick to the facts. Then the buyer can decide whether she's still interested in your property or not.

You must tell the potential buyers about any disputes with a neighbour that you have formally reported to the local council or police. If you don't inform the buyer, you could be legally challenged or even sued at a later date if the buyer can persuade a court that, had she known the true situation, she wouldn't have bought your property.

Coming back for more

If your prospective buyer rings you after the viewing and asks to come back and take another look, rejoice – this is a very good sign. A second viewing indicates that the buyer is very interested in purchasing your property and either wants to clear up a couple of things in his mind or just wants to reassure himself that he has made the right decision to buy your property.

As with first viewings, arrange the second viewing at a mutually convenient time. You may feel that you don't need a chaperone this time because your prospective buyer seemed like such a nice person during your first meeting, but we still advise that you arrange for someone to be at the property with you. It's better to be safe than sorry.

With a second or third viewing, you can leave the prospective buyer to look around on his own; simply tell him that you'll be in the lounge if he has any questions. He'll be familiar with the layout from his first visit, and you'll have already highlighted the key features of the property. He is likely to have some specific aims: he may want to double check that the second bedroom is big enough for a double bed, for example. He may also have some questions he forgot to ask on his first viewing because they went out of his mind.

At the end of the second viewing, the prospective buyer may make an offer or say he'll be in touch. If it's the latter, you may want to chivvy him along a bit; perhaps mention you've had a lot of interest in the property and you wouldn't want him to miss out by taking too long to get back to you. Even if this isn't strictly true, it may instil a sense of urgency in the prospective buyer, resulting in a quicker sale, which is obviously good for you.

Dealing with Offers

Of course, in the best scenario, the prospective buyer makes an offer on your property. That doesn't mean you should immediately accept it. In fact, you should resist the temptation to accept the first offer you get, particularly if it's well below the asking price. If you have only just put your property on the market, wait a bit longer to see whether another buyer offers you the full asking price. For information on negotiating a deal, go to Book VI, Chapter 4.

Book VI

Selling Up at a Profit

If someone offers you the full asking price, your property may be under-priced. You can either accept the offer if you are happy with the sum or hold out for a higher offer from another buyer, who may offer more if they know someone has already offered the full asking price.

Don't accept an offer from one buyer and then later accept an offer from another buyer – this is gazumping and is very distressing and expensive for buyers. Although you may be tempted to go for the higher offer – and it isn't illegal to accept another offer after you've already accepted someone else's – gazumping is a bad practice. It can be expensive for the first buyer, who may have forked out for a valuation and survey and instructed a solicitor. Treat others as you'd like to be treated: Imagine how you'd feel if you were gazumped – understandably furious. Stick with a buyer whose offer you accepted.

If you've shown several buyers around your property, and they are all keen to make an offer, consider opting for *sealed bids*. In this situation, you ask all interested parties to submit an offer to you in writing by a deadline. You then open all the offers and decide which one you're going to accept. You don't have to opt for the highest bid – you may prefer to go for the first-time buyer who isn't caught up in a chain – and you don't have to accept any of the offers you receive. Getting sealed bids is a good way to speed up the process *and* get a good price for your property – usually more than you put it on the market for in the first place.

Chasing Prospective Buyers

Once you've accepted an offer, you need to instruct your solicitor, who will set the wheels in motion. The prospective buyer needs to arrange his financing, arrange a survey, and instruct his own solicitor. In addition, you may need to *chase the buyer,* that is, ensure that he's doing what he needs to do and when. (For those who use estate agents to sell their property, the agent assumes this role.)

Make yourself familiar with the various stages of the conveyancing process so that you know when something is taking longer than it should. Remember that purchasing a property in England, Wales, and Northern Ireland can take 10 to 12 weeks. If the process is dragging on for several months, you have a right to know why. After all, you will have taken your property off the market and you may have missed out on other potential buyers who could have moved more quickly.

The hold-up may be on your side. Your solicitor may be dragging his heels for one reason or another. So while you are harrying the buyer, remember to put in a call to your solicitor, too.

Gentle reminders are a whole lot different from harassment. Don't turn into a stalker, bothering your buyer at all hours of the day and night. Try not to call more than once a week for an update, otherwise you'll put the buyer off and he may well pull out of the sale. Remember, in England, Northern Ireland, and Wales, a sale is not binding until exchange of contracts (in Scotland an offer is binding; see Book I, Chapter 5 for more details on the Scottish house-buying process).

Under the Hammer: Selling at Auction

If you're privately selling a property that has complications such as subsidence or isn't in tip-top condition, or you need a quick sale for whatever reason, you may want to consider selling at auction. Selling at auction offers these possible advantages:

✔ **Auctions are good places to sell homes that have problems.** This is because the sale goes through much more quickly so buyers may be less likely to notice problems. And because they usually get a good price, they may be prepared to overlook a bit of damp or subsidence.

✔ **If a bidding war breaks out among interested buyers, you could end up getting a better price for your property.** In such a situation, you could end up with more than you would have if you'd gone the 'normal' route and sold through an estate agent.

✔ **Selling at auction gives you a great deal of marketing exposure.** Most big auction houses advertise in national, trade, and local press, as well as on the Internet. Your property will also feature in the sale catalogue, usually with a photograph and detailed description.

Before you decide that an auction is the way to go, keep these things in mind:

✔ **Not all properties are suitable for sale at auction.** If yours is in pristine condition and you've spent a lot of time cultivating the garden and expect the sale price to reflect this, you may be better off trying to sell via an estate agent or on your own.

Book VI

Selling Up at a Profit

To find out whether your property is suitable for auction, consult an auctioneer who has an MRICS/FRICS qualification. The Royal Institution of Chartered Surveyors (RICS) has a detailed list of auctioneers in each area. Contact the RICS on 0870 333 1600 or the Web site (www.rics.org.uk). Or try The Essential Information Group, which works with 150 auction houses and provides lists of future auctions (www.eigroup.co.uk).

✔ **Once the auctioneer has brought down her hammer, the sale is binding and neither you nor the bidder can withdraw.** You can change your mind about selling your property up until the auction and the property will be withdrawn from sale. But once someone has accepted your offer it's too late to change your mind about selling. The buyer pays a 10 per cent deposit on the day of the sale.

✔ **The sale must also be completed within a set date.** The buyer usually has 28 days to pay the balance of the purchase price to the auction house and the sale is complete.

✔ **If you sell your property at auction, you must ensure that it is vacant by a fixed date – usually four weeks after the auction.**

Going about it

If the auctioneer thinks your property is suitable for auction, discuss what you need to do before the sale. The auctioneer can tell you all about viewing arrangements and a possible sale date.

Most sales have a closing date for entries, which is six weeks before the date of auction. Make sure you get all your searches done and your details submitted to the auction house in plenty of time.

Price

The auctioneer will discuss the *guide price* with you. This guide gives buyers an idea of how much you're expecting. You will also need to come up with a *reserve price* – the minimum price you're prepared to sell your property for – prospective bidders know that there is a reserve price, but they don't know what it is. Only you and the auctioneer are party to this information.

As the auction date approaches, you may have to adjust the reserve price if market conditions change dramatically. If a lot of people have shown interest in your property, you may decide to increase the reserve price.

Instructing your solicitor

Once the reserve is set, you have to instruct a solicitor to obtain the title deeds and the details of the lease (if there is one), and to prepare the special conditions of sale. Some auctioneers also request that you get local authority and Land Registry searches carried out on the property (see Book I, Chapter 4 for more details on the searches and costs involved). All this information is made available to prospective buyers through your solicitor.

Viewings

The auctioneer arranges viewings of your property with prospective bidders. Interested parties are also likely to commission a survey of the property – and their surveyor needs access to compile this report.

If the property is vacant such viewings won't really affect you. But if you are living at the property, you have to be patient and flexible. Many auctioneers arrange group viewings for popular lots to cut back on the time and hassle. If this is the case with your property, we suggest you go out and leave them to it.

Sold!

If you manage to successfully sell your property at auction, the auctioneer signs a contract on your behalf in the saleroom. The purchaser has to pay a 10 per cent deposit on the day of the sale (see Book I, Chapter 3 for more information about buying a property at auction). The buyer loses this 10 per cent deposit if he doesn't pay the remainder of the sale price, usually within 28 days. But while you get to keep the buyer's forfeited deposit, you also have the hassle of trying to sell your property again.

If your reserve price isn't met at auction, you have a couple of options: you can try selling your property privately instead. Or you may have to face the fact that you have to accept less than your reserve price.

Cost of selling at auction

The auction house is paid by commission – usually around 2 per cent of the sale price, plus VAT. Many auctioneers also charge sellers an entry fee for including their property in the sale. This fee covers the original inspection of the property by someone from the auction house (to ensure it is suitable for auction), as well as marketing and catalogue production costs. The price of this depends on the space you take up in the catalogue, which in itself depends on the value of your property; the bigger the property, the more space you should buy in the catalogue to give it prominence over fellow lots.

If you are tempted to go ahead with the auction, obtain an estimate from the auctioneer, in writing, stating how much you're expected to spend. Also remember that, even if you fail to sell your property, you may have to pay certain auction costs, such as the entry fee. Check with your auctioneer before the sale as to exactly what these fees are likely to be.

The auctioneer's bill for his commission and other expenses is usually sent to your solicitor, who pays it on your behalf. After your mortgage and solicitor's fees have been paid, you receive the balance of the money.

Book VI

Selling Up at a Profit

Chapter 3

Creating the Right Impression

In This Chapter

▶ Cleaning and de-cluttering your property

▶ Deciding what needs repairing or replacing

▶ Financing your improvements

*F*irst impressions count, particularly when you're selling a property. You want prospective buyers to be in no doubt that yours is the one for them – and you can't do that with a bad first impression.

The better your house looks, and the more care you take presenting it, the more likely you are to get the price you want – and quickly. Take time and effort to clean thoroughly, remove clutter and questionable furnishings, and give your property a fresh lick of paint.

In this chapter, we discuss how you can make it easy for prospective buyers to see the potential of your property – and envisage themselves living there.

Ensuring Your Property Is Irresistible

As soon as you decide to sell your property, you need to get it up to scratch. How much work is required depends on the condition you normally keep your property in. Tackle the necessary tasks in the following order:

1. General cleaning

2. Ditching the clutter

3. Making repairs and improvements

4. Painting and wallpapering

5. Cleaning carpets and floors

6. Final cleaning

General cleaning

A good spring clean not only makes your property look better, it also gives you the opportunity to assess whether further work is needed. Only by scrubbing the dirt off the skirting boards, for example, can you assess whether they need repainting or simply cleaning.

Clean thoroughly so that everything is left gleaming. Anything still dull, worn, or tarnished needs replacing. Pay special attention to the following:

- **The windows and glass panels in doors:** Hire a window cleaner to do the outside of the property and tackle the inside yourself. Clean windows let in more natural light and create a good impression. Remember that on a sunny day, dirty windows are even more obvious. While you're washing windows, note any cracked panes that need replacing. Check wooden frames too. Do they need repainting or replacing?

- **Windowsills, especially those at the front of the house:** Because they are visible from the street, they are one of the first things the prospective buyer sees. A cluttered windowsill gives an untidy impression, so make sure yours are clear. The one thing you can get away with on a windowsill is a nice big bunch of freshly-cut flowers.

- **Curtains and blinds:** Clean, iron, and re-hang curtains and nets. Use a mild detergent diluted with water to wipe blinds clean.

- **Floors:** Scrub and clean all floors.

- **Light fittings and lampshades:** These can be easy to forget, so make sure you give them a good wipe down.

- **The bathroom:** Make sure baths, toilets, sinks, or showers are sparkling clean. Thoroughly disinfect the toilet with bleach, and make sure all drains are unblocked and not omitting foul odours. Make sure tiles are clean (re-grout them where necessary).

- **The kitchen:** The cooker and oven should be spotless – a task that's likely to require a lot of elbow grease. Don't forget to scrub the floor, and clean out the fridge and defrost the freezer just in case prospective buyers take a look in there.

Ditching the clutter

A successful seller is someone who sees her property through the eye of a buyer. One person's idea of vital furnishings and ornaments is another's idea of clutter.

If prospective buyers can't imagine their belongings – and themselves – in your highly individualistic house, they won't buy it. Keep surfaces clear. If there is a lot of furniture, store some of it until you sell.

Making repairs and improvements

Fix anything that's broken. If you're lucky, most of the repairs will be minor – fixing broken cupboard doors, replacing broken tiles in the bathroom, or re-grouting. Some properties may require fairly major work, such as dealing with a damp patch on the bedroom ceiling.

If carpets are worn or threadbare, think about replacing them, as this will create a much better impression. But don't get too carried away: recarpeting the house from top to bottom is unnecessary and expensive. Likewise, don't buy the priciest carpet available, as you are unlikely to recoup the cost. Opt for medium quality instead.

If you are unsure about replacing the bathroom or kitchen, ask the agent for advice before spending a lot of money. She will have a good idea what improvements appeal to buyers and which don't. This will prevent you from spending money unnecessarily.

Painting

After you've completed the necessary repairs, the property is ready for a lick of paint. Depending on when you last painted and your preference when it comes to colour, you'll either be facing a lot of work or a little.

You need to think about two things when you paint – your choice of colours and the quality of the work. Both can have an impact on how quickly you sell your property. Walls should be painted in light, neutral colours so if you have garish wallpaper or dark-coloured walls, you should consider painting over these.

Make sure you do the job right. There is nothing worse than a botched paint job, with splashes of paint on floorboards or on skirting boards. If you can't afford to get in the professionals, make sure you prepare the walls carefully first. Remove nails and screws and fill any holes with plaster filler. Clean the walls so they are free of dirt before you begin. And don't forget dust sheets to cover floors and furniture.

Book VI

Selling Up at a Profit

Don't forget to paint doors, doorframes, skirting boards, window frames, and ceilings (in white!) or they will look dirty next to your bright, newly painted walls. And don't forget to remove splattered paint from the floor, windows, woodwork, and cabinets, using white spirit as necessary.

Final cleaning

Once you've done the general cleaning, made any necessary repairs, and painted where required, you are ready to re-clean everything. Although another spring clean may be the last thing you feel like doing, cleanliness is next to godliness, and you can't beat a sparkling clean, fresh-smelling house.

As you do your final clean, keep these points in mind:

- ✔ **If your kitchen and bathrooms are dirty or grimy, buyers wonder about the state of the rest of the property.** Nobody wants to spend the first day in their new home scrubbing the previous owner's grime off the bath. See 'General cleaning' for suggestions on cleaning bathrooms.

  Clear the crumbs and clutter from work surfaces in the kitchen, but don't leave them so bare that they look clinical. A couple of strategically placed, expensive-looking appliances (like a stainless steel kettle or a blender) and a pretty fruit bowl kept topped up create interest and give a bit of a lived-in feel.

- ✔ **Buyers really do open the kitchen cupboards and the fridge door.** Make sure you give them a thorough clean.

- ✔ **Smell is important.** Prospective buyers will be put off if your house smells bad, even if it is spotless. So while you're cleaning the property, pay special attention to whiffs. Open windows to get rid of cigarette smoke and use natural-smelling air fresheners: not ones with a nasty artificial smell.

Once you've done the final cleaning, your job is not finished because you still have to keep your house this clean all the while it's for sale. This can be a hassle if it's on the market for ages. But you must ensure that your property is ready for viewings at short notice. Although estate agents try to give you a call to warn you that they're bringing a buyer round, this call may come only half-an-hour before they arrive.

Heavenly scents

Do you need to go as far as baking your own bread to encourage buyers to put in an offer? It certainly smells delicious, but if scores of prospective buyers are traipsing round at all hours of the day, evening, and weekends, you probably don't have time to crank up the oven and get up to your elbows in dough. And in summer, an oven going at full blast is simply going to make prospective buyers think you're mad.

So what about freshly brewed coffee? It smells great and is easier to make than fresh bread. But the smell can be overpowering and isn't to everyone's tastes. Also be wary of using air-fresheners, because these usually smell very artificial and can be a bit overpowering.

Instead, I suggest you dot as many freshly-cut flowers as you can afford around the house. Very fragrant flowers such as freesias smell wonderful and have the added benefit of brightening up a room and giving it a fresh appearance. If you prefer, choose flowers in a single colour that ties in with the colour scheme of the room. You can't go wrong with flowers because they add a touch of class to your décor.

Just make sure they're fresh – few things are worse than dead flowers dropping all over the carpet. Dead flowers are far worse than no flowers at all and create a poor impression because it looks like you simply don't care.

Salesman's Tour Part 1: Assessing the Impression Created by Each Room

As well as general cleaning and repairs, carefully assess each room to ensure it has a clearly defined purpose. Buyers can be easily confused by a bedroom that doubles as a gym, or a dining room that's used as a bedroom. Make sure each room serves its original purpose. If you've converted the dining-room into a fourth bedroom, remove the bed, wardrobe, and other clutter and bring in a table and chairs to turn it back into a dining room, which is a much bigger selling point than a downstairs bedroom.

As you tour your property, jot down work that you need to do to ensure that everything is as it should be in that type of room. As you assess each room, bear in mind your target audience and think about how you can appeal to them. If your property is a modern apartment likely to appeal to young professionals, for example, is your furniture and décor in keeping with that? If the current furniture looks out of place, think about putting it into storage and hiring items more in keeping with the surroundings and the demands of your target market.

Here's a quick list to help you make your property appear at its best:

- ✔ **The hallway:** The hallway is the first room that the prospective buyer sees, so it's vital that the hallway creates the right impression. Remove bikes and junk which could trip prospective buyers up and simply look untidy. If you paint one room, make it the hallway, as it's the first room the buyer sees.

- ✔ **Kitchen:** Paint tired-looking cupboards in light, neutral colours and replace door handles with modern, expensive-looking ones. Ensure cupboards and doors fit well and aren't hanging off their hinges. Replace grubby work surfaces and broken or missing tiles. Worn-out flooring can also be replaced relatively inexpensively with some bright lino.

- ✔ **Sitting-room:** Make sure the furniture looks right. If you've got chintz sofas in an open-plan warehouse space, they will appear out of place. If the current furniture is old or tatty, hire more appropriate sofas, tables, and so on while you are selling. And remember that soft lighting can make a big difference. Opt for lamps rather than a harsh bulb without a lampshade in the middle of the room.

- ✔ **Dining-room:** A real selling point, show it off to its best advantage if you have one. Lay the table with a smart dinner service and cutlery and use fresh flowers as an inviting centrepiece.

- ✔ **Bathroom:** Get rid of carpet unless it is brand new. Lino looks better, is more hygienic and is cheaper than tiling the floor. Think about installing a shower attachment if there isn't one as most buyers expect one. Expect to pay around £100 for a basic power shower from a DIY store. Invest in fluffy white towels, which look great – and you can take them with you when you complete the sale. Buy a new shower curtain.

  Most buyers want a white bathroom suite and won't accept a coloured one. If you have a coloured suite, consider replacing it with a new white, modern suite. A standard white suite, including basin, bath, and toilet starts at around £300, which won't break the bank and could result in a quicker sale.

- ✔ **Bedrooms:** Masculine bedrooms are a big turn-off for women buyers so try to make them more inviting. Make the beds. Bedding should be clean, ironed, matching and of good quality. And opt for soft lighting.

Salesman's Tour Part II: Getting the Outside Ready

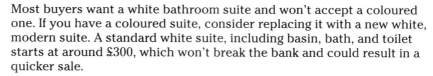

The exterior of the property creates the first impression in the mind of the prospective buyer. And a messy exterior doesn't do justice to a beautiful interior. Here, we explain what you should pay attention to when preparing the *outside* of your property for viewings.

Kerb appeal

Don't underestimate the importance of *kerb appeal* – the appearance of the property from the street. To enhance this, do the following:

- Make sure that the gate opens easily and closes properly (if you have one). If it's hanging off its hinges the buyer will wonder whether the rest of the house is in a similar state. Give it a fresh lick of paint as well and replace any broken panels.

- If you have a fence or wall, ensure it is in good repair and isn't leaning to one side. Give it a fresh lick of paint if necessary.

- Trim hedges and prune trees. Get rid of weeds and make sure the lawn is free of rubbish and cut the grass. You might favour the wild look with waist-high grass, but prospective buyers probably won't share your taste.

- If you have a driveway, make sure no weeds are poking up through the gravel or tarmac.

- Give the garage door a lick of paint, if necessary.

- Spruce up the front door and the area around it. Paint it, if necessary, and polish the knocker, letterbox, and number. If you have a doorbell, make sure it's working. You don't want to leave prospective buyers standing on the doorstep pressing a broken buzzer in vain.

A new door mat is a nice touch: it encourages people to wipe their feet and gives the impression that you care about your property. Steer clear of tacky slogans – you can't beat a *plain* mat.

Window boxes full of colourful flowers are also welcoming, as are well-maintained hanging baskets. Create some balance by putting matching boxes or baskets either side of the front door.

- If there's a caravan on your drive or a clapped out old banger, remove them. Some people have an aversion to caravans, and most people have a dislike of junk. They also detract attention from the property and in the case of the caravan, may make it difficult for the buyer to actually see the house properly. Store these in the garage or away from the property until you've sold it.

- Take a good look at the roof and make arrangements for any needed repairs as soon as possible. Also check the guttering to make sure that it isn't broken or detached from the exterior. Prospective buyers are put off by these problems because they'll have to get them fixed as soon as they move in.

Back garden

Overgrown, unkempt gardens full of weeds are no selling point. So if you're lucky enough to have a back garden, make the most of it. The garden doesn't need to look like it's had a *Ground Force* makeover; just make sure it's neat and well-kept. Simply by cutting the grass, weeding the flowerbeds, pruning the trees, and trimming the hedges, you give the impression that you care – and make it easy for buyers to imagine themselves relaxing and entertaining friends.

You don't have to spend a fortune on expensive shrubs and flowers – and we wouldn't bother unless they're portable, that is, in pots so you can move them from property to property.

Chapter 4

Negotiating a Successful Sale

. . . .

. . . .

*W*hen selling your property, one of the most important aspects of the process is negotiating the price. Rarely does a buyer offer the asking price without attempting to haggle first. Negotiation is part and parcel of the process, so both seller and buyer should be prepared for this. From the seller's point of view, a successful transaction is achieved when you find a buyer who is prepared to pay close to the asking price for your property – and the sale is completed within a reasonable timeframe.

Negotiating the price with a buyer and trying to get her to pay as much as possible for a property is a central part of the estate agent's role – the higher the price he achieves, the greater his commission. If you're selling through an estate agent, you don't have to get involved in negotiations if you don't want to. Your agent will simply ask whether you're prepared to accept an offer. But if you're selling privately, you have to negotiate directly with the buyer.

In this chapter, we look at how to negotiate the best price for your property if you're selling in England, Wales, or Northern Ireland. We also help you decide when to spot a timewaster, when to accept an offer, and when to hold out for a higher one. (For details on selling property in Scotland, see Book VI, Chapter 5).

You Don't Always Get What You Ask For: Negotiating the Price

Sellers have to settle on an asking price when they put their home up for sale (unless the property is at the top end of the market and offers are invited instead). Yet few properties are sold for the asking price. Your property may fetch many thousands of pounds above the asking price in a buoyant market, or it may fetch thousands of pounds below the asking price in a slow market. Buyers expect to pay less than the advertised price for a property and sellers tend to set the price higher than the amount they would happily accept to allow for this.

The asking price is usually considered by both parties to be negotiable. Even so, you must set it carefully because it affects what you end up getting. If you fix it too low in the first place, you're likely to get much less than you had hoped for. Buyers nearly always offer less than the asking price unless they face a lot of competition from other buyers. If you price your property at the minimum you'd be happy to accept, you won't be happy going any lower, yet the buyer will expect to knock you down a little. So when setting the asking price, always ask for several thousand pounds more than the minimum you would happily accept.

Typically, this is how offers are made:

1. **The buyer makes an offer through the estate agent, if you're using one, and directly to you if you are selling your property privately.**

   Buyers tend to make offers verbally, but the estate agent should put them in writing when conveying them to you.

2. **You must decide whether to accept or reject the offer.**

   The first offer is usually turned down as a matter of course because it's likely to be a fair way below the asking price. The buyer may be chancing his luck to see how you react. If it's a ridiculous offer, you should have no qualms about rejecting it. See the later section 'Contemplating Offers' for information on what to consider when you make your decision to accept or reject.

3. **The estate agent conveys your decision to the buyer.**

   If you reject the offer, the buyer can make another offer or give up and look for another property. If the buyer makes an improved offer, you should consider it carefully, even if it's still below the asking price.

   When deciding whether to accept an offer you should take into account whether it's higher than the minimum you're prepared to accept (which you should never reveal to the buyer) and how quickly you want to sell.

4. **If you decide to accept an offer, tell your estate agent.** He will inform the buyer who will then contact his solicitor and pass on details of the property, the agreed price, your contact details and those of your solicitor. The conveyancing process then begins.

5. **You should also inform your solicitor that you have accepted an offer on your property.** Once he has received a written offer from the buyer's solicitor, he will draw up the draft contract.

Here are some important points to remember as you negotiate:

- ✔ **Nothing is guaranteed until exchange of contracts (when both you and the buyer sign the contract).** Before then, both sides can pull out.

- ✔ **The price you agree with a buyer is not necessarily what you will end up getting.** Much can happen between agreeing to a price and exchange of contracts. Offers are made 'subject to contract and survey' and if the survey reveals any major structural problems, the buyer will want to pay less for the property. You don't have to agree to this, but you will have to be flexible if you are to achieve a successful sale.

- ✔ **If you are personally negotiating with the buyer, be firm but reasonable.** You, as the seller, have the upper hand; if you don't want to accept an offer, you don't have to – and the deal's off. But you need to weigh up whether the offer you've got is the best you're likely to get or whether you're prepared to hold out for another offer, which could take months.

- ✔ **Weed out the timewasters by checking that the buyer can afford your property, has already got a firm buyer for his own home – if he is selling one – and wants to move in around the time you were hoping to complete.** Only then should you accept his offer and take your property off the market.

- ✔ **There is no need to rush into a decision.** You can reasonably take a day or two to consider an offer before responding. You may even get a better offer from another buyer in the meantime!

Contemplating Offers

Whether you get one offer or several, you need to work out a strategy for dealing with them. Most sellers want to get the best price for their property in the shortest possible time. But this is not always the case. No two property transactions are the same, and your personal circumstances can go a long way towards dictating how you handle offers for your property. If you need a quick sale, you may have to accept a lower offer than you would if you weren't in a hurry.

Considering the first offer that comes along

Getting an offer is thrilling because it means someone wants to buy your property and you move one step closer to your next investment. But try not to get carried away. If the offer is close to the asking price, you may be very tempted to accept it. But beware of accepting the first offer that comes along, particularly if your property has only been on the market for a day or two. If you've managed to attract a serious buyer in that time, you either have an extremely desirable property, the market is buoyant, or the asking price is too low. If you can, wait a little longer to see whether you get any other – higher – offers.

Before accepting or rejecting an offer, ask your estate agent whether he thinks you are likely to get other – higher – offers. He should have a good understanding of current market conditions and be able to advise whether waiting a little longer for a better offer is worth your while.

If you are genuinely prepared to wait, you may find that the buyer raises his original offer if he's genuinely keen on your property. The new and improved offer may convince you to accept it. But don't reject an offer simply as a ploy to spur the buyer to offer more. He may not make an improved offer – maybe he decided the property isn't worth it – and you may have to wait many months for another buyer to come along.

Receiving offers from several buyers

Most sellers would love to receive several offers for their property so they can choose the most desirable buyer offering the highest price. Not only should this enable you to get a buyer who isn't in a chain (see the section 'Buyers in chains' later in this chapter), with his financing already arranged, but you may also get more than the asking price.

Part of the estate agent's job is to get the best – that means the highest – asking price for your home. If several buyers are interested in one property, your estate agent usually plays them off against one another. For example, if a property is on the market at £150,000 and one buyer is prepared to pay the asking price, the agent informs other buyers of this and asks if they're prepared to beat it. If a second buyer offers £155,000, this information is relayed back to the first buyer who has to decide whether to increase her offer. This continues until one buyer is left in the frame – and you end up with a purchase price that is higher than your original asking price.

Dealing with offers significantly below the asking price

You may find that prospective buyers are only happy to offer significantly less than the asking price on your property. There are several reasons why they may do this and you need to weigh up whether the reasons are good ones and whether you should accept a much lower offer:

- ✔ **Your property has been on the market for several months without a bite.** You may have despaired of ever receiving an offer and then when you do get one, it's much less than the amount you are hoping to receive. You have a choice: either reject this offer and hang on, possibly for several more months, until a better one comes along, or accept it. If you can afford to wait, you may eventually achieve a better price. But if you need to sell as soon as possible, you have to accept the lower price.

- ✔ **Your property is on the market at a much higher price than similar properties in the area.** Prices may have fallen since you first put your property on the market. If your asking price starts to look expensive, you may have to reduce it – or at least be prepared to accept a lower offer.

- ✔ **Your property needs major structural work.** Many people don't want to take on a property requiring major structural renovations. You must be realistic. If the next owner of your property will have to spend a lot of money putting things right, it's only reasonable that the purchase price should be lower to reflect this fact.

If you receive an offer significantly below the asking price, the action you take depends on your personal circumstances. If you desperately need to sell, you may have to accept a lower offer. But if this is the case, don't let the buyer know you are desperate or he will take advantage of this fact and offer even less.

Using sealed bids or 'best and final offers'

If several buyers are keen to purchase your property, one way of deciding between them and achieving the highest price is through *sealed bids* or *best and final offers*. These are very common in Scotland and some parts of the UK when the property market is booming. The big advantage of sealed bids is that there is a chance you'll get a few thousand pounds above the asking price.

Outfoxing the timewasters

A friend of mine rented out her two-bedroom flat in east London when she moved in with her boyfriend. She had no trouble finding good tenants, but when she became pregnant, she and her boyfriend decided to sell both flats and buy a house with more space.

Unfortunately, they made the decision at a time when the housing market was depressed. They received offers on the flats, but they were ridiculously low. Although my friend's flat was for sale at £270,000 – well in line with what she would easily have got several months before – prospective buyers were offering more than £40,000 below the asking price. Even in a quiet market, these offers were ludicrous. The buyers weren't interested in upping their offers. It seemed that they weren't really serious about buying; just trying to see how low an offer they could get away with.

Luckily, my friend and her boyfriend were far from desperate. They decided to take both flats off the market and carry on renting out her flat. Once the market picks up a bit, the plan is to try selling both flats again. It's a bit of a squeeze living in a small flat with a new baby, but they'd rather do that than lose out on thousands of pounds.

Remember: If you've got the option of waiting, you're in a stronger position and are more likely to get the price you want – eventually.

With sealed bids, or best and final offers, buyers interested in purchasing your property must make an offer in writing to your estate agent or solicitor by a certain deadline. Once the deadline has passed, the agent or solicitor opens the bids and informs you of what they are. You get to decide which one you accept (if any).

The highest bid isn't necessarily always the successful one. A lower offer from a buyer who is in a position to move quickly could work out better for you. Look for offers from buyers who are chain-free, have found a buyer for their own home, or have a mortgage agreed in principle.

No gazumping!

Even if you have accepted an offer nothing is guaranteed until exchange of contracts and both buyer and seller can pull out before this stage is reached. The price can change if the buyer's survey reveals problems with the property or the seller accepts a higher offer from another buyer after agreeing on a price with someone else. This latter situation is known as *gazumping*.

Although it's perfectly legal to accept an offer from another buyer before contracts are exchanged, even if you have already accepted an offer, it isn't fair – at least not without giving the original buyer a chance to match the new offer. Think how you'd feel if you were gazumped (which, since you've certainly bought a property yourself, isn't so unlikely). In addition, gazumping can be expensive for the buyer who may have already instructed a solicitor or arranged a survey.

You may be tempted to accept a higher offer from another buyer, but resist doing so. Price isn't everything, and if someone made an offer that you were happy to accept at the time, be decent enough to stand by your agreement. Here's a good rule to follow – treat others as you would like to be treated yourself.

Not All Buyers are Equal

Price is important when it comes to selling your property, but it isn't the be all and end all. Whether the purchase is successfully completed or not depends on a variety of factors including the buyer's financial position, if he is in a chain, and whether the survey uncovers serious problems with the property.

Buyers to avoid

Some buyers spell trouble. They mess you about and hold up the sale, sometimes through no fault of their own but because they are in a complicated chain. Either way, they can make your life a misery and delay your sale. Below, we look at how you can spot them.

Those who've yet to sell their own homes

Avoid accepting an offer from a buyer who has yet to find someone to purchase his home. If a prospective buyer tells you that he has an interested buyer but she hasn't made a firm offer, wait until she has before taking your property off the market. If his 'buyer' falls through, you could hang around for months waiting for him to find another one when you could have found a serious buyer during that time. And in the interim, you may miss out on a property that you had your eye on.

Buyers who haven't arranged financing

If a buyer hasn't already got her finances arranged when she makes an offer on your property, there's a chance she may not be able to get that funding. If this is the case, you're wasting your time accepting her offer. Several wasted weeks could pass before you're finally able to pin the prospective buyer down about her lack of finances, during which time you could have sold your property to someone who'd sorted all this out in advance.

One of the best ways of ensuring that this doesn't happen is to ask the prospective buyer for evidence of her ability to raise the necessary funds. Most lenders will issue a certificate – known as *an agreement in principle* – stating that it will lend the buyer a certain amount of cash, subject to survey. While an agreement in principle isn't an absolute guarantee, it is useful as it demonstrates that the lender can't see anything glaringly wrong with the applicant. It also shows that the buyer is serious about purchasing a property because she's gone to the trouble of consulting a lender.

Make sure you know a buyer's financial status before accepting an offer. This is a vital part of the estate agent's job.

Buyers in chains

Most people who sell a property buy another one at the same time. If your buyer is relying on someone else to buy his home so that he can purchase yours – he's part of a *chain*. If you accept his offer, you become part of the chain. If someone pulls out, the chain is broken and you, along with everyone else in the chain, are affected. With several people in the average chain, the chain can dominate transactions in England and Wales. A lot of juggling has to go on between solicitors to ensure that exchange of contracts and completion happens at the same time on all properties in a chain.

Chains – especially long ones – can easily be broken because there is more of a chance of complications arising. The shorter the chain you're involved in, the better. It might not seem important when you find an enthusiastic buyer who is prepared to pay the asking price for your property, but if the buyer is the first in a long and complicated chain, you could be asking for trouble.

If at all possible, opt for someone who isn't part of a chain, such as a first-time buyer. They may have more trouble financing their purchase than a homeowner – although this doesn't always follow – but this is likely to be the only potential hiccup. If you have several interested buyers to choose between, someone who is buying their first home – or anyone else not involved in a chain – should be top of the list.

Buyers you want

Just as there are prospective buyers you should avoid, there are those that you should be looking to attract. These are buyers who have gone to the trouble of arranging their finances in advance, aren't tied up in complicated chains, and want to move as quickly as possible (if this happens to suit you too). Below, we run through what you should look for in a buyer.

Cash is king

Any reasonable offer made by someone who can afford your property is worth considering, but the most desirable buyer is one who has the cash ready to buy. He doesn't need to get a mortgage beforehand, nor does he have to sell a property before he can buy yours. He has the cash – whether it is from investments, an inheritance, or other source – and he is ready to make an offer.

Cash buyers can move quickly because they don't have to wait for money to come through from a lender or for their home to be sold. They may also be more prepared to pay close to the asking price if they really want your property, as they have funds at their disposal.

First-time buyers

If you're selling a studio, one-bedroom flat, or small house, your property may be suitable for a first-time buyer – an attractive option for a seller. First-time buyers aren't caught up in complicated chains because they aren't selling a property (see the section 'Buyers in chains' for information on why a chain is a bad thing).

Pay particular attention to a first-time buyer's finances. With property prices rocketing in the early 2000s, many first-time buyers have been priced out of the market. They can only afford to purchase a property with help from parents and family or by borrowing many times their income. Ask for evidence that a mortgage lender has agreed in principle to lending them the money, subject to survey.

Because first-time buyers are new to the house-buying process, they may not be aware of the order in which things are done. Ensure your agent keeps an eye on them so they know when to send what to the solicitor. If you aren't using an agent, be sure to do this yourself.

Buyers between homes

Some people choose to sell their home and move into rented accommodation while they look for another. Maybe they made this decision because of a booming housing market; they want to get the best price for their home but don't want to buy another until prices fall. Or they may be considering moving to a new area and want to rent before committing to a permanent move. Either way, these buyers have cash in the bank, so are perfect candidates for a quick sale.

Landlords

The growth of the buy-to-let market means an increasing number of people are setting themselves up as landlords. It's good news if a buyer intends to rent your property to tenants, particularly if he already owns several properties: He probably has a good relationship with his lender, so arranging financing shouldn't be a problem. And because he won't be living in the property, he won't have to sell his own home – speeding up the process.

If you are dealing with a professional landlord with scores of properties, he is likely to be hard-nosed about the price he pays. He is running a business after all and is unlikely to allow emotions to play a part in his decision. Bear this in mind, and don't feel pressurised into accepting a lower price than you're happy with.

Taking Action When You Aren't Getting Any Offers

The nightmare scenario for sellers is when no one shows an interest in their property. There could be many reasons for this, including a depressed market, an overpriced house, or the rundown property next door. If you find yourself in this unenviable position, work out what's causing a lack of offers before you take action, such as lowering your price. You may discover that price isn't the issue at all.

Give it time. Some top-end or unusual properties can take months to shift. And if the market is slow, you'll struggle to sell your property. Don't panic if your property has been for sale for two weeks and you haven't had a buyer round. These things don't happen overnight, so don't rush into taking remedial action before giving it a chance.

Seeking advice

If your property hasn't sold after several weeks, there may be a problem. Seeing what could be causing a lack of offers can be hard. What may be a glaring fault to a prospective buyer you may not even notice. If nobody is biting your hand off to purchase your house, you need to find out from others why that is.

Prospective buyers

One of the best sources of feedback is a prospective buyer who viewed your property but didn't make an offer. The agent should give you feedback after viewings. If several buyers make the same complaint – about the caravan in the drive or the poky garden, for example – you can rectify the situation by removing the caravan or thinning out the plants. Recurring complaints need attention if you are going to find a buyer.

Estate agent

If you haven't had any viewings, ask the agent why. She may suggest that the price is too high or that business is slow and you have to be patient. She may also suggest improvements you can make to the property to increase the chances of a sale.

If you are unhappy with your agent's efforts and have given him several weeks to prove his worth, you should consider switching agents. Check your contract to see when you can instruct another agent without incurring a penalty or having to pay two lots of commission if the second agent manages to sell your property.

Holding tight – for now

If prospective buyers willing to pay close to the asking price are few and far between, you may decide to take your property off the market for now. If you aren't in a hurry to sell, this may be the best plan. Once the market picks up a bit, you can put it up for sale again. This way you are more likely to get the price you want.

Lowering the price

Sitting tight and waiting for a buyer prepared to offer the asking price isn't always convenient. If you're short of time and need to sell quickly, or haven't had any offers in several months, you may have to reduce the price. If the market is quiet and many sellers are reducing their asking price, you're even less likely to get a sale if you don't reduce the price.

Lower the price by a few thousand pounds initially to see whether this generates more interest. If it doesn't, think about reducing it further. Try not to make the mistake of knocking too much off initially because you could end up under-selling your property when it's not necessary.

Lowering the price should be your last resort for these reasons. First, buyers who sense desperation try to take advantage and knock the price down further. Second, after the asking price has been reduced, warning bells start to sound. Buyers will wonder what's wrong with your property and think twice about making an offer at all.

Chapter 5

Selling in Scotland

The house-selling process in Scotland is quite different from the rest of the UK. But if you're selling in Scotland, at least you probably have some idea of what to expect, as you will also have bought a property there (unless you inherited a house).

As with buying in Scotland, a solicitor gets involved much earlier on in the selling process than in England, Wales, or Northern Ireland. And unlike the rest of the UK, solicitors offer an integrated service. Not only do they offer legal advice, they also play the role of estate agents in advertising and helping you sell your property. This means you don't have to deal with an agent at all if you don't want to – information which is likely to be music to the ears of many sellers (and buyers)!

The main advantage of the Scottish selling process is that it's far quicker than the process in the rest of the UK. And because neither party can pull out once missives are concluded, you can make an offer on another property, confident that your sale won't fall through. It all makes for less stress – and a better night's sleep!

In this chapter, we offer tips on finding a solicitor and advertising your property. We also look at what to consider when setting the asking price and deciding which offer to accept.

For details of the selling process in England, Wales and Northern Ireland, see Book I, Chapter 4.

The Preliminaries

The house-selling process moves so much quicker in Scotland than the rest of the UK and the transaction is legally binding much earlier. For these reasons, you must get everything ready *before* you put your property up for sale otherwise you can find yourself accepting an offer before a solicitor has made sure everything is in order.

Finding a solicitor

Just as you need to find a solicitor before you view properties if you are buying in Scotland, you must also instruct a solicitor as soon as you decide to sell. This should done *before* you put your property on the market because your solicitor has work to do before you can do this.

Personal recommendation is the best way of finding a solicitor. If a friend or relative has had a good experience with one, try to instruct her as well. Or if you were happy with the solicitor you used to purchase your home and he's available again, use him. Finding a good solicitor can be hit and miss so if you have a head start, take advantage of it.

Because most Scottish properties are sold through solicitors' property centres, you may also want your solicitor to help find a buyer for your property – usually the estate agent's role in the rest of the UK. If so, opt for a solicitor who uses a big property centre so that your property gets plenty of exposure. That way, you could find a buyer more quickly.

If you're buying a property as well as selling one, we suggest you use the same solicitor for both transactions. Not only is this likely to be cheaper, it also saves you the hassle of having to deal with – and chase up – more than one person.

As you look for a solicitor, get quotes, in writing, for fees and charges. If you contact several solicitors, get quotes from all of them. As you choose, however, keep in mind that the cheapest solicitor may not be the best choice. A solicitor who's been recommended to you may be worth a little bit extra. You don't want to end up paying in the long run because you skimped on advice at this stage.

Once you've found a solicitor, he has a number of tasks to complete before you can put your property on the market. These include:

✔ **Checking whether the property is yours to sell in the first place:** The title deeds are your proof of ownership; your mortgage lender usually keeps these safe. Your solicitor applies to borrow this document so that he can check that you have *clean title* – that is, you can sell the property. You may not be able to if you share title with a spouse, friend, or sibling, for example, and need to get that person's permission before you can sell. This can slow things down if you're divorced or separated or in the process of being so.

✔ **Finding out how much you owe on your mortgage:** When you sell your property, you have to repay the outstanding sum on your mortgage. Your solicitor finds out from your lender how much you owe. He takes this money out of the purchase price (which the buyer's solicitor transfers to him on the date of settlement) and repays the lender for you. Knowing what you owe is important so that you can work out how much cash you'll have left over after you clear the balance, because the leftover amount is what you can put towards your next investment.

✔ **Undertaking various local authority searches:** Your solicitor checks with the local authority on a range of matters, such as your right of way, restrictions, outstanding proposals, and so on.

✔ **Getting you to complete a property information form and fixtures, fittings, and contents form:** The property information form is a standard questionnaire. You have to provide details of boundaries, whether you've had disputes with neighbours, and other information about your property. As for fixtures, fittings, and contents, you have to decide what is and isn't included in the sale.

Book VI

Selling Up at a Profit

Setting the asking price

You can put your property on the market for a fixed price but most sellers go for *offers over*. The asking price – or upset price – is usually the very minimum you expect to get for the property, and bids are invited above this amount.

In setting the asking price, discuss the issue with your solicitor or an agent. They should have a good idea what price similar properties are fetching in your area. Your asking price should be set with this in mind. You don't have to listen to their advice – the ultimate decision is yours. But they should know what they are talking about, so at least consider their advice.

If you're selling privately, you will have to set the price yourself. Check what similar properties in your area are fetching and price your property accordingly. The alternative is to commission a chartered surveyor to value it; however, that isn't always that useful because the report doesn't take prevailing market conditions into account.

In England, Wales, and Northern Ireland, most sellers ask two or three estate agents what they should set the asking price at. In Scotland, however, nearly half of buyers ask their solicitors. According to a survey from the Scottish Executive, 48 per cent of sellers sought advice from an agent, while 38 per cent asked a solicitor what he thought they should put their property on the market at. The remainder asked a surveyor or valuer, or simply didn't seek any advice.

Picking Someone to Sell Your Property

You can sell your property yourself, but most people prefer to get somebody else to do it for them. Estate agents sell most property in England, Wales, and Northern Ireland but in Scotland, most sellers use a solicitor.

Whether you use an agent or solicitor to sell your property, read the contract carefully before signing. Pay particular attention to these things:

- ✔ **Whether you can cancel the contract and how long the contract runs.** Don't sign any contract that ties you to the agent or solicitor for longer than about eight weeks.

- ✔ **How much the solicitor or estate agent is going to charge you.** You should get a complete breakdown of the cost, including extra fees for advertising, if applicable, and VAT. If you aren't happy with the price you're quoted, try negotiating, or if the agent or solicitor won't budge, take your business elsewhere.

Using a solicitor

When you use a solicitor to sell your property, he does your legal work in addition to providing a full estate agency service and dealing with offers from prospective buyers. The only thing he won't do is show buyers round. You can ask him to if you'd rather not do this yourself, but you will have to pay extra.

Solicitors sell property through solicitors' property centres. These are located in most main cities throughout Scotland, and only solicitors can advertise in them. The advantage of selling your property through a solicitor who has access to a property centre is that you get much greater exposure to potential buyers than if you opt for an estate agent.

Your solicitor writes the property particulars – a description of your property and the number and type of rooms – and includes the asking price. Also included are arrangements for viewing and your contact details. Prospective buyers contact you, not your solicitor.

Your solicitor pays the property centre a fee for advertising your property, which varies from centre to centre. To give you an idea of the likely cost, the Glasgow Solicitors Property Centre (GSPC) charges a one-off fixed fee upwards from £195.00, including VAT. Your property is advertised until it is sold – or for six months, whichever happens sooner. The fee covers advertising in the GSPC Property Guide (a mailing list); an advert on the Web site; and another in the property centre. For more details on the GSPC's services, go to www.gspc.co.uk.

Book VI

Selling Up at a Profit

This fee is just the cost of advertising your property. You also have to pay your solicitor commission (usually between 1 per cent and 1.5 per cent of the selling price) if he sells your property. Some solicitors charge a separate conveyancing fee for handling the transfer of property from you to the buyer, and you also have to pay VAT on this.

Using an estate agent

If you opt for an agent to handle your sale, he deals with all aspects of the sale from writing the property particulars, to advertising, showing people round (sometimes he charges an extra fee for this), and negotiating. This is ideal for sellers who prefer to keep their distance from prospective buyers. The Office of Fair Trading produces a guide to using an agent to sell your property. Go to www.oft.gov.uk/Consumer.

Finding the right agent is crucial for a successful sale. Opt for one who is registered with the National Association of Estate Agents (NAEA) or a member of the Royal Institute of Chartered Surveyors (RICS); that way you've got some comeback if you aren't happy.

Expect to pay 1.5 per cent of your property's selling price in commission to the agent who achieves the sale. Make sure you get these charges in writing before signing a contract so there are no nasty surprises. Some agents charge extra for advertising the property (although how they hope to achieve a sale without this is anyone's guess!) or for a 'For Sale' board. Some agents charge a fixed fee rather than commission. Check what your agent prefers before instructing her. Fees are usually paid on conclusion of missives, so make sure the contract states this.

Try to negotiate lower commission and fees with the agent, particularly if it's a quiet time of year, and she's desperate for the business.

Estate agents' contracts often contain a number of confusing technical terms. Make sure you fully understand them before you agree to anything.

Whatever happens, don't sign over sole selling rights to an agent; this means you have to pay commission even if *you* manage to find a buyer. Also avoid the phrase 'Ready, willing, and able purchaser' which means you still have to pay the agent's commission even if you withdraw from the sale, and unconditional missives are not exchanged.

If you use an agent, you will still have to deal with a solicitor when you get to the conveyancing stage. So don't forget that, in addition to the agent's commission, you also have to pay a solicitor for the legal work and searches. For that reason, most people prefer to use a solicitor to sell their property in the first place and be done with it.

Doing it yourself

Some sellers try to save money by selling their property themselves, rather than using a solicitor or agent. This may save you money but it's also time-consuming, stressful, and may ultimately turn into a disaster if you get it wrong. If you have never sold a property before using a solicitor or agent, we don't recommend doing it yourself because you haven't got a clue how things work.

Have you got the time and energy to devote to selling your property? You have to set the asking price, write the particulars, do the advertising, and handle viewings. You also need to negotiate a purchase price. This is a lot to take on, and if you can't do it properly, it's better not to attempt it at all. We discuss going it alone and selling your property privately in more detail in Book VI, Chapter 2.

Even if you sell your property yourself, you still need to employ a solicitor to do your conveyancing – unless you fancy an even bigger challenge and want to do it all yourself! But unless you really want your life to be that much more difficult, get a professional to handle the legal side of things.

If you use a solicitor for the conveyancing, give him notice that you're planning on selling your property, just as you would if you were using a solicitor or agent to handle the sale. You must also clarify in advance, in writing, what he is going to charge you for the conveyancing.

Handling Viewings

If you use a solicitor or agent to sell your property, you will still probably end up showing prospective buyers around yourself. Handling your own viewings makes sense because you know more about the property than anyone else and can field questions from interested buyers. Of course, not everyone is comfortable doing this. If you don't want to, your solicitor or agent will do it – although you have to pay extra.

Before you show anyone around your property, make sure you present it in its best light.

The easier you make it for prospective buyers to view your property, the quicker you are likely to find one ready to make you an offer. Accept evening and weekend viewings, even though it will upset your family's routine. And make sure you give the prospective buyer space on second and subsequent viewings. She should already know her way round and may want to measure up. She will appreciate it if you don't breathe down her neck so remain in the background, ready to answer questions if needed.

Receiving Offers

If a buyer is interested in making an offer for your property, his solicitor will *note interest* with your solicitor. This means you have to give him an opportunity to make an offer – in other words, you can't accept an offer from another buyer until you have given him a chance to bid.

When you get only one offer

If only one prospective buyer notes interest, you should wait until he makes an offer. As this should be above the upset, it is likely to be acceptable to you. (If it is below the upset, there may be a reason for this – perhaps the survey reveals lots of problems. You don't have to accept this offer but you may want to negotiate with the buyer until you agree on a price that you are both happy with.) The prospective buyer also includes the date of entry (when he proposes to move in) and what extras, such as carpets and curtains he also wants to buy. Even if you are happy with the price, you may want to negotiate the other details.

Going with sealed bids

If more than one buyer notes interest, it can go to sealed bids – where you are likely to get more than the asking price. Your solicitor sets a deadline by which interested parties must submit their bid for your property. They don't know what the other buyers are offering (hence, this is sometimes referred to as *bidding blind*).

The deadline for bids should be far enough ahead to give buyers time to arrange a survey and mortgage. Once the deadline has passed, your solicitor or agent tells you what the bids are. As well as a price, the buyer includes a proposed entry date and whether he wants any of your fixtures and fittings. Take all these factors into consideration when considering offers.

The advantage of sealed bids is that the offer process isn't long and drawn out. You know that by a certain time on a certain day you will have some serious offers on the table.

When you work with sealed bids, keep these points in mind:

✔ You get to choose which bid to accept – or you can reject all of them. The highest bid is usually successful, but not always – particularly if the bidder has some unacceptable conditions. You may choose a lower bid if the buyer can move quickly and has picked an entry date in line with your expectations.

✔ If none of the offers are as high as you'd hoped, you can ask all the bidders to improve their offers; there's no guarantee any of them will though. Remember that it's unethical to ask one bidder to increase her offer without giving the others an opportunity to do the same.

✔ A buyer usually only gets the chance to make one bid so he is under pressure to make sure it is a good one. If your property generates a lot of competition, one of the buyers may bid a lot more than the upset in order to secure the property. This is excellent news for you.

Entering the Home Straight

Once you have decided to accept an offer, your solicitor or agent informs the successful buyer's solicitor over the telephone and then follows this up with a formal qualified acceptance, saying which terms in the offer you accept and which ones you don't. Your solicitor also contacts unsuccessful buyers.

The exchange of missives

The buyer's offer isn't set in stone at this stage. Even though your solicitor has informed the buyer's solicitor that you've accepted the offer, you and the buyer can still negotiate the fine points through your solicitors, who send letters backwards and forwards to hammer out an agreement. This is known as *exchange of missives*.

The buyer's solicitor responds with his comments to your proposed changes and your solicitor responds to the buyer's solicitor's response, and so on, until both parties are happy. This usually takes days rather than weeks.

Both you and the buyer can pull out of the deal while missives are being exchanged. You don't have to pay compensation if you pull out.

Conclusion of missives: No going back

When both of you are happy with the contract, missives are *concluded* and the contract is legally binding on both sides. If either party pulls out after this, considerable compensation must be paid to the other party. So make sure you know what you are getting into before this stage.

If you use an agent, he now passes details of the successful offer onto your solicitor. The agent's work is done, and he's usually paid at this stage; it is now down to your solicitor to do the conveyancing. By now, you know what the date of entry is (usually a month after the sale is concluded) – the date by which you must give your solicitor the keys. The buyer can then move in.

Completing the Sale

Once missives are concluded, your solicitor must send the title deeds to the buyer's solicitor. The buyer's solicitor checks these to ensure the deed is in your name and that you can sell the property. If all is correct, he prepares the disposition – the document transferring your property to the buyer.

Your solicitor also informs your lender that missives have been concluded and asks for a redemption statement detailing the outstanding balance on your mortgage. He arranges for this to be paid on completion. At this stage, he also prepares the discharge document and gets the lender to sign it before the date of entry. He also searches the Registers to ensure nothing untoward is noted against you or the property.

Your solicitor adjusts the terms of the disposition, if necessary, once he receives it from the buyer's solicitor, and you have to sign it. On the date of entry, your solicitor delivers the keys to the buyer's solicitor and the signed disposition – in return for the money to buy your property. Your solicitor deducts his fee and the outstanding mortgage. The remainder of the cash is transferred to your account, and the transaction is complete. Congratulations! You've just completed a property deal!

Index

FOR DUMMIES®

Do Anything. Just Add Dummies

PROPERTY

UK editions

978-0-7645-7027-8

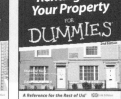

978-0-470-02921-3

Buying a Property in Eastern Europe

978-0-7645-7047-6

PERSONAL FINANCE

978-0-7645-7023-0

978-0-470-51510-5

978-0-470-05815-2

BUSINESS

978-0-7645-7018-6

978-0-7645-7056-8

978-0-7645-7026-1

Answering Tough Interview Questions For Dummies
(978-0-470-01903-0)

Arthritis For Dummies
(978-0-470-02582-6)

Being the Best Man For Dummies
(978-0-470-02657-1)

British History For Dummies
(978-0-470-03536-8)

Building Self-Confidence For Dummies
(978-0-470-01669-5)

Buying a Home on a Budget For Dummies
(978-0-7645-7035-3)

Children's Health For Dummies
(978-0-470-02735-6)

Cognitive Behavioural Therapy For Dummies
(978-0-470-01838-5)

Cricket For Dummies
(978-0-470-03454-5)

CVs For Dummies
(978-0-7645-7017-9)

Detox For Dummies
(978-0-470-01908-5)

Diabetes For Dummies
(978-0-470-05810-7)

Divorce For Dummies
(978-0-7645-7030-8)

DJing For Dummies
(978-0-470-03275-6)

eBay.co.uk For Dummies
(978-0-7645-7059-9)

English Grammar For Dummies
(978-0-470-05752-0)

Gardening For Dummies
(978-0-470-01843-9)

Genealogy Online For Dummies
(978-0-7645-7061-2)

Green Living For Dummies
(978-0-470-06038-4)

Hypnotherapy For Dummies
(978-0-470-01930-6)

Life Coaching For Dummies
(978-0-470-03135-3)

Neuro-linguistic Programming For Dummies
(978-0-7645-7028-5)

Nutrition For Dummies
(978-0-7645-7058-2)

Parenting For Dummies
(978-0-470-02714-1)

Pregnancy For Dummies
(978-0-7645-7042-1)

Rugby Union For Dummies
(978-0-470-03537-5)

Self Build and Renovation For Dummies
(978-0-470-02586-4)

Starting a Business on eBay.co.uk For Dummies
(978-0-470-02666-3)

Starting and Running an Online Business For Dummies
(978-0-470-05768-1)

The GL Diet For Dummies
(978-0-470-02753-0)

The Romans For Dummies
(978-0-470-03077-6)

Thyroid For Dummies
(978-0-470-03172-8)

UK Law and Your Rights For Dummies
(978-0-470-02796-7)

Writing a Novel and Getting Published For Dummies
(978-0-470-05910-4)

FOR DUMMIES®

Do Anything. Just Add Dummies

HOBBIES

978-0-7645-5232-8

978-0-7645-6847-3

978-0-7645-5476-6

Also available:

Art For Dummies
(978-0-7645-5104-8)

Aromatherapy For Dummies
(978-0-7645-5171-0)

Bridge For Dummies
(978-0-471-92426-5)

Card Games For Dummies
(978-0-7645-9910-1)

Chess For Dummies
(978-0-7645-8404-6)

Improving Your Memory
For Dummies
(978-0-7645-5435-3)

Massage For Dummies
(978-0-7645-5172-7)

Meditation For Dummies
(978-0-471-77774-8)

Photography For Dummies
(978-0-7645-4116-2)

Quilting For Dummies
(978-0-7645-9799-2)

EDUCATION

978-0-7645-7206-7

978-0-7645-5581-7

978-0-7645-5422-3

Also available:

Algebra For Dummies
(978-0-7645-5325-7)

Algebra II For Dummies
(978-0-471-77581-2)

Astronomy For Dummies
(978-0-7645-8465-7)

Buddhism For Dummies
(978-0-7645-5359-2)

Calculus For Dummies
(978-0-7645-2498-1)

Forensics For Dummies
(978-0-7645-5580-0)

Islam For Dummies
(978-0-7645-5503-9)

Philosophy For Dummies
(978-0-7645-5153-6)

Religion For Dummies
(978-0-7645-5264-9)

Trigonometry For Dummies
(978-0-7645-6903-6)

PETS

978-0-470-03717-1

978-0-7645-8418-3

978-0-7645-5275-5

Also available:

Aquariums For Dummies
(978-0-7645-5156-7)

Birds For Dummies
(978-0-7645-5139-0)

Dogs For Dummies
(978-0-7645-5274-8)

Ferrets For Dummies
(978-0-7645-5259-5)

Golden Retrievers
For Dummies
(978-0-7645-5267-0)

Horses For Dummies
(978-0-7645-9797-8)

Jack Russell Terriers
For Dummies
(978-0-7645-5268-7)

Labrador Retrievers
For Dummies
(978-0-7645-5281-6)

Puppies Raising & Training
Diary For Dummies
(978-0-7645-0876-9)

FOR DUMMIES®

The easy way to get more done and have more fun

LANGUAGES

978-0-7645-5193-2

978-0-7645-5193-2

978-0-7645-5196-3

Also available:

Chinese For Dummies
(978-0-471-78897-3)

Chinese Phrases
For Dummies
(978-0-7645-8477-0)

French Phrases For Dummies
(978-0-7645-7202-9)

German For Dummies
(978-0-7645-5195-6)

Hebrew For Dummies
(978-0-7645-5489-6)

Italian Phrases For Dummies
(978-0-7645-7203-6)

Japanese For Dummies
(978-0-7645-5429-2)

Latin For Dummies
(978-0-7645-5431-5)

Spanish Phrases
For Dummies
(978-0-7645-7204-3)

Spanish Verbs For Dummies
(978-0-471-76872-2)

MUSIC AND FILM

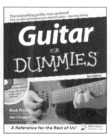

978-0-7645-9904-0

978-0-7645-2476-9

978-0-7645-5105-5

Also available:

Bass Guitar For Dummies
(978-0-7645-2487-5)

Blues For Dummies
(978-0-7645-5080-5)

Classical Music For Dummies
(978-0-7645-5009-6)

Drums For Dummies
(978-0-471-79411-0)

Jazz For Dummies
(978-0-471-75844-9)

Opera For Dummies
(978-0-7645-5010-2)

Rock Guitar For Dummies
(978-0-7645-5356-1)

Screenwriting For Dummies
(978-0-7645-5486-5)

Singing For Dummies
(978-0-7645-2475-2)

Songwriting For Dummies
(978-0-7645-5404-9)

HEALTH, SPORTS & FITNESS

978-0-7645-7851-9

978-0-7645-5623-4

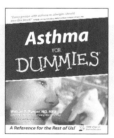

978-0-7645-4233-6

Also available:

Controlling Cholesterol
For Dummies
(978-0-7645-5440-7)

Dieting For Dummies
(978-0-7645-4149-0)

High Blood Pressure
For Dummies
(978-0-7645-5424-7)

Martial Arts For Dummies
(978-0-7645-5358-5)

Pilates For Dummies
(978-0-7645-5397-4)

Power Yoga For Dummies
(978-0-7645-5342-4)

Weight Training
For Dummies
(978-0-471-76845-6)

Yoga For Dummies
(978-0-7645-5117-8)

Available wherever books are sold. For more information or to order direct go to www.wiley.com or call 0800 243407 (Non UK call +44 1243 843296)

FOR DUMMIES®

Helping you expand your horizons and achieve your potential

INTERNET

978-0-470-12174-0

978-0-471-97998-2

978-0-470-08030-6

Also available:

Building a Web Site For
Dummies, 2nd Edition
(978-0-7645-7144-2)

Blogging For Dummies
(978-0-471-77084-8)

Creating Web Pages All-in-
One Desk Reference For
Dummies, 3rd Edition
(978-0-470-09629-1)

eBay.co.uk
For Dummies
(978-0-7645-7059-9)

Web Analysis For Dummies
(978-0-470-09824-0)

Web Design For Dummies,
2nd Edition
(978-0-471-78117-2)

DIGITAL MEDIA

978-0-7645-9802-9

978-0-470-04894-8

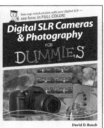

978-0-7645-9803-6

Also available:

BlackBerry For Dummies
(978-0-471-75741-2)

Digital Photo Projects
For Dummies
(978-0-470-12101-6)

Digital Photography
All-in-One Desk Reference
For Dummies
(978-0-470-03743-0)

Photoshop CS3
For Dummies
(978-0-470-11193-2)

Podcasting
For Dummies
(978-0-471-74898-4)

Zune For Dummies
(978-0-470-12045-3)

COMPUTER BASICS

978-0-7645-8958-4

978-0-470-05432-1

978-0-471-75421-3

Also available:

Macs For Dummies,
9th Edition
(978-0-470-04849-8)

Office 2007 All-in-One Desk
Reference For Dummies
(978-0-471-78279-7)

PCs All-in-One Desk
Reference For Dummies,
3rd Edition
(978-0-471-77082-4)

Upgrading & Fixing PCs For
Dummies, 7th Edition
(978-0-470-12102-3)

Windows Vista All-in-One
Desk Reference For Dummies
(978-0-471-74941-7)

Windows XP For Dummies,
2nd Edition
(978-0-7645-7326-2)
